EXPERT RESUMES FOR COMPUTER AND WEB JOBS

THIRD EDITION

Wendy S. Enelow and Louise M. Kursmark

DISCARD

Works
America's Career Publisher

Expert Resumes for Computer and Web Jobs, **Third Edition**

© 2011 by Wendy S. Enelow and Louise M. Kursmark

Published by JIST Works, an imprint of JIST Publishing
7321 Shadeland Station, Suite 200
Indianapolis, IN 46256-3923
Phone: 800-648-JIST   Fax: 877-454-7839   E-mail: info@jist.com

Visit our Web site at **www.jist.com** for information on JIST, free job search information, tables of contents, sample pages, and ordering instructions for our many products!

Quantity discounts are available for JIST books. Please call our Sales Department at 800-648-5478 for a free catalog and more information.

Trade Product Manager: Lori Cates Hand
Development Editor: Heather Stith
Interior Designer: Trudy Coler
Page Layout: Toi Davis
Cover Designer: Amy Peppler Adams
Proofreaders: Laura Bowman, Jeanne Clark
Indexer: Joy Dean Lee

Printed in the United States of America
15 14 13 12 11 10   9 8 7 6 5 4 3 2 1

Library of Congress Cataloging-in-Publication Data

Enelow, Wendy S.
  Expert resumes for computer and Web jobs / Wendy S. Enelow and Louise
  M. Kursmark. – 3rd ed.
        p. cm.
  Includes index.
  ISBN 978-1-59357-811-4 (alk. paper)
 1. Computer science–Vocational guidance. 2. Electronic data processing–Vocational
  guidance. 3. Electronic data processing personnel–Employment.
   4. Résumés (Employment) I. Kursmark, Louise. II. Title.
   QA76.25.E525 2011
   650.14'2'024005–dc22
                                    2010047791

We have been careful to provide accurate information in this book, but it is possible that errors and omissions have been introduced. Please consider this in making any career plans or other important decisions. Trust your own judgment above all else and in all things.

Trademarks: All brand names and product names used in this book are trade names, service marks, trademarks, or registered trademarks of their respective owners.

ISBN 978-1-59357-811-4

TABLE OF CONTENTS

ABOUT THIS BOOK

The technology revolution of the past two decades has impacted the employment market on a scale even more dramatic than the Industrial Revolution. As a result of technology innovation, three remarkable things have happened:

1. **Virtually everyone can be part of the technology revolution,** from the 22-year-old video-game programmer to the 55-year-old systems and software engineer. Opportunities abound for both permanent employment and freelance/consulting work.

2. **There are now thousands of new careers in technology.** Twenty years ago, who had heard of Web site designers, Java scripters, C++ programmers, database administrators, CIOs, CTOs, and CKOs? Now, there is a wealth of opportunity, and every economic projection indicates continuous growth in the demand for technology professionals.

3. **Hundreds of new industries have emerged,** from Web site hosting to the design of advanced telecommunications and networking technologies. Many of these industries did not exist a decade or so ago but have become major contributors to the number and diversity of careers now available in technology.

These new technology professions exist across all businesses and industries, from old-line manufacturing to emerging health-care ventures; from major retail conglomerates to small real estate brokerages; from Ivy League colleges to multinational technology companies. Most important, there are dramatically more employment opportunities than there are qualified professionals, and that's great news for you!

Learning to write a powerful resume that positions you as a competitive candidate in the employment market is what this book is all about. As you read through the early chapters, you'll learn that a resume is much more than just your job history, academic credentials, technical skills, and awards. A truly effective resume is a concise yet comprehensive document that focuses on your achievements, contributions, and the value you bring to a company. Read this book, review the scores of samples, and you'll have the tools you need to create your own winning resume.

Once you have written your resume, this book will instruct you in the methods for preparing resumes for electronic distribution, as well as the traditional printed resume.

By using *Expert Resumes for Computer and Web Jobs* as your guide, you will succeed in developing a powerful and effective technology resume that opens doors, gets interviews, and helps you land your next great career opportunity!

INTRODUCTION

Job search and career management become remarkably more complex and more competitive with each passing year. One major contributor to the new complexity is technology itself, which has created entirely new methods and systems for job search, recruitment, hiring, and lifelong career development.

Fortunately, this new employment landscape offers a host of opportunities for everyone employed in the technology and allied industries and occupations. What's more, that trend is projected to continue through the year 2018.

According to the U.S. Department of Labor's Bureau of Labor Statistics, technology continues to be one of the fastest-growing industries. Consider these impressive statistics:

Specialization	*Percentage of Growth Through 2018*
Network Systems and Data Communications Analysts	53%
Computer Software Engineers, Applications	34%
Computer Software Engineers, Systems Software	30%
Computer and Information Scientists, Research	24%
Network and Computer System Administrators	23%
Operations Research Analysts	22%
Database Administrators	20%

In total, the Bureau projects 22 percent overall growth within the technology sector between now and 2018. What great news for you and everyone else employed in a technology position or a technology industry!

To take advantage of these opportunities, you must be an educated job seeker. That means you must know what you want, where the hiring action is, what additional skills you might need to reach your career objectives, and how best to market yourself. It is no longer enough to be a talented game programmer, user support specialist, or CIO. Now you have to be a strategic marketer, able to package and promote your experience to take advantage of this wave of employment opportunity.

The employment market has changed dramatically over the past decade, and you should expect to hold between 10 and 20 different jobs during your career. No longer is stability the status quo. Today, the norm is movement, onward and upward, in a fast-paced and constantly changing technology market. To stay on top of all of the changes and capture the right opportunities, you must take control of your career. The first step in that process is to write a powerful resume that is rich in content, achievements, and visual appeal, because this document will be at the very forefront of your job search and career management efforts.

Read on to learn how to do that and do it well.

The What, How, Which, and Where of Resume Writing

Without a clearly defined career objective, resume writing becomes much more difficult because there is no direction for the resume. To define your career objective, ask yourself these four critical questions:

- **What type of position/career track are you going to pursue?** Your current career goals dictate the entire resume writing and design process. If you're looking for a position where you will have responsibilities similar to what you do now as a software engineer, you'll write your resume with one strategy and format. However, if you're now interested in pursuing IT project management opportunities or e-commerce systems development opportunities or any one of a host of other positions, then your resume will be focused in a different direction and will showcase different skills, qualifications, projects, and achievements.

- **How are you going to paint a picture of your skills and qualifications that will make you an attractive candidate for your targeted position?** What information are you going to highlight about your past experiences that ties directly to your current objectives? What accomplishments, skills, and qualifications are you going to "sell" in your resume to support your new career objectives? Always remind yourself that your objective drives the entire resume writing process—what you write, where you write it, and why you write it.

- **Which resume format are you going to use?** Is a chronological, functional, or hybrid resume format going to work best for you? Which format will give you the greatest flexibility to highlight the skills you want to bring to the forefront to support your current career goals?

- **Where are you going to look for a job?** Once you have decided what type of position you are interested in, how do you plan to identify and approach those companies and organizations that offer those positions?

When you can answer the what, how, which, and where, you'll be prepared to write your resume and launch your search campaign.

Use chapters 1 and 2 to guide you in developing the content for your resume and selecting the appropriate design and layout. Your resume should focus on your skills, achievements, and qualifications, demonstrating the value and benefit you bring to a prospective employer. The focus should be on the role you want to fill now and not necessarily what you have done in the past.

Chapter 3 will lead you through the preparation of multiple formats of your resume that you'll need for both online and offline job search. The well-designed resume that you print and hand to someone is not the same document that you'll upload to an online resume database. We'll walk you through the various formats, explaining what you'll need, why and when you'll need it, and how to prepare each version.

Review the sample resumes in chapters 4 through 10 to see what other people have done—people in similar situations to yours who faced similar challenges. You'll find interesting formats, unique skills presentations, achievement-focused resumes, project-focused resumes, and much more. Most importantly, you'll see samples written by the top resume writers in the world. These are real resumes that got real interviews and generated real job offers. They're the "best of the best" from us to you.

Next, review chapters 11 and 12 for best-in-class cover letter strategies and samples. As you'll read, your cover letter is an essential partner to your resume and your entire job search effort.

Finally, don't overlook the appendices. We've provided two highly useful resources for managing your career now and in the future. Appendix A is a resume worksheet that you can use to develop your resume and capture career information in the years ahead to make updating your resume faster and easier. In Appendix B, you'll find every resume writer's secret weapon—a list of powerful, distinctive, and descriptive verbs that you can use to add meaning, impact, and variety to your resume.

Job Search Questions and Answers

Before we get to the core of this book—resume writing and design—we would like to offer some practical job search advice that is valuable to virtually every job seeker, whether you are currently employed in the technology field or looking to enter the profession for the first time.

How Do You Enter the Technology Industry?

As with any other industry, education, credentials, and experience are the keys to entry and long-term success. It is difficult to obtain a position in the technology industry without some related work experience, relevant education, or technical credentials. Here are a few pointers:

- **If you're just starting to plan and build your career,** consider a four-year degree in a technology-related discipline—such as Information Systems, Information Technology, Computer Science, or Engineering—or the completion of a technology certification program. Be advised, however, that you must stay current on new technical certification programs and how they are accepted in the market. What's hot one day is passé the next!

- **If you're a technology professional who wants to make the move to a true technology company,** sell your technology knowledge and experience to "connect" yourself to the industry. Perhaps you're a network administrator, database administrator, programmer, or MIS manager in a traditional, nontechnology industry. The technical skills and experiences you've acquired are real and valuable to others. Make the case that you're not an outsider, but rather an insider who understands technology and its applications.

- **If you're a successful sales and marketing professional, customer service specialist, or trainer seeking to enter the technology market** but have no technology experience, focus your resume on your revenue performance and the people skills you bring to an organization. "Sell" the fact that you built and managed customer relationships, improved revenues, designed innovative training programs, and the like. Place the emphasis on you and your performance, not unrelated products or services.

- **If you're an experienced business manager or executive** but have never worked in the technology industry, highlight the value you bring to an organization: your leadership skills, achievements, financial contributions, and more. Many companies seeking talented and effective leadership are more than willing to provide technical training to the "right" candidate.

WHAT IS THE BEST RESUME STRATEGY IF YOU'RE ALREADY IN THE TECHNOLOGY INDUSTRY?

If you're already employed in the technology field but are interested in moving onward and upward, remember one critical fact:

> **Your resume is a marketing tool written to sell YOU!**

If you're a computer systems programmer, *sell* the fact that you've helped to manage development projects; restored nonperforming systems; and created new, user-friendly applications. If you're a technical consultant, *sell* major projects, key clients, and innovative technologies. If you're a CIO, *sell* your achievements—financial, operational, and technological.

When you are writing your resume, your challenge is to create a picture of knowledge, action, and results. In essence, you're stating, "This is what I know, this is how I've used it, and this is how well I've performed." Success sells, so be sure to highlight yours. If you don't, no one else will.

WHERE ARE THE JOBS?

The jobs are everywhere—from technology giants such as IBM, Cisco, and Hewlett-Packard seeking well-qualified hardware, software, and network engineers to the small manufacturing company recruiting a Webmaster or MIS director.

- The jobs are in **development** of new products, technologies, systems, and applications.

- The jobs are in the **manufacture** of these products and technologies.

- The jobs are in the **sale, marketing,** and **support** of these products and technologies.

- The jobs are in the **installation, operation, maintenance,** and **management** of these technologies in nontechnology companies—virtually *every* other company in the world.

- The jobs are in the **delivery** of technology services, as either an employee or a contractor/consultant.

Technology jobs are in every market sector, every industry, and every profession. Technology is everywhere.

How Do You Get Technology Jobs?

To answer this question, we need to review the basic principle underlying job search:

> **Job search is marketing!**

You have a product to sell—yourself—and the best way to sell it is to use all appropriate *marketing channels* just as you would for any other product.

Suppose you wanted to sell office furnishings, systems, and technologies. What would you do? You would market your products using newspaper, magazine, and radio advertisements. You would create a company Web site to build your e-business, and perhaps you would hire a field sales representative to market to major retail chains. Each of these is a different marketing channel through which you would be attempting to reach your target audience.

The same is true for job search. You must use every marketing channel that's right for you. Unfortunately, there is no single formula. What's right for you depends on your specific career objectives—position, industry, geographic restrictions, salary requirements, and more.

Following are the most valuable marketing channels for a successful job search in technology. These are ordered from most effective to least effective, as a general rule. Just remember that everyone's job search is different and what works for your colleague may not work for you and vice versa.

1. **Referrals.** There is nothing better than a personal referral to a company, organization, or person, either in general or for a specific position. Referrals can open doors that, in most instances, would never be accessible any other way. If you know anyone who could possibly refer you, contact that person immediately and ask for his or her assistance.

2. **Offline networking.** Networking is the backbone of every successful job search. Although you might consider it a chore, it is essential that you network effectively with your professional colleagues and associates, past employers, past coworkers, neighbors, friends, and others who might know of opportunities that are right for you. Another good strategy is to attend meetings of technology associations in your area to make new contacts and expand your professional network.

In today's nomadic job market, where you're likely to change jobs every few years, the best strategy is to keep your network "alive" even when you're *not* searching for a new position. Reach out and communicate once, twice, or three times a year with your contacts to find out what's happening in their careers, bring them up-to-date on your career, and share any potential opportunities.

3. **Online networking.** Because of online networking and communication capabilities, it has never been easier to connect with someone you don't know or share information about yourself to a wide group of contacts. Use these capabilities wisely to shorten your job transition time and remain visible throughout your career.

   As of this writing, the predominant online networking tools are LinkedIn (the top site for professional networking) and Facebook (the top site for social networking). The fastest-growing social sharing site is Twitter, which has prompted an entire book (*The Twitter Job Search Guide,* JIST Publishing, 2010) about using the power of Twitter to advance your career. In addition, countless blogs and online communities offer opportunities for you to share your opinions and connect with others.

   We suggest that you make full use of these amazing capabilities! Our brief recommendations will get you started:

   - **LinkedIn: Build your professional profile.** Create a powerful profile based on your new resume. Join appropriate groups to share your expertise, ask questions, and benefit from group wisdom. Build your connections and use LinkedIn's capabilities to connect with people at your target organizations. Compile strong recommendations from colleagues, supervisors, and others who have seen you at work.

   - **Facebook: Develop an appropriate personal profile.** Even if you choose to use Facebook primarily for social networking, be certain that everything you post is appropriate and will not damage you should it be read by a professional contact or a potential employer. Use Facebook's enormous network to connect with people at your target organizations, and make sure your personal contacts know what you're looking for so they can refer appropriate people, opportunities, and information to you.

   - **Twitter: Showcase your expertise.** Use your Twitter persona to share knowledge about your profession, keep colleagues and followers informed of your activities, and build your visibility. Let the network work for you by sharing what you're looking for and who you're trying to connect with.

   - **Additional forums: Strengthen your online identity.** More and more, employers and recruiters are searching online to find new employees who have the right mix of skills, knowledge, attitude, and expertise. The more visible and knowledgeable you appear to be online, the more easily they'll find you. By creating a robust and professional online image, you'll open yourself up to opportunities you wouldn't hear about otherwise, and you'll make every aspect of career management easier and more seamless.

4. **Responses to online job postings.** One of the greatest advantages of the technology revolution is an employer's ability to post job announcements online

and a job seeker's ability to respond immediately via e-mail. In most (but not all) instances, these are bona fide opportunities, and it's well worth your effort to spend time searching for and responding to appropriate postings. However, don't make the mistake of devoting too much time to searching the Internet. It can consume a huge amount of your time that you should spend on other job search marketing efforts.

To expedite your search, here are the largest and most widely used online job-posting sites—presented alphabetically and not necessarily in order of effectiveness or value. We've expanded this list to include some of our favorite sites designed specifically for people employed in the technology professions:

> www.americanjobs.com
>
> www.careerbuilder.com
>
> www.employmentguide.com
>
> www.execunet.com
>
> www.dice.com
>
> www.flipdog.com
>
> www.hirediversity.com
>
> www.informationtechnologycrossing.com
>
> www.job-hunt.org
>
> www.monster.com
>
> www.netshare.com
>
> www.net-temps.com
>
> www.tech-centric.net
>
> www.theladders.com

5. **Responses to newspaper, magazine, and journal advertisements.** Although the opportunity to post online has reduced the overall number of print advertisements, they still abound. Do not forget about this tried-and-true marketing strategy. If they've got the job and you have the qualifications, it's a perfect fit.

6. **Targeted e-mail campaigns (resumes and cover letters) to recruiters.** Recruiters have jobs, and you want one. It's pretty straightforward. The only catch is to find the recruiters who have the right jobs for you. Therefore, you must devote the time and effort to finding the "right" recruiters. There are many resources on the Internet where you can access information about recruiters (for a fee), and then sort that information by industry and profession (technology, computer science, software development, and so on). This allows you to identify the recruiters who would be interested in a candidate with your qualifications. What's more, because these campaigns are transmitted electronically, they are easy and inexpensive to produce.

When working with recruiters, you must keep in mind that they *do not* work for you! Their clients are the hiring companies that pay their fees. They are not in business to "find a job" for you, but rather to fill a specific position with a qualified candidate, either you or someone else. To maximize your chances of finding a position through a recruiter, don't rely on just one or two, but distribute your resume to many who meet your specific criteria.

7. **Online resume postings.** The Internet is swarming with reasonably priced (if not free) Web sites where you can post your resume. It's quick, easy, and the only passive thing you can do in your search. All of the other marketing channels require action on your part. With online resume postings, once you've posted, you're done. You then just wait (and hope!) for some response.

8. **Targeted e-mail and print campaigns to companies.** Just as with campaigns to recruiters (see item 6), you must be extremely careful to select just the companies that would be interested in a candidate with your qualifications. The closer you stick to "where you belong" in relation to your specific experience, the better your response rate will be.

9. **In-person "cold calls" to companies and recruiters.** We consider this the least effective and most time-consuming marketing strategy for any job, including technology positions. It is extremely difficult to just walk in the door and get in front of the right person or any person who can take hiring action. You'll be much better off focusing your time and energy on other, more productive channels.

WHAT ABOUT OPPORTUNITIES IN TECHNOLOGY CONSULTING AND CONTRACTING?

Although, of course, most people will have (and want) full-time jobs, there are now a wealth of opportunities for work as a technology consultant or contractor. According to the U.S. Bureau of Labor Statistics, the demand for consultants is strong and growing at an unprecedented rate. The government's projections indicate a 24 percent increase in the number of consulting opportunities between the years 2008 and 2018.

The term *consultant* or *contractor* generally refers to an individual who moves from one organization to another, from project to project, where his or her particular expertise is most needed and most highly rewarded (and compensated). More and more people in technology, telecommunications, and related occupations are flocking towards these types of working arrangements because of the tremendous flexibility they offer. And what a great phenomenon for companies! They can now hire the staff they need, when they need them, and only when they need them.

If you are seriously considering a consulting career, keep in mind that no matter your area of consulting expertise, one of your most vital functions as an independent consultant will be to market yourself. Consider the computer systems operator who now wants to pursue a career in developing Web applications. Her success as a consultant will not only be tied to her technology expertise but, just as significantly, to her ability to proactively market her consulting practice, establish her clientele, and build a strong revenue stream. If you're not an astute marketer and not willing to invest the time and resources essential to market your consulting practice, then consider joining an established consulting company where the firm itself will capture the clients and you'll only be responsible for product and/or service delivery.

As part of your ongoing efforts to market your consulting practice, you'll need to invest your time in targeted online and offline networking. Initially, you may devote an extraordinary amount of time to rekindling past business relationships and building new ones. In order to establish yourself within the consulting marketplace, you must commit yourself to a structured networking and relationship development program.

The income streams of consultants often vary widely from month to month. There will be good months where money will be flowing in, and there will be slow months where money may only trickle in. Established consultants know that this fluctuation is the norm and have learned to manage their money accordingly. Learning to manage your financial resources can be an extremely difficult lesson and may require some practice, but it is critical to your long-term consulting success.

Learning to "live with the risk" and the volatility of a consulting career can also be an extreme challenge. Unpredictability is the status quo for most consultants, so you must learn to live comfortably with that risk and not allow the stress associated with it to overtake your life and your mental health!

Before you proceed any further in evaluating your potential opportunities in consulting, be sure to take advantage of the thousands of online resources devoted to consulting. If you do an extensive Internet search, you'll find Web sites where you can search for consulting opportunities, sites where you can post your resume for review by companies seeking consultants, hundreds of sites with articles about consulting, other sites that offer the many tools you'll need to manage your practice, and much more. Many of these resources are free; others have a small fee associated with them.

Give careful thought and consideration to the prospect of "contract" work. This rapidly emerging career track is becoming extremely prevalent in technology-related professions. How great to be able to work on the projects that interest you and then move on to something else! There are definite benefits to consider as well as perceived negatives of "not having a permanent job." However, in today's transitory work culture, not having a permanent job is not such a negative! Working as a contractor or consultant allows you, not a company, to control your own career destiny.

Conclusion

Career opportunities abound within technology industries and professions today. What's more, it has never been easier to learn about and apply for jobs. Arm yourself with a powerful resume and cover letter, identify your most appropriate marketing channels, and start your search today. You're destined to reach the next rung on your career ladder.

PART I

Resume Writing, Strategy, and Formats

CHAPTER 1

Resume Writing Strategies for Technology Professionals

If you're reading this book, chances are you've decided to make a career move. It may be because

- You're graduating from college or technical school and are ready to launch your professional career.

- You've just earned your graduate degree or advanced technical certification and are ready to make a step upward in your career.

- You're ready to leave your current position and move up the ladder to a higher-paying and more responsible position.

- You've decided on a career change and will be looking at opportunities in mobile applications and other emerging technology sectors.

- You're unhappy with your current company or management team and have decided to pursue opportunities elsewhere.

- You've been laid off or downsized, or otherwise lost your position, and you must find a new one.

- You've completed a contract assignment and are looking for a new "free-agent" job or perhaps a permanent position.

- You're relocating to a new area and need to find a new job.

- You're returning to the workforce after several years of unemployment or retirement.

- You're simply ready for a change.

No matter the reason for your career transition, a powerful resume is an essential component of your search campaign. In fact, it is virtually impossible to conduct a search without a resume. It is your calling card that briefly, yet powerfully, communicates the skills, qualifications, experience, and value you bring to a prospective employer. It is the document that will open doors and generate interviews. It is the first way people will learn about you when you forward it in response to an advertisement, and it is the last thing they'll remember when they're reviewing your qualifications after an interview.

Your resume is a sales document, and you are the product! You must identify the *features* (what you know and what you can do) and *benefits* (how you can help an employer) of that product, and then communicate them in a concise and hard-hitting written presentation. Remind yourself over and over as you work your way through the resume process that you are writing marketing literature designed to sell a new product—*you*—into a new position.

Your resume can have tremendous power and a phenomenal impact on your job search. So don't take it lightly. Rather, devote the time, energy, and resources that are essential to developing a resume that is well-written, visually attractive, and effective in communicating *who* you are and *how* you want to be perceived.

Resume Strategies

Following are the nine core strategies for writing effective and successful resumes.

RESUME STRATEGY #1: WRITE TO THE JOB YOU WANT

Now that you've decided to look for a new position, the very first step is to identify your career interests, goals, and objectives. This task is critical, because it is the underlying foundation for *what* you include in your resume, *how* you include it, and *where* you include it. You cannot write an effective resume without knowing, at least to some degree, what type or types of positions you will be seeking.

There are two concepts to consider here:

- **Who you are:** This relates to what you have done professionally and/or academically. Are you a programmer, network administrator, systems analyst, or telecommunications engineer? Are you a technology sales professional, field support specialist, or technical training manager? Are you a recent graduate from the DeVry Institute of Technology with a certificate in computer programming? Who are you?

- **How you want to be perceived:** This relates to your current career objectives. If you're a computer analyst looking for a position in project management, don't focus just on your technical qualifications. Put an equal emphasis on projects, personnel, schedules, team leadership, and more. If you're a technical sales engineer interested in a product-management position, highlight your involvement in product development, product support, multidisciplinary teaming, and other skills related to the design, creation, commercialization, and launch of new products.

The strategy, then, is to connect these two concepts by using the *Who you are* information that ties directly to the *How you want to be perceived* message to determine what information to include in your resume. By following this strategy, you're painting a picture that allows a prospective employer to see you as you wish to be seen—as an individual with the qualifications for the type of position you are pursuing.

> **WARNING:** If you prepare a resume without first clearly identifying what your objectives are and how you want to be perceived, your resume will have no focus and no direction. Without the underlying knowledge of "This is what I want to be," you do not know what to highlight in your resume. In turn, the document becomes an historical overview of your career and not the sales document it is designed to be.

RESUME STRATEGY #2: SELL IT TO ME... DON'T TELL IT TO ME

We've already established the fact that resume writing is sales. You are the product, and you must create a document that powerfully communicates the value of that product. One particularly effective strategy for accomplishing this is the "Sell It to Me... Don't Tell It to Me" strategy that impacts virtually every single word you write on your resume.

If you "tell it," you are simply stating facts. If you "sell it," you promote it, advertise it, and draw attention to it. Look at the difference in impact between these examples:

Tell It Strategy: Assisted in development of company Web site and e-commerce capability.

Sell It Strategy: Member of 8-person technology team credited with the design and implementation of company Web site and launch of e-commerce capability (now generating $2.1 million in annual product sales).

Tell It Strategy: Increased sales revenues within the Northeastern U.S. region.

Sell It Strategy: Delivered a 45% revenue increase and 22% gain in customer base while managing technology sales throughout the $8.4 million Chicago sales territory.

Tell It Strategy: Improved systems performance, reliability, and functionality.

Sell It Strategy: Reengineered all system hardware and software, implemented quality assurance standards, upgraded supporting business processes, and significantly improved overall IT performance, reliability, and functionality.

What's the difference between "telling it" and "selling it"? In a nutshell...

Telling It	Selling It
Describes features.	Describes benefits.
Tells what and how.	Sells why the "what" and "how" are important.
Details activities.	Includes results.
Focuses on what you did.	Details how what you did benefited the company, department, team members, customers, and so on.

RESUME STRATEGY #3: USE KEYWORDS

No matter what you read or who you talk to about job search, the concept of keywords is sure to come up. Keywords (or, as they were previously known, buzz-words) are words and phrases specific to a particular industry or profession. For example, keywords for technology include *architecture, artificial intelligence, C++, functionality, hardware, Internet, software, systems analysis, technical training, user support,* and many, many more.

When you use these words and phrases—in your resume, in your cover letter, or during an interview—you are communicating a very specific message. For example, when you include the words "software development" in your resume, your reader will most likely assume that you have experience in user needs analysis, software engineering, testing, prototype development, troubleshooting, hardware interface, and more. As you can see, people will make inferences about your skills based on the use of just one or two individual words.

Here are a few other examples:

- When you use the words **multimedia technology,** people will assume you have experience with videoconferencing, teleconferencing, CD-ROM, graphic interfaces, Internet broadcasting, and more.

- When you mention **e-commerce,** readers and listeners will infer that you have experience with the Internet, online technology, online advertising and promotion, secure shopping carts, and more.

- By referencing **systems architecture** in your resume, you convey that you have experience with hardware, software, systems configuration, systems migration, applications, functionality, systems performance, and more.

- When you use the word **network,** most people will assume you are familiar with LAN and WAN technology, network protocols, network interfaces, network administration, and the like.

Vocab

Keywords are also an integral component of the resume scanning process, whereby companies and recruiters electronically search resumes for specific terms to find candidates with the skills, qualifications, and technical expertise for their particular hiring needs. In many instances, electronic scanning has replaced the more traditional method of an actual person reading your resume (at least initially). Therefore, to some degree, the *only* thing that matters in this instance is that you have included the "right" keywords to match the company's or the recruiter's needs. Without them, you will most certainly be passed over.

Of course, in virtually every instance your resume will be read at some point by human eyes, so it's not enough just to throw together a list of keywords and leave it at that. In fact, it's not even necessary to include a separate "keyword summary" on your resume. A better strategy is to incorporate keywords naturally into the text within the appropriate sections of your resume.

Keep in mind, too, that keywords are arbitrary; there is no defined set of keywords for a Web site developer, network administrator, or any other profession. Employers searching to fill these positions develop a list of terms that reflect the specifics they desire in a qualified candidate. These might be a combination of technical skills, education, length of experience, and other easily defined qualifications, along with "soft skills," such as leadership, problem solving, and communication.

> **NOTE:** Because of the complex and arbitrary nature of keyword selection, we cannot overemphasize how vital it is, especially in the technology industry where precise technical qualifications are often the primary hiring criteria, to be certain that *all* of the keywords that represent your experience and knowledge are included in your resume!

How can you be sure that you are including all the keywords and the right keywords? Just by describing your work experience, projects, technical qualifications, and the like, you will naturally include most of the terms that are important in your field. To cross-check what you've written, review online job postings for positions that are of interest to you. Look at the precise terms used in the ads and be sure you have included them in your resume (as appropriate to your skills and qualifications).

RESUME STRATEGY #4: USE THE "BIG" AND SAVE THE "LITTLE"

When deciding what you want to include in your resume, try to focus on the "big" things—new products, new technologies, system enhancements, productivity and quality gains, major projects, major customers, improvements to functionality, new applications, sales increases, profit improvements, and more. Give a good broad-based picture of what you did and how well you did it. Here's an example:

> Managed a $12 million robotics development project in cooperation with the company's largest retail customer. Orchestrated the entire project, from initial planning and design through prototype development and final customer delivery. Matrix-managed a 42-person development team.

Then, save the "little" stuff—the details—for the interview. With this strategy, you will accomplish two things: You'll keep your resume readable and of a reasonable length (while still selling your achievements), and you'll have new and interesting information to share during the interview, rather than merely repeating what is already on your resume. Using the above example, when discussing this experience during an interview, you could elaborate on the design process, your involvement with marketing, the specific technologies that were involved, and the long-term benefits of the system.

RESUME STRATEGY #5: MAKE YOUR RESUME "INTERVIEWABLE"

One of your greatest challenges is to make your resume a useful interview tool. Once you've passed the keyword scanning test and are contacted for a telephone or in-person interview with a real person, the resume becomes all-important in leading and prompting your interviewer during your conversation.

Your job, then, is to make sure the resume leads the reader where you want to go and presents just the right organization, content, and appearance to stimulate a productive discussion. To improve the "interviewability" of your resume, consider these tactics:

- Make good use of Resume Strategy #4 (Use the "Big" and Save the "Little") to invite further discussion about your experiences.

- Be sure your greatest "selling points" are featured prominently, not buried within the resume.

- Conversely, don't devote lots of space and attention to areas of your background that are irrelevant or about which you feel less than positive; you'll only invite questions about things you really don't want to discuss.

- Make sure your resume is highly readable—this means plenty of white space, an adequate font size, and a logical flow from start to finish.

RESUME STRATEGY #6: ELIMINATE CONFUSION WITH STRUCTURE AND CONTEXT

Keep in mind that your resume will be read *very quickly* by hiring authorities! You may agonize over every word and spend hours working on content and design, but the average reader will skim quickly through your masterpiece and expect to pick up important facts in just a few seconds. Try to make it as easy as possible for readers to grasp the essential facts:

- Be consistent. For example, put job titles, company names, and dates in the same place for each position.

- Make information easy to find by clearly defining different sections of your resume with large, highly visible headings.

- Define the context in which you worked (for example, the company, your department, the specific challenges you faced) before you start describing your activities and accomplishments.

RESUME STRATEGY #7: USE FUNCTION TO DEMONSTRATE ACHIEVEMENT

When you write a resume that focuses only on your job functions, it can be dry and uninteresting and will say very little about your unique activities and contributions. Consider the following example:

> Responsible for the development and administration of all database functions for the company.

Now, consider using that same function to demonstrate achievement and see what happens to the tone and energy of the sentence. It becomes alive and clearly communicates that you deliver results.

> Reengineered the corporation's database systems, introduced new applications, and improved user satisfaction by 18%.

Try to translate your functions into achievements and you'll create a more powerful resume presentation.

RESUME STRATEGY #8: REMAIN IN THE REALM OF REALITY

We've already established that resume writing is sales. So, as any good salesperson would, you might feel somewhat inclined to stretch the truth just a bit. However, be forewarned that you must stay within the realm of reality. Do not push your skills and qualifications outside the bounds of what is truthful. You never want to be in a position where you have to defend something that you've written on your resume. If that's the case, you'll lose the opportunity before you ever get started.

RESUME STRATEGY #9: BE CONFIDENT

You are unique. There is only one individual with the specific combination of employment experience, technical qualifications, achievements, and educational credentials that you have. In turn, this positions you as a unique commodity within the competitive job search market. To succeed, you must prepare a resume that is written to sell *you* and to highlight *your* qualifications and *your* success. If you can accomplish this, you will have won the job search game by generating interest, interviews, and offers.

There Are No Resume Writing Rules

One of the greatest challenges in resume writing is that there are no rules to the game. There are certain expectations about information that you will include: principally, your employment history and your educational qualifications. Beyond that, what you include is entirely dependent upon you and what you have done in your career. What's more, you have tremendous flexibility in determining how to include the information you have selected. In chapter 2, you'll find a complete listing of each possible category you might include in your resume, the type of information in each category, preferred formats for presentation, and sample text you can edit and use.

Although there are no rules, there are a few standards to live by as you write your resume. The following sections discuss these standards in detail.

CONTENT STANDARDS

Content is, of course, the text that goes into your resume. Content standards relate to the writing style you should use, items you should be sure to include, items you should avoid including, and the order and format in which you list your qualifications.

Writing Style

Always write in the first person, dropping the word "I" from the front of each sentence. This style gives your resume a more aggressive and more professional tone than the passive third-person voice. Here are some examples:

First Person

> Manage 12-person team in the design and market commercialization of next-generation SAP technology.

Third Person

> Mr. Jones manages a team of 12 in the design and market commercialization of next-generation SAP technology.

By using the first-person voice, you are assuming "ownership" of that statement. You did such-and-such. When you use the third-person, "someone else" did it. Can you see the difference?

Stay Away From...

Try *not* to use phrases such as "responsible for" or "duties included." These words create a passive tone and style. Instead, use active verbs to describe what you did.

Compare these two ways of conveying the same information:

Duties included the development, implementation, and marketing of an innovative intranet system offering a secure portal with centralized access to records, test results, and medical information. *Responsible for* training and customer-service staff, vendor-employed network engineers, and Web developers. *Also responsible for* $1.3 million operating budget.

Managed the development, implementation, and marketing of an innovative Intranet system offering a secure portal with centralized access to records, test results, and medical information. *Supervised* training and customer-service staff. *Directed* the activities of vendor-employed network engineers and Web developers. *Developed and administered* $1.3 million operating budget.

Resume Style

The traditional **chronological** resume lists work experience in reverse-chronological order (starting with your current or most recent position). The **functional** style de-emphasizes the "where" and "when" of your career and instead groups similar experiences, talents, and qualifications regardless of when they occurred.

Today, however, most resumes follow neither a strictly chronological nor strictly functional format; rather, they are an effective mixture of the two styles, usually known as a "combination" or "hybrid."

Like the chronological resume, the hybrid includes specifics about where you worked, when you worked there, and what your job titles were. Like a functional resume, a hybrid emphasizes your most relevant qualifications—perhaps within chronological job descriptions, in an expanded summary section, in several "career highlights" bullet points at the top of your resume, or in project summaries. Most of the examples in this book are hybrids and show a wide diversity of organizational styles you can use as inspiration for your own resume.

Resume Format

Resumes, principally career summaries and job descriptions, are most often written in a paragraph format, a bulleted format, or a combination of both. Following are three job descriptions, all very similar in content, yet presented in each of the three different formats. The advantages and disadvantages of each format are also addressed.

Paragraph Format

Team Leader—Client/Server Implementation Project   2007 to 2010

VERIZON, Baltimore, Maryland

Co-led $950 million investment to develop client/server order-entry system to service operations in 50 locations throughout 6 northeastern states and

(continued)

(continued)

> support 1,600 users processing 140,000 orders per year ($32 billion in revenue). Directed a staff of 73. Wrote and presented the business case for $7.9 million in board-approved funding.
>
> Planned and orchestrated a successful technology development and implementation project, achieving all performance goals and objectives and delivering the project on time and within budget. Most notably, increased billing accuracy from 80% to 91% and coordinated integration of $1.2 million of capital equipment into existing data center. Delivered major cost reductions including 66% savings in development of technical specifications (through competitive RFP and subsequent negotiation of offshore development contract) and 15-person reduction in client staffing expense.

Advantages:

Requires the least amount of space on the page. Brief, succinct, and to the point.

Disadvantages:

Achievements get lost in the text of the second paragraph. They are not visually distinctive, nor do they stand alone to draw attention to them.

Bulleted List Format

> **Team Leader—Client/Server Implementation Project**   2007 to 2010
>
> **VERIZON,** Baltimore, Maryland
> - Co-led $950 million investment to develop client/server order-entry system to service operations in 50 locations throughout 6 northeastern states and support 1,600 users processing 140,000 orders per year ($32 billion in revenue). Directed a staff of 73.
>
> - Wrote and presented a business case for $7.9 million in board-approved funding.
>
> - Planned and orchestrated a successful technology development and implementation project, achieving all performance goals and objectives and delivering the project on time and within budget. Most notably, increased billing accuracy from 80% to 91%.
>
> - Coordinated integration of $1.2 million of capital equipment into existing data center.
>
> - Delivered major cost reductions including 66% savings in development of technical specifications (through competitive RFP and subsequent negotiation of offshore development contract) and 15-person reduction in client staffing expense.

Advantages:

Quick and easy to peruse.

Disadvantages:

Responsibilities and achievements are lumped together with everything of equal value. In turn, the achievements get lost further down the list and are not immediately recognizable.

Combination Format

Team Leader—Client/Server Implementation Project   2007 to 2010

VERIZON, Baltimore, Maryland

Co-led $950 million investment to develop client/server order-entry system to service operations in 50 locations throughout 6 northeastern states and support 1,600 users processing 140,000 orders per year ($32 billion in revenue). Directed a staff of 73.

- Wrote and presented a business case for $7.9 million in board-approved funding.

- Planned and orchestrated a successful technology development and implementation project, achieving all performance goals and objectives and delivering project on-time and within budget. Most notably, increased billing accuracy from 80% to 91%.

- Coordinated integration of $1.2 million of capital equipment into existing data center.

- Delivered major cost reductions including 66% savings in development of technical specifications (through competitive RFP and subsequent negotiation of offshore development contract) and 15-person reduction in client staffing expense.

Advantages:

Our recommended format. Clearly presents overall responsibilities in the introductory paragraph and then accentuates each achievement as a separate bullet.

Disadvantages:

If you don't have clearly identifiable accomplishments, this format is not effective. It also may shine a glaring light on the positions where your accomplishments were less notable.

E-mail Address and URL

Be sure to include your e-mail address prominently at the top of your resume. E-mail is one of the most preferred methods of communication in job search, particularly within the technology industry.

We advise against using your employer's e-mail address on your resume. Not only does this present a negative impression to future employers, it will become useless once you make your next career move. Instead, obtain a private e-mail address that will be yours permanently. A free e-mail address from a provider such as Yahoo!, Hotmail, or Gmail is perfectly acceptable to use on your resume.

In addition to your e-mail address, if you have an online portfolio, online profile, or other site that shares additional information about yourself and your career, be sure to display the URL at the top of your resume. For more information on Web resumes, refer to chapter 3.

PRESENTATION STANDARDS

Presentation is the way your resume looks. It refers to the fonts you use, the paper you print it on, any graphics you might include, and how many pages your resume should be.

Font

Use a font (typestyle) that is clean, conservative, and easy to read. Stay away from anything that is too fancy, glitzy, curly, and the like. Here are a few recommended fonts:

Tahoma	Times New Roman
Arial	Bookman
Krone	Book Antiqua
Soutane	Garamond
CG Omega	Century Schoolbook
Century Gothic	**Lucida Sans**
Gill Sans	Verdana

Although it is extremely popular, Times New Roman is our least preferred font simply because it is overused. More than 90 percent of the resumes we see are typed in Times New Roman. Your goal is to create a competitive, distinctive document, and, to achieve that, we recommend an alternative font.

Your choice of font should be dictated by the content, format, and length of your resume. Some fonts look better than others at smaller or larger sizes; some have "bolder" boldface type; some require more white space to make them readable. Once you've written your resume, experiment with a few different fonts to see which one best enhances your document.

Type Size

Readability is everything! If the type size is too small, your resume will be difficult to read and difficult to skim for essential information. Interestingly, a too-large type size, particularly for senior-level professionals, can also give a negative impression by conveying a juvenile or unprofessional image.

As a general rule, select type from 10 to 12 points in size. However, there's no hard-and-fast rule, and a lot depends on the font you choose. Take a look at the following examples:

Very readable in 9-point Verdana:

Designed an easy-to-navigate Web page for a retail company, using Adobe Dreamweaver; included a home page, product page, and order form, with strong graphics and hyperlinks.

Difficult to read in too-small 9-point Gill Sans MT:

Designed an easy-to-navigate Web page for a retail company, using Adobe Dreamweaver; included a home page, product page, and order form, with strong graphics and hyperlinks.

Concise and readable in 12-point Times New Roman:

Primary focus: European rollout of SAP system, implementing new functionality into a live, productive system. Project manager and chief architect of euro currency conversion project: security, systems testing, and training. Manage virtual, cross-functional team of 20.

A bit overwhelming in too-large 12-point Bookman Old Style:

Primary focus: European rollout of SAP system, implementing new functionality into a live, productive system. Project manager and chief architect of euro currency conversion project: security, systems testing, and training. Manage virtual, cross-functional team of 20.

Type Enhancements

Bold, *italics,* <u>underlining,</u> and CAPITALIZATION are ideal to highlight certain words, phrases, achievements, projects, numbers, and other information you want to draw special attention to. However, do not overuse these enhancements. If your resume becomes too cluttered, nothing stands out.

> **NOTE:** Resumes intended for electronic transmission and computer scanning have specific restrictions on font, type size, and type enhancements. We discuss these details in chapter 3.

Page Length

A one- or two-page resume is preferred. Use three or more pages only in a particularly unusual circumstance. For instance, if you're an experienced CIO with a 25-year career and a host of major accomplishments in every position, don't shortchange yourself by insisting on a two-page resume. If you're a free agent with many diverse projects under your belt, a longer resume that includes just about all of your projects could give you a competitive edge over other, less-experienced freelancers.

If you must create a resume that's longer than two pages, consider making it more reader-friendly by segmenting the information into separate components. For instance, you might summarize your project-management experience on page 1 of the resume, and then create an addendum that provides more detail about each project. Or you could write an all-encompassing technical summary, and then detail a long list of specific technologies on a separate page.

Paper Color

Be conservative. White, ivory, and light gray are ideal. Other "flashier" colors are inappropriate for individuals in the technology industry.

Graphics and Color

An attractive, relevant graphic can really enhance your technical resume. When you look through the sample resumes in chapters 4 through 10, you'll see some excellent examples of the effective use of graphics to enhance the visual presentation of a resume. Just be sure not to get carried away… be tasteful and relatively conservative.

Similarly, do feel free to use color in your resume. Just be certain that it is tasteful and does not detract from readability. We recommend that you use color for borders and graphics, but not for text. You want to be certain that all of the text on your resume can be clearly read on-screen and when printed, and color can sometimes compromise readability.

White Space

We'll say it again—readability is everything! If people have to struggle to read your resume, they simply won't make the effort. Therefore, be sure to leave plenty of white space. It really does make a difference.

ACCURACY AND PERFECTION

The final step, and one of the most critical in resume writing, is the proofreading stage. It is essential that your resume be well written; visually pleasing; and free of any errors, typographical mistakes, misspellings, and the like. We recommend that you carefully proofread your resume a minimum of three times, and then have two or three other people also proofread it. Consider your resume an example of the quality of work you will produce on a company's behalf. Is your work product going to have errors and inconsistencies? If your resume does, it communicates to a prospective employer that you are careless, and this is the "kiss of death" in a job search.

Take the time to make sure that your resume is perfect in all the little details that do, in fact, make a big difference to those who read it.

CHAPTER 2

Writing Your Resume

For many technology professionals, resume writing is *not* at the top of the list of fun and exciting activities! How can it compare to solving a programming bug, developing a new technology, advancing a mobile application, cracking a longstanding systems malfunction, or launching a global systems upgrade? In your perception, we're sure that it cannot.

However, resume writing can be an enjoyable and rewarding task. Once your resume is complete, you can look at it proudly, reminding yourself of all that you have achieved. It is a snapshot of your career and your success. When it's complete, we guarantee you'll look back with tremendous self-satisfaction as you launch and successfully manage your job search.

The very first step in finding a new position or advancing your career, resume writing can be the most daunting of all tasks in your job search. For most of you in technology, writing may not be your primary skill. In fact, writing is a right-brain skill, the exact opposite of what you do when you use your left brain to develop theories, analyze, synthesize, extrapolate, plan a process, or handle a variety of other functions related to the technology industry.

Therefore, to make the writing process easier, more finite, and more "analytical," we've consolidated it into six discrete sections.

- **Contact Information.** This data uniquely identifies you and provides the end user of your resume (the hiring manager) a means of access.

- **Career Summary.** Think of your Career Summary as the *architecture* of your resume. It is the accumulation of everything that allows the system (you) to work. It is the backbone, the foundation, of your resume.

- **Technical Qualifications.** Your technical qualifications are equivalent to the functionality, the underlying foundation of the system and of your career. This section is a consolidated yet comprehensive summary of your specific technical qualifications and expertise.

- **Professional Experience.** Professional Experience is much like the software and applications of your system. It shows how you put all of your capabilities to work… in ways that benefit "users" (employers).

- **Education, Credentials, and Certifications.** Think of this section as the *system specifications,* the specific qualifications of the system and of your career.

- **The "Extras"** (Professional Affiliations, Civic Affiliations, Publications, Public Speaking, Honors and Awards, Personal Information, and so on). These are the *bits and bytes* of your resume, the "extra stuff" that helps distinguish you from others with similar technical qualifications.

Step-by-Step: Writing the Perfect Resume

In the preceding section, we outlined the six resume sections. Now, we'll detail the particulars of each section—what to include, where to include it, and how to include it.

CONTACT INFORMATION

Let's briefly address the very top section of your resume: your name and contact information.

Name

You'd think this would be the easiest part of writing your resume… writing your name! But there are several factors you should consider:

- Although most people choose to use their full, formal name at the top of a resume, it has become increasingly more acceptable to use the name by which you prefer to be called.

- Bear in mind that it's to your advantage to have readers feel comfortable calling you for an interview. Their comfort level may decrease if your name is gender-neutral, difficult to pronounce, or very unusual; they don't know who they're calling (a man or a woman) or how to ask for you. Here are a few ways you can make it easier for them:

> Lynn T. Cowles (Mr.)
>
> (Ms.) Michael Murray
>
> Tzirina (Irene) Kahn
>
> Ndege "Nick" Vernon

Address

You should always include your home address on your resume. If you use a post office box for mail, include both your mailing address and your physical residence address. However, if you upload your resume to an online site, it's a good practice to remove the address, leaving just your e-mail address and phone number as contact information.

Telephone Number(s)

We recommend that you include just one phone number on your resume—the number where you can be reached most readily and where callers can leave a voice mail message for a speedy return call. For many people, this number is a cell phone number; for others, it is a home number.

In certain cases, you should include more than one number on your resume. If cell coverage is spotty or you are often unable to take calls on your cell phone, include your home number as well as your cell number. Be sure to have a brief, professional-sounding voice mail greeting for all phone numbers that appear on your resume and to regularly monitor your messages.

E-mail Address

Always include your e-mail address on your resume. E-mail is now often the preferred method of communication in job searches, particularly in the early stages of each contact. Do not use your employer's e-mail address, even if you access e-mail through your work computer. Instead, obtain a free, accessible-anywhere address from a provider such as Yahoo!, Hotmail, or Gmail.

As you look through the samples in this book, you'll see how resume writers have arranged the many bits of contact information at the top of a resume. You can use these as models for presenting your own information. The point is to make it as easy as possible for employers to contact you!

Now, let's get into the nitty-gritty of the core content sections of your resume.

CAREER SUMMARY

The Career Summary is the section at the top of your resume that summarizes and highlights your knowledge and expertise.

You might be thinking, "But shouldn't my resume start with an Objective?" Although many job seekers still use Objective statements, we believe that a Career Summary is a much more powerful introduction. The problem with Objectives is that they are either too specific (limiting you to a "Flash Developer position" or too vague (doesn't everyone want a challenging opportunity with a progressive organization offering the opportunity for growth and advancement?). In addition, Objectives can be read as self-serving, because they describe what *you* want rather than suggesting what you have to offer an employer.

In contrast, an effective Career Summary allows you to position yourself as you wish to be perceived and immediately "paint a picture" of yourself that supports your current career goals. It is critical that this section focus on the specific skills, qualifications, and achievements of your career that are related to your current objectives. Your summary is *not* a historical overview of your career. Rather, it is a concise, well-written, and sharp presentation of information designed to *sell* you into your next position.

This section can have various titles, such as the following:

Career Achievements	Management Profile
Career Highlights	Professional Qualifications
Career Summary	Professional Summary
Career Synopsis	Profile
Executive Profile	Summary
Expertise	Summary of Achievement
Highlights of Experience	Summary of Qualifications

Or, as you will see in the first sample format (Headline Format), your summary does not have to have any title at all.

Here are five sample Career Summaries. Consider using one of these as the template for developing your Career Summary, or use them as the foundation to create your own presentation. You will also find some type of Career Summary in just about every resume included in this book.

Headline Format

SENIOR INFORMATION TECHNOLOGY EXECUTIVE

Information Systems / Telecommunications / Web / Voice & Data

Harvard MBA—Specialization in Information Systems and Technologies

Paragraph Format

PROFILE Highly skilled and experienced **Database Developer / Technical Project Lead** with a track record of managing on-time, on-budget projects that deliver substantial business benefits. Solid business background and innate understanding of how technology systems impact business processes. Known for ability to rapidly assess business needs and quick-start technology solutions.

Core Competencies Summary Format

PROFESSIONAL SUMMARY

PRODUCT DEVELOPMENT, SALES & MARKETING PROFESSIONAL

Product Leadership

Technology Development & Commercialization ~ Technology Design, Engineering & Manufacturing ~ Technology Transfer & Commercialization ~ Integrated Systems & Technology Solutions ~ Advanced Telecommunications & Satellite Systems ~ New Product & New Technology Launch

Sales & Marketing Leadership

Marketing & New Business Development ~ Market Planning & Competitive Positioning ~ Negotiations, Presentations & Consultations ~ Sales & Customer Management~ Sales Team Building & Team Leadership ~ Key Account Development & Management ~ Multimedia Customer Communications ~ Territory Development & Management

Business Leadership

P&L Management ~ Partnerships, Alliances & Joint Ventures ~ Operating Management ~ Reengineering & Process Improvement

Industry Leadership

Guest Speaker, 2009 Roundtable Conference
Winner, 2008 Technology Sales Council Award for Excellence

Bulleted List Format

PROFESSIONAL QUALIFICATIONS

- Business analyst with a track record of translating business requirements into technical specifications for projects executed on target, on time, and within budget.

- Particular skill in facilitating interactive cooperation, consensus, collaboration, and commitment with stakeholders, business users, and team members.

- Diverse industry expertise that includes banking, education, financial trading, consumer market research, e-commerce, retail markets, insurance, and commercial software.

- Advanced-level knowledge of development methodologies—Waterfall, Spiral, Scrum, Extreme Programming—and processes—Software Development Life Cycle (SDLC) and Rational Unified Process (RUP).

Category Format

<table>
<tr><td colspan="2" align="center">**CAREER HIGHLIGHTS**</td></tr>
<tr><td>**Experience:**</td><td>12 years in IT Systems Design, Analysis, Programming & Operations</td></tr>
<tr><td>**Education:**</td><td>MS—Information Technology—University of California</td></tr>
<tr><td></td><td>BS—Computer Operations—California Institute of Technology</td></tr>
<tr><td>**Publications:**</td><td>"Enhancing Systems Functionality," *AITP Annual Journal,* 2010</td></tr>
<tr><td></td><td>"Power In Performance," *Computing Weekly,* 2008</td></tr>
<tr><td>**Awards:**</td><td>Technologist of the Year, Dell Corporation, 2010</td></tr>
<tr><td></td><td>Product Design Award, Dell Corporation, 2008</td></tr>
<tr><td></td><td>Recognition of Outstanding Project Leadership, Dell Corporation, 2007</td></tr>
</table>

TECHNICAL QUALIFICATIONS

The Technical Qualifications section is a vital component of just about every technology professional's resume. It is here that you will summarize all of your technical skills and qualifications to clearly demonstrate the value and knowledge you bring to an organization.

There are instances, however, for which a Technical Qualifications section may *not* be appropriate. These may include the following:

- Senior technology executives (CIO, CTO, CKO, MIS Director, VP of Information Technology)

- Technology sales and marketing professionals

- Technology support professionals

For these individuals, technical qualifications are not the *focus* of the resume, although their technical experience is vital. For senior executives, the resume should focus on organizational development and leadership, financial and operational achievements, and other general management functions and achievements. For sales and marketing professionals, the resume should highlight performance, numbers, and revenue/market growth. For support professionals, the emphasis is on customer relationship management, troubleshooting, and problem solving.

For all of the rest of you who will include this section in your resume, here are five samples of Technical Qualifications that you can use as a model. More inspiration can be found in the sample resumes in chapters 4 through 10.

Technical Skills Summary Format

TECHNICAL PROFILE

Requirements Management	Rational Requisite Pro and Telelogic DOORS
Database & Reporting	Access, Oracle, SQL, Sybase, and MicroStrategy
Languages	MySQL, DHTML/HTML, JavaScript
E-commerce	IBM WebSphere Administrator, Web site integration with richrelevance, bazaarvoice Mercado, ForeSee, and Omniture
Quality Assurance	Rational ClearQuest and Hewlett-Packard Quality Center

Double-Column Bullet Format

TECHNOLOGY PROFILE:

Programmer / Systems Analyst / Project Manager with expert qualifications in

- Systems specification, design & analysis
- Voice & data communications
- Data systems engineering & integration
- Application architecture & deployment

- Multimedia & videoconferencing systems
- Internet & intranet solutions
- C++ programming, HTML & Flash coding
- Project planning & team leadership

Multiple-Column List Format

PROJECT SUMMARY

Range of Applications Developed

- Product Evaluation
- Quality Assurance
- Defect Tracking
- Clinical Testing
- Notification Reporting
- Component Catalog
- Production Scheduling

- Vendor/Contract Management
- Timesheet/Expense Accounting
- Facilities Relocation
- Lead Generation/ Tracking
- Market Segment Tracking

- Rates and Booking
- Employee Skills Inventory
- Training/ Certification Tracking

Partial List of Clients

- Kraft
- UPS
- ConAgra
- Solo Cup Corporation
- Motorola
- Baxter International

- McGraw-Hill
- Sara Lee Corporation
- Nalco
- Northwestern Hospital
- Abbott Laboratories

- Hewitt Associates
- University of Illinois
- DePaul University
- State of Illinois

Combination Technical Qualifications/Education Format

TECHNICAL EXPERTISE & EDUCATION

Technical Knowledge: Comprehensive know-how of frameworks, project methodologies, and development tools including C#, .Net, Web services, WCF, Oasis WS, and SQL2008 • e-business multitiered hardware and software • requirements gathering and functional specifications • performance and capacity planning • security threat modeling

Project Skills: Project planning • project management • Waterfall & Agile methodologies • SDLC & SDL integration

Education: B.S. program in physics, Wayne State University, Detroit, MI

Completed 172 out of 180 credit hours

Certifications: CISSP, CISSP-ISSAP, CSSLP • Certified BizTalk/MCAD/ MCSD.net

Combination Career Summary/Technical Skills Summary Format

— TECHNOLOGY PROFILE —

Visionary IT leader, inventor, and network security expert with 18 years of experience developing software, architecting systems, and implementing very large-scale projects. Awarded 2 spam-filtering patents while managing technical operations for Gmail. Consistently demonstrated ability to accomplish more with less by making optimal use of existing staff and resources. Technical expertise includes

Databases: Oracle (10g, 9i), DB2, MS SQL Server, MySQL

Operating Systems: Solaris, HP-UX, AIX, Windows XP, RedHat Linux (and other distributions), Ubuntu

Packaged Software: Business Objects, Oracle tools, BEA Tuxedo, BEA WebLogic, Symantec i3, Wily Introscope, Quest TOAD, Quest STAT, Oracle PeopleSoft CRM/Financials and related PeopleSoft tools, IBM WebSphere, EMC Patrol, Mercury

Languages/Frameworks: SQL, PL/SQL, PeopleTools, UNIX shell scripting, PHP, CakePHP, Symfony, PERL, JavaScript, HTML, Java, .NET, C#, C++, XML, BPEL, Ruby on Rails, Ant, Python, Apache, JBoss, Hibernate, JDeveloper, Eclipse

PROFESSIONAL EXPERIENCE

The Professional Experience section is the meat of your resume—the "software and applications," as we discussed before. It's what gives your resume substance, meaning, and depth. It is also the section that will take you the longest to write. If you've had the same position for 10 years, how can you consolidate all that you have done into one short section? If, on the opposite end of the spectrum, you have had your current position for only 11 months, how can you make it seem substantial and noteworthy? And, for all of you whose experience is in between, what do you include?

These are not easy questions to answer. In fact, the most truthful response to each question is, "it depends." It depends on you, your experience, your achievements and successes, and your current career objectives.

Here are five samples of Professional Experience sections. Review how each individual's unique background is organized and emphasized, and consider your own background when using one of these as the template or foundation for developing your Professional Experience section.

Achievement Format

Emphasizes each position, overall scope of responsibility, and resulting achievements.

PROFESSIONAL EXPERIENCE

ABC TECHNOLOGY INTERNATIONAL, INC., Tokyo, Japan

Board Member / Senior Consultant (2009 to Present)

President & Chief Executive Officer (2007 to 2009)

Recruited by corporate joint-venture partners to launch the start-up of a new technology company to market remote radar systems technology and imagery worldwide. Given full leadership, negotiating, and decision-making responsibility for creating a strategic business plan, negotiating complex government approvals and funding, developing market vision and tactical business development plans, staffing, establishing a global distributor network, and building an operating infrastructure.

- Created and commercialized Japan's first radar satellite company (replacing less reliable optical/solar technology), requiring a massive initiative to educate the marketplace in the functionality of this pioneering technology. Far exceeded the financial, technological, and operational objectives of investors, the Japanese government, and the industry.

- Devoted five years to obtaining government funding ($600 million), negotiating sales and distribution rights, establishing business operations, and developing advanced technologies.

- Launched operations in 2007 and achieved profitability by end of first year. Built sales to $25 million with a staff of 150. Major clients included Georgia Pacific, BP, Lockheed Martin, Canadian Coast Guard, and Swedish and Norwegian governments. Won business in Indonesia, Singapore, and Colombia.

- Structured and negotiated a second round of government financing ($250 million) to fund the development of a second satellite system. Spurred further growth and expansion throughout new markets.

EXCEL TECHNOLOGIES, Washington, DC

Vice President—Marketing (2003 to 2007)

Recruited to provide executive marketing and business-development leadership for an innovative RCA / Sony joint venture to commercialize satellite remote-sensing technology from government to the private sector. Created the entire marketing organization, established a "for-profit" business culture, and recruited talented sales professionals.

- Established a worldwide sales and marketing division and built revenues to $22 million. Delivered phenomenal growth in international markets (60% of total company sales). Negotiated profitable sales in China, Germany, UK, Spain, Israel, Japan, and Brazil.

- Personally structured and negotiated marketing agreements, partnerships, and alliances with foreign governments, international sales agents, and product/technology development firms worldwide.

- Built in-house software and applications development group to eliminate reliance on third-party vendors.

- Reduced workforce from 300 to 150, recruited 70+ professional staff, introduced field sales automation, and restructured field sales teams. Rationalized and balanced technology offerings.

Challenge, Action, and Results (CAR) Format

Emphasizes the challenge of each position, the action you took, and the results you delivered.

PROFESSIONAL EXPERIENCE

Director of Networking & Telecommunications (2006 to Present)

Telecommunications Project Manager (2005 to 2006)

Telecommunications Engineer (2002 to 2005)

PACBELL TECHNOLOGY SERVICES CORPORATION, Los Angeles, California

Challenge: To transition an antiquated organization into a state-of-the-art telecommunications organization to support PTSC's rapid market growth and services expansion. Working to position the company as one of the top 5 players in the global technology market.

Action: Built an entirely new telecommunications organization with new architecture, hardware, software, and network protocols. Restaffed with experienced telecommunications operators, engineers, and project managers. Full P&L responsibility.

(continued)

(continued)

Results:

- Orchestrated the selection and implementation of a T1 backbone to support the implementation of a global telecommunications network. Invested more than $2.8 million to build one of the nation's most sophisticated networks.

- Achieved/surpassed all corporate objectives for system performance, functionality, reliability, and quality. Earned top rankings from internal and external audit teams evaluating the corporation's technological competencies.

- Dramatically increased user/customer responsiveness and satisfaction. Closed 2010 with less than .2% customer complaints and a better than 98.7% customer retention rate.

- Partnered with HP, IBM, and Dell to integrate their systems architecture with proprietary networks and network protocols.

- Contributed to a more than 125% increase in annual gross sales and a 150%+ increase in bottom-line profitability.

Functional Format

Emphasizes the functional areas of responsibility within the job and associated achievements.

TECHNOLOGY MANAGEMENT & LEADERSHIP EXPERIENCE

HEAD OF ENTERPRISE IT SERVICES, *The Hyland Insurance Group,* Worcester, MA (2008 to present)

Develop IT strategy to promote long-term business growth and align processes/systems with business needs. Direct cross-functional team with up to 55 employees and manage $15 million budget. Report to CTO.

Performance Milestones

- **Technology Planning & Direction:** Formulated a comprehensive IT strategy and introduced a $20 million, 3-year roadmap to align emerging technologies with long-range business objectives.

- **Profitability Enhancement:** Decreased project management and process methodology costs 40% by eliminating process overhead and integrating iterative software development practices.

- **Cost Reduction:** Eliminated approximately $5 million in system maintenance costs and reduced lost productivity by restructuring more than 33,000 database applications, reports, and reporting tools.

- **Process Improvement:** Increased work productivity 30% and generated $2 million in annual savings by partnering with offshore company for application development services.

- **Standard Policies & Procedures:** Instituted standard policies/ procedures and streamlined selection processes for reporting tools that helped company avoid $700,000 in annual costs.

DIRECTOR ARCHITECTURE & STRATEGY, *The Bell Insurance Group*, Hartford, CT (2006 to 2008)

Selected as one of top 100 executives to serve on company's business strategy group. Tasked with application and information infrastructure evaluations and enterprise IT strategy development. Reported to the CIO and business unit COO.

Performance Milestones

- **Capacity Planning:** Assembled and chaired an Enterprise IT governance program that decreased IT development costs 15% and eliminated redundant capabilities in just 8 months.

- **Cost Reduction:** Slashed application development costs 40% by pioneering cosourcing and offshore outsourcing strategies.

- **IT Direction & Initiatives:** Secured $10 million in technology funds to formulate a 3-year business strategy program for the company. Devised a 5-year, $40 million strategic IT roadmap and execution plan.

Consulting and Project Format

Emphasizes clients and project highlights.

PROJECT HIGHLIGHTS

DEVELOPER: Maxx Data Applications

CLIENT: Value Enhancement Services, Inc., June 2009–Present

PROJECT:
- Prepare system and design requirements for the Maxx system.
- Write specifications and database definitions.

(continued)

(continued)

- Work with development team and end users to complete system development.
- Continue to modify and enhance the system.

PLATFORMS:

- Microsoft Access XP, VBA, ADO, SQL Server
- Microsoft Excel XP, UML Use Case Studies, UML Use Case Diagrams

BENEFITS:

- System helps clients recover "lost" money by identifying oversights, overpayments, and missed opportunities following an expense audit conducted by Value Enhancement.
- On the first project following implementation, slashed audit time in half—from 3 months to 6 weeks—and doubled recovered funds, thereby doubling revenue to the firm.

DEVELOPER: Microsoft Access Database

CLIENT: City of Plano, Texas, May 2006–June 2009

PROJECT:

- Stepped in on short notice to identify enhancement requirements and then define, specify, and complete enhancements to the Construx project-management system.

PLATFORMS: MS Access XP, VBA, MS Excel XP

BENEFITS:

- Responded to client urgency to complete system modification within a rapid timeframe...completed using only 23 of the 40 hours allocated.

Technology Skills Format

Emphasizes technological expertise and notable projects/achievements.

—PROFESSIONAL EXPERIENCE—

HONEYWELL IAC   2008–2011

Applications Engineer, Specialty Chemicals Division, Cincinnati, OH

Procter & Gamble Shampoo and Conditioner Plant Expansion, Mariscala, Mexico—2011

- Assisted in definition of HPM and PLC logic for core control box.
- Developed software (CL, control language) to simulate batch production of shampoo and conditioner.

B.F. Goodrich Carbopol Plant Upgrade Project, Paducah, KY—2010

- Implemented and adapted old TDC 2000 MFC database, interlocks, and complex control loops into current TPS (Total Plant System) control system.
- Implemented and adapted old GE FANUC PLC ladder logic to a series of logic points in the Honeywell system that wrote and read to the PLC through a serial interface.
- Developed installation qualification and operational qualification documentation for testing procedures.
- Assisted in startup and commissioning of new control system—loop checking, troubleshooting wiring problems, and testing complex control schemes.

Control System Engineer, North American Projects Division, Phoenix, AZ

TCO Project, Tengiz, Kazakhstan—2009

- Translated and then implemented Control Bailey control schematics into current TPS control system.
- Assisted in creating serial interface points on Honeywell system to connect to Wonderware system.
- Developed software to simulate a nitrogen-generation unit for expansion area added to Tengiz plant.
- Assisted in establishing termination drawings that entailed segregation of IS and non-IS field wires.

(continued)

(continued)

- Created intelligent P&IDs of the refinery using Rebis and AutoCAD software.
- Came on board midstream while project was in danger of being lost due to client dissatisfaction. Met critical deadlines through intensive team efforts; contract extended for contingency phase.

Control System Engineer, CSCC, Ashland, KY

Ashland Petroleum Steam Project, Catlettsburg, KY—2008–2009

- Established real-time steam model for Catlettsburg refinery using G2-based Visual-MESA (a steam optimization program).
- Developed real-time control schematics for G2-based ASM (Abnormal Situation Management).
- Created a search program for ASM using G2 code.
- Calculated boiler efficiency curves for all boilers in the refinery.
- Worked with interface technology between G2 and Microsoft products.
- Rapidly learned G2 programming on the job. Became primary project engineer midstream. Contract extended.

EDUCATION, CREDENTIALS, AND CERTIFICATIONS

Your Education section should include college, certifications, credentials, licenses, registrations, and continuing education. Be succinct, and be sure to bring any notable academic credentials or certifications to the forefront—either in your Education section or in your Career Summary, as demonstrated in the first Career Summary example shown previously. If you have attended numerous continuing education programs, list only the most recent, most relevant, and most distinguishing.

Here are five sample Education sections that illustrate a variety of ways to organize and format this information.

Academic Credentials Format

EDUCATION

MBA—Information Systems & Technology—Xavier University—2008

BSEE—Electronics Engineering & Systems Design—The Ohio State University—2004

Highlights of Continuing Professional Education:

- Robotics & Systems Automation, Rensselaer Polytechnic University, 2010

- Advanced Computer Science Applications, The Ohio State University, 2010

- Executive Leadership Skills, Dale Carnegie, 2009

- Web Systems Design & Integration, University of Cincinnati, 2008

Microsoft Systems Certified Engineer (MSCE), 2002

FCC Registered Mobile Radio Operator, 2001

Executive Education Format

EDUCATION

Executive Development Program	STANFORD UNIVERSITY
Executive Development Program	UNIVERSITY OF CALIFORNIA AT IRVINE
Bachelor of Science Degree	UNIVERSITY OF CALIFORNIA AT LOS ANGELES

Certifications Format

TECHNICAL CERTIFICATIONS & EDUCATION

Microsoft Certified Systems Engineer (MCSE), 2009

Microsoft Certified Professional (MCP), 2007

Cisco Certified Network Associate (CCNA), 2007

Computer Systems Management Major, University of Michigan, 2004

A.A.S. Degree in Computer Technology, Michigan Community College, 2002

Professional Training Format

> ### PROFESSIONAL TRAINING & DEVELOPMENT
>
> **Computer Statistics & Methodologies,** Baruch College, 2008
>
> **Computer Operations Management,** Baruch College, 2008
>
> **C++ Programming for Technology Professionals,** University of Maryland, 2007
>
> **Voice & Data Systems Design,** New York University, 2006
>
> **Network Administrator,** New York University, 2008
>
> **Anne Arundel Community College,** Arnold, Maryland, 2004–2006

Nondegree Format

> ### TECHNICAL TRAINING & EDUCATION
>
> **UNIVERSITY OF ILLINOIS,** Urbana, Illinois
>
> **BBA Candidate—Management Information Systems** (senior class status)
>
> **UNIVERSITY OF MICHIGAN,** Ann Arbor, Michigan
>
> **Dual Major in Computer Systems & Programming** (2 years)
>
> **Graduate,** 200+ hours of continuing professional and technical education through AITP, Chicago Technology Institute, IBM, HP, and DePaul University

THE "EXTRAS"

The primary focus of your resume is on information that is directly related to your career goals. However, you also should include things that will distinguish you from other candidates and clearly demonstrate your value to a prospective employer. And, not too surprisingly, it is often the "extras" that get you the interviews.

Following is a list of the other categories you might or might not include in your resume, depending on your particular experience and your current career objectives. Review the information. If it's pertinent to you, use the samples for formatting your own data. Remember, however, that if something is truly impressive, you might want to include it in your Career Summary at the beginning of your resume to draw even more attention to it. If this is the case, it's not necessary to repeat the information at the end of your resume.

Affiliations—Professional

If you are a member of any professional, leadership, or technology associations, be sure to include that information on your resume. It communicates a message of professionalism, a desire to stay current with the industry, and a strong professional network. Here's an example:

PROFESSIONAL AFFILIATIONS

- Member, Association of Information Technology Professionals (Training Program Chairperson—2010)

- Member, Institute for Technology Enterprise (Convention Chairperson—2008)

- President, Project Management Institute (New York Chapter—2006–2007)

Affiliations—Civic

Civic affiliations are fine to include if they fall into one or more of the following categories:

- Are with a notable organization
- Demonstrate leadership experience
- May be of interest to a prospective employer

However, things such as treasurer of your local condo association and volunteer at your child's day care center are not generally of value in marketing your qualifications. Here's an example of what to include:

- Volunteer Chairperson, United Way of America—Detroit Chapter, 2008 to Present

- President, Lambert Valley Conservation District, 2005 to Present

- Treasurer, Habitat for Humanity—Detroit Chapter, 2002 to 2004

Public Speaking

Experts are the ones who are invited to give public presentations at conferences, technical training programs, symposia, and other events. So if you have public speaking experience, others must consider you an expert. Be sure to include this very complimentary information in your resume. Here's one way to present it:

- Keynote Speaker, 2010 Conference of Internet Executives—Las Vegas
- Presenter, 2009 International AITP Conference—Dallas
- Presenter, 2007 IBM Technology Training Symposium—New York

Publications

If you're published, you must be an expert (or at least most people will think so). Just as with your public speaking engagements, be sure to include your publications. They validate your knowledge, qualifications, and credibility. Publications can include books, articles, Web site content, manuals, and other written documents. Here's an example:

- Author, "Winning Web Marketing Strategies," *TechBusiness Magazine,* January 2010
- Author, "Web Marketing 101: Compete To Win," *TechBusiness Online,* February 2008
- Coauthor, "Op-Cit Technology Training Manual," Op-Cit Corporation, December 2007

Honors and Awards

If you have won honors and awards, you can either include them in a separate section on your resume or integrate them into the Education or Professional Experience section, whichever is most appropriate. If you choose to include them in a separate section, consider this format:

- Winner, 2009 **"President's Club"** award for outstanding contributions to new product development.
- Winner, 2006 **"Innovator's Club"** award for outstanding contributions to technology innovation.
- Named **"Graduate Student of the Year,"** Hofstra University, 2002
- **Summa Cum Laude Graduate,** Washington & Lee University, 2000

Teaching and Training Experience

Many professionals in the technology industry also teach or train at institutions and organizations other than their full-time employer. If this is applicable to you, you will want to include that experience on your resume. If someone hires you (paid or unpaid) to speak to an audience, it communicates a strong message about your qualifications and credibility. Here's a format you might use to present this information:

- Adjunct Faculty—Information Technology, Contra Costa Community College, Spring 2009

- Instructor—Programming Principles, Contra Costa Community College, Fall 2007

- Instructor—Systems Architecture, Valley Mead University, Fall 2005–Spring 2006

NOTE: If teaching or training is your primary occupation, don't include this section in your resume. Rather, include your teaching and training in your Professional Experience section.

Personal Information

We do not recommend that you include such personal information as birth date, marital status, number of children, and related data. However, there may be instances when personal information is appropriate. If this information will give you a competitive advantage or answer unspoken questions about your background, then by all means include it. Here's an example:

- Born in Argentina. U.S. Permanent Residency Status since 2000.

- Fluent in English, Spanish, and Portuguese.

- Competitive Triathlete. Top-5 finish, 2008 Midwest Triathlon and 2010 Des Moines Triathlon.

Consolidating the Extras

Sometimes you have so many extra categories at the end of your resume that spacing becomes a problem. You certainly don't want to have to make your resume a page longer to accommodate five lines, nor do you want the "extras" to overwhelm the primary sections of your resume. Yet you believe the "extra" information is important and should be included. Or perhaps you have a few small bits of information that you think are important but don't merit an entire section for each "bit." In these situations, consider consolidating the information using one of the following formats. You'll save space, avoid overemphasizing individual items, and present a professional, distinguished appearance.

PROFESSIONAL PROFILE

Affiliations	American Management Association
	Association of Information Technology Professionals
	Information Technology Executives Leadership Council

(continued)

(continued)

Public Speaking	Keynote Speaker, AMA Leadership Conference, Dallas, 2010
	Presenter, AITP National Conference, San Diego, 2010
	Panelist, AITP National Conference, Chicago, 2008
Foreign Languages	Fluent in English, Spanish, and German

ADDITIONAL INFORMATION

- Founder and Program Chair, Detroit Technical Professionals Association
- Bilingual—Spanish/English
- Available for relocation

Writing Tips, Techniques, and Important Lessons

At this point, you've done a lot of reading, probably taken some notes, highlighted samples that appeal to you, and are ready to plunge into writing your resume. To make this task as easy as possible, we've compiled some "insider" techniques that we've used in our professional resume writing practices. These techniques were learned the hard way through years of experience! We know they work; they will make the writing process easier, faster, and more enjoyable for you.

Get It Down—Then Polish and Perfect It

Don't be too concerned with making your resume "perfect" the first time around. It's far better to move fairly swiftly through the process, getting the basic information organized and on paper (or on-screen), rather than agonizing about the perfect phrase or ideal formatting. Once you've completed a draft, we think you'll be surprised at how close to "final" it is, and you'll be able to edit, tighten, and improve formatting fairly quickly.

Write Your Resume from the Bottom Up

Here's the system:

- **Start with the easy things**—Education, Professional Affiliations, Public Speaking, and any other extras you want to include. These items require little thought, other than formatting considerations, and can be completed in just a few minutes.

- **Write short job descriptions for your older positions, the ones you held years ago.** Be very brief and focus on highlights such as rapid promotion, project highlights, notable achievements, technology innovations, industry recognition, or employment with well-respected, well-known companies.

Once you've completed this, look at how much you've written in a short period of time!

- **Write the job descriptions for your most recent positions.** This will take a bit longer than the other sections you have written. Remember to focus on the overall scope of your responsibility, major projects, and significant achievements. Tell your reader what you did and how well you did it. You can use any of the formats recommended earlier in this chapter, or you can create something that is unique to you and your career.

  Now, see how far along you are? Your resume is 90 percent complete with only one small section left to do.

- **Write your career summary.** Before you start writing, remember your objective for this section. The summary should not simply rehash your previous experience. Rather, it is designed to highlight the skills and qualifications you have that are most closely related to your current career objective(s). The summary is intended to capture the reader's attention and "sell" your expertise.

That's it. You're done. We guarantee that the process of writing your resume will be much, much easier if you follow the "bottom-up" strategy. Now, on to the next tip.

INCLUDE NOTABLE OR PROMINENT "EXTRA" STUFF IN YOUR CAREER SUMMARY

Remember the "bits and bytes" sections that are normally at the bottom of your resume? If this information is particularly notable or prominent—for example, you won a notable award, spoke at an international technology conference, invented a new product, or taught at a prestigious university—you may want to include it at the top in your Career Summary. Remember, the summary section is written to distinguish you from the crowd of other qualified candidates. As such, if you've accomplished anything that clearly demonstrates your knowledge, expertise, and credibility, consider moving it to your Career Summary for added attention. For examples, refer to the sample Career Summaries earlier in the chapter and in chapters 4 through 10.

USE RESUME SAMPLES TO GET IDEAS FOR CONTENT, FORMAT, AND ORGANIZATION

This book is just one of many resources where you can review the resumes of other technology professionals to help you in formulating your strategy, writing the text, and formatting your resume. These books are published precisely for that reason. You don't have to struggle alone. Rather, use all the available resources at your disposal.

Be forewarned, however, that it's unlikely you will find a resume that fits your life and career to a "t." It's more likely that you will use "some of this sample" and "some of that sample" to create a resume that is uniquely "you."

STICK TO THE HIGHLIGHTS

If you have more information than will fit comfortably into a single category on your resume, include just the highlights. This is particularly relevant to the "extra" categories such as Professional Affiliations, Civic Affiliations, Foreign Languages, Honors and Awards, Publications, Public Speaking, and the like. Suppose you have won 10 different awards throughout your career, but you're limited in the amount of space available at the bottom of your resume. Instead of listing all 10 and forcing your resume onto an additional page, simply title the category "Highlights of Honors & Awards" or "Notable Honors & Awards" and include just the most impressive and relevant ones. By using the words "highlights" and "notable," you are communicating to your reader that you are providing just a partial listing.

INCLUDE DATES OR NOT?

Unless you are over age 50, we recommend that you date your work experience and your education. Without dates, your resume becomes vague and difficult for the typical hiring manager or recruiter to interpret. What's more, it often communicates the message that you are trying to hide something. Maybe you haven't worked in two years, maybe you were fired from each of your last three positions, or maybe you never graduated from college. Being vague and creating a resume that is difficult to read will, inevitably, lead to uncertainty and a quick toss into the "not interested" pile of candidates. By including the dates of your education and your experience, you create a clean and concise picture that one can easily follow to track your career progression.

If you are over age 50, dating your early positions must be an individual decision. On the one hand, you do not want to "date" yourself out of consideration by including dates from the 1970s and 1980s. On the other hand, it may be that those positions are worth including for any one of a number of reasons. Further, if you omit those early dates, you might feel as though you are misrepresenting yourself (or lying) to a prospective employer.

Here is a strategy to overcome those concerns while still including your early experience: Create a separate category titled "Previous Professional Experience" in which you summarize your earliest employment. You can tailor this statement to emphasize just what is most important about that experience.

If you want to focus on the reputation of your past employers, include a statement such as this:

- Previous experience includes several programming, applications-development, and project-management positions with **IBM, Tandem, and Hewlett Packard.**

If you want to focus on the rapid progression of your career, consider this example:

> • **Promoted rapidly through a series of increasingly responsible project management positions** with Digital Equipment Corporation, earning six promotions in eight years.

If you want to focus on your early career achievements, include a statement such as the following:

> • Led the design, development, and market launch of X-TEL's second-generation software, now a **$2.1 million profit center** for the corporation.

By including any one of the above paragraphs, under the heading "Previous Professional Experience," you are clearly communicating to your reader that your employment history dates further back than the dates you have indicated on your resume. In turn, you are being 100 percent above-board and not misrepresenting yourself or your career. You're focusing on the success, achievement, and prominence of your earliest assignments without specifying exact dates.

If you are over age 50, we generally do not recommend that you date your education or college degrees. Simply include the degree and the university with no date. Why exclude yourself from consideration by immediately presenting the fact that you earned your college degree in 1969, 1976, or 1982—about the time the hiring manager was probably born? Remember, the goal of your resume is to share the highlights of your career and open doors for interviews. It is *not* to give your entire life story. As such, it is not mandatory to date your college degree.

However, if you use this strategy, be aware that the reader is likely to assume there is *some* gap between when your education ended and when your work experience started. Therefore, if you choose to begin your chronological work history with your first job out of college, omitting your graduation date could actually backfire, because the reader will assume you have experience that predates your first job. In this case, it's best either to *include your graduation date* or *omit dates of earliest experience*, using the summary strategy discussed above.

NEVER INCLUDE SALARY HISTORY OR SALARY REQUIREMENTS ON YOUR RESUME

Your resume is *not* the proper forum for a salary discussion. First of all, you will never provide salary information unless a company has requested that information and you choose to comply. (Studies show that employers will look at your resume anyway, so you may choose not to respond to this request, thereby avoiding pricing yourself out of the job or locking yourself into a lower salary than the job is worth.)

When contacting recruiters, however, we recommend that you do provide salary information, but again, only in your cover letter. With recruiters, you want to "put all of your cards on the table" and help them make an appropriate placement by providing information about your current salary and salary objectives. For example, "Be advised that my current compensation is $75,000 annually and that I am interested in a position starting at a minimum of $85,000 per year." Or, if you would prefer to be a little less specific, you might write, "My annual compensation over the past three years has averaged $50,000+."

Finally, in some instances you will not have the option for omitting salary information. A good example is an online application that requires you to submit your salary history and/or salary requirements along with your resume. In that case, be truthful and know that all candidates will be revealing similar information.

ALWAYS REMEMBER THAT YOU ARE SELLING

As we have discussed over and over throughout this book, resume writing is sales. Understand and appreciate the value you bring to a prospective employer, and then communicate that value by focusing on your achievements. Companies don't want to hire just anyone; they want to hire "the" someone who will make a difference. Show them that you are that candidate.

CHAPTER 3

Producing Your Resume for Online and Offline Distribution: Printed, Electronic, and Web Resumes

If you're like most job seekers (and professional resume writers), you will have worked long and hard to write a powerful resume that proudly showcases your career, your promotions, your achievements, and other highlights of your professional life. You've probably reviewed and edited your resume over and over, making certain that the wording is accurate and positions you precisely for your targeted career objectives.

Your next challenge is the design, layout, and presentation of your resume. It's not enough that your resume reads well; your resume also must have just the right look and feel for the right audience. As such, you must make a few choices and decisions about what your final resume presentation will look like.

In decades past, this would have been only a brief discussion during which we would have told you how important it was to use a "nice" typestyle and to leave plenty of white space so that hiring managers and recruiters could easily peruse your resume. Resume production and distribution were easy. You typed (maybe even word processed!) your resume; printed it on white, ivory, or light gray paper; put it into an envelope; and mailed it. There were few decisions to be made. Even with the introduction of the fax machine, the process was largely the same.

Today's job search looks nothing like it did even a decade ago, because the Internet and e-mail have forever changed how job seekers distribute resumes and look for jobs! These technological tools now provide job seekers with a variety of methods to distribute their resumes.

How you produce your resume will depend entirely on how you will be using and distributing it. Ask yourself these questions:

1. Will you be e-mailing your resume to colleagues and network contacts?

2. Will you be e-mailing your resume in response to specific employment opportunities?

3. Will you be posting your resume on various job boards?

4. Will you be pasting sections of your resume into online employment applications?

5. Will you be uploading your entire resume into a recruiter's database?

For most of you reading this book, the answer to each of those five questions is yes. Yes, you will be e-mailing, posting, pasting, and uploading as you manage a combination of both online and offline resume distribution efforts. As such, you will need at least two different versions of your resume: one for online use and one for offline use.

The Three Types of Resumes

In today's job search and employment world, there are three basic types of resumes:

- The printed resume (Word and PDF files)

- The electronic resume (text files)

- The Web resume

The following sections give details on how to prepare each type of resume and when you will most often use it.

Just as in all other industries and professions, you will need—at a minimum—both a printed and an electronic resume. This is true for everyone reading this book, whether you are a systems analyst, network engineer, programmer, website designer, vice president of information technology, or CIO. In fact, because everyone reading this book is a "technologist" of one sort or another, a Web resume should also be a strong consideration as it might allow you to demonstrate your technical expertise and might give you a competitive edge over others in the employment market.

Different employers have different preferences regarding resumes. Some prospective employers will request a printed copy of your resume, a copy that you might actually mail to them. More often, companies will ask you to e-mail your resume, at which point the recipient might print a copy and/or import it into the company database. Finally, other organizations will ask you to upload your resume (and, sometimes, cover letter) into their online applicant tracking and candidate management systems. The bottom line is, today's job seeker needs both a printed resume and an electronic resume to manage a successful job search and career marketing campaign.

The Printed Resume

The printed resume is what we all know as the "traditional resume," the one that looks good on paper and might include graphic elements such as borders or shaded boxes. This is the version that you mail to a recruiter, take to an interview, use at networking events, and forward by mail and/or e-mail in response to a job posting. It's rare, and becoming more so with each passing year, that organizations would ask you to fax your resume to them. Faxing is, largely, a technology of the past when it comes to efficient job search and career management.

THE PURPOSE OF A PRINTED RESUME

When preparing a printed resume, your objective is to create a sharp, professional, and visually attractive presentation that will stand out from the crowd of other candidates' resumes without going "over the top." A distinctive typestyle such as Tahoma, Verdana, Calibri, Georgia, or Arial Narrow and a few bold lines or boxes can transform a resume from blah to brilliant! If you can make someone notice your resume, you'll instantly move your candidacy forward.

Always keep in mind that a few pieces of paper convey the first impression of you to a potential employer or recruiter, and that first impression goes a long, long way. Either it's sharp and distinctive, or it's lost in the crowd. Only you can make that difference, and you must. Never be fooled into thinking that just because you have the strongest technical qualifications, the most impressive industry certifications, or the ultimate employment history and career path that the visual presentation of your resume does not matter. It is a key factor in elevating you above the crowd of other candidates, and that's an important step in the job search process.

E-MAIL ATTACHMENTS

Most likely, the vast majority of resumes you distribute will be through e-mail, so pay special attention to the following information.

E-mailing is so easy. Simply attach the Microsoft Word version of your resume to your e-mail message and you're set. Because the vast majority of businesses use Microsoft Word, this is the most acceptable format and will present the fewest difficulties in "translation" when attached. Be certain that you save and send your resume in the .doc format, not the .docx format that is standard with newer computer systems. You certainly don't want to send a resume that can't be opened or read by the recipient, and older systems cannot read .docx files.

If you do have a resume with a strong design component, graphics, charts, tables, or other visuals, you might prefer to attach a PDF (portable document format) version of your resume to ensure 100 percent integrity of the presentation. Even if you don't have the capability to create PDF files on your computer, you'll find it's quick, easy, and free to do so by using readily available online resources such as BCL Technologies' PDF Online at www.pdfonline.com.

By using a PDF file, you're certain that your resume appears exactly as you created it. The downside to PDF files is that they cannot be read into a company's resume-storage system unless they are printed and scanned in. In today's fast-paced world of job searching and hiring, you can be rather confident that this will not happen. Therefore, we recommend that you use Microsoft Word .doc files as your everyday standard and only use the PDF format when absolutely necessary.

Be sure you take the time to test your resume by e-mailing it, in .doc and/or PDF formats, to several friends or colleagues. Ask them to both view it and print it on their systems to be sure that everything at their end looks like it does at your end. You could bypass this step if you're sending a PDF file, but why would you? It's always a good strategy to test everything before you let it go "live"!

The Electronic Resume

An electronic resume is a plain-text version of your printed resume, stripped of all of the design, formatting, and other enhancements that you've used to make your resume sharp, attractive, and distinctive. All of the things that you would normally do to make your printed resume look attractive—bold print, italics, multiple columns, sharp-looking typestyle, and more—are stripped away to create a document that can be easily read and/or scanned.

UNDERSTANDING THE USES FOR AN ELECTRONIC RESUME

A plain-text resume makes professional resume writers cringe, but it does have several very important uses that you will, most likely, encounter during your job search campaign:

- You can easily copy and paste the plain-text version into online job applications and resume databases, with no concern that formatting glitches will cause confusion. In today's technology-driven job search and employment landscape, this will be something you will do frequently when reaching out to both companies and recruiters. Don't make the mistake of copying and pasting your Word file into these applications! Often the formatting will be lost and/or presented incorrectly, and your information might not be accurately communicated.

- You can paste the plain-text version of your resume into the body of an e-mail message rather than sending it as an attachment. Some people are hesitant to open attachments from people they don't know, and you might encounter that situation. If so, the text file comes in handy and avoids any potential formatting problems.

- Although unattractive, the plain-text version is 100 percent scannable. It's rare anymore for a company or a recruiter to ask you to e-mail a scannable version of your resume. However, you never know when the situation may arise, and at least you'll be prepared.

CREATING A TEXT FILE

To create a plain-text version of your resume, follow these simple steps:

1. Open the Word file of your resume and create a new version using the Save As feature. Select Text Only, Plain Text, or ASCII in the Save As option box.

2. Close the new file.

3. Reopen the file, and you'll find that your resume has been automatically reformatted into the Courier font, all formatting has been removed, and the text is left-justified.

4. Review the resume very carefully and fix any formatting "glitches"—of which there will probably be quite a few! Pay special attention to the following formatting recommendations:

   • Position your name, and nothing else, on the top line of the resume.

   • Replace odd characters that may have been inserted to take the place of "curly" quotes, dashes, accents, or other nonstandard symbols.

   • Feel free to use *common* abbreviations (for instance, *B.S.* or *BS* for Bachelor of Science degree). But when in doubt, spell it out.

   • Eliminate graphics, borders, and horizontal lines.

   • Avoid columns and tables, although a simple two-column listing can be read without difficulty.

   • Spell out symbols such as % and &.

   • If necessary, add extra blank lines to improve readability. Length doesn't really matter because people see the entire document and not a certain number of pages.

   • Consider adding horizontal dividers to break the resume into sections so that people can easily skim and review the document. You can use any standard typewriter symbols (such as *, -, (,), =, +, ^, or #).

To illustrate what you can expect when creating these versions of your own resume, the following figures show the same resume in a printed Word format, a printed PDF format (allowing inclusion of additional graphics), and an electronic (text) format.

Eileen Gaffney

34 Holly Lane, Darien, CT 06820
egaffney@choiceapplications.com • 203.868.4675

Adobe-Certified Flex Developer

Delivering Impeccably Designed Applications That Fulfill Client Needs

Clarify client needs and translate them into well-designed, cost-effective applications. Execute all life-cycle phases, incorporating solid understanding of OOAD principles and routinely creating efficient, transparent, and maintainable code.

Architect database-enabled applications. Build frameworks that allow nonprogrammers to create and update content.

Possess excellent communication skills, a quick learning style, strong attention to detail, and a hardworking ethos. Transitioned to the Adobe Flex platform in 2006; Adobe Certified Developer in Flex 2.

Technical Qualifications

Languages: ActionScript • MXML • XML • ASP • CSS • HTML • SQL • Java

Architecture: OOAD • Cairngorm • Design Patterns • MVC • UML

Platforms & Tools: Adobe AIR • Adobe Flex 2 & 3 • Ant • Antennae • BlazeDS • Dreamweaver • Eclipse/Flex Builder • Flash • FlexUnit • Fluint • Illustrator • Jira • LCDS • MySQL • Photoshop • SoundEdit • SQL Server • SQLite • SVN/TortoiseSVN • Tomcat • Visual FlexUnit

Selected Flex Projects

☑ Currently developing a **foreign language learning tool for use on next-generation cell phones** (a Choice Applications in-house project). An Adobe AIR application will drill users, who can indicate which content is mastered. Users can also upload their own language-learning modules with an Adobe Flex RIA. Cairngorm architecture will implement AIR player and RIA. Technical challenges include synchronization of a local SQLite database with the master database on server and creation of custom Flex components.

☑ Developed Visual FlexUnit, an open-source Adobe AIR-based FlexUnit extension for **automated testing of the visual appearance of Flex components.** Integrated project into CompuWrite's automated build process and wrote documentation. Published project on Google code, including a simplified build process using Antennae. See http://code.google.com/j/visualflexair/wiki/VisualFlexAIR.

☑ Created **example of Flex's data visualization and mapping capabilities.** See www.choiceapps/map.com.

☑ Implemented the **Fluint testing framework** (for Generative).

Employment

President, Choice Applications   http://www.choiceapps.com   Darien, CT, 1997–Present

Software development consultancy helping clients create desktop and Web-based applications. In addition to Flex projects described above, highlights of professional role in Choice Applications' projects include:

Application Architect and Programmer, CASTLE LEARNING AND DEVELOPMENT, INC., Stamford, CT

Hired during company emergency when data errors threatened sales of 1.0 version of key new product. Successfully analyzed and fixed product before customer complaints mounted. Continued on to develop version 2.0. The product tested reading skills in fine detail and allowed teachers to tailor lessons for maximum impact. It implemented intelligent branching that made decisions similar to those made by a human expert testing a child.

Page 1

The Word version of a developer's resume.

☑ Wrote and used Flash components to prototype complex UI features.

☑ Created a Lingo profiler framework and a functional testing framework for project.

☑ Delivered a complete, functioning product.

Application Architect and Lead Programmer, WEINSTEIN INSTITUTE FOR EDUCATION, New York, NY

Challenged to develop "The Virtual Patient," a series of case-based educational modules for medical students that simulated examinations and interviews of virtual patients; enabled students to order tests, therapies, and consults; and provided feedback. Created a unique framework to provide both the flexibility needed to develop multiple modules and the structure required to make it cost-effective.

☑ Designed program with a Director front-end and a FileMaker database back-end so that most data could be entered directly into the database by content authors.

☑ Collaboratively planned UI and overall program design with Institute staff and teamed with other programmers to plan program architecture.

☑ Wrote functional and technical specs; wrote much of the actual Lingo programming.

Architect and Programmer, NEW YORK UNIVERSITY SCHOOL OF MEDICINE, New York, NY

Developed and implemented Rich Internet Application allowing doctors and medical students to specify patient symptoms, view information and images, and posit diagnoses. Brainstormed program and UI design with author. Designed architecture. Wrote functional and technical specs.

☑ Implemented ASP/IIS/SQL Server back-end.

☑ Wrote ActionScript 2.0 client code that communicated with ASP.

☑ Implemented with Director Shockwave in 2000 and reimplemented with Flash in 2003.

Lead Programmer, INNOVATIONS IN SCIENCE EDUCATION, Stamford, CT

Delivered interactive components for Houghton Mifflin's earth science website that included on-screen drawing, a distance measurement tool, drag and drop, graphing, and other features. Executed full life cycle quickly and under budget.

☑ Developed cost-effective framework that allowed less-advanced developers to efficiently create interactive Shockwave modules using a combination of Macromedia Director's GUI, preconstructed behaviors, and an XML configuration file.

Profile

Affiliations
Stamford Flex Application Incubator Group (mentor/coordinator), Adobe Stamford User Group (cochair), Stamford Flash Platform User Group (e-mail list moderator), and CairngormDocs.org (webmaster).

Online Publications
Author, *FlexAbility* (blog). http://www.choiceapps.com/flex_ability/

Lead author, "Visual FlexUnit (documentation page)," December 2007.
http://code.google.com/p/visualflexair/VisualFlexAIR

Author, *Setting Up a Windows Apache/Tomcat/LCDS Server,* December 2007.
http://www.choiceapps.com/technology/choiceapps_articles/setting_up_a_windows_tomcat_fds_server.html

Selected Presentations
Using the Strategy Pattern: A Simple Audio Sequencing Example, Stamford Flash Platform Design Patterns Group, February 2009.

Visual FlexUnit, Stamford Flash Platform Design Patterns Group, January 2008.

The Command Pattern & Cairngorm, Stamford Flash Platform Design Patterns Group, December 2006.
http://www.choiceapps.com/technology/presentations/command_pattern_and_cairngorm/

Interests
Skydiving, carpentry, 19th-century literature.

Eileen Gaffney

34 Holly Lane, Darien, CT 06820
egaffney@choiceapplications.com • 203.868.4675

CERTIFIED PROFESSIONAL
Adobe® Flex™ Developer

Delivering Impeccably Designed Applications That Fulfill Client Needs

Clarify client needs and translate them into well-designed, cost-effective applications. Execute all life-cycle phases, incorporating solid understanding of OOAD principles and routinely creating efficient, transparent, and maintainable code.

Architect database-enabled applications. Build frameworks that allow nonprogrammers to create and update content.

Possess excellent communication skills, a quick learning style, strong attention to detail, and a hardworking ethos. Transitioned to the Adobe Flex platform in 2006; Adobe Certified Developer in Flex 2.

Technical Qualifications

Languages: ActionScript • MXML • XML • ASP • CSS • HTML • SQL • Java

Architecture: OOAD • Cairngorm • Design Patterns • MVC • UML

Platforms & Tools: Adobe AIR • Adobe Flex 2 & 3 • Ant • Antennae • BlazeDS • Dreamweaver • Eclipse/Flex Builder • Flash • FlexUnit • Fluint • Illustrator • Jira • LCDS • MySQL • Photoshop • SoundEdit • SQL Server • SQLite • SVN/TortoiseSVN • Tomcat • Visual FlexUnit

Selected Flex Projects

☑ Currently developing a **foreign language learning tool for use on next-generation cell phones** (a Choice Applications in-house project). An Adobe AIR application will drill users, who can indicate which content is mastered. Users can also upload their own language-learning modules with an Adobe Flex RIA. Cairngorm architecture will implement AIR player and RIA. Technical challenges include synchronization of a local SQLite database with the master database on server and creation of custom Flex components.

☑ Developed Visual FlexUnit, an open-source Adobe AIR-based FlexUnit extension for **automated testing of the visual appearance of Flex components.** Integrated project into CompuWrite's automated build process and wrote documentation. Published project on Google code, including a simplified build process using Antennae. See http://code.google.com/j/visualflexair/wiki/VisualFlexAIR.

☑ Created **example of Flex's data visualization and mapping capabilities.** See www.choiceapps/map.com.

☑ Implemented the **Fluint testing framework** (for Generative).

Employment

President, Choice Applications   http://www.choiceapps.com   Darien, CT, 1997–Present

Software development consultancy helping clients create desktop and Web-based applications. In addition to Flex projects described above, highlights of professional role in Choice Applications' projects include:

Application Architect and Programmer, CASTLE LEARNING AND DEVELOPMENT, INC., Stamford, CT

Hired during company emergency when data errors threatened sales of 1.0 version of key new product. Successfully analyzed and fixed product before customer complaints mounted. Continued on to develop version 2.0. The product tested reading skills in fine detail and allowed teachers to tailor lessons for maximum impact. It implemented intelligent branching that made decisions similar to those made by a human expert testing a child.

Page 1

The PDF version of a developer's resume.

☑ Wrote and used Flash components to prototype complex UI features.
☑ Created a Lingo profiler framework and a functional testing framework for project.
☑ Delivered a complete, functioning product.

Application Architect and Lead Programmer, WEINSTEIN INSTITUTE FOR EDUCATION, New York, NY

Challenged to develop "The Virtual Patient," a series of case-based educational modules for medical students that simulated examinations and interviews of virtual patients; enabled students to order tests, therapies, and consults; and provided feedback. Created a unique framework to provide both the flexibility needed to develop multiple modules and the structure required to make it cost-effective.

☑ Designed program with a Director front-end and a FileMaker database back-end so that most data could be entered directly into the database by content authors.
☑ Collaboratively planned UI and overall program design with Institute staff and teamed with other programmers to plan program architecture.
☑ Wrote functional and technical specs; wrote much of the actual Lingo programming.

Architect and Programmer, NEW YORK UNIVERSITY SCHOOL OF MEDICINE, New York, NY

Developed and implemented Rich Internet Application allowing doctors and medical students to specify patient symptoms, view information and images, and posit diagnoses. Brainstormed program and UI design with author. Designed architecture. Wrote functional and technical specs.

☑ Implemented ASP/IIS/SQL Server back-end.
☑ Wrote ActionScript 2.0 client code that communicated with ASP.
☑ Implemented with Director Shockwave in 2000 and reimplemented with Flash in 2003.

Lead Programmer, INNOVATIONS IN SCIENCE EDUCATION, Stamford, CT

Delivered interactive components for Houghton Mifflin's earth science website that included on-screen drawing, a distance measurement tool, drag and drop, graphing, and other features. Executed full life cycle quickly and under budget.

☑ Developed cost-effective framework that allowed less-advanced developers to efficiently create interactive Shockwave modules using a combination of Macromedia Director's GUI, preconstructed behaviors, and an XML configuration file.

Profile

Affiliations   Stamford Flex Application Incubator Group (mentor/coordinator), Adobe Stamford User Group (cochair), Stamford Flash Platform User Group (e-mail list moderator), and CairngormDocs.org (webmaster).

Online Publications   Author, *FlexAbility* (blog). http://www.choiceapps.com/flex_ability/

Lead author, "Visual FlexUnit (documentation page)," December 2007. http://code.google.com/p/visualflexair/VisualFlexAIR

Author, *Setting Up a Windows Apache/Tomcat/LCDS Server,* December 2007. http://www.choiceapps.com/technology/choiceapps_articles/setting_up_a_windows_tomcat_fds_server.html

Selected Presentations   *Using the Strategy Pattern: A Simple Audio Sequencing Example,* Stamford Flash Platform Design Patterns Group, February 2009.

Visual FlexUnit, Stamford Flash Platform Design Patterns Group, January 2008.

The Command Pattern & Cairngorm, Stamford Flash Platform Design Patterns Group, December 2006. http://www.choiceapps.com/technology/presentations/command_pattern_and_cairngorm/

Interests   Skydiving, carpentry, 19th-century literature.

```
EILEEN GAFFNEY
34 Holly Lane, Darien, CT 06820
egaffney@choiceapplications.com
203.868.4675


========================================
ADOBE-CERTIFIED FLEX DEVELOPER
----------------------------------------
Delivering Impeccably Designed Applications That Fulfill Client Needs

Clarify client needs and translate them into well-designed, cost-
effective applications. Execute all life-cycle phases, incorporating
solid understanding of OOAD principles and routinely creating efficient,
transparent, and maintainable code.

Architect database-enabled applications. Build frameworks that allow
nonprogrammers to create and update content.

Possess excellent communication skills, a quick learning style, strong
attention to detail, and a hardworking ethos. Transitioned to the Adobe
Flex platform in 2006; Adobe Certified Developer in Flex 2.

========================================
TECHNICAL QUALIFICATIONS

Languages: ActionScript * MXML * XML * ASP * CSS * HTML * SQL * Java

Architecture: OOAD * Cairngorm * Design Patterns * MVC * UML

Platforms & Tools: Adobe AIR * Adobe Flex 2 & 3 * Ant * Antennae *
BlazeDS * Dreamweaver * Eclipse/Flex Builder * Flash * FlexUnit * Fluint
* Illustrator * Jira * LCDS * MySQL * Photoshop * SoundEdit * SQL Server
* SQLite * SVN/TortoiseSVN * Tomcat * Visual FlexUnit

========================================
SELECTED FLEX PROJECTS

* Currently developing a foreign language learning tool for use on next-
generation cell phones (a Choice Applications in-house project). An Adobe
AIR application will drill users, who can indicate which content is
mastered. Users can also upload their own language-learning modules with
an Adobe Flex RIA. Cairngorm architecture will implement AIR player and
RIA. Technical challenges include synchronization of a local SQLite
database with the master database on server and creation of custom Flex
components.

* Developed Visual FlexUnit, an open-source Adobe AIR-based FlexUnit
extension for automated testing of the visual appearance of Flex
components. Integrated project into CompuWrite's automated build process
and wrote documentation. Published project on Google code, including a
simplified build process using Antennae. See
http://code.google.com/j/visualflexair/wiki/VisualFlexAIR.
```

The electronic version of a developer's resume.

```
* Created example of Flex's data visualization and mapping capabilities.
See www.choiceapps/map.com.

* Implemented the Fluint testing framework (for Generative).

=========================================
EMPLOYMENT

President, Choice Applications, Darien, CT, 1997 to Present
http://www.choiceapps.com
Software development consultancy helping clients create desktop and Web-
based applications. In addition to Flex projects described above,
highlights of professional role in Choice Applications' projects include:

-------------------------------------------
Application Architect and Programmer
CASTLE LEARNING AND DEVELOPMENT, INC., Stamford, CT

Hired during company emergency when data errors threatened sales of 1.0
version of key new product. Successfully analyzed and fixed product
before customer complaints mounted. Continued on to develop version 2.0.
The product tested reading skills in fine detail and allowed teachers to
tailor lessons for maximum impact. It implemented intelligent branching
that made decisions similar to those made by a human expert testing a
child.

* Wrote and used Flash components to prototype complex UI features.
* Created a Lingo profiler framework and a functional testing framework
for project.
* Delivered a complete, functioning product.


-------------------------------------------
Application Architect and Lead Programmer
WEINSTEIN INSTITUTE FOR EDUCATION, New York, NY

Challenged to develop "The Virtual Patient," a series of case-based
educational modules for medical students that simulated examinations and
interviews of virtual patients; enabled students to order tests,
therapies, and consults; and provided feedback. Created a unique
framework to provide both the flexibility needed to develop multiple
modules and the structure required to make it cost-effective.

* Designed program with a Director front-end and a FileMaker database
back-end so that most data could be entered directly into the database by
content authors.
* Collaboratively planned UI and overall program design with Institute
staff and teamed with other programmers to plan program architecture.
* Wrote functional and technical specs; wrote much of the actual Lingo
programming.


-------------------------------------------
Architect and Programmer
NEW YORK UNIVERSITY SCHOOL OF MEDICINE, New York, NY
```

Developed and implemented Rich Internet Application allowing doctors and medical students to specify patient symptoms, view information and images, and posit diagnoses. Brainstormed program and UI design with author. Designed architecture. Wrote functional and technical specs.

* Implemented ASP/IIS/SQL Server back-end.
* Wrote ActionScript 2.0 client code that communicated with ASP.
* Implemented with Director Shockwave in 2000 and reimplemented with Flash in 2003.

Lead Programmer
INNOVATIONS IN SCIENCE EDUCATION, Stamford, CT

Delivered interactive components for Houghton Mifflin's earth science website that included on-screen drawing, a distance measurement tool, drag and drop, graphing, and other features. Executed full life cycle quickly and under budget.

* Developed cost-effective framework that allowed less-advanced developers to efficiently create interactive Shockwave modules using a combination of Macromedia Director's GUI, preconstructed behaviors, and an XML configuration file.

==
AFFILIATIONS

Stamford Flex Application Incubator Group (mentor/coordinator), Adobe Stamford User Group (cochair), Stamford Flash Platform User Group (e-mail list moderator), and CairngormDocs.org (webmaster).

==
ONLINE PUBLICATIONS

Author, FlexAbility (blog). http://www.choiceapps.com/flex_ability/

Lead author, "Visual FlexUnit (documentation page)," December 2007. http://code.google.com/p/visualflexair/VisualFlexAIR

Author, Setting Up a Windows Apache/Tomcat/LCDS Server, December 2007. http://www.choiceapps.com/technology/choiceapps_articles/setting_up_a_win dows_tomcat_fds_server.html

==
SELECTED PRESENTATIONS

Using the Strategy Pattern: A Simple Audio Sequencing Example, Stamford Flash Platform Design Patterns Group, February 2009.

Visual FlexUnit, Stamford Flash Platform Design Patterns Group, January 2008.

```
The Command Pattern & Cairngorm, Stamford Flash Platform Design Patterns
Group, December 2006. http://www.choiceapps.com/technology/presentations/
command_pattern_and_cairngorm/

=========================================
INTERESTS

Skydiving, carpentry, 19th-century literature.
```

The Web Resume

The newest evolution in resumes combines the visually pleasing quality of the printed resume with the technological ease of the electronic resume and the amazing capabilities of the Web. Instead of seeing only the information you can include on your Word, text, or even PDF resume, the full-fledged Web resume is richer and deeper. What's more, it can be interactive and visually exciting as well.

THE REASONS FOR A WEB RESUME

Why should you develop a Web resume? Nowadays, employers routinely search the Web for information about candidates at every stage of the selection process, from early identification of prospective employees to reference and character checks before hire.

Thus, it makes sense for you to know what employers will find when they search for you online. Of course, what will crop up is any public or published information about you—things as mundane as when you placed in the top 10 in a road race or as potentially damaging as an arrest or criminal conviction. Regardless of what's online now, you can add to the weight of positive information by creating a Web resume that reinforces all of the messages you've conveyed in your print resume.

From simplest to most complex, your Web resume can be a profile on various social and business networking sites such as Facebook or LinkedIn; a complete portfolio posted through an online service such as VisualCV; or a full-blown personal Web site that you create and manage. For everyone reading this book—for every "technologist"—a Web resume can be a very valuable tool where you can often demonstrate your technical expertise. For example, if you're an expert in HTML programming, you don't just have to write about it; you can show it on your Web resume.

For all of these options, you can begin with your existing resume and add appropriate material to expand, reinforce, and complement your resume. Consider adding lists of all of your technology skills, achievements, career highlights, project highlights, consulting engagements, publications, public speaking engagements, education, professional and/or technical credentials, management skills, and more. Your portfolio might include a page of online graphics that you've designed or a demonstration of a sophisticated e-commerce transaction system that you developed and commercialized. A video of you "in action" in the tech center, in the field, or in the boardroom would also be a great addition.

A Web resume or portfolio will not only showcase your skills, it will raise your online profile so that when potential employers search for you, they'll find information of value. At the very least, we strongly recommend that you create a professional profile on LinkedIn (www.linkedin.com), which is the most widely used professional networking site, and explore and use LinkedIn's extensive capabilities to build your online visibility and expand your network.

Finally, if you use Facebook or other sites for social networking, never include anything that could be damaging to your professional reputation. You might think these sites protect your privacy, but you can't be 100 percent certain, so don't risk your career success by sharing inappropriate content online.

THE NEW VIDEO BIO PHENOMENON

One of the newest technology additions to the portfolio of tech tools for job search and career management is the video biography. These bios allow you, the job seeker, to present yourself "live" to prospective employers and recruiters. Bios are growing in popularity because they can be very helpful to companies in evaluating prime candidates. They can give you a truly competitive edge if your video bio shows that you are articulate and attractive.

Video bios are sometimes mistakenly labeled "video resumes." In fact, they are very different. You certainly don't want to record yourself reading or reciting your resume—that would not make for a very interesting video! The video bio instead allows you to showcase yourself in a different way by briefly sharing interesting information and demonstrating your communication skills. Intended as an adjunct to your resume, never as a replacement, the video bio can be very effective in today's visually and technologically oriented culture.

The use of video bios is somewhat controversial because of the potential for bias and discrimination based on ethnicity, race, size, age, and other personal characteristics. You'll have to make a decision for yourself as to whether a video bio would be a positive addition to your portfolio of career and job search communications. You can read much more about video bios at videoBIO (www.videobio.com), one of the leaders in this emerging technology as it relates to personal marketing and branding for job searches.

The Three Resume Types Compared

This chart quickly compares the similarities and differences between the three types of resumes we've discussed in this chapter.

	PRINTED RESUMES (WORD AND PDF FILES)	ELECTRONIC RESUMES (TEXT FILES)	WEB RESUMES
TYPESTYLE/ FONT	Sharp, conservative, and distinctive (see our recommendations in chapter 1).	Courier.	Sharp, conservative, and distinctive. Attractive on-screen and when printed from an online document.
TYPE ENHANCEMENTS	**Bold,** *italics,* and <u>underlining</u> for emphasis.	CAPITALIZATION is the only enhancement available to you.	**Bold,** *italics,* <u>underlining</u>, and color available for emphasis.

(continued)

(continued)

	PRINTED RESUMES (WORD AND PDF FILES)	ELECTRONIC RESUMES (TEXT FILES)	WEB RESUMES
TYPE SIZE	10-, 11-, or 12-point preferred. Larger type sizes (14, 18, 20, 22, and even larger, depending on typestyle) will effectively enhance your name and section headings.	12-point.	Use type sizes that are readable on-screen and off.
TEXT FORMAT	Use centering and indenting to optimize the visual presentation.	Type all information flush left.	Use centering and indenting to optimize the visual presentation.
PREFERRED LENGTH	One to two pages; three if essential.	Length is immaterial; almost definitely, converting your resume to text will make it longer.	Length is immaterial; just be sure your site is well organized so viewers can quickly find the material of greatest interest to them.
PAPER COLOR	White, ivory, light gray, light blue, or other conservative background.	Not applicable for e-mailed documents. White for documents printed for scanning.	Paper is not used, but do select your background carefully to maximize readability.
WHITE SPACE	Use appropriately for best readability.	Use white space to break up dense text sections.	Use appropriately for best readability both on-screen and when printed.

Resume Checklist

Before you sit down to write your resume, carefully review the following checklist to be certain that you've addressed everything. Each item is a critical step in writing, formatting, and designing a powerful resume, the foundation of every successful job search campaign. Every item is applicable to just about any active job seeker:

❑ Clearly define who you are and how you want to be perceived (for example, mobile app developer, business analyst, test developer, project manager, CIO). The perception you want to create will align directly with your current career objectives, which may or may not be aligned with your past experience.

❑ Document your key skills, qualifications, competencies, and knowledge. You can create a Word file for this, write it on a piece of paper, or use the resume questionnaire in Appendix A.

❑ Document your career achievements, project highlights, contributions, honors and awards, and other notable accomplishments. As above, you can create a Word file for this, write it on a piece of paper, or use the resume questionnaire in Appendix A.

❑ Document all of your technology skills, including hardware, software, applications, networks, programming languages, telecommunications systems, Web and Internet technologies, and more.

❑ Identify one or more specific job targets and positions that you will pursue. With these in hand, you're much better prepared to write your resume because you know where you're headed and what you want to showcase about your career.

❑ Identify one or more industries and companies that you will target. Just as with identifying target positions, once you've outlined this, you're much better prepared to write your resume because you know where you're headed and what to highlight about your career, responsibilities, achievements, and more.

❑ Research and compile a list of keywords and keyword phrases for the industries and professions that you are targeting, and then be certain to incorporate as many of them as you can in your resume (and cover letter).

❑ Collect several job postings or announcements that are similar to jobs you'll be applying for. Review carefully to be certain you understand the core qualifications as well as the "extras" so that you can highlight both in your resume.

❑ Determine which resume format will work best for you and your career—chronological, functional, or combination, often referred to as a hybrid resume, as discussed in chapter 1.

❑ Get a personal e-mail address if you don't already have one. Using your employer's e-mail address on your resume is never appropriate. You can easily get a Gmail, Hotmail, or other free e-mail address.

❑ Write your resume using the strategies, guidelines, suggestions, and samples you'll find throughout this book.

❏ Select an attractive font (typestyle) that's appropriate for the industries and professions that you're targeting.

❏ Review resume samples for up-to-date ideas on resume styles, formats, fonts, organization, and content. You might like part of one resume and part of another. Great! Do not feel limited or believe that you have to format and structure your resume in exactly the same style as one of the sample formats.

❏ Determine which final versions of your resume you will need: PDF, Word, and/or text. This decision will depend entirely on how you plan to execute your search campaign.

❏ Ask several colleagues and/or friends to review and proofread your resume. Start by e-mailing a copy to them so you can see what they see. Ask for a critique of the content, formatting, presentation, and any other ideas they'd like to share with you.

❏ Proofread. Proofread. Proofread. Then have one or two other people proofread. It's amazing how easy it is to overlook small grammar, punctuation, or format errors. Don't let a misspelled word stand in the way of getting an interview!

PART II

Sample Resumes for Computer and Web Jobs

CHAPTER 4

Resumes for Computer Operators and Technicians

- Computer Operations and Systems Professionals
- Computer Technology and Electronics Technicians
- Technology Operations Support Professionals
- Computer Analysts
- Computer Systems Technicians
- Technical Support Professionals
- Field Service Technicians
- Field Engineers
- Network/PC Technicians
- Information Technology/Systems Technicians

John B. Lankford

2020 West Main Street, Apt. 231 — Hendersonville, Tennessee 37075

615-555-5466 — jblankford@home.com

Computer Operations and Systems Professional

Windows XP/7 – Linux – Mac OS

DSU/CSU – Routers – Hubs

Microsoft Office

Qualifications Summary

Solid computer operations background involving installation, maintenance, and troubleshooting of PC hardware, operating systems, LAN and WAN equipment, and numerous software applications.

Experience as a technical trainer/instructor with strong knowledge in hardware repair and technical training.

Ability to translate technical information and make it more easily understood by nontechnical audiences.

Talent for readily learning new systems and software. Strong desire to expand computer knowledge and apply it to improving business performance.

Professional Experience

Field Engineer / Inside Sales Support 2010–Present
DIGITAL COMMUNICATIONS, INC. — Hendersonville, Tennessee

Configure, install, and troubleshoot PC and network issues.

Work with inside sales staff to determine customer needs and provide sales support.

Serve as in-house expert on LAN and WAN connectivity, assisting as needed on all client sites.

Senior Field Engineer 2007–2010
TECH SYSTEMS — Marietta, Georgia

Tested and repaired hardware for both personal users and small- to medium-sized businesses.

Installed, operated, and troubleshot hardware and software, providing on-site support.

Personal Systems Help Center / Technical Support Group 2003–2007
IBM — Marietta, Georgia / Research Triangle Park, North Carolina

Provided information and technical support via telephone for users with software problems.

Accurately and successfully identified customer problems and offered solutions.

Served as an effective team leader and liaison between Technical Support Group and management.

Education

Bachelor of Science, Economics — 2003..Florida State University, Tallahassee

This individual's years of directly related experience are summarized in brief "responsibility" statements, whereas his qualifications are presented "front and center" as his greatest selling points.

Jeremiah Best

32 Andrews Street, Livingston, NJ 07039
(973) 740-5555 ▪ jerbest@net.com

Objective

A technical support position in computer technology and electronics

Education

Certificate, Electronics and Computer Technology
December 2010   The Computer Institute, Rahwah, NJ
- 60-week, 96-semester-credit-hour program
- GPA 3.93 / Director's List every semester
- Worked part-time to fund education while taking classes

Courses

- ✓ Basic Electricity I & II
- ✓ Microcomputer Fundamentals
- ✓ Semiconductor Devices and Circuits
- ✓ Personal Computer Repair
- ✓ Integrated Circuits and Digital Logic
- ✓ Data Communications and Fiber Optics
- ✓ Systems and Networking

Technical Skills and Equipment

AC/DC Power Supply	PC Repair / Troubleshooting
Digital Logic Probe	Networking Media Installation
Breadboarding Circuits	Networking Server Installation
Digital Voltmeter AC/DC	Workstation Software Installation
Oscilloscope	Data Communications
Function Generator	Microprocessing
Novell NetWare / OES	Windows and Mac OS

Work History
2009–present

Grand Central Theatre, Livingston, NJ
Kitchen Help / Concession Help

- Prepare fast food for theatre clientele, often cooking for 200–300 orders per shift per night, as part of a team of six kitchen and concession workers.

- Serve as cashier for concession sales, filling in for absent workers; handle and reconcile $3K–$4K in sales per night.

- Selected by manager as "Employee of the Month" in October 2010 for cooperative attitude, perfect attendance, and willingness to work double shifts on short notice.

Testimonials

"Jeremiah is an exceptional person, and I know that anything he is a part of will be a success."
—Ellery Williams, Managing Director, Grand Central Theatre

"Jeremiah is punctual and eager to work..."
—William McCarthy, Manager, Grand Central Theatre

This individual is a new graduate whose education and technical capabilities take up most of the resume. His work experience is less important; it is not technology based, but it does show strong capabilities and achievements. Note the effective testimonials at the bottom.

Lisel Roemmele

11034 Highway 1247
Waynesburg, KY 40489
(606) 595-1029
liselr@aol.com

PROFILE

"Lisel is at the top of her class, showing a great deal of insight and enthusiasm for networking, trouble-shooting, and administration.

"I feel she can be of considerable help in a school environment, as she has good people skills, is willing to work wherever needed, and is tenacious in solving problems that come up day-to-day."

— *Roger Angevine, Chair, Physical Sciences and Mathematics*

Innovative, achievement-oriented computer professional with exceptional abilities in the areas of technical and systems support. Immediate goal is to provide comprehensive, high-quality support to meet the needs of a growing organization. Personal and professional strengths include

- Conscientiousness and dependability in completing systems projects accurately and independently in zero-error-tolerance environment.
- Experience in system management disciplines including disaster recovery.
- Proven ability to meet and maintain time requirements.
- Experience developing applications/solutions for ad hoc assignments.
- Ability to grasp and master new concepts easily.
- Equal effectiveness in working independently or as part of a team.
- Strong work ethic; dedication to enhancing personal computer skills.

PROFICIENCIES

Operating Systems:
Windows XP, Vista, 7; Windows Server; Linux

Languages:
Java, C#, Flash

INTERNSHIP EXPERIENCE

2009–2010   **Somerset Community College**   **Somerset, KY**
On-call consultant. Installation of software, networks, and workstations for lab units and associates as required. Strengths in troubleshooting and technical support.

EDUCATION

"If there is a network problem that is not easily discovered, Lisel is willing to go the extra mile to find and resolve it.

"She is quite knowledgeable and has the ability to troubleshoot many PC platforms. Her extensive knowledge of operating and network systems will be an asset to any company."

— *Troy Schlake, Network Administrator, Bondtech Corp*

Network Information Systems Technology
Somerset Community College, Somerset, Kentucky
Degree anticipated in May 2011

CERTIFICATIONS HELD

Microsoft Certified Professional, MCPID 1465546
Microsoft Server Certified (2010)
Windows 7 Certified (2010)

Excellent personal and professional references will be made available on request.

An interesting layout makes this resume attractive and fun to read. The testimonials in the left column are highly visible, yet they don't detract from the standard format of the rest of the resume.

Vanessa Smith

6882 Leavenworth Street #3C
San Francisco, CA 94108

Mobile: 415.887.1218
van.smith@gmail.com

TECHNOLOGY OPERATIONS SUPPORT PROFESSIONAL
**Information Systems / Voice & Data Networks / Telecommunications & Wireless Technology
Print Media / Broadcast Media / Digital Media / New Media**

Talented technologist with a unique combination of experience in planning, testing, configuring, installing, training, troubleshooting, and supporting advanced technologies in both B2B and B2C organizations. Equally strong performance in managing customer relationships, building collaborative partnerships with key business allies, and providing one-on-one technical support to top business executives. Expertise includes:

Technical Ideation & Innovation	Fixed & Mobile Phone Technology
Applications & Software Support	Remote Access & Virtual Environments
Desktops, Laptops & Mobile Computing	Computer Scripting & Imaging
Help Desk Training & Operations	Disaster Recovery & Data Recovery
User Training & Documentation	Systems Security & Software Compliance

Outstanding performance documented by reviews noting strong skills in project planning and delivery, staff training and mentoring, scheduling, organization, and decision making. Consistent record of achieving or surpassing all project deadlines and technology milestones. Reputation as an independent thinker and team player.

TECHNOLOGY PROFILE

Certifications: Mac OS X v10.5 Directory Services, Apple Certified Macintosh Technician

Software: Microsoft Office, iWork, iLife, Apple Remote Desktop, Google Apps, Adobe Creative Suite, Final Cut Studio, Final Cut Server, Adobe/K4, Quark/QPS, Active Directory, Open Directory, LANDesk, KBOX by KACE, Symantec AntiVirus, Kaspersky, Netboot, InstaDMG, Ghost, PxeBoot, Filemaker Pro, Extensis Suitcase, Blackberry Enterprise Server, Citrix, Parallels, PeopleSoft, Lotus Notes, Apple Scripts, Shell Scripts, Automator, CalDav, IMAP, SSH, FTP, VNC, DNS, DHCP

Hardware: Apple, Dell, IBM

Networks: LAN/WAN, VPN, Juniper, AT&T, Verizon, T-Mobile

OS: Mac OS X, Mac OS X Server, Windows XP, Windows 7, UNIX, Linux

PROFESSIONAL EXPERIENCE

Senior Application Support Specialist
WORLD CULTURE SOCIETY, San Francisco, CA

February 2009 to Present

High-profile, fast-paced position supporting 800+ Macintosh and 1,200+ Dell computers on LAN/WAN, VPN, and satellite technologies around the globe. Provide hardware and software training and support to users organization-wide, from front-line staff to top executives and board members. Work in partnership with technical project managers to expedite seamless technology transitions.

continued

Following a strong summary and technical profile, relatively short-term work experience is expanded to make the most of significant projects, which are organized into two sections to promote readability.

Vanessa Smith   Page 2
415.887.1218
van.smith@gmail.com

Project Highlights – World Culture Society:

- Facilitated planning, configuration, testing, deployment, and support of new software and applications (for example, Adobe/K4, Quark/QPS, Parallels, Google Apps, Citrix, KBOX 2000).

- Spearheaded successful transition from LANDesk to KBOX, affecting every aspect of client management including help desk, asset management, scripting, security, software distribution, imaging, and reporting.

- Rolled out iPhone and other wireless devices to board members, top executives, and senior managers and continue to provide instant technical response and support. Collaborated with AT&T, purchasing, and internal tech resources to facilitate voice and data transfers and installs.

- Led project to extend Active Directory schema to support global network of Macintosh computers.

Business Process & Operating Improvements – World Culture Society:

- Reduced new technology installation times through improved planning and system configurations.

- Assisted with server room relocation projects, rack recabling, server monitoring, and switch patching. Coordinated tech support for office moves for up to 100 users.

- Coordinated a series of process automation and simplification projects utilizing Apple Scripts, Shell Scripts, and Automator to streamline and expedite workflow throughout the organization.

Mac Genius   November 2007 to February 2009
APPLE COMPUTER, INC., Mill Valley, CA

Provided technical troubleshooting and customer support in high-stress, time-sensitive environment. Diagnosed hardware and software problems, replaced components, installed new applications, and tested systems performance. Demonstrated outstanding skills in customer relationship management.

- Appointed **Acting Lead Mac Genius** for 3 months in absence of business leader. Supervised a team of 20, coordinated staff scheduling, and designed/led in-house technical training programs.

- Provided technical support for launch of iPhone, MacBook Air, and other innovations.

- Led customer quality control team and implemented improved customer service standards.

EDUCATION

B.S., Information Technology & Digital Media, University of San Francisco, 2007
Concentration in Communications & Advertising

THOMAS LEMKE

5555 Dove Drive
Citrus Heights, California 95621
(916) 788-9993

tlemke@att.net

Computer Analyst

PROFILE

More than six years of experience in advanced computer diagnostics and on-site system analysis and service. Strong skills in troubleshooting and installing hardware/software, operating systems, and networks. Proven capabilities in the following:

- Quality Standards
- Commitment and Reliability
- Interpersonal Relations
- Team Building
- Problem Solving
- Customer Service
- Purchasing
- Staff Training
- Business Solutions

TECHNICAL EXPERTISE

- Windows 7, XP
- Mobile Applications
- Technical Support/Service
- PC Hardware/Software & Networking
- Basic Integrated Circuit Repair
- Computer Peripherals/Equipment

RELATED EXPERIENCE

ASPER COMPUTER COMPANY, Sacramento, CA   2004 to Present

Field Technician/Lead Technician
Comanage computer sales, service, and business processes. Assist as resource and problem solver for customers and local businesses (*Holly Cleaners, Sacramento School District, Modular Buildings, Inc.*) to maximize benefit from equipment and applications development. Focus on providing a high level of customer service. Troubleshoot a full range of technical issues related to installations by telephone or in person.

Selected Accomplishments
- Supervised and developed highly involved, self-directed technicians.
- Worked closely with online technical support to ensure quality installation of hardware, operating systems, and software programs.
- Built strong reputation as Morris High School's resource for diagnosing and analyzing technical problems on the SASI program.
- Consistently planned and completed projects on schedule.

ALDA COMPUTER, Sacramento, CA   2003 to 2004

Manufacturing Associate
Highly motivated participant/team player of 20-member team. Focused on problem solving and decision making through working together. Maintained safety standards and quality control for each job on production line.

EDUCATION

A+ Service Technician (2008)
Heald Institute of Technology, Sacramento, CA (2008)
Courses: Integrated Circuit Repair and Computer Science

This resume uses a traditional format and clean typestyle to present quite a bit of information on one page without sacrificing readability. The headline is centered and set off by borders to attract immediate attention.

Marguerite P. Baker

2487 N. Snelling Avenue

651-555-6921   Falcon Heights, MN 55108   maggieb@isp.net

PROFILE

More than 12 years of experience in computer systems installation, maintenance, and repair. Technical knowledge encompasses multiple manufacturers' equipment. Commitment to fixing problems permanently, saving customers time and money. Exceptional customer service skills; ability to calm disgruntled customers and explain problems understandably to nontechnical users.

TECHNICAL SUMMARY

Hardware:	*Manufacturers:*	*Operating Systems/Software:*
Medium to Large Data Centers	HP	HP-UX11i
Storage Systems Hardware	Dell	Linux
Point of Sale (POS) Equipment	NCR	HP Insight Dynamics – VSE
Printers	IBM	Systems Insight Manager

CAREER HISTORY

HP • Bloomington, Minnesota ....**System Services Representative**........................2000–2011
Performed on-site installation, maintenance, repair, and deinstallation of HP and multivendor systems and components including hardware, networking products, operating systems, and software. Quickly analyzed problems and presented solutions to customers with goal of minimizing disruption of service.

Selected Customers

General Mills
Land O'Lakes, Inc.
Gander Mountain
Target Corporation
Excel Energy
Medtronic, Inc.
Deluxe Corp.
Minnesota Vikings
Best Buy

*Performed Installations
Valued at $1+ million*

Bethesda Hospital
3M Company
U.S. Bancorp
Cargill

Maintenance/Repair:
- Assigned to geographic territory as primary representative. Provided backup for technicians in other areas.
- Managed maintenance and repairs for POS equipment in 200+ retail chain stores in the Twin Cities.
- Performed maintenance and repair services as transparent representative of third-party vendors.
- Installed multimillion-dollar systems.
- Completed cross-training in all services and equipment.

Operational Support:
- Advised customers on preventative maintenance, configuration, and operational and environmental factors.
- Consulted with management and developed multiple-year forecasts for customers' IT needs, including lease-versus-own scenarios.
- Developed cost estimates for repairs. Reviewed warranty and service contracts to determine applicability.

Internal:
- Collaborated with HP escalated support to diagnose and resolve complex problems.
- Acted as mentor to new employees. Shared expertise and tips to enhance new hires' understanding and performance.
- Received the company's Platinum Star for outstanding performance.

continued

The most notable feature of this resume is the shaded box that highlights large clients and major projects.

651-555-6921   Marguerite P. Baker   maggieb@isp.net

CAREER HISTORY, continued

General NanoSystems • Edina, Minnesota ....**Bench Tech Engineer**...1998–2000
- Supervised quality assurance.
- Analyzed board blueprints.
- Repaired logic cards at board level.

Stark Electronics • St. Paul, Minnesota ....**Customer Service Representative**....................1996–1998
- Problem-solved equipment issues and developed repair cost estimates.

EDUCATION, CERTIFICATIONS & TECHNICAL TRAINING

Macalester College • St. Paul, Minnesota ....**Bachelor of Science** 2000

Dunwoody College • Minneapolis, Minnesota......**Associate of Computer Technology** 1997

Certification
NARDA ....**Refrigeration Type 1 Tech Certification** 2007

Selected Technical Training
(comprehensive list available on request)

Binary and Hexadecimal (2009)	Gentran EDI (2002)
Servicing Fiber Optic Links (2008)	Phillips LMS Tape Systems (2002)
ESD Prevention (2006)	AS/400 Architecture (2001)
Client/Server Hardware & Software Clustering (2005)	Qualstar Tape Drives (IBM-060) (1999)

ANTHONY E. CALAVETTI

1501 Crosswicks Landing • Port Monmouth, NJ 07758 • 732-706-1341
E-mail: acala@aol.com

OBJECTIVE: Position in Technical Support

SUMMARY

- Self-directed, confident professional with effective troubleshooting, customer relations, interpersonal, and leadership skills and experience installing and configuring a variety of operating systems.
- Familiar with network management tasks, including user and security administration, file/directory access, and remote access service; experience with TCP/IP and NetBIOS protocols.
- Entrusted with highly confidential information; security clearance.
- Strong academic performance (93% grade average) at a highly regarded technical school.

O/S: Novell NetWare and OES, Windows XP, Windows 7
Software: MS Office (Word, Access, Outlook, Excel, PowerPoint) for Mac and Windows; WordPress
Hardware: PCs, Hard Drives, CD-ROMs, Video Boards, NICs, Multimedia Devices, Printers

EXPERIENCE

Technical Support Representative, A.N.B., Inc., Irvington, NJ   2009–Present
Provide hardware and software support for clients of a computer service and retail organization.

- Install and configure computers and peripherals for clients throughout the Northeast.
- Perform a wide range of troubleshooting and repair work, including hard drive replacement, restoration of files, and video card replacement.
- Set up a peer-to-peer network with 5 workstations.
- Provide explanations for clients and demonstrate appropriate facets of system/software.

Secure Documents Handling Clerk, U.S. Army, VA   2007–2009
Entered, maintained, and tracked confidential information, including personal records, achievements, salaries, benefits, and education, for 400+ military personnel. Supervised a data entry clerk.

- Reviewed records for accuracy and thoroughness, entered data into computer system, and submitted electronically to superiors for review.
- Instructed 12 trainees in various clerical functions.
- Received 2 awards for outstanding performance.

Administrative Clerk, U.S. Army, SC   2005–2007
Performed diverse clerical functions, including data entry, correspondence preparation, and record keeping.

- Assisted with installation of Novell operating system and applications software after a hard drive crash.

EDUCATION / HONORS

Computer Technical Support Program, 2006 • Computer Institute, Jersey City, NJ • 93% grade average
A.S. Business Administration, 1995 • Randall Community College, Randall, NJ

Technical / Leadership Achievements

- Performed network management and administration functions using Windows XP. Set up and managed user accounts; handled security issues (file/directory access); configured print queues, network printers, and remote access service. Maintained registry profiles for local and roaming users and provided disk administration support.
- Designed an easy-to-navigate Web page for a retail company, using WordPress; included a home page, product page, and order form with strong graphics and hyperlinks.
- Installed and configured operating systems and applications.
- Assisted in network cable layout and installation.
- Recognized frequently as a team leader; selected to summarize project work and answer questions.
- Encouraged other students to focus on project objectives and provided technical guidance.

This individual has both recent education credentials and relevant work experience, so both are described in detail. Note how the Summary combines both overall qualifications and specific technical skills.

JASON DE MARCO

1030 Saddlehorn Drive
Hendersonville, TN 37075

615-555-1097
jdemarco@aol.com

A+ CERTIFIED SERVICE TECHNICIAN

Highly skilled technical professional demonstrating knowledge and skill with various PC-based operating systems, networks, and software applications. Trained to support end users in a Windows environment via telephone and hands-on support. Diagnose and troubleshoot PC and basic network problems. Install and configure software onto individual and networked systems. Set up PCs, printers, modems, monitors, and other ancillary equipment and attach them to networks.

An effective communicator with solid professional abilities, a strong work ethic, and a commitment to excellence.

TECHNICAL SKILLS

Operating Systems
Windows 7, XP

Applications
Microsoft Office (Word, Excel, PowerPoint, Outlook)
Mobile Device Connectivity and Applications

ABILITIES

- Help Desk Support / Customer Service
- On-Site Technical Support
- Installation / Configuration
- Troubleshooting / Repair

CERTIFICATIONS

A+ Service Technician Certification – August 2005
Career Blazers Learning Center – Delray Beach, Florida

PC Applications – May 2005
Edward Ross Career & Employment Institute – Deerfield Beach, Florida

EDUCATION

Degree Program: Associate of Applied Science (45 credit hours) – 1999 to 2002
Broward Community College – Fort Lauderdale, Florida

WORK EXPERIENCE

Computer Technician – 2005 to Present
Wireless Innovations – Nashville, Tennessee
- Perform troubleshooting, repairs, and upgrades for company's LAN system.
- Provide on-site software training and technical support to end users using full array of Windows software, hardware, and mobile devices.

Route Salesman – 1996 to 2005
Blanding Brothers – Fort Lauderdale, Florida
- Serviced commercial accounts, primarily supermarkets, delis, and convenience stores.
- Prepared daily log to track inventory, sales, collections, and payment receipts.

This individual successfully transitioned from a nontechnology sales job to a computer technician position and is ready for advancement. His resume highlights his solid and current technical skills.

EVAN FLANDERS

1159 Danlette Drive   (631) 888-4000
North Bridge, NY 11703   eflanders229@aol.com

A+ Certified Technician seeking to expand career within the information technology arena

B.A. degree in Economics, continuing education in information technology, and a combination of technical and diversified administrative experience gained over 10 years in positions of increased responsibility.

Select strengths encompass…

Project Management / Help Desk Support / End-User Training / PC/LAN Service and Support
Systems Integration / Sales and Marketing / Procedural Documentation / Client Needs Assessment
Business and Technical Problem Resolution / Inventory Control / Vendor Relations / Cost Management

PROFESSIONAL EXPERIENCE

PC/LAN Technician   2009–2011
FINANCIALLY SOUND, INC. (FSI), Merlin, NY

Technical Support

- Successfully rolled out Windows 7 and newly developed FSI software to 80 nationwide branch locations.

- Installed and configured 50 Windows workstations at Dallas branch office, providing comprehensive postinstallation support, including client training and provision of procedural documentation.

- Attached corporate personnel to Novell and Windows network; performed network backups.

- Provided remote and on-site end-user support on a broad scope of hardware/software problems and printing/network connectivity issues; delivered effective training and practical solutions.

- Developed procedural documentation to streamline and optimize departmental/company-wide workflow.

- Built and maintained workstations and laptops; replaced and upgraded peripherals and components.

- Proficiently utilized diagnostic tools to assess and troubleshoot hardware and software performance to sustain the effective use of existing and newly implemented systems technology.

- Retrieved borrower-related data for underwriters and processors through remote server management.

Office Management

- Sourced and negotiated with resale vendors, achieving total cost savings of $25,000 in license renewal fees for first and second quarters of 2010.

- Handled all aspects of IT cost center and inventory control at the corporate and company-wide level with direct responsibility for distribution of accurate and timely documentation to all impacted departments.

- Created batch files to automate pulling of monthly pipeline reports for senior management review.

- Maintained and updated equipment tracking data for accounting and reporting functions.

- Supervised and maintained company-wide user activity to ensure integrity of multiple licensing software.

— Page 1 of 2 —

The Select Strengths section combines with the technical skills summary on page 2 to create a strong "keyword summary" for this individual.

EVAN FLANDERS

Page 2 of 2

ADDITIONAL WORK HISTORY

HH GROUP, Woodland, NY   2004–2009
New Accounts / Parts Administrator

RECOVERY HOME SYSTEMS, Centralville, NY   2001–2004
Administrative Assistant

COMPUTER / NETWORKING SKILLS

Operating Systems: Windows 7, Windows XP, Mac OS

Protocols/Networks: TCP/IP, NetBIOS, HTTP

Hardware: Hard drives, printers, scanners, CD-ROMs, Cat5 cables, hubs, NIC cards, mobile devices

Software:

Commercial:	*Industry-specific:*
Microsoft Office Modules (Windows/Mac),	e-Credit, ICC Credit, Energizer, Midanet, Flood Link,
Norton Internet Security, Symantec pcAnywhere	Greatland Escrow, Allregs, Echo Connection Plus

EDUCATION

CAREER CENTER, Garden Grove, NY
MCSE Windows 7 track, Fall 2010 enrollment

Completed Coursework, 2010–2011:
Windows 7 / Networking Technologies
Flash / Java / HTML
Microcomputers I & II / PC rebuilding, upgrading, and repairing

THE UNIVERSITY AT OLD WESTERN TOWN, Old Western Town, NY
Bachelor of Arts, Economics, 2008
Graduated with honors — GPA 3.77

CENTER COMMUNITY COLLEGE, Bendwood, NY
Associate of Arts, Liberal Arts and Science, 2002
Graduated with honors — GPA 3.5

LICENSES / CERTIFICATIONS

Comp TIA A+ Certified Technician

New York State Notary Public

CHARLES SALONGO

2741 East Broadway
Phoenix, AZ 85048

480-549-2309
csalongo@home.com

SUMMARY OF QUALIFICATIONS

- Experienced field engineer with strong business, marketing, and customer service background, coupled with experience in troubleshooting, installing, and repairing electrical and electronic systems. Proficient in

  > **System Installation**   ▸ **System Development**
  > **IT Service / Support Management** ▸ **System Troubleshooting**
  > **Client Relations / Support**   ▸ **End-User Training**

- Extensive technical hardware and software background, with ability to independently master new software and hardware, initiate troubleshooting process, and solve variety of technical support issues.
- Expertise in network design, configuration, and integration. Ability to assist in all facets of hardware and software conversion, including customization, support, cabling, training, and installation.
- Reliable member of team, assessing problems and system requirements, developing effective solutions to meet end user needs. Network with other computer experts regarding hardware and software problems.
- Education in computer science, with 3,000 hours of lab and theory training.

TECHNICAL EXPERTISE

Systems:	Windows XP/7	Novell	Linux
Software:	Microsoft Office	Symantec pcAnywhere	Mobile Applications
Certification:	Microsoft Certified Desktop Support Technician (MCDST)		
	Microsoft Certified Systems Administrator (MCSA)		

PROFESSIONAL EXPERIENCE

Service Engineer — MYRIAD COMPUTER, Phoenix, Arizona — 2005 to Present
- Analyze and assess problems; recommend hardware, software, and office integration; determine use in order to make relevant recommendations on upgrading and networking, using LAN/WAN networks and web/mobile connectivity as appropriate.
- Train clients in all aspects of system, from basic instruction in operating hardware to more complex software applications.
- Purchase computer components, maintain and control inventory levels, and implement cost controls to ensure profitability.

Field Engineer — FIBERMESH SYSTEMS (Division of Visys, Inc.), Phoenix, Arizona — 2002 to 2005
- Served as primary contact for technical support to client base of 90 medical and 60 commercial clients.
- Supported / operated personal computers for up to 700 end users and devices.

Field Engineer — HVM CORPORATION, Phoenix, Arizona — 2000 to 2002
- Developed and integrated electronic alarm control system designs and programs for gas distribution networks per client requirements.
- Installed diffusion equipment in U.S. and Mexico. Experience included diffusion furnaces, temperature / pressure indicators and controllers, relay / solenoid control, and programmable logic controllers integrated into Novell network for controlled shutdowns.

EDUCATION

Associate's Degree — Electronics Technology — 2000
LONG TECHNICAL COLLEGE, Phoenix, Arizona

The extensive Summary of Qualifications section sells this candidate with a list of keywords along with both an experience summary and "soft" skills.

DON G. SHELLEY

65 Lake Green Circle ~ Stafford, TX 77477
Home: (281) 992-0663 ~ Cell: (281) 565-4999 ~ dgs1159@mccn.net

NETWORK / PC TECHNICIAN

More than 10 years of broad-based experience encompassing installation, upgrades, troubleshooting, configuration, support, and maintenance of third-party software applications, hardware, servers, and workstations. Skilled at determining company and end-user requirements and designing architecture to meet or exceed those requirements. Effective leadership and training skills combined with extensive technical expertise. Highly organized, with the ability to efficiently manage projects and resources.

Competencies:

TROUBLESHOOTING, ANALYSIS & RESOLUTION ~ IMPLEMENTATION PLANNING & MANAGEMENT
END-USER TRAINING ~ SYSTEM UPGRADES ~ DATABASE ADMINISTRATION ~ IT PURCHASING
STAFF SUPERVISION & TRAINING ~ EXPENSE TRACKING & CONTROL ~ VENDOR RELATIONS

TECHNICAL SKILLS

Hardware: All relevant hardware, including servers, bridges, routers, LANs, WANs, and switches as well as fiber-optic connections and network printers

Networks: Windows Server, Novell NetWare and OES

Operating Systems: Windows XP, 7; Linux

Software: Microsoft Office Suite, Aspen Plus Simulation Software, Kemma Bridge, EPOCH, Engineer's Aid, Microsoft Exchange, Visio, Enterprise Administrator, Weather View 32, Performance 2000

PROFESSIONAL EXPERIENCE

MODERN INFORMATION SYSTEMS – Houston, TX   2004 to Present
(Contracted to Sitico Chemical Corporation)

PC / Application Technician

Sole on-site technician with full accountability for hardware, software, and network support for a manufacturing plant with 300 end users. Perform system administration to include installations, maintenance, upgrades, troubleshooting, and support for servers, fiber optics, printers, software applications, and all workstations.

Manage installation and upgrade project schedules and work closely with management to control project risks involving schedule, technical issues, and personnel. Communicate with vendors and suppliers to purchase parts and coordinate warranty service. Provide training to system users and new technicians. Set up and maintain individual user and group accounts. Work closely with help desk to ensure all issues are quickly resolved and to maintain optimal system performance.

- Planned and managed migration from Windows XP to Windows 7, with no loss of data or drop in productivity.
- Resolved a long-standing problem of slow connectivity by troubleshooting network settings.

(continued)

This traditional, comprehensive resume for an experienced professional devotes two full pages to his 13+-year career. The Competencies and Technical Skills sections are effective keyword listings.

Cell: (281) 565-4999   DON G. SHELLEY ~ PAGE 2   dgs1159@mccn.net

PROFESSIONAL EXPERIENCE
(continued)

COMPUTER INNOVATIONS – Houston, TX   2003 to 2004
(A local computer manufacturer)

Service and Production Manager

Tested and troubleshot hardware and software problems of completed systems and corrected deficiencies in assembly or manufacturing. Supervised, scheduled, and trained 20 technicians. Scheduled production, work flow, and customer repairs to ensure a high level of customer satisfaction. Maintained and updated two Novell networks.

- Created database for tracking parts and service, enabling more-efficient repairs and improving customer service.

JLM COMPUTERS, INC. – Houston, TX   2000 to 2003
(A national computer manufacturer)

PC Evaluation and Test Engineer

Evaluated all new computer systems and internal peripherals before shipment to mass merchants such as Sam's Club and Walmart. Supervised 14 production personnel. Provided installation, maintenance, and support for systems at administrative offices. Installed and configured Microsoft's HCT (Hardware Compatibility Testing) on all systems to ensure complete compatibility with JLM systems. Installed EDI (Electronic Data Interface) to allow for more efficient and accurate communication with trading partners. Maintained current knowledge of major hardware and software manufacturers and technology changes.

TETRAMAX, INC. – San Jose, CA   1998 to 2000
(A plastics manufacturer specializing in fluorocarbons)

Process Engineer

Created and administered databases for all materials, log numbers, and material properties for the Isostatic Molding Research and Development department. Interfaced all CNC machines to a common terminal. Created bar and chart graphs to exhibit control limits for major companies such as Lockheed, Boeing, and Hughes. Oversaw R&D development of the isostatic molding process to improve material properties.

- Designed and built first machine on the West Coast to skive six-foot wide tetrafluoroethylene.

TRAINING

NETWARE 6.5 ADMINISTRATION – certificate
MICROSOFT WINDOWS SERVER – certificate
MICROSOFT EXCHANGE SERVER – certificate

Please keep this inquiry confidential at this time.

ADAM TYLER, Austel Licensed No. 55555

220 Citizen Street, PCVILL 2615 ACT • 0404 555 555 • (02) 5555 5555 • adam@adam.com.au

"I can honestly say that Adam would be in the top 5 percent of people I have offered positions to and, by far, the best installer/technician." Manager's reference

Telecommunications/IT installation specialist with 9+ years of experience troubleshooting faults, installing systems and components, laying cables, restoring services, and refining technical expertise. Poised for leading technician or supervisory role where client interaction is integral to ongoing client retention and satisfaction.

- Cited by management for demonstrating high-level, enthusiastic customer service and willingness to achieve time-critical deadlines, resulting in increased productivity and business revenues.
- Exceptional track record for quality, safety, and team leadership.

KEY STRENGTHS

High-level technical competencies.
Install, repair, diagnose, and troubleshoot the following:

- Personal Computers and Networks
- Telecommunications Cables
- Security Systems
- Printers and Scanners
- Software
- Plotters
- Modems

Articulate in communicating problems and solutions to people at all levels. Noted for the following:

- Customer Relations Attitude
- Intuitive Hardware/Software Support
- Team Leadership/Team Building
- Rapid Conflict Resolution
- Safety and Quality Compliance
- Productivity in Deadline-Dependent Environments

QUALIFICATIONS AND ADVANCED TRAINING

AUSTEL CABLING LICENSE (General Premises), Australian Telecommunications Authority

QUALIFIED ELECTRONIC SECURITY INSTALLER, Australian Institute of Technology

PROFESSIONAL EXPERIENCE

HEAD INSTALLER/NO. 1 TECHNICIAN, ICU Home Security   2007–Present

Install, test, maintain, and service security systems in homes across Canberra. Despite no previous experience in this industry, attained security installer's certificate and was elevated to leadership role in recognition of technical expertise, thoroughness, and customer-focused communication style.

- Frequently requested to contribute fault-finding expertise on troublesome or complex project assignments; quickly gained reputation for ability to identify persistent and elusive faults.
- Instructed new customers on the use, operation, features, and benefits of security systems; shared information on emergency procedures, company policy, servicing schedules, and routine equipment care.
- Contributed to business revenues by recommending extended warranties and maintenance plans.

"Adam's honesty, integrity, work ethic, organization, and people skills are to be envied by most....His workmanship has always matched his own personal high standards....This office constantly receives mail from Adam's clients heralding his praises." Reference excerpt from manager, ICU Home Security

FIELD ENGINEER, Tekkoworld   2002–2007

Hands-on technical role installing, configuring, and troubleshooting personal computers and peripherals (printers, scanners, plotters, modems). Established outstanding customer relationships, acquiring business-wide reputation for strengths in resolving the most complex of technical challenges.

"We found Adam to be responsive, efficient, and meticulous in all his work activities. Indeed, one of his skills lies in the rapport he had with our customers." Reference excerpt from managing director, Tekkoworld

REFERENCES AVAILABLE UPON REQUEST

Because this individual's hands-on work was repetitive (he installed only telecommunication cables and security systems), in his resume it was essential to express his broader capabilities, including a customer service focus and team leadership skills.

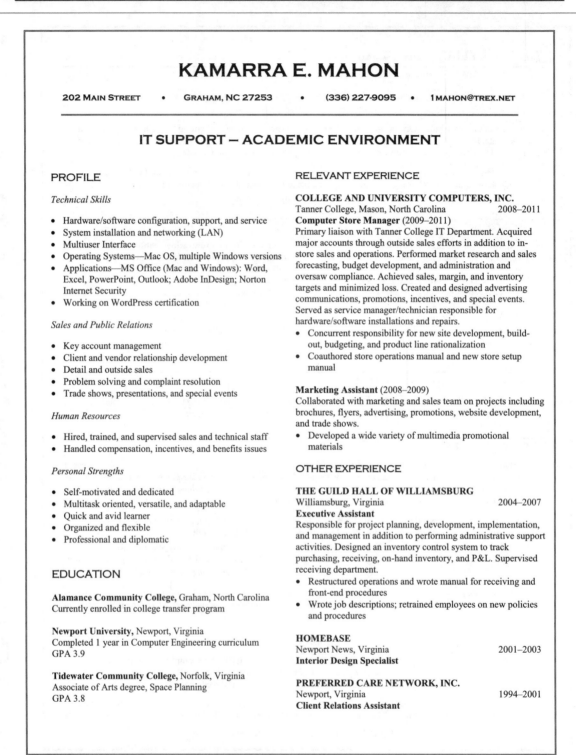

KAMARRA E. MAHON

202 MAIN STREET • GRAHAM, NC 27253 • (336) 227-9095 • 1MAHON@TREX.NET

IT SUPPORT – ACADEMIC ENVIRONMENT

PROFILE

Technical Skills

- Hardware/software configuration, support, and service
- System installation and networking (LAN)
- Multiuser Interface
- Operating Systems—Mac OS, multiple Windows versions
- Applications—MS Office (Mac and Windows): Word, Excel, PowerPoint, Outlook; Adobe InDesign; Norton Internet Security
- Working on WordPress certification

Sales and Public Relations

- Key account management
- Client and vendor relationship development
- Detail and outside sales
- Problem solving and complaint resolution
- Trade shows, presentations, and special events

Human Resources

- Hired, trained, and supervised sales and technical staff
- Handled compensation, incentives, and benefits issues

Personal Strengths

- Self-motivated and dedicated
- Multitask oriented, versatile, and adaptable
- Quick and avid learner
- Organized and flexible
- Professional and diplomatic

EDUCATION

Alamance Community College, Graham, North Carolina
Currently enrolled in college transfer program

Newport University, Newport, Virginia
Completed 1 year in Computer Engineering curriculum
GPA 3.9

Tidewater Community College, Norfolk, Virginia
Associate of Arts degree, Space Planning
GPA 3.8

RELEVANT EXPERIENCE

COLLEGE AND UNIVERSITY COMPUTERS, INC.
Tanner College, Mason, North Carolina   2008–2011
Computer Store Manager (2009–2011)
Primary liaison with Tanner College IT Department. Acquired major accounts through outside sales efforts in addition to in-store sales and operations. Performed market research and sales forecasting, budget development, and administration and oversaw compliance. Achieved sales, margin, and inventory targets and minimized loss. Created and designed advertising communications, promotions, incentives, and special events. Served as service manager/technician responsible for hardware/software installations and repairs.

- Concurrent responsibility for new site development, build-out, budgeting, and product line rationalization
- Coauthored store operations manual and new store setup manual

Marketing Assistant (2008–2009)
Collaborated with marketing and sales team on projects including brochures, flyers, advertising, promotions, website development, and trade shows.

- Developed a wide variety of multimedia promotional materials

OTHER EXPERIENCE

THE GUILD HALL OF WILLIAMSBURG
Williamsburg, Virginia   2004–2007
Executive Assistant
Responsible for project planning, development, implementation, and management in addition to performing administrative support activities. Designed an inventory control system to track purchasing, receiving, on-hand inventory, and P&L. Supervised receiving department.

- Restructured operations and wrote manual for receiving and front-end procedures
- Wrote job descriptions; retrained employees on new policies and procedures

HOMEBASE
Newport News, Virginia   2001–2003
Interior Design Specialist

PREFERRED CARE NETWORK, INC.
Newport, Virginia   1994–2001
Client Relations Assistant

A two-column format equally showcases skills, education, and relevant experience that helped this job seeker land a new position providing technical support for a school district.

James M. Pantell

3409 Blue Tree Drive, Baltimore, MD 21047
Tel: 410.575.5095   Email: JMP@yahoo.com

Information Technology & Information Systems Technician
Clearance: TS/SCI

Certified through Microsoft: MCSE, MCIPT
Certified through Novell: CNA and CNE

Skilled communications technician incorporating 14 years of in-depth knowledge of complex communications, computer, network, digital imagery processing, and local and worldwide intelligence systems. Highly skilled with scores of network operating systems, hardware, software, networks, servers, workstations, LAN, WAN, fiber optics, and a wide variety of attached peripherals from military, commercial, and proprietary manufacturers.

Full scope of responsibilities includes installation, integration, configuring, diagnostic testing, repair, and maintenance of systems, servers, fiber optic termination, worldwide data communications, routers, workstations, digital, satellite, multiplexers, and cryptographic equipment.

Skills

Systems Administrator	Satellite Communications Systems	Encryption Equipment
Systems Analyst	Technical Hardware Support	Technical Authority
Secure Systems		Troubleshooting

Professional Experience

Verizon, Baltimore, MD   2005 to Present
Systems Field Representative (Europe)

- Currently participating in the implementation and administration of a Top Secret Windows network integrated with the in-place UNIX environment.
- Manage baselining and daily desktop maintenance of Secret and Unclassified Windows networks.
- Install and maintain Sun enterprise servers, storage devices, workstations, and many personal computers. Plan and install fiber optics, Thinnet, and Cat 5 cabling.
- Efficiently provide residential, on-call, and deployed maintenance support throughout Europe. Maintain an extensive knowledge of complex U.S. military command, control, communications, computer, and intelligence systems. Conduct troubleshooting and maintenance on a wide variety of systems and provide technical hardware support.

Science of Computers International, Germany   2000 to 2005
Systems Administrator

- Provided technical support to Novell and Microsoft networks utilizing three different Network Operating Systems (NOS) supporting classified and unclassified Local Area Networks (LANs).
- Conducted systems analysis on the networks, servers, and workstations.
- As member of critical integration team, installed and configured new hardware and software into existing networks. Conducted a full range of testing and analysis of the compatibility of new and old components, configurations, functionality, and expandability, ensuring full support for new system.

continued

In this resume, extensive lists of technical training and proficiencies are relegated to page 2 to allow the individual's high-level experience to shine on page 1. Note the brief "a short list" notation under Technical Training; this is an effective way to convey only the highlights.

James M. Pantell, Page 2
JMP@yahoo.com

Verizon, Baltimore, MD   1995 to 2000
Field Service Representative (Europe)

- Installed, integrated, and conducted diagnostic testing and repair at the European Node of the Joint Worldwide Communication System (JWCS). The system included secure high-speed data communications and simultaneous video-teleconferencing.
- Installed, tested, and repaired communication circuits and maintenance of 3 separate videoconferencing studios.
- Precisely calculated and ensured that the sparing level for the system was properly maintained.
- Installed and terminated fiber optic cables, Sun workstations and servers, and Cisco routers.
- Instrumental in the critical installation and integration of an Ethernet LAN and ATM, connecting more than 150 Sun workstations.
- Ensured the security of highly classified materials by installing, testing, and repairing encryption devices.
- Managed a team responsible for installation, integration, testing, and repair of a prototype Sun-based classified message handling system. Ensured continuous, uninterrupted networks.

Education

A.A. in Computer Studies, Central Texas College, 1995

Technical Training

A short list

- *Certified through Comp TIA: Network+ Certification, 2009*
- *Certified through Microsoft: MCSE, 2008; MCIPT, 2009*
- *Certified through Novell: CAN, 2001; CNE, 2009*
- Windows Network Training, 2007
- Novell NetWare Administration & Advance Administration, 2005
- Novell Service and Support & Design and Implementation, 2005
- Novell NetWare Installation and Configuration Workshop, 2004
- Fiber Optic Installation and Termination, 2004
- Cryptologic Equipment Limited Maintenance, 2004
- LAN Cabling Systems, 2001

Computer Proficiencies

Software: Microsoft Office Suite, Novell GroupWise, Microsoft Exchange, Microsoft Exchange Server, Visio

Operating Systems: Microsoft Windows XP, 7; Novell NetWare / OES

Hardware Families: Sun Servers, Cisco Routers, HP ProLiant Servers, Network Equipment Technologies

CHAPTER 5

Resumes for Computer Systems Professionals

- Database Specialists
- Database Designers
- Database Administrators
- Applications Programmers
- Programmer Analysts
- Software Engineers
- Quality Assurance Experts
- Business Analysts
- Software Architects
- Software Test Developers

VIVIAN ROMANO

10 Mathews Drive ◆ Bridgeport, CT 06604 ◆ (203) 237-5345 ◆ vivromano@gmail.com

IT DATABASE SPECIALIST/SYSTEMS ADMINISTRATOR

Recognized "go-to" resource, quick learner, and eager teacher

Well-regarded IT specialist with broad-based background and extensive experience in administrative roles. Forward-thinking professional with a record of success in researching and implementing technology solutions to improve/automate processes and maximize operational effectiveness. Organized, effective leader with meticulous attention to detail. Adaptable, solution-oriented team player actively seeking to improve the status quo.

Core Expertise:

Database Processing / Database Analysis / Network Management / Systems Training
Training & Documentation / Problem Solving / Organizational Improvement

PROFESSIONAL EXPERIENCE

EMERGENCY SERVICES, INC., Clinton, CT   2003 to present
Systems Administrator
Serve as system administrator for 5,000-record work-order database system. Manage records, train end users, and create ad hoc reports. Maintain servers, computers, printers, and mobile phones used by employees in 5 locations. Monitor e-mail systems and identify/implement solutions to improve efficiency and productivity.

- Introduced new Corrigo database system to manage work-order requests in office that saw 300+ new work orders per month. Successfully transitioned company to paperless environment while improving efficiency.
- Trained internal and field staff in use of new system, creating customized training materials that included 6 separate training guides adapted to need and experience level. Facilitated development of training tools by acquiring and utilizing new screen-shot software to capture frame-by-frame views on handheld PPC phones.
- Developed well-received daily status reports for client, designing an intricate solution that drew information from 2 distinct databases before running a query that ultimately generated the required results.
- Created automated process for checking accuracy of data in 3,000 files by conducting comparison to master files. Identified Excel add-on tool that reduced processing time, allowing what used to be a 3-day manual process to be completed in 20 minutes.
- Facing need to rename hundreds of files, researched and implemented solution that simplified and automated what would have proven to be a very time-consuming process highly subject to errors.
- Gained justification for and implemented file backup, e-mail storage, emergency e-mail access, and e-mail spam filtering solutions.

EDUCATION

BA, University of Connecticut, Storrs, CT, 2000

COMPUTER SKILLS

Access, Excel, Corrigo, Word, PowerPoint, Project, Outlook, WordPerfect, Lotus

One job and one primary accomplishment—introducing a new database system—make up the bulk of this resume, which includes detailed achievements that show the value of the new database.

John Percello

303 Treepark Lane   (847) 345-7811
Palatine, Illinois 60067   johnpcl@aol.com

DATABASE DESIGNER

- Designed database for customer history
- Designed database for machine shop
- Integrated spreadsheets into a database
- Programmed procedures to update records

- Designed database to store heat numbers
- Designed database for inspection services
- Created database to track outbound shipments and incoming freight

EMPLOYMENT

R.W.O. METAL, Arlington Heights, IL   2001–Present
Shipping/Receiving Manager, 2005–Present

- Help company meet ISO 9001 requirements.
- Utilize software for truck bills of lading and UPS shipments.
- Continue to perform production scheduler duties.

Production Scheduler, 2001–2005

- Created and maintained multiple MS Access databases:
  1. To track production, document history, produce shipping manifests, and print out production reports and charts
  2. For customer quality certification
  3. For machine shop inspection histories
- Assisted in the creation of an Excel spreadsheet used to schedule orders.

Note: Throughout my career with this company, I have assisted coworkers with all computer-related problems whether software, hardware, or network. For example, I created a backup routine when the tape drive on the server failed. I also have built numerous spreadsheets and small databases for others or taught them how to do it themselves.

EDUCATION   WILLIAM RAINER-HARPER COLLEGE, Palatine, IL
- Certificate in Information Systems
- Completed courses in Visual Basic, C, MS Access, MS Excel, MS Word, MS PowerPoint, Paradox, WordPress
- Currently enrolled in Web Design
- Studying for MCSD certification

A strong element of this resume is the personal note below the employment summary that calls out technology-related activities in a nontechnology job.

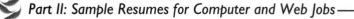

DAVID SUZUKI

145 West Rosecliff Court   414-629-3676
Saukville, WI 53080   davidsuzuki@yahoo.com

TECHNICAL PROFILE

A dedicated and loyal systems professional with 25+ years of hands-on experience as a **database administrator and application developer.** Solid understanding of relational databases. Excellent designing, coding, and testing skills. Strong oral and written communication abilities.

Databases:	Oracle, MySQL
Languages:	C++, Perl, Visual Basic, Java
Operating Systems:	Windows XP, 7
Third-Party Software:	IBM Cognos, Informatica, Microsoft Access

PROFESSIONAL EXPERIENCE

Midwest Staffing, Inc. Milwaukee, WI   1986 to Present
(A global employment services organization with annual sales in excess of $10 billion)

LEAD DATABASE ADMINISTRATOR AND DEVELOPER

Lead database administrator with 24/7 responsibility for performance, tuning, recovery, and planning. Administer mission-critical payroll and billing database that bills $5+ million per week. Use various utilities to transfer data to other platforms and build tables/indexes. Respond to end users' requests for information and resolve discrepancies in data reports. Research and interact with vendors in the purchase of third-party software. Train and supervise assistant DBAs. Write user manuals, operating procedures, and internal documentation.

Selected Database Development Projects and Achievements

- Designed, developed, and implemented Oracle data bank, allowing access to data via easy-to-use desktop tools.

- Developed and maintain franchise-fee billing application.

- Developed central billing consolidation application that bills $4 million per month.

- Researched and recommended purchase of Informatica utility. Data movement to the data repository, the Internet, and databases is now accomplished in one step. Previously, data movement involved large amounts of development time.

- Reduced data transfer time by 50% by designing new cross-platform processes.

- Selected by management to train assistant database administrator. Assistant is now a reliable backup on all database issues.

EDUCATION

Oracle and Oracle Tuning, Certificate Courses, University of Wisconsin–Milwaukee, 2009

Note how your attention is drawn to the Selected Database Development Projects and Achievements section—the hands-on experience that sells this candidate.

Tanya Kirkpatrick

578 14th Street, #3
Tampa, FL 33609

(813) 967-1408
tanya.kirk@browsenet.com

PROGRAMMER / SOFTWARE ENGINEER

PROFILE OF QUALIFICATIONS

Cited as *"a keen technical intellect who consistently makes the grade through innovation and the perfect eye for finding coding flaws."*—Jerry Drake, Director

- Results-oriented software engineer who adapts easily to shifting requirements.
- Consistently commended for ability to work as a team member or independently while achieving critical deadlines. Strong project leader.
- Recognized for performance and project contributions. Consistently achieve highest rating in annual evaluations for top 2% of total company personnel.

TECHNICAL APPLICATIONS

- **Programming Languages:** C, C++, SQL, CICS, C shell, Java, Perl, HSPICE, MATLAB.
- **Platforms:** Unix, Macintosh OS, Windows XP, Windows 7.
- **Software:** MS Word, Excel, PowerPoint, and Access; various other programs.
- Experienced in developing Graphical User Interfaces (GUIs).

EDUCATION & TRAINING

B.S. in Computer Information Systems, University of South Florida, Tampa, FL
- Courses: **Coding for Tomorrow, Java, SQL and Images, Copyrights and the Web**

PROFESSIONAL EXPERIENCE

Senior Programmer, Carco Corporation, Orlando, FL—2004 to Present
Perform multifaceted programming and analysis from code development through acceptance testing on a number of projects.

- Develop special applications in C++ to customize office business systems.
- Enhance existing software subsystems to accommodate new requirements.
- Lead a consulting team in the analysis of customer operating systems and software applications. Make suggestions for software changes and customization to existing programs.

Software Analyst and Programmer I, Carco Corporation, Orlando, FL—2002 to 2004

- Developed a graphical user interface (GUI) for an analog design automation tool in a Unix environment. Interface communicated with a range of C programs to transfer input parameters provided by user and to display programs' output on the screen.

The attractive boxed headline and excellent testimonial are strong lead-ins to this resume.

JEFFREY J. VANBEEK

555 – 200 Masters Road West
Augusta, Ontario A2B 2B2

Phone: (905) 555-6666
Email: vanbeek@imail.com

Profile

Highly motivated and enthusiastic **IT professional** with proven experience in both team and project management capacities. Outstanding analysis, programming, and debugging capabilities. Ability to work autonomously and as a team player, with demonstrated strengths in leadership and mentoring. Easily adaptable to change and eager to learn and expand capabilities. Industry expertise includes:

- **2D / 3D Graphing**
- **Speech Recognition**
- **Geometry Management**
- **Taxation Software**

Languages

C++, C, Visual C++, ASP, Java, COM, Windows SDK, Visual Basic, Object Pascal

Experience

2008–Present

C++ / ActiveX Template Library / Microsoft Foundation Classes / COM / ASP

TECHNICAL PROJECT MANAGER — XYZ Group Inc., Augusta, Ontario
- Managed programmers, technical writers, and release engineers from design and implementation through testing and delivery during several major release cycles.
- Produced charting and geometry management components for Windows developers.
- Researched and prototyped geometry management tool based on design by chief technology officer.
- Led development of an ASP version of the charting components.
- Provide estimates and technical expertise to sales force to develop and close source code deals and arrange custom consulting work.

2006–2008

Visual C++ / Windows SDK / Microsoft Foundation Classes

SENIOR SPEECH RECOGNITION PROGRAMMER — VoiceTech Inc., Augusta, Ontario
- Used C++, Object Pascal, and Windows SDK to build a natural language interface to office productivity tools such as Microsoft Word, Excel, and Outlook.
- Controlled office tools through programmable APIs while processing speech input from programs such as Dragon NaturallySpeaking.
- Worked on VoiceMate for the Internet, which allowed control of Internet browsers by voice control.

2006

SENIOR PROGRAMMER — Rybena Corporation, Pinehurst, Ontario
- Developed photo-realistic desktop communications center using Visual C++ and SDK.
- Mentored team members in debugging skills.
- Interacted with internal QA and usability groups to design and improve components.

continued...

This resume uses the attractive, clean, highly readable Tahoma font along with a clever design to make it a visual standout.

JEFFREY J. VANBEEK   (905) 555-6666 • vanbeek@imail.com   Page 2

2004–2006 LEAD PROGRAMMER/ANALYST — TaxSystems Canada, Pinehurst, Ontario
- Guided UI subsystem development while building core tax calculation routines.
- Developed shared class libraries in C++ for personal, corporate, and trust tax products.
- Connected TaxSystems' data structures to MFC's document/view architecture using a multiple document/multiple view interface (MDI).

DOS / C

2001–2004 TAX SOFTWARE PROGRAMMER/ANALYST — TaxSystems Canada, Pinehurst, Ontario
- Conducted full overhaul of TaxSystems' system platform to improve performance and stability.
- Performed troubleshooting, maintenance, optimization, and enhancements.

2000–2001 TAX SOFTWARE PROGRAMMER/ANALYST — ABC Systems Corp., Medina, Ontario
- Reimplemented core of existing tax programs to rectify limitations caused by existing segmented architecture design.
- Highlight was design and implementation for "E-Tax," allowing preparation and transmission of electronically filed tax returns with Revenue Canada, Taxation.

Education
1998 **University of Waterloo**
Bachelor of Mathematics – Honours Computer Science / Information Systems option
Awards:
Brad J. Sokol Award for Student Leadership
Gates Foundation Scholarship 1997–1998
René Descartes Entrance Award

Training
2010 **People Management Course**
- 3-day in-house program conducted by Canadian Management Association
2009 **Microsoft Professional Developer's Conference**
2007 **Project Management Course**
- 2-day in-house program developed for SHL and BC Tel

References
Personal and professional references available upon request.

CHARLES G. SHORT

▶ ▶ ▶ ▶ ▶ ▶ ▶ ▶ ▶ ▶ ▶ ▶ ▶ ▶ ▶

11906 Charter Parkway • Ballwin, MO 63011
636.962.8453/mobile • 636.965.8299/home
cgshort01@att.net

SUMMARY ▶

Focused **Senior Programmer/Analyst** with a proven record of contribution in team leadership, system analysis, design, development, and implementation. Particular expertise in client-side and mainframe development. Knowledge of supply chain management, financial accounting, manufacturing, production, asset management, and transportation functions.

- ▶ Confident rapport builder; skilled in building positive working relationships based on sincerity, helpfulness, mutual respect, and trust.
- ▶ Skilled, versatile communicator and facilitator; effective with business and technical participants at all levels.
- ▶ Goal-oriented, systematic planner with a big-picture perspective.
- ▶ Relaxed, collegial, and supportive team leader and mentor.
- ▶ Adaptable, creative, and tactful problem solver; skilled in identifying the best options and solutions.
- ▶ Engaged learner; well-read on current technologies and applications.
- ▶ Enthusiastic contributor with a collaborative spirit, a strong work ethic, and a passion for seeing a quality job through to fruition.

Tools	XMLSpy, IntelliJ IDEA, Toad, TSO/ISPF, IMS Expert, Data Expert/FileAid
Databases	Oracle, MySQL, DB2
Languages	Java, Java Swing, XML, XSL, XSLT, HTML, DOM, JavaScript, SQL, Flash, PHP
Software	Weblogic, WordPress, MS Office

EDUCATION ▶

M.A., Computer Resources and Information Management
Maryville University, St. Louis, MO

B.S., *with honors,* Information Systems and Data Processing; Minor: Business
Bowling Green University, Bowling Green, OH
- • Earned 100% of college expenses.

EXPERIENCE ▶

2001–present   DYNAQUIP CONTROLS, INC., Washington, MO

Lead Programmer/Analyst 1/07–present
Provide team leadership for design/development of supply-chain/inventory-management system incorporating Cayenta Frameworks Java client and Weblogic J2EE EJB server. Participate in task and navigation analysis, paper prototyping, usability testing, and results analysis, providing liaison to human factors/usability project team. Ensure 8–10 developers conform to standards, specifications, and quality expectations.
- • Developed graphical user interface (GUI) using Cayenta's Java-based controllers.
- • Facilitated user testing and led implementation of user-centered design.
- • Mentored several junior developers on standards and principles.
- • Maintained server-side EJB (Enterprise Java Beans) components.

Page 1 of 2

This candidate's early work experience, while seemingly unrelated to his new career in technology, provides him with diverse knowledge of business functions—just the kind of practical information a programmer/analyst needs to deliver accurate software solutions.

CHARLES G. SHORT   cgshort01@att.net   Page 2

Senior Programmer/Analyst 10/04–1/07
Participated in a variety of design/development and enhancement projects.

- Created GUI for asset-management/tracking system, using Java, Java Swing, and Model-View-Controller framework.
- Coded tracking system to accommodate internationalization.

Programmer/Analyst 5/01–10/04
Developed and maintained mainframe revenue-accounting systems.

- Participated in developing and testing COBOL/IMS/DB2 interface to Revenue Systems Processing (RSP) client/server front-end for existing batch-accounting and waybill-tracking system.
- Provided primary support for Accounts Receivable Autocash System accommodating receipt and processing of bank transmissions (Electronic Fund Transfers).
- Enhanced and maintained IMS/DB2 revenue-accounting, waybill-processing and collection systems.

1998–2001   PC MALL, Toledo, OH

Warehouse Support Assistant
Retrieved, verified, packaged, and shipped computer/electronic equipment to domestic and international locations (part-time during college).

1992–1998   COTTON CLUB, INC., Toledo, OH

Plant Team Technician
Learned and performed bottling operations, purchasing, materials management, equipment troubleshooting/maintenance, and distribution functions. Met with vendor sales representatives.

1988–1991   UNITED STATES NAVY

Sonarman
Installed and maintained submarine sonar systems. Trained new personnel on procedures, documentation, and equipment handling for surveillance and precision navigation systems; managed up to 5 sailors.

TRAINING ▶

Maryville University, Center for the Application of Information Technology (CAIT):
Enterprise Java Beans, Graphical User Interface Using Java, Java Servlet Programming, Advanced Java Programming

Object Computer Incorporated (OCI):
Extensible Markup Language (XML), Extensible Stylesheet Language Transformations (XSLT)

Dale Carnegie Course

CHRISTOPHER RYAN

119 Dorothy Place, Lynbrook, New York 11563 • 516-472-8953 • cryan2003@hotmail.com

SOFTWARE ENGINEER / PROGRAMMER

C++, Perl, and Java / Object-Oriented Design and Development / Windows, UNIX, and GNU/Linux

Professional Profile

Software engineering and honors program graduate with 4+ years of hands-on programming and application design experience. Track record reveals exceptional skills in effective and error-free programming, system debugging, and customer-centered service. Demonstrated creativity in utilizing various software tools to develop and perform testing and analysis.

Core Skills

- Program & Instruction Coding
- System Analysis
- High-Level Design
- User Training
- Program Logic Development
- Program Documentation
- Web Design & Maintenance
- Database Design
- System Administration

Strengths

➤ Software design and development in C++, C, Java, Perl, and PHP in Windows, UNIX, and Linux.

➤ Experience working with Microsoft Foundation Classes, OpenGL, and Windows Sockets in C++ and Swing and JDBC in Java.

➤ Effective testing of software applications and submission of clear problem reports with solution recommendations.

Computers

Languages:	C++, C, HTML, Java, JavaScript, Perl, ASP, PHP, Assembly, UNIX Shell Script, and SQL
O/S:	Windows XP/7, UNIX, GNU/Linux (Debian), and Macintosh
Applications:	MS Office Suite, Visio, Visual C++, Visual SourceSafe, GNU Dia, GIMP, Adobe Photoshop, CVS, GCC, DDD, Nedit, vim, Dreamweaver, and WordPress

Experience

KINGSTON REYNOLDS & ASSOCIATES, Far Rockaway, New York   2009–Present
Programmer
- Create and use Perl script to generate XML documentation of SQL stored procedures and ASP pages.
- Develop HTML Web pages and modify ASP forms.
- Perform software testing of ASP pages and standalone Visual Basic applications.
- Perform research, analysis, and client support.

COLUMBIA UNIVERSITY, New York, New York   2005–2007
Web Team / Teaching Assistant / Tutor and Grader
- Designed Web pages for the University.
- Assisted with Software Engineering classes and labs.

CONTINUED

This individual has an outstanding education but has been working at a basic job since graduation. This resume is designed to show off all of his computer skills, briefly mention his work experiences, and list all of his academic achievements because he is practically entry-level.

CHRISTOPHER RYAN   CRYAN2003@HOTMAIL.COM   PAGE TWO

LIFE SCIENCE TECHNOLOGY, INC., Valley Stream, New York   Summers 2006–2008
Administrative Assistant
- Maintained product database and assembled drug master file for submission to the FDA.
- Designed Regulatory Affairs Department brochure.

COLUMBIA UNIVERSITY, New York, New York   Summer 2005
Information Technology Intern
- Created Web pages for the Development Office.
- Set up networked computer lab.

Education

Columbia University, New York, New York
Bachelor of Science—Software Engineering   May 2009
➢ Columbia University Honors Program
➢ GPA 3.9—Graduated with Highest Honors
➢ Presidential Scholar for three semesters
➢ Tau Beta Pi Engineering Honors Society
➢ Phi Kappa Phi Honors Society

Career Solutions, Lynbrook, New York
Computer Support and Maintenance Program   2004–2005
➢ CompTIA Certified A+ Service Technician

Hofstra University, Hempstead, New York
HTML Web Page Design   Summer 2003

JONATHAN P. WOODRIDGE

41 Chatham Avenue • Cherry Hill, NJ 08034 • 609-714-8020 • jpw@aol.com

Programming / Software Training / Technical Support

SUMMARY

- High-energy, self-directed professional with a technical / business academic background and 10+ years of successful business experience.
- Frequent recognition for outstanding performance in positions requiring strong planning, analytical, problem-solving, and customer service skills.
- C++ programming experience, using class functions and conversions, inheritance and dynamic memory location, I/O file streams, data files, and data structures: arrays, strings, addresses, and pointers.
- Developer of programs that integrated Visual Basic with Access.
- Extensive background in training and customer service; talent for clearly conveying information.
- Strong troubleshooting skills; proven ability to assess and hurdle complex obstacles.

Programming Languages: C++, Visual Basic
Software: Excel, Access, PowerPoint, MS Word, Visio
Operating Systems: Windows XP / 7

EDUCATION / PROFESSIONAL DEVELOPMENT

A.S., Computer Science / Business Administration: Dumont County College, Dumont, NJ

Professional Seminars / Training Programs
Customer Service, Training, Interviewing, Employee Relations / Coaching

SKILLS AND ACCOMPLISHMENTS

Programming

- Developed an amortization chart in C++ that allowed user to enter input to calculate payments, balances, and interest paid.
- In C++, created a bowling program that recorded score data input by user and stored it in an output data file for later use.
- Developed programs for the real estate and fast food industries that integrated Visual Basic with Access, utilizing the database in the interface and retrieving it using SQL statements.

Technical Writing

- As project manager, led a team of 6 in the development of a software manual.
- Conducted an analysis of the software program and typical users, assigned responsibilities, completed a task list, developed task completion dates, and performed frequent reviews to assess progress.
- Ensured clarity and integrity of document and use of appropriate terminology.

Planning / Leadership / Training / Troubleshooting

- Managed the operations of multimillion-dollar retail locations, with responsibility for sales, customer service, cost containment, recruiting, training, scheduling, and inventory.
- Received frequent regional and district recognition for sales volume and expense control.
- Evaluated problems at various sites and devised and implemented solutions.
- Trained managers throughout the region while maintaining responsibility for store management.
- Conducted group orientation and training sessions for seasonal sales associates.

Customer Service

- Focused on creating customer-centered environments that inspired repeat business.
- Emphasized quality service with management trainees and staff.

PROFESSIONAL EXPERIENCE

Store Manager, The Man's Shop, Sea Girt, NJ	2003–2009
Store Manager, Carltons of California, Freehold, NJ	1996–2003

INTERESTS

Investing and financial management

This is one of the few purely "functional" resumes you'll find in this collection. Notice how the Professional Experience section is bare-bones, whereas the Skills and Accomplishments section is categorized and detailed.

Mary G. Rodriguez

4411 East Maryland Avenue — Gilbert, AZ 85234
(480) 781-0710 — MRodriguez@gmail.com

FOCUS Position as **Software Engineer** where a B.S. in Computer Science, experience in object-oriented programming, and knowledge of Internet technology are desirable.

TECHNICAL EXPERTISE

Program Design / Development / Maintenance

Database & Network Administration

System Upgrades & Enhancements

Hardware & Software Evaluation / Support

Programming Languages / Platforms:
Java, C++, Visual C++, HTML, JCL, CICS, SQL, Pascal, Windows, UNIX

Software:
MS Office, Adobe InDesign, WordPress, Novell NetWare

RELATED EXPERIENCE

Programmer / Analyst   STATE OF ARIZONA, Phoenix, AZ — 2009–2011
Used a variety of programming languages to develop interdepartmental programs. Analyzed data and wrote basic requirements documentation to create databases and applications. Assisted in training end users.
   Achievements:
   — Assisted in upgrading 20-system linked network in Novell.

Programmer   ANALYTICAL RESEARCH, INC., Sacramento, CA — 2007–2009
Directly accountable for all facets of programming and system maintenance for market research company providing services for major travel and leisure accounts throughout the world, including US Airways, Lufthansa, United Airlines, and Ritz-Carlton Hotels.

Developed and implemented custom marketing research programs; administered 30,000+-record database; coordinated user additions, deletions, and system back-up functions for Novell network. Participated in all phases of hardware and software upgrades, enhancements, and maintenance. Occasionally supervised temporary employees.
   Achievements:
   — Developed presentations for visual aids and company books utilizing a variety of graphic packages.
   — Managed 200-slide presentation to major clients.

Desktop Publisher   ARTISTRY, INC., Los Angeles, CA — 2004–2007
Assisted customers in the development of custom brochures and other marketing materials. Determined client requirements, assisted in selection of special graphic designs and programs, designed materials, and processed orders.
   Achievements:
   — Developed strong skills in computer operations and creative design.

EDUCATION / TRAINING

B.S. in Computer Science, 2008   CALIFORNIA STATE UNIVERSITY, Northridge, CA
Emphasis: Software Engineering & Computer Mathematics

Java, Intermediate Java, C++, Visual C++   SCOTTSDALE COLLEGE, Scottsdale, AZ
   — Currently attending
   — Developed a mortgage calculator utilizing Java applets

This efficient, one-page format uses good organization and formatting to clearly communicate the individual's qualifications. The Focus statement at the top is another way of stating an objective.

DEBORAH WOOD

4209 Brower Road, P.O. Box 325, Anderson, MA 56209
Phone: (345) 295-7810 ▪ Mobile: (345) 505-5621 ▪ E-mail: dwood@aol.com

SOFTWARE DEVELOPMENT MANAGER / SENIOR SOFTWARE ENGINEER
25+ years of experience in all phases of the software development life cycle

Exceptionally well-qualified senior software engineer and manager with sophisticated programming skills and a sincere passion for resolving complex problems and business challenges through technical innovation. Solid portfolio of vertical market software products proving expert hands-on ability in all phases of the software development life cycle—conception to customer delivery and support. Dedicated, results-driven, and energetic leader; extensive experience in small start-up environments. Core strengths in:

- Product Conception, Design, & Development
- Project Management
- Product Quality Assurance
- Troubleshooting & Customer Support
- Contract & Licensing Negotiations
- Custom Software Engineering
- Team Building & Leadership
- General Business Management

TECHNICAL QUALIFICATIONS

Languages:	Borland Delphi, Borland C++ Builder, MS C/C++, MS Assembler, MS VC++, MS Visual Basic, Borland C/C++, Turbo Pascal, HP Assembler, Access, dBASE, Clipper
Libraries & APIs:	Windows 16/32 API, ActiveX, Inso OEM Viewer API, Quick View, Aztec Copy Protection, Cimmetry AutoCAD API, TurboPower Series, Raize, LMD, WPTools, Dream Inspector, Topaz, Rainbow Technologies Hardware Lock, Essentials Series, Genus Series, Greenleaf, and more
Development Tools & Applications:	Wise InstallMaster, MS Visual SourceSafe, Multi-Edit, EC, WinBatch, CodeView Debugger, CodeSmith Debugger, MS Office (Word, Excel, PowerPoint, Outlook, Project), Adobe Acrobat, Norton Utilities, PowerDesk, Photoshop, and more
Operating Systems:	Windows XP, Windows 7, Windows Server, Mac OS

CAREER HIGHLIGHTS

Alsiksek Software Solutions, Boston, MA	2008–2011
New Technologies, Inc., Boston, MA	1998–2008

VICE PRESIDENT OF ENGINEERING / DIRECTOR OF PRODUCT ENGINEERING

Cofounded New Technologies, Inc., and directed all software product development, shipping, and customer support efforts. Conceptualized, designed, and managed the development of vertical market software products targeted to the industrial and manufacturing industries. Formulated and implemented quality assurance policies, procedures, and methodologies. Negotiated favorable contracts and licenses for third-party software modules and libraries. Led teams of up to 7 programmers and technicians.

Retained by Alsiksek as Director of Product Engineering following acquisition of New Technologies in 2008. Continued in previous product engineering, project management, and support role; focused on refining and upgrading the cutting-edge document management product developed by New Technologies.

- Conceptualized, designed, developed, and delivered a full line of software products meeting industrial and manufacturing industry needs for computer-based training, file organization and document management, troubleshooting, and shop floor utilities.
  - Products included Trainer Series, Assistant Series, Technical Toolbox, Portable HGR, and the company's most notable product, Virtual Library.

- Earned reputation for exceptionally solid, high-quality, and supportable software products through stringent oversight of specifications, code version control, code reuse, documentation, and testing.

continued…

Extremely appropriate for a senior software engineer, this resume includes a detailed profile, lengthy technical skills summary, and experience that highlights accomplishments and contributions.

DEBORAH WOOD • dwood@aol.com • Page 2

- Invented, designed, and integrated new technologies within software products, utilizing special talent for analyzing customer requirements and creating new, marketable products to meet needs.

- Specified and developed troubleshooting products and played an instrumental development role in custom computer-based training covering a wide range of general and specific industrial topics for Allen-Bradley, GE Fanuc, and Reliance Electric. Assisted in structuring third-party reseller licensing agreements with Rockwell Software and Taylor Software for New Technologies' products.

- Delivered fully functional software applications; oversaw licensing enforcement, setup utility development, documentation and packaging creation, and manufacturing/shipping processes.

- Developed a minimally intrusive licensing enforcement/copy protection strategy that enabled the ability to meter software product users in a multiuser environment.

- Redesigned, upgraded, and enhanced Virtual Library for the latest Windows 64-bit platform, achieving complete backward compatibility and the ability to coexist with earlier versions.

- Created totally innovative feature for Virtual Library that utilizes dynamic pointer technology to provide an advanced, nondatabase-driven document revision control system with e-mail support for companies seeking to achieve and maintain ISO 9001 status.

Wood and Associates, Inc., New York, NY   1995–1998

PRESIDENT / PRINCIPAL SOFTWARE CONSULTANT

Built and managed this software consulting company, working under contract with Allen-Bradley to handle CNC custom software engineering engagements as well as support customers through troubleshooting and enhancements for previously developed custom software. Directed a 10-person team of subcontractors. Simultaneously managed other computer consulting projects for a wide range of clients.

- Designed, developed, and tested a platform for an Allen-Bradley hardware line, which was implemented to improve the human interface front end. Created and integrated new features such as real-time task scheduling and task switching.

- Conceived and developed a software product to facilitate hardware development and documentation.

Allen-Bradley Co., Highland Heights, OH / Dusseldorf, West Germany   1986–1995

CNC SOFTWARE GROUP SUPERVISOR, MILLS AND ROBOTICS (1993–1995)
CNC SOFTWARE QUALITY ASSURANCE SUPERVISOR (1992–1993)
COMPUTER CENTER SUPERVISOR (1991–1992)
SOFTWARE ENGINEER / TECHNICIAN (1986–1991)

Advanced rapidly through positions of increasing responsibility as a software engineer and supervisor to final management position, leading a team of 5 directly reporting supervisors and approximately 70 indirect reports. Managed all standard and custom software development projects for mill and robotics applications.

- Measurably improved "as shipped" software quality through the implementation of new policies and procedures for testing and shipping. Analyzed and isolated problem areas and developed an innovative preventative method to eliminate problems in new shipments.

- Developed a fully operational and self-sustaining CNC computer department in Dusseldorf, West Germany, achieving corporate goal of establishing a local CNC software development engineering presence in Europe. Completed assignment in just 19 months, 5 months ahead of schedule.

EDUCATION

COMPUTER PROGRAMMING – Institute of Computer Management, Boston, MA – 1986

Extensive continuing education includes college-accredited courses in software development languages/ techniques, operating systems, and network administration, as well as vendor training with Microsoft, Borland, and IBM/Lotus. Certified as ISO 9001 Facilitator Specialist through Cleveland State University.

CAROLYN HE

321 Westminster, Apt. #4
Los Angeles, CA 90020

310-787-8232
carolyn.he@ymail.com

QUALITY ASSURANCE | CONFIGURATION MANAGEMENT
Delivering quality, performance, reliability, and absolute integrity.

Dedicated and motivated technologist with 20+ years of progressive experience in quality assurance, configuration management, and testing to further the success of any organization's business goals and objectives. Subject matter expert in applying methodologies, processes, and procedures in the execution of a full life-cycle approach. Fact-based decision maker with excellent analytical abilities, a demonstrated aptitude to learn and utilize new and complex technologies, and the ability to establish trust-based rapport.

Qualification Highlights:

- Chosen by a committee of peers and management as *'most valuable contributor'* during 2-year installation, test, and acceptance project for a large-scale air traffic control system. Quiet, confident demeanor greatly facilitated final acceptance.

- Proved to government agencies that newly developed QA manual, process, and procedures fulfilled all requirements, providing the organization the means to satisfy contract requirements for new business with the government.

- Appointed leader on QA and CM/DM workshop committees for well-known industry associations (EIA and IEEE) to develop new requirements and standards for Department of Defense (DOD) contractors.

- Increased value to the customer through corrective and preventive action, including reducing life-cycle time, cost, and defects. Developed a comprehensive matrix of CMMI and ISO requirements that mapped to all engineering organizations and the CM/QA organizations.

- Performed analysis of Statement of Work (SOW) requirements and specifications to cost and developed a test satisfaction matrix for both performance and acceptance details.

PROFESSIONAL EXPERIENCE

LENERA FEDERAL SYSTEMS   2008–Present
Contractor to U.S. Bureau of Labor Statistics
Configuration Management Analyst

Certify that all software, hardware, and other components constituting the IT infrastructure common operating environment are developed, maintained, and compliant with external regulatory and nonregulatory agencies.

- Perform required internal audits, providing recommendations for process improvements and updates.

- Develop and maintain configuration baselines to support diverse systems, utilizing best-practice configuration management (CM) processes and procedures to provide the right balance.

- Train team on new processes and restructuring of the electronic repositories.

LOCKHEED MARTIN CORPORATION   2003–2008
Software Quality Assurance/Configuration Management Engineer and Technical Lead

Performed the roles of a lead SQA and CM Engineer for a site of 100 programmers and testers designing, coding, implementing, and testing a large-scale air traffic control system.

- Instrumental in developing and implementing standards, processes, and procedures to fulfill ISO 9001/AS9100B and SEI/CMMI Level 4 (progressing to Level 5) requirements, always meeting or exceeding customer expectations. Results: on-time deliverables.

- Conducted independent assessments covering requirements and process compliance, risk identification, testing, adequacy and suitability, and effectiveness and efficiency of engineering processes.

Continued

For this software quality assurance/configuration management professional, a strong Qualification Highlights section introduces a detailed, well-organized, accomplishment-rich resume.

CAROLYN HE   310-787-8232
Page 2   carolyn.he@ymail.com

LOCKHEED MARTIN CORPORATION   1998–2002
Quality Assurance/Configuration Management Manager

Recruited for expertise in critical systems integration and customer acceptance. Assigned to new development of FAA terminal systems air traffic programs for 200 U.S. and 4 off-shore airports. Scope of responsibilities encompassed system hardware and software design/development, production, and "sell off" to the FAA.

- Developed strong customer relationships and actively participated in contract negotiations, guaranteeing customer acceptance of tasks and associated funding.
- Performed QA and CM for terminal control programs, including development site, initial hardware first articles, and final integrated system and acceptance testing.
- Designed and implemented QA and CM/DM audit checklists for ISO and CMMI requirements.

CORALE CORPORATION   1994–1997
Remote Site Acceptance Test and Operations Management

Won customer acceptance of a large air traffic control system, deployed on schedule to 200 U.S. airports.

- Performed all QA-CM/DM and test management on-site while providing technical and managerial direction to the home-based employees.
- Worked hands-on to complete all tasks: Performed all factory audit activity and vendor surveillance and provided on-site system integration and test oversight/support.
- Hired and trained personnel to support a 3-shift, 24/7 operation at a remote site.
- Conducted on-site user acceptance testing and training, utilizing a large contingent of transient software, hardware, and test engineers as well as program management and support personnel.

SYSMAXRIX CORPORATION   1991–1993
Quality Assurance/Configuration Management Manager

Drove development of quality management procedures and systems and improvised plans to improve upon the existing quality standards.

- Convinced project engineers and program managers to accept newly developed QA functionality as "value-added" services, significantly reducing time to completion.
- Authored a comprehensive implementation manual for functional and physical audits necessary to prove acceptability of computer systems equipment and software, resulting in a revised implementation method that reduced total time and cost.
- Conducted concurrent product acceptance at 3 large manufacturing locations in 3 different states while controlling schedule slips and eliminating budget overruns.

UNISYS CORPORATION, **Quality Assurance Manager and Vendor Surveillance**   1986–1990

SPERRY UNIVAC CORPORATION, **Software Quality Assurance Manager**   1983–1986

Education and Teaching

University of Minnesota, Bachelor of Arts in Sociology

Self-Taught: Performance of audits for required physical and functional satisfaction.

Teaching: Adjunct professor, software design and development, University of St. Thomas, master's program

RESUME 26: BY ROBYN FELDBERG, NCRW, ACRW, CCMC, CJSS, TCCS, WTVCIC

LOUISE P. KENDALL

~ Willing to travel and open to the possibility of relocation ~

LKP

8656 Frontier Drive, Lakewood, Colorado 80227
lpkendall@gmail.com ♦ Home: (303) 744-2829 ♦ Cellular: (303) 731-9283

BUSINESS ANALYST / PROGRAM MANAGER

~ Expert in driving profits and controlling costs by making software do things it wasn't meant to do ~

Hardworking, organized, and analytical professional with a proven background delivering sensible software solutions on time and at or under budget while working as part of a team or alone. Exceptional project management and problem-solving skills. Known for figuring out the most cost-effective ways to solve problems using resources that are already in place. Subject matter expertise in television broadcasting software. Experience designing and implementing Web-based applications.

CORE COMPETENCIES

- Project Management & Documentation
- Usability Testing / User Acceptance Testing
- Bug Tracking / Fault Reporting
- Product Roadmap Development
- Gap Analysis / Market Analysis
- Cost Control / Efficiency Improvement

- User Documentation Review
- Solution Delivery
- Quality Assurance
- Requirements Scope Management
- Software Development & Deployment
- Internal & External Training / Consulting

CAREER CHRONOLOGY

Cyrus Corporation, Denver, Colorado   1989–Present
Publicly held global company that manufactures digital radios, wireless local-loop telephony systems, broadband wireless access products, radios for defense, secure communications systems, HF modems, and digital imaging systems.

BUSINESS ANALYST III, *Innovacast* (07/2008–Present)

Challenged by employer to take newly acquired 2-piece broadcasting software offering from a concept to a working demo in time for International Broadcasting Convention and deliver it for general field release in 16 months. Working independently, learned how to use software and identified its capabilities. Wrote gap analysis, product roadmap, and market analysis.

Re-architected software to be more functional and user friendly than original offering. Worked with marketing department to develop trade show materials.

- Honored with "The Patent Award" in February 2010 for successfully filing a patent on the Innovacast software and playing a key role in competitively positioning company in the industry.
- Recognized with "Certificate of Achievement" in September 2008 for delivering a working demo in less than 2.5 months and in time for the International Broadcasting Convention.
- Reduced product delivery time 80% and saved the company thousands of dollars by repurposing code released in previous software and using software we owned to create user-friendly interface.
- Proposed and implemented requirements management solution that significantly improved communication and understanding between development team and stakeholders.

BUSINESS ANALYST III, *Discovery* (10/2005–07/2008)

Designed interchange between Discovery (a broadcast sales tracking system) and H-Class (a platform that allowed communication between various software packages).

- Independently learned how to use Discovery software and Mercury Quality Center testing tool.
- Improved reporting capabilities, saved company time, and reduced product defects by developing an innovative methodology that identified what bugs required testing.
- After only 4 months, assigned to create and lead training sessions and mentor a team of 4.
- Singled out for high-profile global assignments in England and South Africa.

... CONTINUED ...

Notable eye-catchers in this resume include the monogram logo and the branding statement. A lengthy career is presented on just two pages through careful selection of material and stronger focus on recent experiences.

LOUISE P. KENDALL – *PAGE 2*
lpkendall@gmail.com ♦ Home: (303) 744-2829 ♦ Cellular: (303) 731-9283

SYSTEM ENGINEER (3/2003–10/2005)

Began working on the H-Class platform, as one of the first 2 business analysts on a team of 5. Used Agile Development strategies to break down software into small, independently developable and testable pieces. As project team grew, oversaw project management and collaborated with other business analysts to ensure designs would mesh with system as a whole.

♦ Designed business requirements for H-Class platform, working on the user interface, security module, and scheduling module.

♦ During a slow time, independently offered to help a previous supervisor whose team was struggling to deliver a product release on time.
  — Initiative resulted in temporary work assignment in England to test outstanding defects.
  — Played a key role in timely product delivery, thereby averting $25,000 penalty for late delivery.
  — Saved employer the expense of contracting additional help to test defects.

♦ Saved employer the cost of purchasing test-planning software by designing database to hold and report requirements for each phase of start-up project.

SPECIAL PROJECTS COORDINATOR (02/2002–03/2003)

Worked across multiple product lines and managed a staff of 2 to convert BMS Traffic System to Web-based application. Created plan to migrate support of Novar Outsourcing to a new office.

♦ Working under a tight deadline, played a key role in creating and delivering Web-based software in time to be demonstrated at NAB—a key industry trade show.

BIAS/SALESLINE TECHNICAL SUPPORT LEAD (04/2001–02/2002)

Functioned in a management role to oversee daily activities of the technical support team of up to 15. Mentored product support team and served as internal escalation point.

BIAS/SALESLINE SPECIAL PROJECTS COORDINATOR (09/1998–04/2001)

Served as development team's client advocate for new broadcast traffic solution. Planned, developed, and executed system testing routines. Developed installation and training plan for new system.

BIAS/SALESLINE TRAINING COORDINATOR (09/1996–09/1998)

Assessed training needs of customer service staff and created training programs to increase ability to serve client base. Designed, planned, and executed internal and external training programs.

BIAS/SALESLINE CUSTOMER SERVICE REPRESENTATIVE (09/1989–09/1996)

Provided training to new clients and consulted with established clients on system setup and use.

EDUCATION, AFFILIATIONS & PROFESSIONAL SERVICE

BACHELOR OF ARTS, BROADCAST PRODUCTION—Auburn University, Auburn, Alabama

MEMBER—International Institute of Business Analysis

SAFETY TEAM LEAD—Cyrus Corporation (current)

♦ Appointed to lead an emergency response team of 8. Work closely with corporate Environmental, Health, and Safety team and the executive committee to ensure emergency preparedness.

♦ ♦ ♦ ♦ ♦

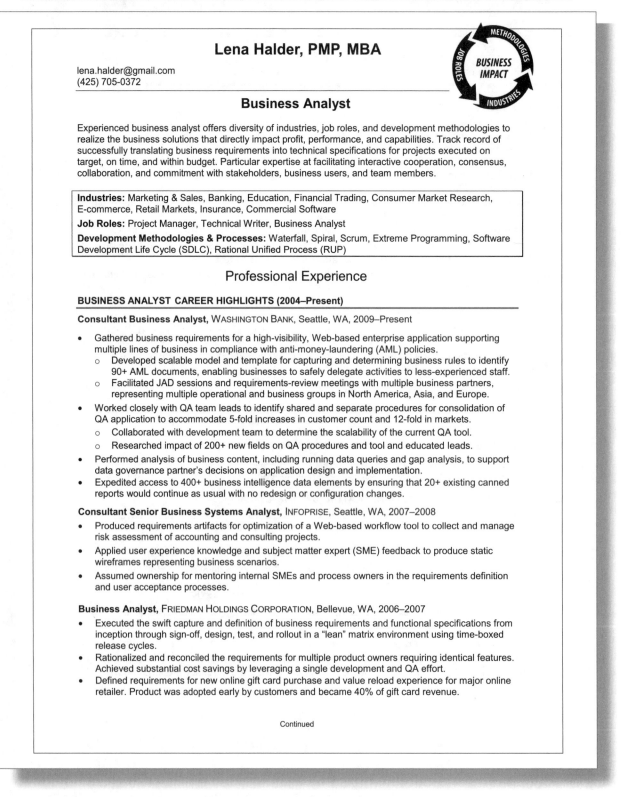

Lena Halder, PMP, MBA

lena.halder@gmail.com
(425) 705-0372

Business Analyst

Experienced business analyst offers diversity of industries, job roles, and development methodologies to realize the business solutions that directly impact profit, performance, and capabilities. Track record of successfully translating business requirements into technical specifications for projects executed on target, on time, and within budget. Particular expertise at facilitating interactive cooperation, consensus, collaboration, and commitment with stakeholders, business users, and team members.

Industries: Marketing & Sales, Banking, Education, Financial Trading, Consumer Market Research, E-commerce, Retail Markets, Insurance, Commercial Software

Job Roles: Project Manager, Technical Writer, Business Analyst

Development Methodologies & Processes: Waterfall, Spiral, Scrum, Extreme Programming, Software Development Life Cycle (SDLC), Rational Unified Process (RUP)

Professional Experience

BUSINESS ANALYST CAREER HIGHLIGHTS (2004–Present)

Consultant Business Analyst, WASHINGTON BANK, Seattle, WA, 2009–Present

- Gathered business requirements for a high-visibility, Web-based enterprise application supporting multiple lines of business in compliance with anti-money-laundering (AML) policies.
  - Developed scalable model and template for capturing and determining business rules to identify 90+ AML documents, enabling businesses to safely delegate activities to less-experienced staff.
  - Facilitated JAD sessions and requirements-review meetings with multiple business partners, representing multiple operational and business groups in North America, Asia, and Europe.
- Worked closely with QA team leads to identify shared and separate procedures for consolidation of QA application to accommodate 5-fold increases in customer count and 12-fold in markets.
  - Collaborated with development team to determine the scalability of the current QA tool.
  - Researched impact of 200+ new fields on QA procedures and tool and educated leads.
- Performed analysis of business content, including running data queries and gap analysis, to support data governance partner's decisions on application design and implementation.
- Expedited access to 400+ business intelligence data elements by ensuring that 20+ existing canned reports would continue as usual with no redesign or configuration changes.

Consultant Senior Business Systems Analyst, INFOPRISE, Seattle, WA, 2007–2008

- Produced requirements artifacts for optimization of a Web-based workflow tool to collect and manage risk assessment of accounting and consulting projects.
- Applied user experience knowledge and subject matter expert (SME) feedback to produce static wireframes representing business scenarios.
- Assumed ownership for mentoring internal SMEs and process owners in the requirements definition and user acceptance processes.

Business Analyst, FRIEDMAN HOLDINGS CORPORATION, Bellevue, WA, 2006–2007

- Executed the swift capture and definition of business requirements and functional specifications from inception through sign-off, design, test, and rollout in a "lean" matrix environment using time-boxed release cycles.
- Rationalized and reconciled the requirements for multiple product owners requiring identical features. Achieved substantial cost savings by leveraging a single development and QA effort.
- Defined requirements for new online gift card purchase and value reload experience for major online retailer. Product was adopted early by customers and became 40% of gift card revenue.

Continued

A powerful graphic illustrates this candidate's value—combining diverse job roles, industries, and methodologies to deliver business impact. Complex projects are summarized clearly and concisely, and a technology summary on page 2 ends the resume on a highly relevant note.

Lena Halder, PMP, MBA

lena.halder@gmail.com   page 2   (425) 705-0372

- Instrumental in improving online merchandising and revenues through integration of customized product recommendations, visitor surveys, visitor tracking and purchase metrics, customer product reviews, and "quick view" product summary information.
- Scoped consumer interaction requirements and briefed IT delivery managers and offshore development leads on requirements approach and progress for each initiative.
- Advised local and offshore development and QA staff during design, development, and validation.

Consultant Business Analyst, WASHINGTON FAMILY INSURANCE, Seattle, WA, 2004–2006

- Derived requirements to modify POS retailer data with a daily volume of 1M to 3M records. Developed modifications to expedite weekly process and release of data to Fortune 1000 customers.
- Drafted and executed functional tests for Web-based claim processing call center application, coordinating resolution of defects to ensure successful user acceptance test (UAT) results.
- Captured requirements for order estimation and order fulfillment processes, delivering use cases, rules, and UI wireframes on time with 100% client acceptance in a demanding scrum environment.
- Led requirements effort to define standard and custom metrics for associated data marts.

TECHNICAL WRITER CAREER HIGHLIGHTS (2001–2004)

Technical Writer/Project Manager, WASHINGTON MERCANTILE EXCHANGE, Seattle, WA, 2003–2004
Senior Technical Writer, DATACENTRIC COMPUTER SYSTEMS, Olympia, WA, 2002–2003
Technical Writer, EAGLE DERIVATIVES GROUP, Seattle, WA, 2001–2002

- Owned, designed, developed, and delivered print and online documentation for developers, end users, and administrators. Implemented single-source tools for fast and flexible deliverables.
- Evaluated tools and made selections based on fit with internal processes and automation goals.

PROJECT MANAGER CAREER HIGHLIGHTS (1997–2001)

Project Manager/Technical Writer, DAVIDSON RETAIL MANAGEMENT, Tacoma, WA, 1999–2001
Senior Project Manager, RPI SOFTWARE, Tacoma, WA, 1998–1999
Project Manager, NETMATRIX MARKETING, INC., Naperville, IL, 1997–1998

- Managed team of developers, consultants, testers, and translation vendor to deliver on-time and on-budget UNIX and Windows setup programs in 6 languages, including Chinese and Japanese.
  - Championed adoption of requirements management tools, improving predictability of releases.
  - Implemented change control procedures, thereby reducing costs and ensuring on-time delivery.
- Managed all aspects of commercial and Web-based documentation projects, including resource constraints management, staffing, delivery date negotiation, and expectation management.
- Collaborated with business and PMO to produce charter, scope, and status documents.

Education, Certifications, and Memberships

Master of Business Administration, University of Washington, Seattle, WA
Bachelor of Arts, Business, University of Washington, Seattle, WA
Project Management Professional (PMP) certificate, Project Management Institute
Certified ScrumMaster (CSM), Scrum Alliance

Technical Profile

Requirements Management	Rational Requisite Pro and Telelogic DOORS
Database & Reporting	Access, Oracle, SQL, Sybase, and MicroStrategy
Languages	MySQL, DHTML/HTML, basic JavaScript
E-commerce	IBM WebSphere Administrator, Web site integration with richrelevance, Bazaarvoice, Mercado, ForeSee, and Omniture
Quality Assurance	Rational ClearQuest and HP Quality Center

DARYL HAYES

235 Weston Court ◆ Madison, CT 06443 ◆ 203-844-1934 ◆ dhayes@gmail.com

SENIOR BUSINESS ANALYST

PROJECT MANAGEMENT/CONTENT MANAGEMENT

Requirements Gathering ◆ Specification Setting ◆ Product Testing ◆ User Documentation

*Leveraging content knowledge, communication skills, and analytical abilities
to drive the success of technology projects.*

Well-regarded business analyst with proven expertise in driving the implementation of system enhancements, collaborating effectively with business stakeholders and developers to bring technology solutions into production. Organized, effective professional known for ability to grasp business needs; translate them into clear, concise specifications; and develop/execute detailed test plans to ensure virtually trouble-free releases. Respected business partner valued for knowledge and accessibility. Dedicated project manager who can be relied on to get the job done.

Core Competencies

➢ Managing technology projects, serving as link between business users and developers to ensure delivery of new solutions according to requirements.

➢ Cultivating productive relationships with diverse groups of people, fostering collaborative work environment based on confidence and trust.

➢ Leveraging analytical nature, strong writing skills, and keen attention to detail to develop comprehensive requirements and test plans that facilitate project completion by minimizing miscommunication.

➢ Authoring well-written, well-received user guides, providing clear documentation of new releases.

➢ Improving value of web-based tools through implementation of new content management technology.

PROFESSIONAL EXPERIENCE

METLIFE   Mar 2005 to Present

Senior Business Analyst

Direct content management projects for key product groups, facilitating implementation of content solutions for marketing and online enrollment websites. Promote the benefits of this technology to business users, and collaborate with developers to design and implement innovative solutions to drive business goals.

**Played instrumental role in rebuilding deficient application...
implementing innovations that transformed it into powerful and sophisticated marketing tool.**

- Established solid record of success as business analyst, planning and executing 4 releases per year while building reputation as knowledgeable and accessible resource, the "go-to" person for getting things done.

- Wrote requirements and test plans for a complex enrollment site redesign project. In testing now, yearlong project is on target to meet launch date, delivering competitive user-friendly tool designed to improve customer experience.

- As a developing subject matter expert in advanced content management technology, have influenced dramatic improvements in website's effectiveness in attracting new enrollments to customer database by using innovative solutions that allowed for real-time delivery of customized messages according to market segment.

- Developed Flash presentation capability to further enhance applications.

continued

*This well-organized and well-designed resume calls attention to impressive achievements in every role.
A Core Competencies section in the summary is balanced by a Technology Skills section at the end.*

DARYL HAYES   DHAYES@GMAIL.COM   PAGE 2

CONSULTING/SELF-EMPLOYMENT   Jan 1999 to Mar 2005
Lead Quality Assurance/Quality Operations Analyst

Took on assignments for finance/banking industry giants, as well as other smaller companies.

- Served as lead QA analyst for apparel company, designing and implementing testing and documentation strategy covering 200 applications to ensure smooth transition from Windows 2000 to Windows XP. Worked with local staff to develop comprehensive listing of applications to ensure complete and flawless execution.

- Played key role in creation and implementation of standardized process for software deployment to be used across financial giant's entire investment banking division. Worked closely with developers to build knowledge of and ensure compliance with new procedures.

- Conducted new-release testing for critical banking application used worldwide to manage funds and securities. Implemented comprehensive test plans following best practices to ensure virtually error-free results.

COLORTEC   Jul 1995 to Dec 1998
Lead Quality Assurance/Help Desk Analyst

Hired to provide help desk support, earned quick promotion to lead quality analyst role. Planned, wrote, and executed test plans and cases for company's proprietary software. Coordinated Y2K testing and remediation efforts.

- Brought new standards to company's QA efforts, minimizing bugs with meticulous, systematic approach. Also brought documentation efforts to new level of excellence.

CITIBANK   Jul 1993 to Jun 1995
Security Software Help Desk Analyst

Provided user support related to software security and network access.

- A self-taught help desk analyst, quickly built reputation for service excellence.

EDUCATION

Bachelor of Arts Degree, Fordham University, Bronx, NY

TECHNOLOGY SKILLS

Applications: Word, Excel, PowerPoint, Outlook, Visio, MS Visual SourceSafe (VSS), Component Services, Internet Information Services (IIS), Wise for Windows Installer, StarTeam by StarBase-Source Code Control and Project Management/Tracking.

Tools: ATG (Art Technology Group) Email Marketing Interface, Stellent Content Repository Tool, Rational Test Manager and Requisite Pro, iRise Project Management Tool, MS SharePoint Collaboration Tool

Standards: Familiar with Six Sigma and Capability Maturity Model (CMM)

PETER CHIANG

4236 Broadview Avenue
Los Gatos, CA 95030

pchiang2010@gmail.com

408-526-3305 (home)
408-500-2300 (cell)

ENGINEERING MANAGEMENT

Technically astute, hands-on leader with experience spanning startups to established corporations. More than 15 years of innovative high-tech experience, including technical team leadership and complex project management. Consistent record of improving processes, performance, and competitive positioning in a deadline-driven environment, despite the challenges of a difficult world market and a weak economy.

Management Core Strengths

- Team recruitment / management / development
- Technology evaluation and implementation
- Software release and process management

- Performance metrics and trends
- Cross-functional relationship management
- Incisive, problem-solving leadership

Technology Expertise

- Scalable OLTP application modeling, implementation, and performance tuning
- OLAP data-warehouse design, analytics, and data mining
- High-performance data integration (ETL) design

- Programming, including SQL, C/C++, Java, HTML, AJAX, ASP, PHP, and JSP
- Parallel-storage subsystems design and implementation
- Wireless embedded systems

PROFESSIONAL EXPERIENCE

Consumer Online Database Manager
Haverford Software, Inc., Fremont, CA

2008–2011

Managed 9-member, distributed e-commerce team whose performance was initially impacted by 75% turnover rate, low morale, and fear of job loss, which prevented processes and quality of deliverables from meeting business objectives.

- ***Challenge:*** Partner with senior management and leverage available resources to overcome numerous obstacles and turn around an underperforming team.

  Key actions: Introduced the SCRUM and Agile development process to engineering, QA, and business teams within 2 months. Initiated personal contact to build stronger team relationships.

  Result: Retained and recruited key staff to deliver major product releases within 3 months. Redirected team focus to critical projects and milestones. Increased transparency, improved work quality and resource utilization, and helped decrease costs.

Database & Data Warehouse Architect
Powers Consulting, Inc., Belmont, CA

2005–2008

Provided technical vision, strategies, and cross-domain data warehouse design to facilitate business decisions and meet business demands.

- ***Challenge:*** Provide critical expertise to assist the world's largest Flash company, which had previously failed twice on implementation of a key P&L financial data-warehouse project.

  Key actions: Rewrote design and technical specifications and conducted continuous consensus-gathering through high-quality proposals and presentations. Collaborated with corporate IT management and staff early to enhance the design and development process.

  Result: Delivered the first working data model, cube design, and ETL software in 3 months. Achieved 800% performance improvement from the previous generation implementation.

- continued -

The Challenge-Action-Results format is used to highlight key accomplishments of a progressive career in software and systems development. Note that both management and technical expertise are highlighted in separate sections of the summary.

PETER CHIANG, 408-526-3305 (H) / 408-500-2300 (C)   Page 2

PROFESSIONAL EXPERIENCE
(continued)

Senior Engineering Manager   2002–2005
Horizon Communications, Inc., San Jose, CA

Managed a 12-person onshore/offshore meeting component team, 6-person onshore communication server team, and 4-person onshore release team, whose performance had been adversely impacted by departmental turmoil and poorly defined processes and policies.

- *Challenge:* Resolve major issues seriously impacting product releases, testing, and service quality in a group that had not succeeded in completing any major releases in more than a year.

 Key actions: Partnered with senior management to establish policies and milestones. Mentored the team to improve work attitudes. Streamlined and redesigned software component architecture and automated the release process across departments. Researched and designed the first click-stream analysis and mining for meeting services.

 Result: Automation built and released software 95 times faster than before. Greatly improved a dysfunctional situation and enabled a 350-employee group to move forward on major releases.

Director, Product & Business Development   2000–2002
Adelphi Microsystems, Inc., Mountain View, CA

Managed business and product directions, building strategic relationships with Toshiba, Microsoft, and corporate customers.

- *Challenge:* Initiate actions to redirect the focus from overemphasis on engineering and improve recognition of the computing platform by markets and partners.

 Key actions: Initiated joint marketing with Toshiba and Microsoft. Signed up for Windows CE exhibitions. Refocused engineering resources and certified Adelphi as a Windows CE Silver Partner. Aligned company actions with the wireless trend to pull out clear partners and segments.

 Result: Uniquely positioned the company as a leading wireless embedded-system provider. Generated stronger company visibility and significantly increased business referrals from Toshiba and Microsoft. Attracted several dozen leads and NRE projects valued in millions of dollars.

Software Architect   1996–2000
Advantage Technology, Inc., Los Angeles, CA

Designed a video streaming server, real-time content database, and system monitoring programs.

- *Challenge:* Expand the company's ability to capitalize on new software opportunities after the initial target market encountered major copyright issues.

 Key actions: Secured $2+ million in funding by conducting market research, drafting a business plan, and soliciting angel investors. Re-architected TV-on-demand to multimedia-on-demand to refocus on the education market.

 Result: Built a streaming video company with operations in 2 locations. Penetrated the education market and delivered the world's first multimedia-on-demand software system to a high-profile customer in 1998. Laid the foundation for generation of $9+ million in revenue within 4 years.

EDUCATION & CERTIFICATION

Master of Science in Electrical & Computer Engineering (ECE), University of California, San Diego: major in distributed computing, parallel computing, software and hardware architecture, 1994

Bachelor of Science, Computer Science & Information Engineering, Taiwan National University: major in algorithms, computer languages, computer system development and information theory, 1992

Certifications: Oracle Advanced Administration; Sybase Replication Administration

Marvin A. Madorski

Cell: (650) 328-4336   PO Box 3452 • San Mateo, CA 94401   mmadorski@gmail.com

Software Engineering and Systems Architecture
Adept, Inventive, and Driven Technologist
Consultant • Project Manager • Product Developer

Talented software expert and business analyst with special expertise in service-oriented architecture (SOA), data security, Web services, and biometrics. More than 15 years of experience mastering projects that pose progressively more difficult management scope and technical complexity.

- Invented and patented a software queuing mechanism, used worldwide by Unisys clients.
- Won *Microsoft Health Users Group Innovation Award* (MS-HUG) for inventing a biometric authorization system used by companies in the health-care sector.
- Launched M&M Consultants and built a long list of top-tier clients that includes Oracle, Microsoft, Intel, HP, and Adobe.

CERTIFICATIONS AND TECHNICAL SKILLS

Certifications: CISSP, CISSP-ISSAP, CSSLP • Certified BizTalk/MCAD/MCSD.net

Skills: Comprehensive knowledge and know-how of frameworks, project methodologies, and development tools, including C#, .Net, Web services, WCF, Oasis WS, and SQL2008 • E-business multitiered hardware and software • Requirements gathering and functional specifications • Performance and capacity planning • Security threat modeling • Project planning • Project management • Waterfall & Agile methodologies • SDLC & SDL integration

PROFESSIONAL EXPERIENCE

M&M CONSULTANTS, INC., San Mateo, CA   **2001–Present**
Consulting firm that advises clients on IT strategy, application development, system architecture, data security, and best practices for project management.
Consultant and Principal

Design, develop, architect, and deploy software solutions for many of the world's top technology companies, including Oracle, HP, and Microsoft. Advise Mayo Clinic as subject matter expert in healthcare IT. Solve challenging data-security problems for government clients.

Project highlights and accomplishments include:

Oracle
- Developed a technical vision strategy and plan (TVSP) for a major, confidential project. Rearchitected existing plan and cut the number of databases by 60%.
- Created new digital-rights tools and architected a robust enterprise electronic signature server for electronic document signing.
- Designed, developed, and stress-tested a state-driven, stored-procedure system for the Connected Systems Framework (CSF).

Microsoft Corporation
- Developed two versions of Software Assurance Benefits system (SAB 3.1 and SAB 3.5) that saved approximately $1.2 million during SAB 3.5 launch.
- Created sustainable process that validated eligibility of volume-licensing customers when requesting product activation keys for Windows 7.
- Architected and developed an authentication server for SOA applications. Designed and implemented an XML-driven test harness for SOA.

Blue-chip corporate clients are highlighted in the summary and then within several job descriptions both to paint this candidate as a corporate "insider" and to showcase his most notable projects and achievements.

Marvin Madorski ....(650) 328-4336 .... mmadorski@gmail.com ....Page 2

M&M CONSULTANTS, INC., continued

Office of Technology Assessment

- Developed and proved feasibility of a cell phone application for law enforcement. Devised Web service that displays a consolidated view of multiple law enforcement jurisdictions.
- Designed and implemented a Web service and Windows application that analyzed personnel requirements and resources for OTA.

Motorola

- Developed a C++/Java/CORBA–based multithreaded solution that provisioned mobile devices for Motorola Manufacturing and Distribution Centers and EMS/ODM partners.
- Designed and implemented global manufacturing solution that saved up to $56 million, improved uptime 75%, and reduced engineering support resources by 40%.
- Designed and implemented reusable framework for Java based front-end applications that led to 40% reduction in manufacturing development time.

ARCUS PARTNERS, San Jose, CA   **2000–2001**
Private company that provides high-performance Java solutions for application servers worldwide.
Product Development Director

- Managed delivery of a 64-bit Java compiler to Intel for Itanium (IA64) product.
- Organized, staffed, and managed a consulting-services organization.
- Developed performance metrics and methodologies used throughout ARCUS.

M&M CONSULTANTS, INC., Issaquah, WA   **1999–2000**
Consultant

Advised Unisys/Burroughs customers on IT and application development.

- Showed Unisys customers new ways to improve performance analysis, modeling, programming, data security, and IT department organization. Presented technical seminars worldwide.
- Consulted on multiprocessor architecture at the Unisys Pasadena plant. Analyzed efficiency of A Series INTEL-based, C-compiled code. Modeled numerous system configurations using a proprietary capacity-planning tool. Designed and implemented SageAdvice, which analyzed and eliminated bottlenecks.

SENTIENT, INC., Scottsdale, AZ   **1995–1999**
Private company focused on HIPAA-compliant security software.
Program Manager

Hired as program manager to lead development—from design to engineering prototypes—of business-critical programs for the world's first biometric-authentication system. Led program and systems-level design of biometric camera, frame grabber, drivers, and hardware. Collaborated closely with Sentient's manufacturing partner regarding end-to-end manufacturing process.

- Won *Microsoft Health Users Group Innovation Award* (MS-HUG) for design and development of a breakthrough, biometric, single-sign-on security application used by the Mayo Clinic and Scottsdale Hospital (more than 2,800 workstations).
- Architected a complex "master-master" SQL server design that achieved 5-9s reliability of the SSO system (developed as an alternative to the fledgling cluster release).

EDUCATION

B.S. Program in Physics, Wayne State University, Detroit, MI
Completed 172 out of 180 credit hours

JAI SHARMA

JSharma21@gmail.com

20010 Market Street
Baltimore, MD 21202

Cell: 301.444.3333
www.jsharma.com

ORACLE ENTERPRISE ARCHITECT

Visionary Technologist with Legendary Customer Relationship Skills

Expert in Manufacturing IT and Manufacturing Execution Systems (MES)

Life Sciences • Pharmaceuticals • Regulated Industries

Award-winning architect, software developer, and technical leader with 17 years of experience leading product development, system architecture, and extremely large-scale implementations. Fluent in Hindi, Marathi, and English.

- **Award Winner:** Honored by GE for outstanding technical creativity, earning multiple awards and national recognition for inventing a new approach to coding and framework that led to $10M in new business.

- **Top Contributor:** Hands-on manager with strong record of promotion, contribution, and success with every employer. Known for consistently completing projects as promised, on schedule, within budget, and with exceptional quality.

- **Relationship Builder:** Remarkably skilled in client service, sales support, and new business development. Generate follow-up business by doing whatever it takes to deliver results as promised.

Software Development	Project Management	New Business Development
System Architecture	Business Process Reengineering	New Technology Evangelism
MES, SAP, and ERP Systems	New Product Development	Contract Negotiation
Factory and Business Automation	IT Outsourcing (India)	Technical and Sales Presentations

PROFESSIONAL EXPERIENCE

SPERRY CONTROLS, Catonsville, MD   2009–Present

Leading provider of process-control equipment for life sciences, power generation, pulp and paper, gas distribution, and waste processing. Approximately $80 million annual sales and 220 employees.

Senior Solution Architect – MOMI

Currently leading a project in the Manufacturing Operations Management and Intelligence (MOMI) space. Hire and mentor the very best technical talent. Collaborate closely with senior management and account teams. Win new business via creative problem solving, industry buzz, and strong customer referrals.

- Led highly successful implementation of several business-critical projects:
  - Syncade-SAP interface for Johnson & Johnson: Led combined SAP functional and technical integration teams (Sperry and J&J). Analyzed existing system and proposed low-cost opportunities that produced major technical improvements.
  - J&J/Portsmouth electronic batch record (EBR) project: Achieved quick turnaround by leveraging expertise in Manufacturing Execution Systems (MES).
- Devised plan to cut wasted time and duplication 50% for future implementations by meticulously documenting architecture for SAP- and ERP-related integration techniques.
- Strengthened company relationship between Sperry and J&J. Established credibility as trusted advisor and produced follow-up business—valued at $8 million over 5 years—in the data management area.

RMS SYSTEMS, INC., Reston, VA   2007–2009

Acquired by EXCEL Healthcare (2009). Develops perioperative clinical information management systems (PCIMS) for electronic medical record (EMR) compliance and reporting.

Director of Implementations and Special Projects

Continued

This resume leads with a strong summary that clearly distinguishes this software and systems architect as an award-winning top performer.

Jai Sharma   *301.444.3333 • JSharma21@gmail.com • Page 2*

RMS SYSTEMS, INC., continued

Tasked to improve and standardize implementation methodology. Managed a 4-person team of experts that seamlessly implemented major upgrades at customer sites.

- Cut implementation time 55% by developing a unique, artifact-driven methodology.
- Developed $500,000 in follow-up business by reaching out to existing customers and promoting opportunities for system enhancements.
- Created 2 new product offerings, in complementary markets, by repurposing an existing product platform. Managed implementation, marketing, and sales strategy for the new products.
- Saved 40% on manufacturing costs for confidential client—and concurrently increased reliability and performance—by initiating a hardware reengineering project.

GENERAL ELECTRIC PROCESS SOLUTIONS, Cambridge, MA   **1998–2007**

Provides automation and control solutions, equipment, and services that improve customers' business performance.

Promoted to Manager and Chief Architect, Life Sciences Technology (2005–2007)
GE Process Solutions, Cambridge, MA

Promoted to Chief Architect, POMSnet Product Line (2004)
GE Process Solutions, Cambridge, MA (GE acquired POMS Corp in 2004).

Principal Consultant and Project Manager (1998–2004)
POMS Corporation, Cambridge, MA

Designed and developed POMS (Production/Process Operations Management System), an enterprise application that improves manufacturing performance by ensuring that products are consistently manufactured and configured as planned.

Major Awards

Technical excellence and customer satisfaction: BRAVO Gold Award, 2006 • Process Solutions, Operations Quality Award, 2006 • BRAVO Gold Award, 2004 • Major Technical Achievement Award, 2004 • BRAVO Silver Award, 2003 • Outstanding Customer Service Award, 2002 • Outstanding Performance Award, 2001 • Customer Satisfaction Award, 1999

Highlights

- Architected and led development of POMSnet—GE's first 100% Web-based MES application for life sciences—written in ASP.NET and C#.
- Managed development for 3 major releases of POMSnet, including 2.5+ million lines of code that supported more than 250 manufacturing operations.
- Led 3 managers, 9 technical leads, 25 developers, and 5 test resources (including 8 offshore developers in Pune and Banagalore, India).

───────────────**SUMMARY OF ADDITIONAL EXPERIENCE**───────────────

SYNTHTECH, INC., Mountain View, CA (1996–1998), Senior Business Consultant: Led end-to-end implementations and integration projects for MES software (FlowStream) at various client sites.

UNIVERSITY OF PENNSYLVANIA, Philadelphia, PA (1994–1996), Graduate Research Assistant: Implemented FlowStream MES for Monsanto. Created HMIs and device drivers for real-time data capture.

TATA ENGINEERING AND LOCOMOTIVE, Pune, India (1993–1994), Engineer: Worked in tool and die manufacturing; CNC programming, planning and scheduling; and engine assembly and testing.

───────────────────────**EDUCATION**───────────────────────

Master of Science, Electrical Engineering, University of Pennsylvania, Philadelphia, PA (1996)
Integrated Manufacturing Systems Engineering

Bachelor of Engineering, Mechanical Engineering, India Institute of Technology (1993)

PAULA LOPEZ

35 Hemlock Drive ◆ Mount Holly, NJ 08060 ◆ (609) 235-8181 ◆ p.lopez@gmail.com

SOFTWARE TEST DEVELOPER

*Developing and executing meticulous test plans
to help ensure trouble-free software releases.*

Budding software engineer with more than 2 years of experience in software testing and a proven record of success in leveraging analytical mindset and keen attention to detail to develop and execute sound test plans to ensure bug-free software releases. Organized, effective project coordinator known for focused approach and thorough follow-through. Solution-oriented team player with passion for excellence and demonstrated commitment to goals.

Key Strengths

◆ Automated Testing	◆ Test Plan Development/Execution	◆ User Interface Design
◆ Software Engineering	◆ SAP/OLAP Query Applications	◆ Database Development

RELATED EXPERIENCE

COMPUTER HORIZONS   Sep 2010 to Present
Test Specialist
Conduct testing for key healthcare-monitoring system developed in conjunction with noted global healthcare agency. Oversee administration of user access and permissions.

- Hired to support testing of complex health surveillance system; quickly came up to speed to become valuable project contributor.
- Developed considerable expertise in short tenure, becoming go-to resource—even to seasoned veterans—in 2 distinct content areas.
- Facilitated project completion, going the extra mile to help others set up or finish work. A recognized team player, took on extra responsibilities, such as problem-solving and writing documents, to keep testing on track.

ADVANCED ANALYTICS   May 2009 to May 2010
Software Test Developer
Served as core test developer for new data analytics product, developing and executing test plans to ensure product quality. Participated in development of automated test tool for product. Assisted in supporting multiple other product releases and integration add-ons.

- Hired as member of 2-person testing team for new product, subsequently provided sole testing support for standalone software package. Earned praise of manager for excellence in developing and executing test plans that met high standards of completeness and accuracy.
- Researched and mastered creation of universes to enhance testing, providing advanced support judged to be "next-level" performance.
- Set up and maintained multiple test environments to cover various deployment scenarios to provide complete testing of new releases.
- Participated in developing automated test tools for new product.

This resume highlights both relevant professional experience and projects completed while in school to paint the picture of a highly qualified software test developer.

Paula Lopez   p.lopez@gmail.com   Page 2

TURNER MEDICAL SYSTEMS, INC.   Sep 2008 to Apr 2009
Software Tester
Developed test plans for medical software used in hospitals.

- Quickly came up to speed in new environment, developing reputation for efficiency in writing detailed test plans that were highly effective in identifying bugs.

- Developed close working relationships with developers, conducting research before writing test plans to ensure they were the best they could be.

- Garnered praise for outstanding defect reports that clearly delineated location of bugs, making them easy to reproduce and resolve.

EDUCATION

BS Degree, Computer Science (Software Engineering), Fairleigh Dickinson University, 2010

Relevant Class Projects

➤ **Web-based Information System:** Participated on team that designed and built Web-based inventory management system using MySQL in CodeIgniter framework. Created user-friendly application that received high marks for effectiveness and ease of use.

➤ **Database Query Application:** Led team that developed tool to allow users to query and retrieve data from SQL Server database.

➤ **User Interface Design:** Designed user interface to allow users to purchase market analysis reports and user data, implementing easy-to-use electronic cart to facilitate shopping.

➤ **Software Engineering:** Demonstrated mastery of all phases of the software life cycle while developing voting system application.

TECHNOLOGY SKILLS

Languages:	C, C++, Java, HTML, XHTML, CSS, XML, PHP, CodeIgniter, Haskell, SQL
Operating Systems:	Linux/UNIX, Windows
Databases:	MS SQL Server, Oracle DB, DB2
Software:	Jcreator, Redhat, Visio, SQL Server, Kate, Test Director, Visual Studio, GHE, Winhugs, Filezilla, MySQL, Adapt, Universe Designer, Business Explorer Query Designer, Clementine, VMware

CHAPTER 6

Resumes for Technology Support Professionals

- Help Desk Administrators and Analysts

- QA Testing and Network Administrators

- Technical Support Technicians

- Technical Training Specialists

- Technical Writers

- E-business Technology Directors

- Technology Sales and Marketing Professionals

- Technology Business Development Professionals

- Technology Services Managers

James Carro

408 Springmeadow • Holbrook, NY 11741 • 631-567-9183 • jcarro@aol.com

PROFILE

Help Desk / Desktop Support Specialist able to provide theoretical and practical customer/user service and support to diagnose, troubleshoot, and repair hardware, software, and peripheral problems. Skilled in applying analytical and technical skills to produce practical solutions. Experienced in the installation of state-of-the-art hardware and software applications. Knowledgeable about equipment bases, digital switches, hubs, patch cables, routers, servers, administrator stations, network closet wiring, and installation procedures.

TECHNICAL PROFICIENCIES

Install, Upgrade, Migrate, and Configure

Hardware: Pentium, Core
Language: HTML
Operating Systems: Windows XP/7
Software: MS Office (Word, Access, Excel, PowerPoint, Outlook) ~ Lotus Notes ~ Norton Utilities
Protocols: SCSI ~ IDE ~ ESDI • **Interfaces:** Modems ~ Network Cards ~ IO Ports ~ Mobile Devices

EDUCATION

A+ Certification, 2005

**Ongoing professional development in networks, servers, and software
through Long Island Tech Group**

EXPERIENCE

MEDICAL GROUP • Oakdale, NY   **2006 to Present**
Independent Computer Support Contractor
> Install operating systems and software, configure systems, and troubleshoot problems for 300+ users.
> ~ *Researched components for value and reliability resulting in substantial savings to customers.*
> ~ *Specialized in interconnecting components for seamless operability across devices and platforms.*

CERIDIAN PERFORMANCE PARTNERS • Boston, MA   **2002 to 2006**
Fulfillment Coordinator
> Performed as visibility liaison among company and human resource departments of subscribing Fortune 500 clients. Assured timely and cost-efficient fulfillment of material for affiliate and client events. Updated and maintained affiliate and client databases. In conjunction with production department, defined and maintained online inventory system for offsite service facility.

LAURA ASHLEY GLOBAL DEVELOPMENT • Boston, MA   **1999 to 2002**
Mail Services Supervisor
> Distributed U.S. and interoffice mail, including payroll, to a staff of 300. Operated and upgraded Pitney Bowes mailing systems. Maintained database of 200 North American shops, U.K. headquarters, and European satellite offices.
> ~ *Contributed creatively to marketing department's nationwide, window-display advertising.*
> ~ *Trained personnel in applications of UPS Online Shipping and Federal Express PowerShip.*

This resume is easy to skim for essential information—technical qualifications, experience, and achievements.

Furkhunda Rizvi

57 Hofstra Boulevard
Port Jefferson Station, NY 11772
631-555-2425 • frizvi@yahoo.com

Overview

Skilled **Help Desk Analyst** with 7 years of experience providing PC and client/server technical support. Experience in diagnosing and resolving difficult problems in the area of hardware, application, and operating systems. Interface with end users handling inquiries regarding system configuration and operating systems. Effectively render technical advice to nontechnical personnel. Keen ability to address technical issues and close out customer tickets in a timely manner.

Technical Capabilities

<u>Operating Systems</u>:
- Windows 7
- Windows Server 2008
- Windows XP
- Novell Client
- UNIX/Linux
- AS/400

<u>Applications</u>:
- Lotus Notes
- Netview
- Microsoft Office Suite
- Lotus SmartSuite
- PC Anywhere

<u>Hardware</u>:
- Printers & Routers
- Multiplexors
- Serial Connectors
- CATS Cables
- Digi Boxes
- NIC Cards

Professional Experience

Help Desk Analyst, Federal City Bank, Littletown, New York   **2006–Present**
Provide technical support to more than 2,000 branches, back offices, and ATM computer-based systems.

- Provide expedient and appropriate commands to incoming inquiries regarding system malfunctions.
- Dispatch appropriate second-tier support or vendors to solve hardware complications.
- Maintain complete documentation of all daily site outages, LAN outages, and application alerts allowing corporate headquarters to identify high-error-frequency locations.

Accomplishments:
- Identified possible technological glitches and offered solutions for a newly installed GUI program.
- Upheld, as part of a team, the technical integrity of two computer systems during a merger.

Help Desk Representative, Cable USA, Northport, New York   **2004–2006**

- Resolved daily systematic and operational malfunctions, ensuring minimal loss of work productivity.
- Directed support for complex problems to next-level support, simultaneously keeping users informed as to the status of open calls.
- Assisted end users with connectivity problems, computer lockouts, and printer problems.

Education

Associate of Science—Computer Information Systems, Briarcliffe College, Patchogue, New York, 2004

The clean, attractive look of this resume is achieved through font selection, horizontal lines at top and bottom, and the three-column format of the Technical Capabilities section.

SUSAN SCHAEFFER

3 Vineland Road ✧ Hazlet, New Jersey 07730 ✧ 732-555-4278
sschaeffer@verizon.net

QUALIFICATIONS PROFILE

More than 10 years of experience in QA testing, network administration, and customer/technical support and demonstrated expertise in computer installation, configuration, maintenance, and administration. Effectively train end users and perform skilled problem resolution. Accurately assess customer needs and specifications by phone and in person. Quickly identify problems and issues and provide fast troubleshooting and problem resolution.

Highlights include

- Excellent communication and diagnostic skills.
- Ability to rapidly learn new information regarding technology concepts and tools.
- Solid knowledge of computer-based information technologies and their interrelations with business management processes.
- Reputation as a proactive self-starter known to initiate process and system improvements to increase stability and staff productivity.

PROFESSIONAL EXPERIENCE

ABC Financial ✧ Pennsville, NJ   2003–Present
<u>Second-Level Senior Help Desk Technician / QA Tester</u>
Troubleshoot approximately 30 second-level calls per day in regards to application support, remote LAN access, Lotus Notes, Internet access, LAN troubleshooting, operating system support, Microsoft Office, mainframe applications, hardware support, and proprietary financial applications for more than 64,000 employees and vendors worldwide. Document and track status of client inquiries, coordinate appropriate responses, and follow up to ensure client satisfaction. Resolve more than 90% of calls and receive excellent customer satisfaction feedback.

Key achievements:

➢ Prepared, organized, and conducted Remedy Action Request System training enterprise-wide for 1,000+ employees. Created and distributed end-user documentation and training surveys.
➢ Customized, established, and evaluated training criteria for each specific business group.
➢ Wrote biweekly "Remedy Newsletter," ensuring superior support for the application.
➢ Performed QA testing to ensure the product and specifications exceeded standards and were in compliance with business-unit requirements.
➢ Often recognized for superior performance. Named "Employee of the Month" for May 2010.

HKG Pharmaceuticals ✧ Ortley Beach, NJ   1997–2003
<u>Lead Help Desk Technician / Tester / Trainer / Technical Writer</u>
Progressed through the computer and network operations group into a help desk position, eventually supporting more than 2,000 sales representatives and internal marketing employees. Supported proprietary software, various operating systems, upload issues, and software and hardware installations. Tested and error-proofed outgoing software programs in conjunction with designing reference materials for end-user instruction.

Key achievements:

➢ Created and delivered training programs to educate end users on quick solutions to common problems. Resulted in 8% reduction in first-level call volume.
➢ Analyzed CDR (Call Detail Record) data and made final decision to purchase Vision Helpdesk for the issue tracking tool.

continued

A strong Qualifications Profile section sets the tone for this accomplishment-rich resume. Certifications and computer skills are clearly presented in table format on page 2.

Susan Schaeffer	sschaeffer@verizon.net	Page 2

Professional Experience Continued...

Lamar Global Solutions ✧ Allentown, NJ   1996–1997
<u>**Technical Recruiter**</u>

CERTIFICATIONS

• Microsoft Word	• Microsoft PowerPoint	• Microsoft Outlook
• Microsoft Excel	• Microsoft Access	• Mac OS

COMPUTER SKILLS

• Microsoft Word	• Visio	• Vision Helpdesk
• Microsoft Excel	• Adobe Acrobat	• WordPress
• Microsoft PowerPoint	• Windows XP/7	• Lotus Notes
• Microsoft Project	• Windows Server	• Remedy
• Microsoft Access	• Mainframe Applications	• Remote LAN Access

EDUCATION

University of Phoenix ✧ Online   2010
MBA
Technology Management

Kirk Hall University ✧ Gainsville, NJ   1998
Bachelor of Science
Marketing, GPA 3.34

Bill Rupert

118 Ronan Ct • Matawan, NJ 07747 • rupert@optonline.net
(Home) 732-739-2480 • (Mobile) 732-750-4687

INFORMATION TECHNOLOGY LEADER

Talented and accomplished technical professional with 5 years of success in supervising, problem solving, and training. Experienced director of cross-functional teams with diverse technical backgrounds. Dedicated, hard-working individual with intercommunications skills to work at all levels of an organization. Innovative professional with proven ability to identify, analyze, and solve issues to increase customer satisfaction and raise skills sets of team members through expertise in

- Leading Level 1 and 2 technical teams
- Communicating, presenting, and training
- Coaching, mentoring, and managing technical staff
- Developing and implementing projects

PROFESSIONAL EXPERIENCE

TEAM LEADER / TECHNICAL SUPPORT SPECIALIST   2006–Present
CBA Financial, Lafayette, NJ

Team Leader: Guide and supervise team of 7 members in all aspects of technical and procedural support. Compile daily help desk statistics; monitor phone calls; address conflicts or performance issues; create agendas for and lead biweekly team meetings. Provide ongoing feedback to team members to help achieve and exceed performance objectives. Dedicate extensive time and energy to improving communications with help desk analysts, local desktop support, and clientele, while accepting full responsibility for 6-month and annual performance reviews, employee motivation, and morale.

Technical Support Specialist: Built and currently direct the Lotus SmartSuite Level 2 group, supporting internal help desks to resolve end users' questions and issues. Provide training at all levels to help desk analysts via Sametime sessions, conference calls, and classroom programs. Resolve approximately 30 Level 2 issues per day. Monitor Level 1 tickets on a daily basis in search of technical trends to help provide individual or group feedback and update training programs.

Career Highlights:
- ➤ Traveled internationally for 2 months to train new help desk analysts on receiving Level 1 technical phone calls.
- ➤ Created, coordinated, and implemented the new-hire training program. Oversee 10 trainers while maintaining and updating all documentation, including midterm and final exams, training outlines, and end-user reference guides.
- ➤ Developed and currently maintain the department's Lotus SmartSuite troubleshooting guide.
- ➤ Participated on the "Remedy implementation team," which involved pilot testing, evaluating, and providing feedback to the development team.
- ➤ Won help desk "Employee of the Quarter" award for the first quarter of 2009.

SENIOR HELP DESK ANALYST   2004–2006
CBA Financial, Lafayette, NJ
Interpreted, evaluated, and resolved more than 70% of telephone inquiries pertaining to application and network support. Provided technical guidance for domestic, international, and remote end users, along with other systems support units, to identify and resolve complex client problems. Documented and tracked status of client inquiries, coordinated appropriate responses, and followed up to ensure client satisfaction. Participated in the analysis of client-identified issues that required changes to department procedures, standards, or systems.

continued

The Career Highlights section breaks up the position description and calls attention to notable activities and achievements.

Bill Rupert	rupert@optonline.net	Page 2

Professional Experience – continued…

RESELLER COMPUTER CONSULTANT / ACCOUNT EXECUTIVE　　　　　2002–2004
Evax Engineering Corporation, Irvine, NJ
Managed more than 300 accounts nationwide. Negotiated pricing of various computer components with industry leaders of retail and resell. Assisted upper-level management with marketing ideas in accordance with current market conditions and trends both domestically and internationally. Authorized account manager of desktop and laptop computers.

COMPUTER SKILLS

- Microsoft Word
- Microsoft Excel
- Microsoft PowerPoint
- Microsoft Outlook

- Lotus SmartSuite
- Systems Management Server (SMS)
- Windows XP/Vista/7
- Windows Server

- Expert Advisor
- Visio
- Remedy
- Remote LAN Access

EDUCATION

BACHELOR'S DEGREE IN MANAGEMENT SCIENCE　　　　　2001
Kane University, Union, NJ

NETWORKING CLASSES　　　　　2005
Integrated Computer Management (ICM)

Jayne Wharburton

3213 Zenith
Blairsburg, IA 50010

(515) 238-1875
Jaynewharb@prairienet.com

SUMMARY OF QUALIFICATIONS

Solution center professional with two and a half years of experience interacting face-to-face with students, faculty, and staff. Able to clearly understand problems and find positive solutions through use of problem-solving skills, knowledge, and consultation with other technical support staff. Excellent knowledge of policies and procedures. Willing to learn new skills to continue serving the best needs of the customer and the organization.

TECHNOLOGY SKILLS

Microsoft Dynamics, Visual FoxPro, Microsoft Word, Excel, PowerPoint, and Outlook.

WORK EXPERIENCE

Iowa State University, Ames, IA, 2005–present

Computation Center, Clerk III, 2009–present
Interface with walk-in customers (students, faculty, staff) on a daily basis. Explain technical procedures in a clear, precise manner using personal knowledge and expertise, consulting with other support staff, or referring to senior-level technical staff.

→ Understand and apply the center's policies and procedures.
→ Explain Internet and university intranet access registration to students, faculty, and staff.
→ Direct setup of wireless connections for dormitories and off-campus sites.
→ Verify student accounts and enter information into database.
→ Develop excellent client relations with internal and external departments.
→ Prepare invoices and process charge orders, sales, and reference materials.
→ Maintain inventory of computer supplies necessary to meet customer needs.

Extension Distribution Center, Clerk III, 2005–2009
Balanced cash reports to sales on a daily basis, prepared billing and credits, maintained up-to-date database, and processed orders.
→ Applied problem-solving skills to resolve complicated orders in a timely manner.

EDUCATION

Bachelor of Science, Iowa State University, Ames, IA, 2007
Major: Social Work

Note how this individual transitioned from a degree in social work to a career in technology! The resume does a good job of defining her technical activities along with problem-solving and customer-service skills.

ALEXANDER V. MATTESON

1234 Winterberry Crescent	407-678-1234
Winter Park, Florida 32793	AVM123@hotmail.com

OBJECTIVE   Entry-level technical support/programming position utilizing strong computer skills.

QUALIFICATIONS

Programming Experience

- Utilized FoxPro to create inventory/sales analysis tool for retailer. This program identifies customer buying trends and allows user to project sales of various product lines.
- Designed and implemented Just-In-Time ordering system utilizing FoxPro and EDI to directly interface with book publishers' electronic ordering systems. This innovation reduced inventory on hand by 36% for these product lines.
- Proficient in C/C++, Java, Perl, and HTML.

Software Skills

- Implemented and administered Web-based integrated inventory, purchasing, and point-of-sale system for local retailer. System handles 100,000 transactions per year and has substantially streamlined inventory/ordering procedures.
- Installed, revised, and administered "One-Write" accounting system.
- Skilled in Microsoft Office; Microsoft Windows XP/7; and various ordering, accounting, and financial applications.

Business Management Experience

- Administered payroll, accounts payable/receivable, and all tax filings for retail business.
- Managed $120,000 securities portfolio.
- Restructured organization for retailer, redefining job descriptions and reclassifying job responsibilities.
- Reviewed business insurance policies and instituted changes resulting in 34% savings in annual premiums.
- Reduced costs of direct-mail advertising campaign by 43% through analysis of mailing list and programming designed to minimize postage costs.

EMPLOYMENT HISTORY

2001–Present   **Operations Manager/Financial Manager**
Enchanted World of Toys, Inc., Orlando, Florida

EDUCATION

Graduate School of Business Administration
University of Miami, Coral Gables, Florida
Coursework in Accounting and Economics

2001   **Bachelor of Science, Aeronautical Studies**
Florida Institute of Technology, Melbourne, Florida
Dean's List — 5 Semesters; G.P.A.: 3.4/4.0

PERSONAL   Sergeant-at-Arms, Orlando Rotary Club
FAA Certified Commercial Pilot

References Available Upon Request

The lengthy Qualifications section, subdivided into three distinct areas of expertise, places the focus squarely on these essential qualifications while deemphasizing the candidate's current combined operations/financial management position.

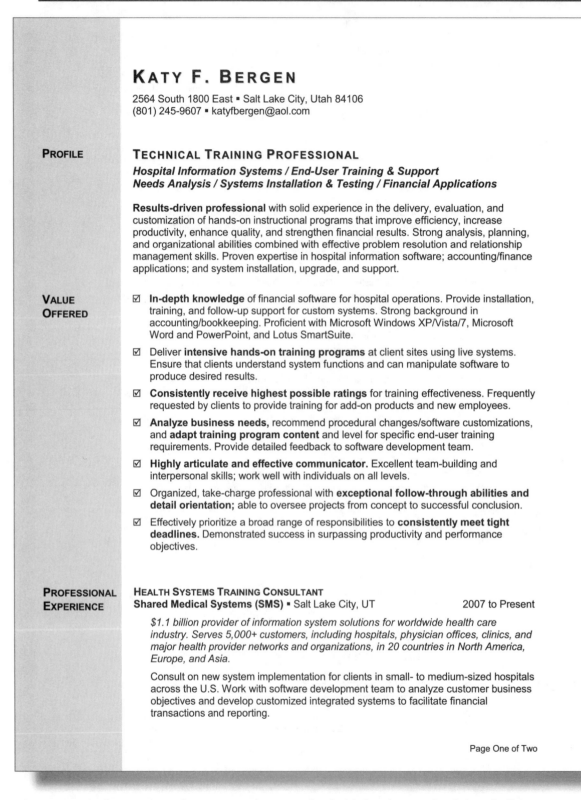

KATY F. BERGEN

2564 South 1800 East ▪ Salt Lake City, Utah 84106
(801) 245-9607 ▪ katyfbergen@aol.com

PROFILE

TECHNICAL TRAINING PROFESSIONAL
Hospital Information Systems / End-User Training & Support
Needs Analysis / Systems Installation & Testing / Financial Applications

Results-driven professional with solid experience in the delivery, evaluation, and customization of hands-on instructional programs that improve efficiency, increase productivity, enhance quality, and strengthen financial results. Strong analysis, planning, and organizational abilities combined with effective problem resolution and relationship management skills. Proven expertise in hospital information software; accounting/finance applications; and system installation, upgrade, and support.

VALUE OFFERED

☑ **In-depth knowledge** of financial software for hospital operations. Provide installation, training, and follow-up support for custom systems. Strong background in accounting/bookkeeping. Proficient with Microsoft Windows XP/Vista/7, Microsoft Word and PowerPoint, and Lotus SmartSuite.

☑ Deliver **intensive hands-on training programs** at client sites using live systems. Ensure that clients understand system functions and can manipulate software to produce desired results.

☑ **Consistently receive highest possible ratings** for training effectiveness. Frequently requested by clients to provide training for add-on products and new employees.

☑ **Analyze business needs,** recommend procedural changes/software customizations, and **adapt training program content** and level for specific end-user training requirements. Provide detailed feedback to software development team.

☑ **Highly articulate and effective communicator.** Excellent team-building and interpersonal skills; work well with individuals on all levels.

☑ Organized, take-charge professional with **exceptional follow-through abilities and detail orientation;** able to oversee projects from concept to successful conclusion.

☑ Effectively prioritize a broad range of responsibilities to **consistently meet tight deadlines.** Demonstrated success in surpassing productivity and performance objectives.

PROFESSIONAL EXPERIENCE

HEALTH SYSTEMS TRAINING CONSULTANT
Shared Medical Systems (SMS) ▪ Salt Lake City, UT   2007 to Present

$1.1 billion provider of information system solutions for worldwide health care industry. Serves 5,000+ customers, including hospitals, physician offices, clinics, and major health provider networks and organizations, in 20 countries in North America, Europe, and Asia.

Consult on new system implementation for clients in small- to medium-sized hospitals across the U.S. Work with software development team to analyze customer business objectives and develop customized integrated systems to facilitate financial transactions and reporting.

Page One of Two

This attractive format—combining a wide, gray-shaded left column, check-box bullet points, and a clean sans-serif font—creates a very professional resume for an experienced technical trainer. Note the unusual Value Offered section.

KATY F. BERGEN katyfbergen@aol.com Page Two

PROFESSIONAL EXPERIENCE

HEALTH SYSTEMS TRAINING CONSULTANT
Shared Medical Systems (SMS), *continued*

Travel to customer sites for 4-week installation jobs. Deliver, install, and test systems; interface with hospital administrators and technical staff for troubleshooting and performance assessments. Train end users on live system, providing on-the-job support/Q&A during final week. Compile thorough reports for management and development team on installation events and training outcomes.

Recent Accomplishments

- Successfully completed training for 35 users at hospitals in 8 states and the Caribbean during 2010. Provided on-site installation, training, and support for 42 weeks of the year.
- Consistently earned *excellent* and *exceeds requirements* ratings on student and supervisor performance evaluations.
- Selected for SMS Installer's Achievement Club—1 of 20 consultants chosen by management among 150 installer/trainers company-wide.
- Assisted 10-member team in documenting policies and procedures for remote computer operations. Wrote hidden command-line policy for system, including user profiles and upgrades. Provided feedback to team on hospital environment/situations, staff responsibilities, and trainer interactions.
- Worked with 12-member process improvement team to rewrite extensive SMS system implementation methodology.
- Mentored 3 new SMS trainers. Routinely served as resource person for colleagues, providing materials and advice on training methods.

PRIOR EXPERIENCE

BOOKKEEPER
Affordable Fabrics ▪ Omaha, NE

RADIO NEWS & PROMOTIONS DIRECTOR/WRITER/BROADCASTER
KLO-AM, Ogden, UT ▪ KSIT-FM, Rock Springs, WY ▪ KTRS-FM, Casper, WY
KALL-FM, Salt Lake City, UT ▪ AEROTRAFFIC, Salt Lake City, UT ▪ KRVI-FM, Salt Lake City, UT ▪ KYNN-FM, Omaha, NE

OFFICE MANAGER
Spring Air Mountain West, Inc. ▪ Salt Lake City, UT
Norm Bishop Volkswagen ▪ Boise, ID

EDUCATION AND TRAINING

Boise State University, Boise, ID, courses in Business Administration

Professional Development
Complete 100+ hours of SMS training annually. Courses have included Consulting Skills, Business Writing, Behavioral Interviewing, Listening Skills, Communications, Sexual Harassment, PowerPoint Presentations.

RESUME 40: BY MYRIAM-ROSE KOHN, CPBS, CCM, CCMC, IJCTC, CPRW, CEIP

Bonita Thomas

27851 Altadena Street, Cacillo, CA 91384 • 661-538-9331 • bthomas@aol.com

Technical Expertise

- Windows XP
- Windows 7
- MS Word
- MS Excel
- MS PowerPoint
- MS Outlook
- Lotus SmartSuite
- LAN
- WAN

Systems Training & Technical Support Professional

Dynamic, passionate, creative, dedicated, and results-driven training and support specialist with proven record of achievement in computer systems training and technical support (groups and individuals).

Outstanding project management, networking, presentation, and follow-up skills. Solid abilities in technical training, team building, management development, and customer service. Extensive background in sophisticated networking, client/server, and telecommunications technologies. Excellent troubleshooter; persuasive communicator; superior motivator. Flexible, loyal, strong work ethic, and a quick learner.

Professional Experience

CACILLO INSURANCE • Southern Valley, CA • 1997–Present

> Senior Fire Claim Automation and Procedures Specialist (3+ years)
> Senior Auto Claim Automation and Procedures Specialist (2 years)
> Auto/Fire Claims Procedure Training Specialist (2 years)
> Agency Field Specialist (7 years)

Consistently promoted based on performance.

As designated **instructor,** design instructional system and manage training program. Train claims employees in the use of automated computer system for effective handling of client claims. Conduct group sessions either in office or at central training facility. Perform work flow analysis on clerical support, professional (claims representatives), and management units in each office by interviewing them and watching them perform, and then reviewing common errors occurring in different situations. Lead monthly discussions with superiors and report findings directly to corporate headquarters. Keep meticulous records as to who (300+ employees) was trained, when, and in which applications.

In **technical support** role, manage, support, troubleshoot, and maintain claims system for 5 offices. Provide on-site training and telephone support (help desk) for multiple offices/departments (clerical, administrative, accounting, claims, agency administration, management). Produce computerized/multimedia presentation materials for employee meetings and other functions. Involved in development, testing, and training of new software programs distributed throughout the region.

- Instrumental in diagnosing major system problem and implementing solution in regional offices affecting 100+ employees. Resolved numerous issues and made recommendations that were adopted officewide.

- Member of system conversion team for numerous software and operating system upgrades.

- Project team leader for setup and operation of mobile disaster operation offices for handling of claims. Set up computers (hardware); train and supervise temporary and permanent staff to process claims.

Community Volunteer

- Big Sisters of Los Angeles
- Santa Clarita Shelter
- United Negro College Fund
- Delhaven Community Center
- Adult Tutor, California Literacy

Education

Bachelor of Arts: University of Redlands, Redlands, CA
- Major: Communications; Minor: Education

Microsoft Office User Specialist Program, IIA (Insurance Institute of America) Designation

Fire and Casualty Broker/Agent, Life Agent: Department of Insurance, State of California

This resume packs a lot of information onto one page, yet in a highly readable format thanks to clear, bold headings, brief bullet-point lists, and a readable serif font. The computer graphic adds interest and helps to break up the text-rich sections.

RESUME 41: BY BARBARA SAFANI, MA, CERW, CPRW, NCRW, CCM

LILY P. CHOY

132-20 82nd St., Ozone Park, NY 11417   Home: 718-275-3232   Cell: 917-848-6627   lilypchoy@mail.com

TECHNICAL ACCOUNT MANAGER / INTEGRATION ANALYST / SALES AND SYSTEMS ENGINEER

IT Logic	B&D Systems	Data Manager, Inc.	CompAmerica

- 20+ years of experience as a liaison to corporate clients, marketing teams, and systems engineers; partner with leading Fortune 100 companies in financial services, media, and government sectors.
- Success gathering competitive intelligence and incorporating partner products into company solutions to deliver best-in-class infrastructure software applications.
- Expertise creating and facilitating demonstrations and prototypes that link product features and benefits to client-specific needs.
- Recognition for ability to absorb multiple technologies in short time frames.

Core Competencies

Multitier Enterprise Systems

Technology Integration

Systems Functionality

Architecture Solutions

Mainframe Applications

Systems Implementation

Competitive Benchmarking

Technical Sales Presentations

Solutions Selling

Pre/Post Sales Support

Proof of Concept

Technical Account Maintenance

Client Servicing

CAREER HIGHLIGHTS

Continuous Process Improvement
- Reengineered IT Logic product demonstration and reduced systems requirements by more than 60%.
- Leveraged industry product knowledge to supply competitive market data for briefing distributed throughout B&D Systems. Recommended procedures for influencing future market share.
- Designed a customer-specific Data Manager product demonstration that streamlined training capabilities and increased client usability by as much as 98%.

Customer Focus
- Turned around 3 at-risk clients at IT Logic by providing "high-touch" service resulting in improved customer service rating and on-time integration testing.
- Spearheaded "tech-day" between customer sales team and IT Logic engineering team; resolved 100% of outstanding systems issues.
- Delivered presales proposal and integration testing on time under extremely tight deadline; applauded by IT Logic and client management for ability to adapt quickly under difficult circumstances.
- Reduced downtime on trading floor by 25% over a 2-year period as B&D's on-site support specialist.
- Requested as CompAmerica's point person for the company's 2 largest accounts.

Technology Solutions
- Promoted to integration specialist for IT Logic's financial accounts from pool of more than 65 SEs nationwide, based on industry knowledge and solid record of achievement in application and data integration.
- Selected by senior management to be liaison in the B&D Integration and mainframe areas of the company product set. Designated regional mainframe expert.

continued

A combined functional/chronological format was used to showcase accomplishments from all phases of this candidate's career. High-profile company names are emphasized in the summary.

LILY P. CHOY
lilypchoy@mail.com   page two

Business Platforms

XYZ Application Server, ABC Integration, XYZ Portal, J2EE, XYZ Enterprise Servers

Operating Systems and Database Products

Microsoft Windows, Microsoft SQL, Oracle, Linux

Integration Connections

Mainframe, Database, HTTP, PeopleSoft, SAP, Siebel

Internet Technologies

HTML, XML, JSP, JavaScript, Web Services, Web Design

Financial Integrations

SWIFT, Omgeo, STP, FIX

Awards/Recognitions

IT Logic Merit Stock Option, 2009

IT Logic Knowledge Transfer Award, 2007

B&D Merit Award, 2003

B&D Innovator Circle Award, 2003

Data Manager Field Systems Engineer of the Quarter, 1999

CompAmerica Solution Award, 1995, 1996

CompAmerica Appreciation Award, 1994

- Integrated B&D mainframe data into emulation Windows software using Oracle product for NBC coverage of presidential election.
- Pioneered B&D demo center to market services to 300+ local users.
- Piloted initiative at Data Manager to replace expensive leased lines with Internet service for a potential cost savings to the client of $1 million.
- Requested by Morgan Stanley as the CompAmerica representative at the prestigious Las Vegas Comdex industry show on three occasions.

Business Development

- Delivered 275+ technical sales presentations to 42 Fortune 100 clients on several business platforms over a 20+ year career.
- Presented CompAmerica's new XYZ Personal System and Operating System to 2,300+ customers over a 2-week period. Persuaded client to purchase 370 computers on day of announcement, enhancing company revenues by $700,000.

CHRONOLOGY

IT Logic, New York, NY   **2004 to 2011**
Third-largest applications infrastructure software company providing enterprise software to 1,200+ customers.
- Integration Specialist (2007 to 2011)
- Senior Systems Engineer (2004 to 2007)

B&D Systems, New York, NY   **1999 to 2004**
Provider of innovative integration web services and portal and analytic solutions for 1,100 enterprise customers worldwide.
- Senior Systems Engineer, Eastern Region

Data Manager, Inc., New York, NY   **1996 to 1999**
Leading supplier of enterprise information access and management software services to major corporations and government agencies worldwide.
- Senior Systems Engineer, Northeast Region

CompAmerica, New York, NY   **1987 to 1996**
Industry leader in IT business and consultative services.
- Account Specialist Systems Engineer (1994 to 1996)
- Specialist Systems Engineer (1992 to 1994)
- Customer Service Representative (1990 to 1992)
- Senior Associate Programmer (1987 to 1990)

EDUCATION

MBA, Information and Communications Systems
Fordham University, New York, NY   1993

BS, Computer Science
Cornell University, Ithaca, NY   1987

KYO TANAKA

75 Hillcrest Drive • East Haven, CT 06512 • 203-469-2320 • kyotanaka@gmail.com

PROFILE

Experienced technical writer / trainer with demonstrated skill in documenting software used for both nontechnical users and technical support staff. Recognized for producing consistently clear, coherent documentation within deadline and with minimal supervision. Accustomed to collaborating closely with programmers during development and testing as an integral part of the software development team.

- Strengths include communication skills (both oral and written), organization and planning, meticulous proofreading, and project/schedule management.
- Expertise using MS Word (Windows and Mac) and Adobe RoboHelp authoring tool.

EXPERIENCE

MAAX INDUSTRIAL AUTOMATION AND CONTROLS, New Haven, Connecticut
AUTO-CONTROLS CORPORATION (purchased by Maax IAC 4/09)
HIGH RIDGE CORPORATION (purchased by Auto-Controls 6/07)

Technical Writer / Trainer, 2007–2011

Wrote detailed online and print instruction manuals for Windows- and UNIX-based industrial gauging equipment.

- Produced a technical reference for setting up and maintaining the hardware as well as in-depth software documentation for daily use and system setup.
- Involved in each product during the development cycle and contributed significantly to software testing.
- Provided software training classes, for both an historical product and newer products, to customers and technical support personnel.

Technical Writer, 2004–2007

Researched, wrote, and often illustrated industrial gauge manuals.

- Manuals include theory, safety requirements, installation and setup procedures, operator guides, and maintenance requirements.
- Also wrote detailed instructions for the computerized electronics or personal computers used to operate the gauges.

(continued)

Professional experience as technical trainer and writer is enhanced by freelance writing and editing activities.

KYO TANAKA   kyotanaka@gmail.com

Page 2

FREELANCE

Writer / Proofreader / Trainer, 2004–Present

Independently generate diverse professional assignments. Recent sampling includes

- Teaching Microsoft Word classes in the Southern Connecticut Community Education program.
- Teaching Windows 7, both basic and intermediate, to employees of Kelly Staffing Service in 2010.
- Revising policies-and-procedures manual for Pratt & Whitney Credit Union, in 2008 and 2009.
- Summarizing market research interviews, editing, and consolidating findings into structured reports for Angus Consultants in 2005.
- Writing a travel article that was published in *Yankee* magazine in 2010.
- Volunteering as a feature article writer for the local Habitat for Humanity newsletter.

YALE–NEW HAVEN LIBRARY, New Haven, Connecticut

Indexer, January 2003–May 2004

Assisted with the development of a local history index generated from newspapers dating back to the early 1800s. Focused primarily on individuals and their connections to events.

BUILDERS REVIEW, INC., Derby, Connecticut

Managing Editor, 2000–2002

Wrote and assigned feature articles, "spotlights" on local home builder associations, and news items as well as promotional material for the company. Proofread 20+ magazines and all printing assignments. Established the editorial, feature, and production schedules for all the magazines.

EDUCATION

UNIVERSITY OF CONNECTICUT, Storrs, Connecticut

Bachelor of Arts, Biology, May 2000

Minored in both Communications and English. Worked sophomore, junior, and senior years as a resident assistant for the University Housing Department. Served one year as a peer assistant. Active in intramural sports.

ACTIVITIES

- Senior Member of the Society for Technical Communication.
- Marathoner (qualified for Boston Marathon 2011).

STEVEN J. THOMAS
E-business Technology Director

CAREER PROFILE

E-business/E-learning Management Professional experienced in the strategic planning, design, execution, and leadership of enterprise-wide technology initiatives that support business systems, strengthen organizational capabilities, and enhance productivity and efficiency. Proven record for delivering cost-effective projects on time and within budget. Expertise in technical training and development, combined with equally strong qualifications in project management, operations/department management, and systems integration. Recognized for building, mentoring, and supervising teams that are responsive to meeting business demands for high-quality training products.

*Nominated for the **2010 Excellence Award** for creating an electronic knowledge base*
for all 300 training personnel across all business lines in company.
*Recognized with the prestigious annual **E-learning Best Practices Award** in 2009.*

PROFESSIONAL EXPERIENCE

RYAN BECK FINANCIAL SERVICES, INC.   SAN DIEGO, CA
Director, E-business Technology Solutions Group   2008–Present
Assistant Manager, E-business Technology Solutions Group   2007–2008

Promoted to pioneer and direct group's development and maintenance of technology-based training initiatives and support functions, including Web-based training, online help, and Electronic Performance Support Systems (EPSS) for 2,000 internal and 20,000 external customers. Provide e-learning expertise and support to technical trainers as well as managers company-wide. Supervise team of 8 and manage vendor relationships and contract negotiations.

Selected Accomplishments:

▶ **Chosen to manage a major corporate initiative for development and implementation of training in the release of a new, higher-end technical product that prepared new teams to meet aggressive sales goals.**
  • Created the project management structure and standards for a complex project that included new product, operating model, and technology components.
  • Led team of 11 in developing and implementing training materials delivered on time and within budget.
  • Forged a collaborative partnership and team environment between 2 separate training departments that had never worked together.

▶ **Introduced, championed, and persuaded senior management to adopt innovative e-learning technologies, processes, and trends company-wide.**
  • Promoted to senior training and business leaders and managed development of a process-based assessment and training method from idea generation to successful pilot implementation. Results led to enhanced workflow processes: Improved accuracy by 20% and time to perform tasks by 246%; 96% of trainees stated that the training program would increase their efficiency.
  • Led research on new simulation tool products, reducing development costs by an estimated $142K+ per year with a 174% EVA. Presented business case and won approval from senior leadership to implement.
  • Spearheaded creation of e-learning standards, processes, and best practices, ensuring application of consistent methodology in program development among new and existing training personnel.

▶ **Led development of and delivered 4 Web-based training programs on time and within budget, effectively overcoming multiple obstacles.**
  • Took charge of the design and implementation of 2 concurrent Web-based training projects that included e-learning, instructor-led training, distance learning, and job aids for loss control system. Implemented with 1,600 users and realized significant savings for the company over prior system rollout strategy.

5889 Sullivan Avenue • San Diego, CA 92128 • 858.487.3100 • sjthomas@yahoo.com

This resume is peppered with documented business results from e-learning programs this executive has led.

STEVEN J. THOMAS   Page 2

Director, E-business Technology Solutions Group *continued...*

- Managed Web-based course design, contributing to successful relaunch of business objects application for 1,400 users. Led training program development for business insurance analytical platform.
- Provided development direction, mentoring, and consultation on a high-priority project for Web-based and online help training initiatives related to a business lines-rating tool.

▶ **Initiated and persuaded management to authorize the revamping of a 1,500-page online product manual that provided key data on 48 states for 50,000 users. Streamlined and produced a searchable, more user-friendly Web format that is also easier and faster to maintain than prior version.**

ARRANSON TECHNOLOGY SYSTEMS, INC.   SAN DIEGO, CA
Training Consultant, Integrated Learning Solutions Group   2005–2007

Collaborated with clients and technical experts to develop Web-based training, computer-based training, and instructor-led training for proprietary ERP systems. Team leader for Web-based training project, including interaction with internal and external clients, project planning, creation of design structure and standards, and instruction evaluation. Analyzed software design documents to determine system functionality.

Selected Accomplishments:

▶ Developed multimedia training for 22,000 users of procurement systems, automating and streamlining strategic contract management support within a complete workflow management solution.
▶ Designed multimedia program to train 8,000+ users of a financial system that managed $36 billion annually.
▶ Codesigned a central record-keeping database, using Access and Active Server Pages.
▶ Developed user guides, job aids, and train-the-trainer materials for an Ariba e-procurement system.

ELECTRONIC INFORMATION TECHNOLOGIES, INC.   NEW YORK, NY
Technical Trainer   2000–2005

Provided end-user training on a proprietary ERP system to the finance and accounting organization of a government agency with 16,000 employees. Led 12 other training instructors.

Selected Accomplishments:

▶ Provided training on accounting systems for paying 5.7+ million people annually; trained personnel on vendor payments (total of $126 billion annually) and computerized accounts payable system.
▶ Contributed to development of instructional design standards for all financial management courses.
▶ Presented numerous courses on vendor pay; created and instructed a Microsoft Office training course.

EDUCATION

M.S., MANAGEMENT INFORMATION SYSTEMS
University of California, San Diego, CA, 2006

B.S., WORKFORCE EDUCATION AND DEVELOPMENT
New York University, New York, NY, 2000

5889 Sullivan Avenue • San Diego, CA 92128 • 858.487.3100 • sjthomas@yahoo.com

LOUIS M. DIAMOND

515 Bay Drive
Residence: (732) 295-9803
Email: lmdiamond@home.com

Brick, NJ 08724
Mobile: (201) 609-2520

TECHNOLOGY SALES / MARKETING AND BUSINESS DEVELOPMENT

Asia, Europe, Middle East, and United States

Solid executive career leading start-up and fast-track growth of high-technology companies. Expert in business development, product positioning, and market expansion with strong operations, financial, and HR skills. Consistent top performer through strengths in identifying opportunities forging strategic, revenue-generating partnerships. Proven "intrapreneur" with a track record in championing new organizational initiatives and employing innovative thinking.

CAREER HISTORY

XYLINK CORPORATION, San Diego, CA (2/06–Present)

Director of Business Development, 7/08–Present

Orchestrate aggressive market and business development initiatives throughout emerging global markets for $400 million corporation. Lead a worldwide business development team in setting tactics for the sale of high-technology products, including security software, standalone WAN/LAN appliances, modules, and components.

Capture vertical industries such as telecommunications (network equipment manufacturers and carriers), health care (payers and providers), and wireless (e-merchants and solution providers). Perform financial evaluation of business development opportunities, including NPV and IRR calculations. Conceive and develop new product distribution channels that increase market penetration. Evaluate competitive activity, competitive products, emerging technologies, and new markets to determine the corporation's global market strategy.

Accomplishments:

- Built a global business development and sales organization, spearheading business development initiatives and marketing strategies that spanned 4 continents. Trained new sales recruits in international liaison, marketing, and business development skills.
- Negotiated an annual $4 million technology license contract with L3 Communications.
- Performed due diligence and negotiated an OEM contract with DICA technologies for the sale of an ISDN product into the Japanese market; captured $3.5 million in annual sales revenues.
- Negotiated and signed a global purchasing agreement with AT&T Solutions, resulting in $6 million in annual sales revenues.
- Established multichannel distribution networks to expand product reach in health care, wireless, and telecommunications markets.
- Negotiated strategic alliances and signed multiple comarketing agreements, including the establishment of partnerships with Symantec and IBM/Tivoli.
- Developed Marconi Communications and ADTRAN as a reseller channel for VPN products; estimated annual revenue of $6.5M.
- Developed business partnership with Nokia and Ericsson to provide wireless security technology.

Global Account Manager, 2/06–7/08

- Drove international sales revenues, launched new business development initiatives, and profitably directed account-development programs throughout emerging markets worldwide, including such accounts as Citigroup, AT&T, Bank of America, Chase, Credit Suisse, and Fidelity Investments.
- Increased sales revenues by 200% over 2-year period.

continued

More than half of the first page of this resume is taken up with sales-related accomplishments. Note that unlike many other computer and Web resumes, technical qualifications are included only within the context of sales achievements.

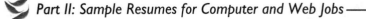

LOUIS M. DIAMOND   lmdiamond@home.com   Page Two

CAREER HISTORY (Continued)

CINCINNATI ELECTRONICS CORPORATION, Mason, OH (1/05–2/06)

Regional Sales Manager, Eastern United States

Oversaw a distribution network and directed marketing and sales activities within a territory extending from the Caribbean to eastern Canada. Boosted both market penetration and company brand recognition. Increased sales by more than 90%.

Revamped regional coverage to maximize productivity and enhance efficiency of the distribution network. Tracked sales and analyzed trends and market conditions to develop annual forecasts. Generated market analysis reports. Developed and implemented application-specific seminars and presentations for value-added resellers. Interfaced with advertising and public relations agencies to maximize marketing efforts.

HUGHES AIRCRAFT CORPORATION (FLIR Systems, Inc.), Carlsbad, CA (12/01–1/05)

District Sales Manager, Northeast Territory

Managed and coordinated infrared imaging system sales to Fortune 500 companies throughout New Jersey and extending to eastern Canada. Cultivated territory by developing and implementing comprehensive marketing strategies. Hired and trained independent factory representatives to exceed targeted sales quotas. Tailored an incentive program to optimize productivity. Increased sales by 74% within a 4-year period.

AGEMA INFRARED SYSTEMS, Secaucus, NJ (9/99–12/01)

Sales/Service Representative

Introduced thermal imaging systems to the medical marketplace. Performed market research prior to product introduction.

DATAGRAPHIX, New York, NY (7/98–9/99)

Customer Engineer

Responsible for the installation and maintenance of complex scanning systems.

EDUCATION

RUTGERS, THE STATE UNIVERSITY OF NEW JERSEY, Newark, NJ
Executive MBA, Finance Concentration
Bachelor of Science Degree, Marketing

GAVILAN COLLEGE, Gilroy, CA
Associate Degree, Electronic Technology

MILITARY HISTORY

UNITED STATES NAVY (Honorable Discharge), 9/92–6/98
Cryptologic Technician Maintenance E-5; received Top Secret SBI Clearance

Dwight D. Stephenson

1082 South Street • Natick, MA 01760
Home: 508-349-9876 • Mobile: 508-209-1234 • dstephenson@xmail.com

IT PROFESSIONAL SERVICES / TECHNOLOGY SALES

- 20 years of experience in information technology and professional service sales.
- Consistently achieve or surpass quota.
- Proficient in learning and selling technical products to sophisticated clients.
- Exceptional ability to build a region through prospecting and missionary selling.
- Strong closer with emphasis on strategic selling to major account market.
- Leadership qualities and a team player.

PROFESSIONAL EXPERIENCE

TECHNOLOGY FOR YOU—Boston, MA   2009–Present
Regional Sales Manager—*IT professional services to Fortune 500 accounts*

- Place teams of consultants to identify/solve issues of client, such as enterprise systems management, software distribution, data management, and data security.
- Exceeded quota ($3 million) with sales to large corporate and government accounts.

SOLUTIONS, INC.—Boston, MA   2005–2009
Account Manager—*Development tools and solutions for major accounts in the New England marketplace*

- Closed sales with large corporate accounts, including Fidelity, Unum, and Allmerica.
- Exceeded quota with 50% of the business coming from new accounts. Developed strong CIO/ CTO relationships with client companies to achieve long-term company success.
- Rebuilt Fortune 500 direct end-user account base in New England.
- Established and managed new systems integration partners throughout New England.

RBN ASSOCIATES, INC.—Boston, MA, and Providence, RI   2003–2005
Account Manager—*Routers, bridges, and other internetworking products*

- Built Rhode Island territory from $400K ('03) to $2.5 million in sales ('05).
- Top producer of new account business in Eastern Region.
- Successfully maintained key end-user accounts, including Bank of America, GTECH, Textron, and State of Rhode Island.
- Developed numerous new accounts and reseller channels.

Continued

With a bold, italic description of specific technologies and environments following each job title, it's very clear that Mr. Stephenson's expertise is in technology sales. Note how many sales keywords (quota, prospecting, missionary selling, closer, and so forth) are included in the summary.

Dwight D. Stephenson, 508-209-1234
Page 2

DATATEL, INC.—Boston, MA   2000–2003
Senior Account Executive—*Networking management systems, multiplexers*

- Represented company products in the public and private sectors.

- Established strong relationships with new WAN and LAN customers, including State of Massachusetts, BBN, Raytheon, and Lotus.

- Rookie of the Year, 2000.

ENTERPRISE DATA SYSTEMS CORP.—Boston, MA   1997–2000
Account Manager—*CPUs and data storage systems*

- Produced more than $10 million in sales to commercial, education, and public sector accounts.

- Developed relationships with highest levels of MIS management in Boston.

- Achieved status as highest-producing representative in Boston District.

- 1999 sales contest winner (#5 out of 135).

VITEM CORPORATION—Albany, NY, and Boston, MA   1993–1997
Sales Representative—*Storage equipment and communication products*

- Sold successfully to Albany-area commercial and New York State government accounts.

- Developed significant volume of new accounts; established strong contacts with 50 area data-processing industry executives.

- Managed all sales functions of remote office.

- Achieved Quota Club status: #1 ('94) and #2 ('95). Sold over $2 million a year from '94 to '97.

SOFTWARE UNLIMITED—Boston, MA   1990–1993
Account Manager—*IBM 34/38-type minicomputers and software for the manufacturing and distribution industry*
Consistently exceeded quota objectives ('91 through '93). Acquired excellent product and industry training.

TRAINING, SEMINARS, AND WORKSHOPS

Holden Associates	– Power-Based Selling (2005)
Target Marketing Associates	– Target Account Selling (2002)
Miller-Heiman	– Strategic Selling (1998)
	– Conceptual Sales (1998)

EDUCATION

MBA, 1996, Bentley College, Waltham, MA
Bachelor of Arts, Economics, 1990, Roger Williams College, Bristol, RI

BARBARA D. LOPATO

415-978-1262 • BarbaraDL@yahoo.com
186 Cliff Side Drive, Milpitas, CA 95034

NETWORK SECURITY SALES EXECUTIVE
Start-ups to Fortune 500 • Midmarket & Enterprise • Solution Sales • Channel Partnerships

Revenue driver and catalyst for aggressive growth—20 years of experience identifying, capturing, and driving business opportunities from concept to multimillion-dollar sales. Keen understanding of the entire technology sales process and buying cycle and an entrepreneurial appreciation for the value of promotion, profitability, and a positive bottom line. Excel at networking and negotiating with C-level decision makers to close complex deals. Skillfully establish, develop, and manage profitable relationships with channel partners. Able to build sales territories from the ground up with little or no resources.

- **Propelled start-up** to valued player in the integrated security solutions and malware arena, driving **multimillion-dollar sales** in the first few years to successfully position the company for $31M acquisition.
- **Inked company's first SaaS account** with major North American telecommunications player, building a **>$3.5M** annual revenue stream.
- **Accelerated sales more than 400%** in just **2** years through definitive sales strategy and execution.

Gaining competitive market advantage and bottom-line profit through innovative, consultative technology sales.

PROFESSIONAL EXPERIENCE

TRANSCO NETWORK SECURITY, 2010   Milpitas, CA
(Award-winning developer of security information and event management technology.)

Regional Account Manager (6-month contract)

Unleashed new business opportunities through aggressive cold calling, email campaigns, and webinars, targeting midtier financial credit unions, banks, utility companies, retail firms, and healthcare organizations. Delivered impressive results in a very short time—pipeline growth of **225%** and two **6-figure contracts.**

PLATFORM CORPORATION, 2009–2010   San Francisco, CA
(Privately held, industry-leading provider of infrastructure software solutions to ensure network security.)

Senior Sales Manager

Key player in establishing proactive approach and systematic roadmap for security device product specifications. Innovated visionary action plan lauded by second-round venture capitalists that ensured access to all resources, including product managers and CTO, necessary to build and close business opportunities.

Business Development & Profitability:

- Formulated strategic prospect list and analyzed each prospect by whiteboarding Platform Corp. products and solutions.
- Won contracts with **Intel, Motorola, Wyse Technology,** and **Aruba Networks.**
- Delivered **156%** revenue growth through partnerships for the device security framework campaign.

CP SECURE, 2006–2009   Cupertino, CA
(Start-up provider of integrated security solutions that protect organizations from Internet-originated Web- and e-mail–based malware threats. Founded by former Trans Micro executives in 2006 and acquired by NETGEAR in 2008.)

Sales Director, North America

Recruited as company's first sales specialist to build and define sales strategy and go-to-market plan for next-generation Web security appliance targeting midsize market. Reported directly to CEO/founder.

Business Development & Profitability:

- Grew start-up from **0 to $1.5M** annual sales to effectively position company for **$31M** acquisition by NETGEAR.
- Identified, developed, and grew **key channel partnerships** to build diverse, loyal, and self-sustaining VAR program.
- Validated the new company and product to shape a channel partner program that generated **50%** of overall business.
- Worked with marketing director to develop and execute innovative programs that expanded revenue pipeline by **225%.**

continued . . . .

All of the borders and lines in this resume were printed in red, providing a splash of color in keeping with the vibrant tone of this strong sales resume. Note position of dates after company names rather than at right margin, effectively downplaying a few short tenures.

BARBARA D. LOPATO   415-978-1262 • BarbaraDL@yahoo.com

TRANS MICRO (NASDAQ: TMIC), 1999–2006   Cupertino, CA
(Japan-based global leader in developing, delivering, and supporting Internet-content security solutions.)

> *Key contributor to repositioning Trans Micro as an Internet security company. Progressed through high-visibility roles to achieve a number of industry and company "firsts." Instrumental in:*
> - *Landing company's first OEM account.*
> - *Establishing industry's first SaaS product.*
> - *Building the sales process that launched the industry's first e-mail gateway antivirus product.*

Business Development Manager, Consumer Products Division (2005–2006)

Created and implemented North American OEM and consumer products sales model. Reported directly to Senior Vice President, Worldwide Operations.

Business Development & Profitability:

- Exceeded annual sales quota by **175%** *in the first year.*
- Negotiated and closed company's **first OEM contract** with Global 500 Sony, complete with worldwide product bundle.

Senior Sales, Managed Security Services (2003–2005)

Hand-selected by Chairman/CEO for team that shaped the vision, strategy, and execution for Internet Outsourcing Services Division. Quickly defined targets (ASPs and major North American telecommunication vertical) and pitched the new model through cold-calling to line up face-to-face presentations by CTO and COO.

Business Development & Profitability:

- Inked company's first SaaS account with major North American telecommunications players, creating a **>$3.5M annual revenue stream.**
- Established **$1.25M** Bloomberg relationship, with an annual support contract on the back end.
- Attained **President's Club,** 2004.

Senior Enterprise Account Manager (1999–2003)

Hired as company's third U.S. employee, reporting directly to VP of Sales to build the sales process that launched InterScan VirusWall, the industry's first e-mail gateway antivirus product. Established stellar record of developing and managing Eastern Regional sales territory, including product line that grew to one of the company's most profitable ever, generating millions of dollars in revenue with deployments worldwide.

Business Development & Profitability:

- Catapulted annual revenues from **zero to $10M.**
- Inked the company's **first enterprise license** to PNC Bank and an enterprise client reference list that included Bloomberg, Chase Manhattan Bank, Citibank, Goldman Sachs, Federal Reserve Bank, Praxair, and State Street Bank.
- Closed **$250K** contract with Chase Manhattan Bank—the company's **first 6-figure contract.**

MCAFEE ASSOCIATES (NYSE: MFE), 1997–1999   Santa Clara, CA
(World's largest dedicated security technology company.)

Senior Enterprise Account Manager

Hired to establish Western Regional sales territory. Recruited, trained, and supervised 5-member sales team. Reported directly to VP of Sales.

Business Development & Profitability:

- Averaged **137%** performance to goal for annual sales.
- Advanced sales **from $11M to $45M** in 2 years.
- Named to **President's Club,** 1998.

EDUCATION
BS, Business Management — San Jose State University
Negotiating Successful Solutions — Huthwaite, 2006
SPIN Selling — Huthwaite, 2005
Sales Advantage — Dale Carnegie, 2004

Michael Roy

5 Fairway Court • Burlington, Ontario, Canada L7M 2S8

(905) 336-5454 • mroy@gmail.com

IT BUSINESS DEVELOPMENT PROFESSIONAL

Experienced business development executive with 17 years of success in formulating and implementing high-level strategic business directions within the pharmaceutical, healthcare, and financial industries. Innovative professional with proven ability to successfully analyze client business issues, recommend IT solutions, and convert opportunities to sales by utilizing the following:

- Program Development & Management
- Product Development & Marketing
- Client Training & Management
- Team Leadership

Demonstrated skill in assimilating new concepts and technology and capitalizing on the primary competencies of technical and design teams.

CAREER HIGHLIGHTS

Compusolutions, Washington, DC   2010–Present
Regional Vice President—Business Development
Manage a multidisciplinary team of technical professionals in offshore/onshore outsourcing of software development to leading-edge technology firms.

- Increased software development outsourcing contracts by $30M in 6 months within the domains of ERP, CRM, document imaging, workflow, airline reservation systems, and e-learning.
- Collaborated with local and international project leaders to achieve best practices in software development life cycle.
- Managed and led multiple teams of professionals such as project managers, business analysts, technical architects, web developers, and quality assurance resources.

ELT, Ottawa, ON   2008–2010
Senior Business Development Executive
Assumed responsibility for software sales (in excess of $10M) and professional services in an 8-state account base for a Fortune 50 healthcare information systems company.

- Collaborated with implementation team to successfully install clinical information, document imaging, and workflow systems in 15 larger hospitals.
- Developed cost benefits and return-on-investment analysis demonstrating the effectiveness of document imaging and workflow on clinical and financial environments.
- Won the approval of key executive stakeholders (CEO, CFO) to convert ROI analysis into sales opportunity.

HighNet Systems Inc., Houston, TX   2006–2008
Technical Account Executive
Consulted with key executives in utilization of IT to solve business issues for a developer of document imaging and workflow systems for the financial and healthcare industries.

- Participated in maintenance of various accounts and projects within the financial and healthcare industries.
- Worked effectively as a team member to assemble new technology and information.

continued

Michael successfully transitioned from design engineer to business development executive. His resume showcases his dual expertise because both are assets for technology sales roles.

Michael Roy	mroy@gmail.com	Page 2

SYmPiatic, Ottawa, ON   2002–2006
Director—Information Technology
Provided technical leadership to a company of 850 employees whose areas of expertise centered on clinical information systems for the healthcare industry.

- Designed, implemented, and maintained the LAN environment at the corporate office and 7 regional offices across Canada.
- Successfully coordinated corporate selection of Customer Relationship Management (CRM) solutions provider.

Technis Ltd., Toronto, ON   1995–2002
Technical Service Engineer
Designed and implemented LAN/WAN-based diagnostic and monitoring systems for hospital critical-care environments.

- Collaborated in the management of multiple complex projects, contributing to profit growth from $2M to $10M in 1 year.
- Provided project management and technical support, on-site diagnosis, and troubleshooting of LAN and wireless cardiac telemetry monitoring systems installations.

J&R Testing, Windsor, ON   1994–1995
Design Engineer
Worked on all phases of design and development of various industrial and pharmaceutical testing equipment.

- Consulted with development team on architecture and development tools that enabled the on-time, on-budget development of the hepatitis testing system.

TECHNICAL SKILLS

Project Management Tools	**Special Operating Systems**	**Network/Infrastructure**
MS Visio 2010	Document Imaging	LAN/WAN/WLAN
MS Project 2010	Automated Workflow	Wireless Cardiac Telemetry
MS Windows Server	Electronic Medical Records	Monitoring Systems

EDUCATION & PROFESSIONAL TRAINING

- **Electrical Engineering Technologist:** Algonquin College, Ottawa, ON
- **Electrical Engineering Technician:** Seneca College, Toronto, ON
- **Project Management Skills:** DigitalThink, Inc.
- **Data Communication and Networking:** Learning Tree International, Ottawa, ON
- **Financial and Management Accounting:** Toronto University, Toronto, ON
- **Executive Presentation Skills:** Communispond, Inc., Chicago, IL

Irina McCarver

513-204-7382
mccarver@gmail.com

1929 Miami Lakes Drive
Loveland, Ohio 45140

Expertise: Technology Services Operations Management

Strategic Analysis & Planning — Management — Performance Improvement —
Marketing & Sales — Staff Development

Performance Highlights

- Spearheaded across-the-board operational improvements that helped a computer company to grow 35% per year, outperforming aggressive goals and successfully positioning the company for acquisition. Retained as operations director following buyout.

- Developed service and customer focus as strong competitive advantages. Motivated staff and successfully instilled a strong client-first orientation in sales and service teams.

- Juggled multiple challenges while maintaining peak performance. Completed MBA while working full-time; took on added consulting position while employed by Nestle. Consistently used exceptional multitasking skills to maintain a high level of personal productivity.

Professional Experience

COM-SOLUTIONS, INC., Centerville, Ohio   2006–Present
Full-service computer solutions firm; purchased by public company (Neolog) in 2010 for $52 million

Operations Director, 2006–Present

Direct all activities for rapidly growing computer services firm offering hardware, software, and network solutions to Fortune 100 clients. Accountable for sales, profitability, customer satisfaction, and all aspects of operations (inventory, purchasing, shipping & receiving), overseeing 12 direct and 60 indirect reports.

Develop and implement strategic plans to achieve corporate goals for growth and profitability.

- Increased sales 35% annually, outperforming aggressive 30% growth goal.

- Improved company-wide skill levels, morale, and teamwork through training, judicious hiring, and weeding out underperforming staff. Developed expert technical staff as a competitive advantage.

- Promoted company image as customer problem-solver able to deliver both long-range solutions and "fast fixes" for immediate productivity.

- Slashed product delivery time from 4 days to 1–2 days by realigning staff schedules and communicating urgency to vendors.

- Created and implemented aggressive sales, marketing, and advertising campaign targeting our key audience, MIS professionals.

- Consistently delivered excellent quality, value, and service to the point that volume of referral business eliminated the need for costly advertising.

Management / Operations Consultant, 2006

Challenged to develop operational improvements to deliver 30% annual growth. Analyzed entire operating structure and identified opportunities for significant improvement in customer service and business development.

- Offered permanent position as operations director as a result of findings and contributions during consulting assignment.

The Performance Highlights section of this resume includes personal traits that have contributed to career success.

Irina McCarver

513-204-7382
mccarver@gmail.com

Professional Experience, continued

NESTLE CORPORATION, Chillicothe, Ohio   2000–2006

Production Supervisor

Managed planning and scheduling for all day-to-day operations in fast-paced candy processing and packaging plant. Responsible for quality control, safety, training, ergonomics, and special projects. Managed 50 employees.

- Over 5 years, achieved savings of $175,000 through cost control and productivity enhancements; decreased absenteeism 75%; reduced defective product rate 10%.

Education

MBA, 2009
Emphasis on Information Systems and International Management
XAVIER UNIVERSITY, Cincinnati, Ohio

BS Management Operations and Systems, 1999
THE OHIO STATE UNIVERSITY, Columbus, Ohio

Additional Information

Strong oral, written, and persuasive communications skills.

Fluent in Russian; understand Polish and Spanish.

CHAPTER 7

Resumes for Network and Systems Technologists

- Network Administrators and Systems Analysts
- Network Engineers
- Network and Computer Specialists
- Systems Administrators
- IT Project Managers
- Certified Professional Systems Engineers

Myra C. Landers, MCTS

1256 GEYERS LANE, ELLICOTT CITY, MD 21046 — 301.555.5555 — MCL@HOTMAIL.COM

Network Administrator / Systems Analyst

Tech Profile

▶ PC Hardware & Software Configurations

▶ LAN/WAN

▶ Windows Server 2008

▶ Exchange Server 2010

▶ ADP

▶ Microsoft Products

▶ Mobile Devices

Awards

Received several notable awards for excellence in the following areas:

▶ Managing Computer Operations

▶ Professionalism

▶ Team Leadership

Endorsements

"… undoubtedly the best systems analyst we have at this facility …"

"… always puts the customer first…"

"… ready for more responsibility… always seeking to learn more, do more, and advance the mission."

Profile

▶ Expert knowledge of all Microsoft products.

▶ Microsoft Certified Technology Specialist (MCTS), Windows Server 2008.

▶ 10 years of direct experience supervising critical computer operations.

▶ Troubleshoot operations, processes, and networks; determine accurate and timely solutions; apply quality assurance measures.

Experience

UNITED STATES ARMY, 2003 to Present   *Top Secret Clearance*
Network Administrator/Systems Analyst, **Germany**   **2007 to Present**

▶ Supervise 2 personnel supporting critical computer requirements and ongoing operations. Effectively manage daily operations in a network with 50 computers, 2 servers (40 offices), and 250 clients.

▶ Implement upgrades and policies regarding network security, researching and figuring new ways to make applications run more smoothly. Keep all automation systems free from viruses. Analyze problems/glitches and recommend or implement viable working solutions.

▶ Provide quality service to all customers, reacting quickly and thoughtfully to problems and applying knowledge/experience to ensure minimal computer problems and downtime.

▶ Maintain comprehensive working knowledge of Windows Server 2008 Workstation and Exchange Server 2010.

▶ Start new accounts for secure Internet access. Manage and issue PKI email encryption software to best secure military email.

Specific Accomplishments

▶ Selected by senior management to colead a diverse team in providing daily customer service and network administration. Instrumental in bringing a new server online.

▶ Developed a system policy and implemented software to upgrade network security, ensuring compatibility with the fast-paced civilian sector, which was running dual operating systems. Ensured programs operated correctly, and then installed more server-based software and services enabling server-based administration of the network, significantly enhancing initial response time to the client.

Power Generation Section, Team Leader, **Texas**   **2003 to 2006**

▶ Supervised a team of 6 mechanics. Performed direct support, maintenance, repair, overhauling, and rebuilding of power generation equipment.

▶ Trained, guided, and offered assistance to a team of mechanics to ensure full mission capability at all times. Reviewed operator's equipment licenses.

▶ Conducted troubleshooting of mechanical, electrical, and hydraulic systems and determined faults.

▶ Prepared status reports for senior management on equipment and parts tracking. Managed inventory and parts tracking databases. Administered quality control measures.

Education and Training

▶ AA in Computer Science, Central Texas College, 2005

▶ Microsoft Windows Server Core Technologies, New Horizons, 2009 (Certificate of Training)

▶ Internetworking Using MS TCP/IP, New Horizons, 2009 (Certificate of Training)

▶ Primary Leadership Development Course, U.S. Army, 2005

▶ Power Generation Management, U.S. Army, 2006

This attractive, unusual format does a good job of organizing and presenting the information in this resume so that it remains highly readable. The left column effectively highlights important and distinguishing qualifications and recommendations.

RAHUL SRIVINISAN

220 East 42nd Street, #4R • New York, NY 10017
Cell: (212) 724-4009 • E-mail: rahulsrivinisan@verizon.net

NETWORK ENGINEERING AND EMERGING TECHNOLOGIES
NEW MEDIA • E-COMMERCE • INTERNET • NETWORK SECURITY

Inventor of ingenious spam filters used by one of the world's biggest Internet companies.

Visionary IT leader, inventor, and network security expert with 18 years of experience developing software, architecting systems, and implementing large-scale projects. Fluent in English, Tamil, and Hindi. U.S. citizen. Top Secret security clearance (currently inactive).

- **Technology:** Awarded 2 spam filtering patents while managing technical operations for Gmail. Repeatedly asked to step in, save the day, and turn around troubled projects.

- **Business Development:** In addition to primary role as technologist, expert at promoting new and emerging technologies to all levels of strategically important accounts, from ultratechnical engineering staff to top executives.

- **Team Leadership:** Exceptional team-building and recruiting skills. Consistently able to find ways to accomplish more and make optimal use of existing staff and resources.

PROFESSIONAL EXPERIENCE

AT&T COMMMUNICATIONS, INC.   Morristown, NJ, 2007–Present

Long-Distance Broadband Division, largest provider of local and long-distance telephone, DSL, and wireless service in U.S.

DIRECTOR, ENTERPRISE ARCHITECTURE AND WEB APPLICATIONS

Brought on board to rescue a complex project with chronic technical problems. Currently lead development of the mission-critical ordering and care business for Broadband DSL, which supports 6,000+ business users on a 24/7 basis. Implement architectural strategies that include third-party software (including Oracle/PeopleSoft CRM) and internal applications.

- Saved $87 million on project investment and turned around the product line (combined value more than $5 billion) by successfully deploying the Broadband Ordering and Care application (previous 3 attempts had failed).

- Architected large-scale implementation of Oracle PeopleSoft CRM that—over a 5-year period —will achieve $610 million in cost savings and generate $300 million in additional revenue.

- Led CRM 2.0 initiative, resulting in product and technical roadmap for next-generation CRM application for a 13-state region—all within 3 months. Cut costs to a bare minimum (under $300,000), expanded system capabilities, and enabled $3 million in new revenue.

SAIC   San Diego, CA, 2005–2007

Global defense, security, and aerospace company with approximately 107,000 employees and $36 billion in annual revenues.

DIRECTOR, INTERNET DEVELOPMENT, NATIONAL SECURITY AGENCY

Tasked to reorganize Web development teams and lead implementation of a collaborative application suite used throughout the intelligence community. Led 70-member team that built a complex Web application involving GIS mapping, meeting planning, personnel tracking, and message parsing.

- Cut outside consultant fees by 20%—and increased development expertise—by assessing and reassigning program staff.

- Cut overall program costs 65% by reorganizing teams, cutting staff, and implementing Agile and other best-practice methodologies.

- Integrated and harmonized disparate technologies: Oracle, Google maps, ArcView, Hibernate, Java, Java Struts, Spring, BEA Aqualogic (Plumtree), WebLogic.

continued

Mentioned right up front, a truly notable achievement—invention of spam filters—distinguishes this candidate from all others.

GOOGLE, INC.   **Mountain View, CA, 1997–2004**

Global "public cloud" computing and Internet search technologies company. Runs 1 million+ servers processing 1 billion+ search requests and 20 petabytes of user-generated data every day.

SENIOR TECHNICAL MANAGER (2000–2004)

Promoted to broader scope of responsibility that included all monitoring, management, and metrics for overall Google infrastructure and application portfolio.

- Assembled and led a 4-team, 35-member development group that designed and built more than 100 reporting applications.
- Devised a comprehensive O&M enterprise-management solution for all Google brands.

TECHNICAL MANAGER, E-MAIL SYSTEMS (1997–2000)

Led a 3-team, 25-person organization that ran all operations for one of the world's largest e-mail systems (up to 300 million e-mails per day).

Architecture and Development

- Listed as inventor on 2 key patents that thwarted online fraud and spamming.
- Built high-volume, high-redundancy coding units based on advanced queuing theory and multilayered code bases. Managed 500 UNIX servers (E4500s and HP N Class).

E-mail Operations

- Decreased event-response times more than 60% by improving event filtering, problem-escalation protocols, and processing procedures.
- Collected and analyzed an extremely large array of metrics (more than 1,000 data points per minute) from all components of the Google Mail system.
- Managed hardware and software assets valued above $500 million. Negotiated hardware contracts (up to $55 million) with top manufacturers.

Spam Fighting

- Achieved one of Google's highest priority business goals by drastically decreasing the impact of spam on subscribers (and minimizing negative publicity for Google).
- Developed applications that analyzed Google mail flows—based on complex queuing theory and volumetric profiling—that led to more than $100M annual savings.

ADDITIONAL EXPERIENCE

NASA AMES RESEARCH CENTER, Sunnyvale, CA (1992–1996): Member of 30-person team that designed the Space Network Control Center for all NASA communications; promoted to Senior Systems Engineer.

TECHNOLOGY PROFILE

Databases: Oracle (10g, 9i), DB2, MS SQL Server, MySQL

Operating Systems: Solaris, HP-UX, AIX, Windows XP, RedHat Linux (and other distributions), Ubuntu

Packaged Software: Business Objects, Oracle tools, BEA Tuxedo, BEA WebLogic, Symantec i3, Wily Introscope, Quest TOAD, Quest STAT, Oracle PeopleSoft CRM/Financials and related PeopleSoft tools, IBM WebSphere, EMC Patrol, Mercury

Languages/Frameworks: SQL, PL/SQL, PeopleTools, UNIX shell scripting, PHP, CakePHP, Symfony, PERL, JavaScript, HTML, Java, .NET, C#, C++, XML, BPEL, Ruby on Rails, Ant, Python, Apache, JBoss, Hibernate, JDeveloper, Eclipse

EDUCATION

M.S., Computer Engineering, University California (UCSD), San Diego, CA (1992)

B.S., Electrical Engineering, University of California (UCLA), Los Angeles, CA (1990)

Yuval Fischel
■ ■ ■

18 Eloura Lane
Rocklin, CA 95677

Email: yuvalfischel@hotmail.com

Telephone: (916) 624-8735
Mobile: (916) 214-9900

IT Professional

MCSE • Technical Support • Networks • Applications • System Security

Generalist **IT professional** with multiple strengths in network administration, system security, and advanced desktop and application support. Microsoft Certified Systems Engineer certification combined with customer support experience, developing a capacity to understand problems intuitively, strategize a course of action, automate daily work tasks, and create robust systems that aid productivity. Acknowledged throughout employment and academic life as an able troubleshooter, a cooperative team player, and an individual willing to share information for improved service delivery. International experience in high-pressure desktop/application support areas; proven skills in dealing with people from a diversity of backgrounds with expediency and courtesy.

Value Offered:

- Network Design, Implementation, Security, and Administration
- LAN/WAN

- Disaster Recovery, Backups
- System Security
- Application Support
- Process Reengineering

- Hardware Configurations and Troubleshooting
- IT Policy Development
- Customer Service

Technology Snapshot

Network: TCP/IP and Internet networking, routers, hubs, wiring

Server Applications: Exchange 2010, Linux Red Hat proxy server, DNS server, Mac OS server, firewalls, Archserve, terminal server

Platforms: Windows XP/7, Mac OS 7 to 10.6, Linux

Desktop Applications: Microsoft Office, Adobe Reader, Adobe Photoshop

Hardware: PC repairs, troubleshooting, peripherals, installations

Experience Highlights

- Streamlined and automated system tasks that **enabled a 33% reduction in staff with no loss of service levels to end users.**

- **Expedited issue resolution** by launching remote access software (VNC) that controlled the network across multiple sites in Israel.

- Cut time in restoring faulty hard drives by hours through use of Ghost disk imaging and regular backups.

- **Instigated a series of preventative maintenance** tasks. Composed scripts that automated everyday work routines, including the deletion of temporary files, regular disk checks, and defragmentation processes.

- **Managed a $20,000 project,** expanding a local area network for a high-tech company. Installed personal computers and laid cables for 5 new stations.

- Influenced clients during on-site visits by displaying professionalism, expediency, and courtesy. **Reputation as a competent technician prompted repeat business** and encouraged word-of-mouth referrals that **increased the client base by 25%.**

Yuval Fischel

Page 1

Confidential

A strong and detailed first page disguises the fact that this candidate had only two jobs and three years of experience. The idea was to get across his understanding of business benefits from his contributions and to show that he had a multitude of IT skills but was not locked into one particular area.

Employment Narrative

CALFORNIAN PUBLICATIONS   2009–2011
Network Technician/Administrator

Confronted upon commencement with a network experiencing substantial problems. Constant crashes and mail congestion from outdated equipment and inadequate security prompted numerous end-user complaints.

In a 24/7 production environment with diverse platforms and specialist editorial software, the need to handle complex issues quickly and competently was paramount. Mastered the systems quickly, achieving daily recognition for high levels of service delivery.

Actions/Contributions:

- Combated lengthy downtimes following system crashes that severely affected the productivity of end users. Introduced Ghost images of central systems that contained critical software—an initiative that allowed rapid restoration. Solution **cut downtime by 35%,** eliminating the need to reinstall operating system and applications.

- Initiated transition from existing virus protection to Norton AntiVirus. After implementation, **90% of virus issues were eliminated.**

- **Instigated a series of preventative maintenance tasks.** Composed scripts that automated the deletion of temporary files, and routinely launched regular disk checks and defragmentation processes. Deployed PoleEdit policy with administrator rights **preventing the installation of unauthorized software.**

- **Expedited issue resolution** by launching remote access software to control the network across multiple sites in Israel. Created educational tools for end users that provided the step-by-step basics of general problem resolution to employ prior to contacting technical support. **Cut technician time on problem resolution by 33%.**

- Assumed control of backups to ensure quick restoration following system crashes.

- Configured a Check Point firewall to **deflect spam.** Expert configuration prevented receipt of spam, prompting **less mail congestion.**

- Streamlined and automated system tasks that enabled a 33% reduction in staff **without loss of service level to end users.** As a team of two remaining technicians, administered the WAN and LAN; oversaw communication lines to 20 branches connected by ATM and ISDN; provided first-, second-, and third-level technical support on a range of office, specialist, and utility software via telephone from customers locally and internationally; troubleshot hardware issues for 300 personal computers, 50 printers, routers, switches, modems, and 25 laptops.

ONLINE LAB   2008
Senior Network Technician

- **Managed $20,000 project,** expanding a local area network for a high-tech company; installed personal computers and laid cables for 5 new stations.

- Selected to form 2-person team to install 40 personal computers in 2 days for a banking institution. **Completed project to deadline without incident.**

Summary

Reported to:
Infrastructure Manager

Supervised:
Computer Technician

Customers: 500 end users

Technologies:
Windows 2010 Server;
Exchange 2010, Linux
Kernel 2.6, DNS
Server.

Position Tasks:
- Defining profiles
- Backups
- LAN/WAN connectivity issues
- PC/peripheral troubleshooting
- Software installations
- First-, second- and third-level desktop support
- Subcontractor liaison
- Systems migration/ integration

Education and Training

Bachelor of Social Science, *Emphasis: Informatics, Computer Research Tools.* Hebrew University of Jerusalem.
MCSE 2010

JUSTIN WILSON

510.653.7542
jwilson@gmail.com

45 N. Winding River Rd.
Oakland, CA 94605

**Microsoft Certified Professional (MCP) / Master Certified Novell Engineer (MCNE)
Cisco Certified Network Associate (CCNA) / A+ Certification**

QUALIFICATIONS SUMMARY

➤ Results-oriented technology engineer with more than 18 years of experience in electronics, computer technologies, and digital commerce.

➤ Extensive customer service background worldwide.

➤ Expertise in multiple protocols and platforms.

➤ Extensive training and experience using Novell NetWare.

➤ Excellent team development, management, and leadership skills.

➤ Multicultural and multilingual. Fluent in German, French, and Italian.

PROFESSIONAL EXPERIENCE

TECHNO-SUPPORT USA, La Jolla, CA   2007 to Present

The largest independent provider of technology support for the digital world.

Senior National Technical Support Engineer

Oversee the development and execution of customized solutions to help established businesses adapt their IT infrastructures to the changing requirements of the rapidly evolving digital marketplace. Assist major providers of broadband, DSL, cable, and wireless technologies meet demands for deployment and support. Manage a team of 92 technicians in a 24/7 operation.

- Manage Sabre travel information support for Novell server-based and Windows peer-to-peer-based networks, including modem and frame relay connectivity.

- Provide direct second-level support for Novell, Inc., under contract. Resolve all aspects of client and server issues dealing with design and repair of directory services (for example, 700 servers for the State of California).

- Managed a series of service and quality improvement projects to enhance the customer experience and create loyalty.

- Conduct monthly classroom instruction in Novell Certification courses.

MEMOREX TELEX, Fresno, CA   2000 to 2007

Product Test Supervisor (2002 to 2007)

Oversaw testing of more than 12 state-of-the-art technology product lines and 30+ technicians.

- Developed and created test plans, organized test resources and schedules, managed execution, and oversaw quality control procedures and processes.

- Interfaced with project leads and engineers to define test requirements and develop a database for streamlining processes.

- Interfaced with customers, engineers, technicians, and senior executives to resolve problems and improve productivity, efficiency, and quality.

Continued

The strong technical credentials leading off this resume are sure to catch the attention of employers. Its inviting appearance and well-written text encourage them to read further.

JUSTIN WILSON   jwilson@gmail.com   Page 2

MEMOREX TELEX (Continued)

Electronics Technician (2000 to 2002)

Instrumental member of an elite electronics team designing and troubleshooting electronic circuits for technologically advanced systems for a series of new product releases.

- Drew schematic circuit diagrams using PC software, designed and built mechanical enclosures, produced drawings for outsourcing, and prepared layout of circuits using PCB layout software.
- Oversaw assembly of fine-pitch surface-mount components and ball-grid arrays on printed circuit boards used in oscilloscopes, digital multimeter, soldering iron, microscope, and vacuum-operated desoldering equipment.

TELETECH/AMERICA ONLINE, Stockton, CA   1996 to 2000

Technical Lead

Supervised a group of 32 technicians in providing customer service and technical support to incoming callers.

- Assisted users worldwide in a diverse range of technical support issues.

BURTEK INC., Sacramento, CA   1993 to 1996

Senior Field Service Engineer

Supervised in-house and on-site assembly, test, and customer acceptance of flight simulation-training devices to British Air, PSA, TWA, and Eastern Airlines.

- Provided close customer contact to resolve product performance issues in a timely fashion.

U.S. NAVY   1990 to 1993

Electronics Technician

Served as communications liaison in NATO fleet exercises. Supervised work of radar and communications technical group at NAS Whiting Field. Top security clearance. Recipient of numerous awards, medals, and commendations.

EDUCATION

BBA, Computer and Information Science, University of CA, 2003
AAS, Industrial Engineering, Tulsa Community College, OK, 1993
AAS, Computer Science, Tulsa Community College, OK, 1990
Graduate, U.S. Naval Electronics School, Great Lakes, IL

Completed 48 technical training, application, systems, and technology courses and seminars. Amplified training addendum available upon request.

PROFESSIONAL AFFILIATIONS

NPA (Network Professionals Association)

NUI (Novell Users International)

SARAH LANCER

155 Crystal Road, Hilltop, NY 11787 • (631) 222-0102 • lancer523@earthlink.net

---

Manager of LAN administration with MCSC, MCITP, and NCE certifications seeking continuous challenge with a progressive organization. Core strengths encompass

— LAN Administration	— Technical Writing	— Expense Control
— Project Management	— Business/Technical Solutions	— Procurement
— System Conversions	— Planning & Development	— Inventory Control
— Help Desk Support	— Team Leadership	— Vendor Relations

PROFESSIONAL EXPERIENCE

MILLER-STENSON FINANCIAL ADVISORS, Miller Place, New York   2005–present
Manager, LAN Administration   2010–present
LAN Administrator   2005–2010

Project Management

- Report directly to the Vice President of Information Services; charged with overseeing the technical support needs of 200 corporate users and 40 users throughout 7 remote branch locations.
- Manage the performance of LAN-based hardware and software, as it relates to multiple versions of Novell and Windows Servers, to support the management of critical financial data.
- Provide technical expertise and support for multiple Microsoft products encompassing Office 2007 and 2010 and various hardware, inclusive of printers, scanners, and mobile devices.
- Directed the complexities of a corporate human resources system conversion involving the purchase, installation, configuration, and migration of confidential information to a Novell server.
- Guided several mass deployments of corporate-based systems through implementation of Novell's ZENworks and provided postinstallation support with client connectivity issues.
- Collaborate with Sprint concerning service issues, user access privileges, and firewall protection for the corporate website. Monitor the integrity of online ethics.
- Remain on call to expeditiously diagnose and troubleshoot a broad scope of technical problems.
- Serve a key role in the execution of disaster recovery plans 24 hours a day, 7 days a week.

Office Administration

- Requisition the purchase of hardware and software. Monitor data and company-wide user activity reports to track equipment and the use of licensed software.
- Participate in audits to ensure LAN activities are fully compliant with regulatory procedures.
- Develop technical manuals and documentation for technical teams and company-wide personnel.
- Prepare biweekly status reports for management review.

— continued —

This resume uses bulleted lists to present diverse experience and accomplishments. It is extremely readable in 12-point Times New Roman font.

SARAH LANCER, lancer523@earthlink.net

— Page 2 —

OLYMPIA UNIVERSAL, Lake Calverton, New York   April–December 2004
Technical Support Engineer
- As part of a team of Technical Support Engineers, provided postinstallation systems support to 6,000 field service engineers, salespeople, and customers for approximately 1,000 networks servicing nationally based medical professionals.
- Diagnosed and supported an extensive product line of video imaging equipment, printers, and voice recognition software utilized during medical procedures.
- Prepared tradeshow exhibit materials, developed technical documentation, and planned LAN designs.
- Compiled field data, maintained activity logs, and prepared monthly reports for management review.

GLOBAL AVIATORS, INC., Unionville, New York   1999–2004
Network Administrator
- Traveled internationally to collaborate with management on the planning of technical breakthroughs.
- Supported diversified network requirements for multiple corporate locations, established data communications capabilities, and implemented data backup procedures.
- Guided the analysis, testing, implementation, and conversion of multiple entities to an A/P and G/L system to facilitate the preparation of budget forecasts, financial statements, and monthly reports.

COMPUTER / NETWORKING SKILLS

Operating Systems: Windows Server; Novell NetWare
Hardware: Extensive hardware and peripheral installation and maintenance
Software: Installation and troubleshooting of various Microsoft applications
Protocols: TCP/IP, IPX/SPX
Cabling: Ethernet 10/100Base-T

EDUCATION AND PROFESSIONAL CERTIFICATION

COMPUTER TRAINING SOLUTIONS, Miller Place, New York
Microsoft Certified Systems Engineer (MCSE), 2010

NAUTICAL HEIGHTS COMMUNITY COLLEGE, Miller Place, New York
A.A.S., Computer Information Systems, 2004

Microsoft Certified Information Technology Professional (MCITP), 2009

Novell Certified Engineer (NCE), 2006

Robert Patel

2456 Rodeo Place | Hayward, CA 94541
C: 650.267.7554 | rpatel@gmail.com

IT SPECIALIST: ARCHITECT | ENGINEER

Enterprise Network Security • Identity Management • Directory & Provisioning

Focused, resourceful IT professional with 10 years of experience in design, development, implementation, testing, change management, and support with multinational companies, including Fortune 200 retail giant Fine Clothes. Hands-on leadership of software development life cycle and enterprise-wide architecture, configuration, infrastructure, and application builds.

Five years of identity management experience designing and implementing complex, sustainable IdM solutions. Outstanding leadership abilities, coordinating all phases of project life cycle while motivating and mentoring team members to deliver results on time and within budget. *Expertise in*

- ☑ IT Roadmap & Strategy Planning
- ☑ Corporate-Based Security Practices
- ☑ Robust Architecture Design
- ☑ Automated & Request-Based Provisioning
- ☑ Sarbanes-Oxley Compliance
- ☑ Custom Deliverables & Reports
- ☑ Benchmarking & Best Practices
- ☑ Customer & Staff Training

Experience | Accomplishments

FINE CLOTHES, INC., San Jose, CA   2000–Present

From original Technical Consultant role, recruited to full-time position as Lead Software Development Engineer based on leadership and technical expertise. Further challenged in 2006 to lay foundation for identity management function as Subject Matter Expert for LDAP and Access Management.

Lead Security Administrator (2006–Present)

Train and mentor team of junior security engineers and operations staff on LDAP processes and tools. Instrumental in access management team's project planning: forecasting, resource allocation, and budgeting. Led implementation of LDAP authentication for UNIX clients as part of PCI compliance initiative.

- **Create** scalable, reliable, and sustainable enterprise-wide IdM solutions and framework.
- **Developed** strategic plan to enable provisioning using request- and role-based access.
- **Designed** custom audit reports to implement compensating controls for quarterly SOX compliance efforts.

Lead Software Development Engineer (2001–2006)
Active Directory & Exchange 2000 Consultant (2000–2001)

Application integration projects to enable Web applications with Shared Storage Option (SSO):

- **Key role** as data architect for the team responsible for data flows, data consistency, and integration for account provisioning purposes.
- **Integrated** PeopleSoft Directory Interface (PDI) with EDS to improve the identity creation SLA in key systems and streamline the on-boarding, modification, and termination processes.
- **Implemented** modular automated provision metadirectory, sourcing information from HRMS system to AD, EDS, and Global Financial system using ITDI managing 150,000+ accounts.
- **Performed** automated TAM-enabling user entries in EDS; load-balanced mailbox creation of user accounts in AD.
- **Developed,** analyzed, and implemented IT security functional requirements and coded auditing and reporting features for SOX compliance.

IT security and architecture projects to enable Web applications with SSO:

- **Developed** integration architecture that set the foundation for enterprise-wide Identity Management (IdM) system, providing solutions to save administrative costs, enhance security, and improve service levels during organizational change and enterprise application implementations.
- **Performed** IdM solutions reviews and analyses of workflows and approval processes.
- **Participated** in IDS strategy for IdM road path, conducted POC and tool evaluation, selected technologies and tools, implemented related projects as technical lead according to company methodologies, SOX, and SDLC.

Continued

Packed full of details and accomplishments, this resume is tightly written in "bites" of material that can be quickly absorbed. Readability is further enhanced by the bold type that leads off each bullet point.

Robert Patel   C: 650.267.7554 | rpatel@gmail.com

Sun ONE Directory Server implementation for point-of-sale registers and key enterprise applications:

- **Implemented** ACIs to restrict and control access to environment, ensuring data is protected.
- **Installed** load-balanced, fault-tolerant, and highly available iDAR servers to control application connections.
- **Developed** and communicated best practices and security design patterns for use across projects.
- **Supported** and troubleshot systems to optimize performance and reliability.
- **Coached** teams to perform production support tasks postdeployment and provide support documentation.

IT SOLUTIONS, INC., Edison, NJ   2000

Systems Engineer

- **Conducted** Active Directory POC and designed Windows 2000 infrastructure for school district.
- **Performed** a Windows 2000 Professional workstation POC with OS deployment for installing 500+ desktops over a network.

MICROSOFT CONSULTING SERVICES, Bangalore, India   1999–2000

Consultant

- **Designed** a highly secure, highly available, fault-tolerant PKI-based messaging system for a banking research organization. Won the job against stiff competition by providing a data transfer solution that worked over the system's very limited bandwidth.
- **Implemented** self-service account management system for ISP customers.
- **Conducted** Windows 2000 and Active Directory on-site training classes for key clients.

MAHINDRA CONSULTING SERVICES, Mumbai, India   1997–1999

Systems Engineer

- **Projects** included implementing a Windows multidomain model with PDC and multiple BDCs, implementing Exchange 5.5 for 5,000 user mailboxes, and deploying software remotely to 2,500 desktops using a centralized administration model.

Professional Profile

Education: **B.S. in Electronics Engineering,** University of Bombay, 1997

Certification: Microsoft Certified Systems Engineer
                     Certified Project Manager, Santa Clara University

Fluency: English, Hindi

Technology Profile

- **Web Technologies:** J2SE, JSP, JDBC, JavaScript, VBScript, XML, HTML, ASP
- **Web Servers:** IBM WebSphere, Resin, Tomcat, Apache, IIS
- **Languages:** Java, Visual Basic
- **PKI:** MS Certificate Server, MS Exchange Key Management System
- **Platforms:** Windows XP/7, Solaris, AIX, Linux
- **Development Tools:** Eclipse, IntelliJ, Visual Studio, IBM WebSphere Studio App Developer
- **Methodologies:** Extreme Programming, Software Engineering, System Analysis and Design Management
- **Applications/Products:** Microsoft—Active Directory, Exchange, MIIS; IBM—Tivoli Directory Integrator, Tivoli Access Manager; SUN—Directory Server, Identity Manager
- **Version Control:** CVS, Dimensions, Visual SourceSafe

RICHARD OLIVER

49 Gregory Way ◆ Easton, PA 18045
215-494-8711 ◆ roliver@gmail.com

NETWORK/SYSTEMS ADMINISTRATOR

Envisioning and implementing technology solutions to meet user needs

Forward-thinking IT professional with broad-based knowledge of network and systems administration. Proven record of success in developing and implementing strategic plans to improve corporate computing environments. Effective at assessing business needs and recommending appropriate technology solutions. Resourceful, take-charge leader recognized for ability to step into any situation and get results. Valued as versatile team player who is quick to pick up new concepts and who thrives on challenge.

TECHNOLOGY SKILLS

Software:	Microsoft Expression Web, Excel, GroupWise, IBM AIX, Microsoft Forefront Threat Management Gateway, Code Master, TPS, Batch Job Server, ARCserve, VMS, MEDITECH, HP Web Jetadmin, Extend Systems, Goldkey
Hardware:	Windows and Novell servers, bridges, routers, LANs, WANs, 3Com hubs, HP and Dell computers, HP Jetdirect, Bay network routers
Operating Systems:	Windows XP/7, Linux

RELATED PROFESSIONAL EXPERIENCE

Network Administrator
PPL, Allentown, PA, 2004 to present

Managed network operations during period of frequent organizational change. Drove network upgrades/modifications to meet constantly changing needs.

Implementing $300,000 network administration budget, capably oversee company networks and servers, providing reliable computing environment that meets the needs of 200 users in 9 locations.

Technology Expertise

- Led complex network integration project, separating networks of 2 sister companies and realigning them with new organizational structures. Developed and executed plans for new network on schedule and within established budget.
- As part of merger activities, set up environment for and integrated customer applications across 4 sites in the United States and Canada.
- Envisioned and designed new computer room, developing plan to accommodate future expansion. Relocated computers to new room, implementing plan that achieved full operability over a single weekend.
- Initiated migration of servers from Novell to Windows soon after hire. Established firewalls and enabled file sharing for first time, enhancing security while providing opportunity for improved efficiency.

Cost Cutting and Other Improvement Initiatives

- Consolidated WAN services, negotiating volume discounts that saved $121,000 per year.
- Initiated RFP that identified alternative vendor for contracted network services, a change that saved $30,000 over 2 years. Negotiated new contract for telephone services that saved as much as $12,000 per year.
- Saved $45,000 in new website development costs by gaining rights to capture and modify existing website of parent company. Adapted site to allow user updates, reducing load on technical resources.
- Developed utility to capture exchange rate for international sales that improved accuracy of transactions.

Continued

To call attention to the top achievement of each position, a bold statement leads off each position description. This strategy creates a distinctive resume and ensures that key accomplishments will not be overlooked.

Richard Oliver   roliver@gmail.com   Page 2

Systems and Network Analyst
SWS Consulting, Bethlehem, PA, 2000 to 2004

Provided outstanding systems and network support to small and midsized businesses. Drove internal changes that improved overall operations and service to clients.

Oversaw computer installations and upgrades for clients. Configured software. Maintained servers and networks.

- Effectively assessed client needs and recommended appropriate hardware and software solutions, building strong relationships based on trust. Leveraged relationships to promote new sales.
- Developed well-received recommendations to improve business and reduce service calls. For example, suggested incorporation of surge protectors in all computer systems sold. Persuaded management of benefits and cost-effectiveness of selling name-brand parts that come with manufacturer warranties.

Help Desk Systems Analyst
Lehigh Valley Hospital, Allentown, PA, 1999–2000

Spearheaded Y2K effort. Mobilized team to assess needs and implement Y2K-compliant solutions.

Led team that supported more than 360 users within main hospital and across several satellite locations.

- Built record of success in keeping servers up and running. Initiated computer inventory system that ensured stock items were at hand to minimize downtime.
- Charged with ensuring Y2K compliance, justified addition of 2 temporary workers to implement necessary upgrades. As part of effort, oversaw large-scale installation of Windows 2000.

Network and Technical Systems Manager
Keystone Medical Group, Philadelphia, PA, 1994 to 1999

Dramatically improved systems while supporting 230 users.

Managed WAN with 13 Novell servers across 5 campuses. Led systems quality improvement team.

- Implemented network enhancements that improved uptime from 83% to 99.8%.
- Revamped disaster-recovery plan and upgraded networks. Rewired entire building using fiber-optic technology, introducing redundancies to ensure continued operation in face of emergency.
- Researched and implemented new technologies, including videoconferencing system, to meet user needs.

EDUCATION

Electronics Certificate, Keystone Technical Institute

JOHN D. JOSEPH

150 Elm Street
Hartford, CT 06107

john.joseph27@yahoo.com

Residence: 860.249.3409
Mobile: 860.505.2301

PROFESSIONAL SUMMARY

*Development, standardization, upgrade, and deployment of enterprise-class IT systems and processes—
UNIX-based, WAN, LAN, and client-server environments.*

IT project manager, team leader, and individual contributor with 13+ years of experience supporting a multibillion-dollar company's growth and expansion. Consistently tapped to manage complex, cross-functional technology initiatives and turn around projects. Tenacious problem solver known for "making things happen" at lower costs within strict time constraints. Skilled relationship builder able to achieve project buy-in from stakeholders. **Combine bottom-line business orientation with technical expertise.** Skills:

- IT Operations & Process Management
- E-business Content Management
- ERP System Implementation (SAP)
- Enterprise-Wide IT Desktop Support
- Budget Development

- Architecture-Standards Development
- Data Conversion
- CRM (Customer Relationship Management)
- Systems Integration & Implementation
- Data Warehouse/Reporting Management

PROFESSIONAL EXPERIENCE

SELECT LIGHTING INC., Hartford, CT   1999–Present
Third-largest lighting manufacturer in the world with $3.7 billion in North American annual sales.

E-business Manager / Data Warehouse Manager (2003–Present)

Direct corporate-enhancement projects to increase functionality of IT operations for 5 major North American divisions. Manage the data warehouse department and projects in support of enterprise business systems and intranet/extranet initiatives. Oversee application development for R&D. Direct 7 technical staff.

CHALLENGE: *SAP reporting/data warehouse upgrade.* Solve serious reliability, reporting, and cost problems. Manage a 2-terabyte, UNIX-based data warehouse including multiple Windows Server–based data marts to optimize reporting for North American operations at 19 sales offices, 3 distribution centers, 17 manufacturing plants, and 1 customer service center.

Actions: Enhanced data warehouse architecture. Designed and implemented a data warehouse application-development methodology. Formalized processes, procedures, and standards for establishing and operating reporting subsystems. Automated report delivery.

Results: Delivered a scalable, efficient warehouse reporting system. Decreased emergency-event frequency from daily failures to once in 3 months. Slashed costs, reduced errors, and increased reliability. Reduced report-development cycle time by 50%. Dramatically grew reporting capability while reducing staffing requirements by 66%. Provided cost-efficient capability for adding new reporting modules.

CHALLENGE: *Document management.* Collect and consolidate information stored in various formats in multiple locations. Meet consumer requirements for a single online source for lighting information. Render operable the extranet's online product catalog.

Actions: Implemented a Web-based corporate-document-management system and product catalog in 3 weeks. Collaborated with a business-side colleague to consolidate data and integrate it into Web systems. Provided intensive technical input into software installation, integration, and testing. Identified need for an alternate storage system, then purchased and adapted a solution using FileNET. Achieved buy-in from 3 contributing divisions. Coordinated upload to the extranet of thousands of pages in standardized format.

Continued

This resume uses a Challenge-Action-Results format to provide significant and relevant detail about major technology projects in a highly readable format.

JOHN D. JOSEPH — PAGE 2

john.joseph27@yahoo.com — 860.505.2301

Results: Automated document management. Played key role in producing a 6-fold increase in Web orders from 5% of North American sales to 30%. Delivered a more-efficient approval process for making document changes, thus ensuring conformity to brand identity. Provided e-commerce product-catalog functionality.

SAP Data Conversion Manager (2002–2003)

Managed the SAP data conversion effort for a division with $1.4 billion in annual sales. Directed team of 10 programmers to convert master data from mainframe legacy systems to a SAP client-server environment.

CHALLENGE: *Conversion to ERP system.* Restore integrity of a mission-critical project that was in disarray and behind schedule. Solve communication problems between business side and IT.

Actions: Closed communication gap, bringing all stakeholders on board with plans. Worked with programmers to extract data from the mainframe, reformat it, and upload it into SAP. Scheduled and implemented tests to establish benchmarks and correct sequencing in preparation for going live.

Results: Successfully converted to a client-server, UNIX-based SAP system within the 3-month deadline. Seamlessly transitioned to SAP over a weekend with full functionality delivered by Monday.

Technical Services Manager (1999–2002)

Managed IT desktop support and operations at headquarters, customer service center, 19 sales offices, and 3 distribution centers. Managed 10 direct reports. Hardware asset management accountability for 600+ PCs.

CHALLENGE: *Hardware asset management.* Correct inefficiencies and inaccuracies.

Actions: Established an automated materials-management system to track inventory and purchasing. Converted from a disorganized system with hundreds of personal printers to network printing.

Results: Delivered $200,000 in cost savings over a 3-year period. Enabled more-accurate planning for hardware obsolescence. Supported improved management decision making and budgeting.

EDUCATION, PROFESSIONAL DEVELOPMENT & SKILLS

UNIVERSITY OF MASSACHUSETTS, Amherst, MA: **Bachelor of Science,** Computer Science

Recent Technical Training—Maintain leading-edge skills in **both technology and management:**
Software/Hardware/Systems: Linux Systems, Server-Side Web Programming in PHP, JavaScript, Visual Basic, Statistics, Apache Server, MySQL
SAP Training: Logistics Information Systems Reporting, Business Information Warehouse Analysis, Business Information Systems
Architecture: Data Warehouse Architecture, Client-Server Architecture

Management Skills Coursework (selected): Process Management, Team-Oriented Problem Solving, Finance, Time and Priority Management, Supervisory Management, Total Quality Management

Technology Skills:
UNIX, Linux, Windows XP/7, Oracle, MS SQL
SAP R/3, FileNET Document Management
ASP.NET, VB.NET, JavaScript, PHP, MySQL, Visual Basic
Microsoft Project, Office, Access, Visio; IBM Cognos PowerPlay and Impromptu

This resume fits the first few lines of important professional experience on page 1, while giving most of the space to technical and professional qualifications.

PETER BROWN, CCIE

234 Hawking Blvd.
Oakville, Ontario L6L 4T2

Phone: 905.342.2525
Email: pete.brown@luringo.ca

Lead the Organization into Tomorrow

SENIOR DESIGN ENGINEER ▪ TECHNICAL ARCHITECT

Detail- and task-oriented professional with an exemplary background in conceiving and developing unique initiatives to propel technology to the limit and optimize performance. **Capable of tackling the most challenging networks and delivering results.** Creative and visionary, recognised for keeping on the leading edge of technology and utilizing the latest applications and hardware. Results- and performance-driven; thrive in an environment of constant challenge and diversity. Articulate; break down the technology barrier and act as the conduit between customer and technical experts. Industrious; exude energy and confidence; motivate and mentor team members to succeed and deliver quality work within strict specifications, timelines, and budgets. Core competencies include:

▪ Project Management	▪ Routers & Switches
▪ Routing Protocols	▪ Internetworking, TCP/IP Services
▪ Cost-Benefit Analysis	▪ Presales Technical Support
▪ Enterprise Architecture Development	▪ Systems Documentation

TECHNICAL ENVIRONMENTS

Operating Systems	MS Windows XP, 7; Windows Server; Novell; OS2
Cisco Routers & Switches	All models and series
Routing Protocols	RIP, IGRP, EIGRP, OSPF, IPX EIGRP, IPX RIP, BGP IS-IS, ISR
Routed/Bridged Protocols	IP, IPX, NetBIOS, SNA
Telco	ISDN, Frame Relay, X25, ATM, T1, Dark Fiber, ASDL
Other Tools	Sniffer Pro, Network General Sniffer, NetView (SNMP), DNS, HTTP

PROFESSIONAL EXPERIENCE

Roma Telecommunications, Inc., Toronto, Ontario   2007–present
SENIOR DESIGN ENGINEERING SPECIALIST, Level II   2008–present
SENIOR DESIGN ENGINEERING SPECIALIST, Level I   2007–2008

- Played key leadership role in conceiving and delivering a national Multi-Protocol Laboratory Switching (MPLS) network for a high-value contract with numerous Government of Ontario ministries secured by Roma, despite fierce competition from Bell Canada. *Initiative now providing a very high SLA for the Government of Ontario.* Process included:
  - Developing the complex system, detailing equipment needed to create the customized and aggregated services, and devising the proof of concept to be accepted by client.
  - Working with the program manager to define the business case to capture $9 million in funding to complete the prestigious project, considered one of the top 5 projects in Roma.
  - Ordering and monitoring delivery of numerous Cisco switches and routers.
  - Leading team in prestaging and configuring equipment before shipping to dispersed offices.
  - Working with space/power/racking group to ensure the power support was adequate.
  - Partnering with transport team to optimize the long-haul connectivity over SONET.
  - Scrutinizing documentation with Last Ride Access designers to establish the processes for commodity devices.

Continued

Attractive and easy-to-skim tables are used to present keywords, technical skills, and extensive training.

PETER BROWN, CCIE   PETE.BROWN@LURINGO.CA   PAGE TWO

Roma Telecommunications, continued

- Directing the knowledge handoff to local Tier I and II designers and acting as the main troubleshooter and providing support to all Tier III network professionals.
- Interacting with vendor to iron out bugs.
- Acted as lead engineer during complex process of moving an MPLS project for the FTM Bank from presales to postsales. Worked with custom solution group to validate functionality of services delivered to FTM Bank. Designed and delivered final product and was dispatched to local design engineers to implement the product on the Roma network, allowing a complete end-to-end solution. *Project recognized as the highest-level initiative undertaken by Roma.*
- Provided design engineering and custom solutions for clients, interacting with cross-functional personnel to complete diverse projects according to mandates.
- Reported to the manager of national service fulfillment; consistently appraised by manager with the highest ratings and given financial remuneration for work.
- Recipient of the 2008 "President's Award" for being the *Leader of Tomorrow.*

Rienwald Services Incorporated, Mississauga, Ontario   2006–2007
SENIOR TECHNICAL ANALYST
- Played a key technical advisory role during the office and systems move from Montreal, Quebec, to Mississauga, Ontario; designed new systems environment work flow and completed transfer without business interruption.
- Moved the Rienwald Data Centre from a layer II network building to a layer III solution, enabling Rienwald to stabilize network operations and allow for expansion.

Systems Intel Services, Toronto, Ontario   2005–2006
TECHNICAL LEAD
- Contracted by Toronto Catholic District School Board to install and roll out the Windows XP network across 50 schools. Project recognized by Microsoft Canada as one of the first dozen production networks in Canada.
- Developed and implemented new desktop software system for the TCDSB.

EDUCATION

Ryerson Polytechnic University, Toronto, Ontario   2000
BACHELOR OF BUSINESS MANAGEMENT—Accounting

CISCO CERTIFIED INTERNETWORKING EXPERT (CCIE #21234)

Strong proponent of continually updating skills and staying on the leading edge. Attended numerous courses, workshops, and seminars, including:

Cisco Secure Pix Firewall Advanced (CSPFA)	Cisco Secure Virtual Private Network (CSVPN)
Implementing Cisco MPLS (MPLS)	Advanced Cisco Router Configuration
NetGun Masters	Expert CCIE Prep
Cisco Internetworking Troubleshooting	Designing Cisco Networks
Designing Windows XP Networking Services	C-Level Systems Integration
Configuration Management for Windows 7	Windows 7 Support

EDWARD NGUYEN, P.E., Ch.Eng.

2498 Dolores Street, Unit 7B
San Francisco, CA 92108

enguyen@mac.com

Mobile: 413-229-1219
Home: 413-781-6554

PROFESSIONAL ENGINEER / ENGINEERING MANAGER / PROJECT DIRECTOR

Active (Q) Top Secret security clearance. Bilingual English/Vietnamese; speaking fluency in French.

Technical Competencies:	Computer Simulation, Technology & Systems Integration, Solutions Engineering
Design & Development:	R&D, Technical Ideation, Human Factors, Human Systems Engineering, Project Management
Business Management:	Process Design & Optimization, Best Practices, Budgeting, Cost Management
Talent Management:	Team Building & Leadership, Collaborative Brainstorming, Mentoring, Technical Recruitment
Global Business:	Cross-Cultural Relations, Multinational Project Leadership, International Client Relations

Twenty-year career leading high-impact design and engineering projects, programs, solutions, and organizations for customers and markets worldwide. Consistently successful in delivering new products and systems that solve complex challenges, capture new opportunities, and exceed customer expectations. Expert in communicating complex technical information to business executives and integrating seemingly disparate data into a logical whole to drive the right business decisions. Creative with a strong portfolio of research, reporting, and regulatory skills.

PROFESSIONAL EXPERIENCE

PRO-SCI CORPORATION, Oakland, CA
(Government contractor with $1 billion in annual revenues)

Assistant Vice President / Principal Engineer (2009 to Present)
Assistant Vice President / Manager – Naval Engineering Division (2006 to 2009)
Director – Naval Engineering Division (1990 to 2006)

High-profile career leading the planning, design, engineering, and delivery of multimillion-dollar, multiyear, technologically sophisticated projects for clients in commercial, government, and military markets throughout North America, Europe, and Asia. Successfully managed projects, led teams, and maintained key customer relationships through periods of significant organizational change and transition. Directed project teams of up to 20 design and engineering professionals.

Recognized as one of the company's leading engineering experts, driving forward new creative ideas, design projects, and other initiatives to develop new client offerings, enhance global market reach, and drive long-term profitability. Personally manage complex customer relationships, negotiations, and briefings.

Technology Projects, Solutions, and Innovations

- Spearheaded design of sophisticated computer tool roadmap to provide U.S. Navy with a precise blueprint for integrated, practical, and cost-effective computer-aided design of all technical systems for next-generation vessels. Project eliminated longstanding issues impeding systems performance and will save billions of dollars in future costs.

- Won executive approval and managed internal R&D project to enhance current computer analysis tool, strengthen company's technical stature, and increase long-term sales and profits.

- Invented novel cost-estimating software that reduced company's financial and design risk exposure.

Industry & Business Leadership

- Appointed to prestigious NATO Industrial Advisory Group 50 to provide technical leadership for environmentally friendly 21st-century defense installations.

- Improved U.S. understanding of European and Asian advances in automated design and production systems by participating in industry-university team exploring promising new technologies.

- Passed all internal and external ISO 9000-2001 quality audits for multiple consecutive years.

Continued

A strong technical summary anchors the top of this resume while the extensive accomplishments of the most recent position are broken up by headings that showcase different areas of expertise.

EDWARD NGUYEN, P.E., Ch.Eng.   Page 2
enguyen@mac.com ... Mobile: 413-229-1219

Global Sales, Marketing & Business Development

- Strengthened global market visibility and credibility of corporate technology profile by authoring and presenting 30+ papers on design, engineering, computer tools and simulation, and more.
- Represented the products, services, and solutions of French software company seeking entry into the U.S. market. Evaluated market potential, demonstrated demand, developed relationships with key customer accounts, and provided critical cross-cultural business guidance to company executives.

ENGINEERING CONCEPTS, INC., San Francisco, CA

Cofounder & CEO (1986 to 1990)

Launched advanced systems design and engineering company. Recruited technical and professional staff, wrote business and marketing plans, handled key account presentations, negotiated contracts, and closed sales. Managed technical projects as well as general business and administrative affairs for the company.

- Closed several projects within first few weeks by leveraging business relationships and strong reputation for technical and engineering expertise.
- Won 2 Small Business Innovation Research (SBIR) contracts to research, evaluate, and recommend new designs with improved materials to enhance operational performance of client products and systems.
- Edited technically complex systems manual to enhance operator effectiveness and safety.

Previous Experience: Stanford University Applied Engineering Lab

- Planned, staffed, and directed design, development, and technical/engineering support projects for DoD, DoT, NOAA, U.S. Armed Forces, and international governments and utilities.
- Led presentations and negotiated and closed multiyear, multimillion-dollar contract with the U.S. Army.
- Redesigned critical management and reporting processes to enhance control of a renewable energy R&D program jointly funded for hundreds of millions of dollars by government and industry.

EDUCATION & PROFESSIONAL CERTIFICATIONS

M.S., Engineering, Stanford University, Stanford, CA
B.S., Mechanical Engineering (Minor in Business), Northeastern University, Boston, MA
Graduate, Naval Officer Candidate School (Commissioned U.S. Navy Officer, Engineering Duty)
Professional Engineer, Massachusetts and California; **Chartered Engineer,** United Kingdom

PROFESSIONAL PUBLICATIONS & PRESENTATIONS

- "The Creative Spark for R&D," TECH-PRO national conference, 2009
- "Leading Technical Teams," IT Executives Forum, 2008
- 34 engineering/technology articles published and presented worldwide

CHAPTER **8**

Resumes for Web, Internet, E-commerce, and Game-Design Professionals

- Video Game Designers
- Web Designers
- Web Graphic Artists
- Web Applications Managers
- Webmasters
- Internet Sales and Marketing Professionals
- E-commerce/Internet Executives

Paula Heaton
VIDEO GAME ARTIST

"I work to evoke emotion and I strive for perfection, but I also know that it takes more than artistic vision to make a great game. I'm very dedicated and I do whatever it takes to get the job done."

professional profile

Creative artist with a recognized talent for conveying personalities, emotions, weight, and motion. Collaborate well with others to generate and execute ideas within tight deadlines. Earned a reputation for dedication, humor, intelligence, and going "above and beyond" to help teammates.

technical skills

Software... 3DS Max, Character Studio, Unreal Editor, Illustrator, Photoshop, InDesign, Dreamweaver, Flash, QuarkXPress, Premier.

Graphics... Low- and high-polygon 3D modeling, texture maps, lighting, camera work, character design, modeling, rigging, animation, concept art, and storyboards.

professional experience

BIG STYLE STUDIOS   2008–2011
ARTIST

Created concept art, sprite animations, and textures for newly formed game developer. Reported to the company's founder and developed cityscape concepts, gadgets, weapons, characters, monsters, and objects for a Wii role-playing game (RPG).

- Created animation sequences for game's lead character within multidirectional control scheme. Produced sprites, created a running sequence in all eight directions, and converted the art into files for programmers to code.
- Transformed company's website to incorporate Flash animation and a more appealing interface. Designed and programmed a cinematic entrance, created custom soundtrack, and highlighted company's development philosophy through stimulating artwork.
- Volunteered to take on additional texturing work under extremely tight deadlines, helping the team members meet their commitments for work on fantasy RPG.

education

Certificate in Multimedia Technology, Ohio Media Institute, Cleveland, OH   2007
Courses: Digital/Audio Video Production, Digital Imagery, Computer Animation, Multimedia Production

- Earned a 4.0 GPA.
- Created a three-minute 3D film within seven weeks. Storyboarded entire film and designed all camera work. Hand-animated biped's actions and applied them using 3DS Max. Independently completed all models, textures, and animation for the four characters. The finished project is now shown to incoming classes to demonstrate what they can accomplish.

Ohio University, Athens, OH   2006
Completed coursework in Studio 2D, Drawing, Art History, and Watercolor Painting

affiliations

Active member, International Game Developers Association (IGDA), Chicago chapter

45 Mark Lane, Cleveland, OH 44101 / heaton@net.net / h: (216) 555-5555 / c: (216) 555-5555

The artist's own work is used to highlight and distinguish this creative resume; the quote beneath her name gives further insight into her unique qualities. Her part-time work for the last three years is the central focus of the resume and helps position her above other recent graduates.

BRENT D. BOATMAN

1836 Tameria Drive, Dallas, TX 75234 ♦ (214) 251-3415 ♦ bboatman@texas.net

GAME PROGRAMMER

C/C++	Open GL	Nintendo Wii
VisualBasic	3D Graphics	Sony PlayStation
Maya MEL	Windows API	Microsoft Xbox
Java	Console Development	iPhone Apps
Assembly	DirectX SDK	

PROFESSIONAL EXPERIENCE

2009–2011 **Koala Game Studio, Dallas, Texas**
Developer and publisher of entertainment software

Game Programmer

♦ Participated as a graphics programmer on a cross-functional development team that published a highly successful, leading-edge sports game for Nintendo Wii. Recognized for strong individual contribution and emerging technical leadership.

♦ Represented company on team partnered with Microsoft to successfully resolve software incompatibility issues inhibiting game development.

♦ Currently creating leading-edge graphics technology for next-generation platforms, including iPhone apps.

Manager's comments: "very hard worker" ... "goes above and beyond to meet schedule" ... "instrumental in creating Wii version of game" ... "very high-quality work."

2008–2009 **University of North Texas, Denton, Texas**
Computer Science Department

Student Intern

♦ Helped design and code an educational game under a research grant; incorporated graphics, sound, and network play into game.
♦ Assisted professor in innovative computer game development lab.

EDUCATION **University of North Texas, Denton, Texas**
Bachelor of Science, 2009
Major: Computer Science; Minor: Mathematics

Attended iPhone Apps Developers' Conference, 2010

This resume is distinguished by the box design that sets off key information—technical skills and manager's endorsements.

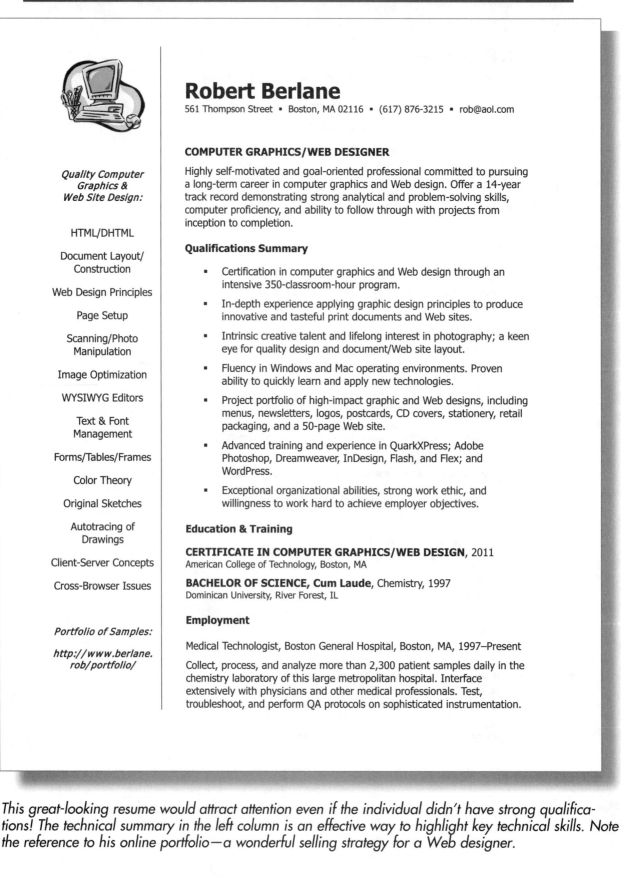

**Quality Computer
Graphics &
Web Site Design:**

HTML/DHTML

Document Layout/
Construction

Web Design Principles

Page Setup

Scanning/Photo
Manipulation

Image Optimization

WYSIWYG Editors

Text & Font
Management

Forms/Tables/Frames

Color Theory

Original Sketches

Autotracing of
Drawings

Client-Server Concepts

Cross-Browser Issues

Portfolio of Samples:

*http://www.berlane.
rob/portfolio/*

Robert Berlane

561 Thompson Street ▪ Boston, MA 02116 ▪ (617) 876-3215 ▪ rob@aol.com

COMPUTER GRAPHICS/WEB DESIGNER

Highly self-motivated and goal-oriented professional committed to pursuing a long-term career in computer graphics and Web design. Offer a 14-year track record demonstrating strong analytical and problem-solving skills, computer proficiency, and ability to follow through with projects from inception to completion.

Qualifications Summary

- Certification in computer graphics and Web design through an intensive 350-classroom-hour program.

- In-depth experience applying graphic design principles to produce innovative and tasteful print documents and Web sites.

- Intrinsic creative talent and lifelong interest in photography; a keen eye for quality design and document/Web site layout.

- Fluency in Windows and Mac operating environments. Proven ability to quickly learn and apply new technologies.

- Project portfolio of high-impact graphic and Web designs, including menus, newsletters, logos, postcards, CD covers, stationery, retail packaging, and a 50-page Web site.

- Advanced training and experience in QuarkXPress; Adobe Photoshop, Dreamweaver, InDesign, Flash, and Flex; and WordPress.

- Exceptional organizational abilities, strong work ethic, and willingness to work hard to achieve employer objectives.

Education & Training

CERTIFICATE IN COMPUTER GRAPHICS/WEB DESIGN, 2011
American College of Technology, Boston, MA

BACHELOR OF SCIENCE, Cum Laude, Chemistry, 1997
Dominican University, River Forest, IL

Employment

Medical Technologist, Boston General Hospital, Boston, MA, 1997–Present

Collect, process, and analyze more than 2,300 patient samples daily in the chemistry laboratory of this large metropolitan hospital. Interface extensively with physicians and other medical professionals. Test, troubleshoot, and perform QA protocols on sophisticated instrumentation.

This great-looking resume would attract attention even if the individual didn't have strong qualifications! The technical summary in the left column is an effective way to highlight key technical skills. Note the reference to his online portfolio—a wonderful selling strategy for a Web designer.

RESUME 62: BY JANICE WORTHINGTON, MA, CPRW, JCTC, CEIP

LYDIA
MOSBACH

lydiamosbach@mindspring.com

3596 Bogart Avenue
Columbus, Ohio 43240
(614) 766-9844

ENTRY–LEVEL WEB DESIGNER

Visionary, creative professional qualified by 5 years of academic and professional achievements in website production and project management. Combined expertise in graphic design and technical editing with exceptional ability to conceptualize and bring project to full fruition.

QUALIFICATION HIGHLIGHTS

- Cutting-edge technical knowledge of HTML, Flash, and Flex programming.
- Extensive graphic layout, design, production, and marketing experience.
- Demonstrated experience in promotion strategies.
- Proven record of effectively managing multiple tasks without compromising quality.
- Innovative, creative, and enthusiastic in approaching projects.
- Recognized for strong work ethic, integrity, and commitment to success.

EDUCATIONAL ACHIEVEMENTS

Master of Arts, December, 2010
University of Reading—Reading, England

Visiting Scholar, 2009
Summer Program in Archaeology, 2008
American Academy in Rome—Rome, Italy

Internationaler Ferienkurs, 2008
Universität Heidelberg—Heidelberg, Germany

Bachelor of Arts, Art, 2007
Mount Holyoke College, South Hadley, Massachusetts

SELECTED PROJECT HIGHLIGHTS

The Parthenet: Internet Resources for Students of Art History—Conceived in 2005 to assist students in online research. Contains numerous sources of information about art history. Award-winning site is highly used and is listed in academic Internet guides worldwide. (2008 to Present) www.mtholyoke.edu/parthenet.html

Digital site emulation at Kenchreai, the Eastern port of Corinth—Studied the applications of technology in the field and created a multimedia website. Manipulated plans into 3D-animated sequences of the site's building phases. (2007 to 2010)

Consultant to the Matrix Project at Yale University and Mount Holyoke College—Worked with team of medieval scholars to create an online database of medieval women's religious communities in Western Europe. (2006 to 2008)

The Travels of Mac and Cheese—Developed as a spoof on the deification of Kraft Macaroni and Cheese. Site involved a "reenactment" of a box of macaroni and cheese traveling around Europe and photographing the journey for the website. (2006 to 2007) www.mtholyoke.edu/mandcc/mandc.html

Page One of Two

This new graduate has a solid portfolio of interesting projects that are highlighted on the resume. Her strong academic credentials take center stage on page 1.

LYDIA MOSBACH

lydiamosbach@mindspring.com

Page Two of Two
(614) 766-9844

Matrix: Resources for the Study of Women's Religious Communities—Developed site's original design, graphics, layout, and database format for presentation at national conference. (2006 to 2007) matrix.bc.edu (Can be viewed in present form at Boston University.)

Hildegard and Clare Resource Center—Identified need and developed site concerning medieval religious women. The site provides resources and links for in-depth study of Hildegard of Bingen (Germany) and Clare of Markyate (England). (2006 to 2007) www.mtholyoke.edu/medieval/resource.html

Mount Holyoke College History Department—Commissioned by the History Department to develop its informational Web page, which is now maintained by the department secretary. (2006 to 2007) www.mtholyoke.edu/acad/hist

Minnie the Mini Cooper—Created original site narrating the travels and tribulations of Minnie the Mini Cooper; provided travelogue, insights, and links to Mini Cooper enthusiast sites. (2005 to 2006) lydiamosbach.mindspring.com/Minnie.html.

EXPERIENCE

Online Editor and Member—*The Journal of the Women's College Art Coalition* (2005 to 2007)
- Published online edition of *The Journal,* an undergraduate scholarly journal concerning women's issues in the fine arts. Designed and maintained websites.
- Generated publicity and outreach programs to 83 other women's colleges in the nation.

Development Office Intern—Mount Holyoke College (2004 to 2007)
- Orchestrated fundraising efforts for the Alumnae Fund of the College. Managed large-scale phone-a-thons; organized callers and donation recordkeeping.
- Developed incentive strategies and events to encourage and maintain caller morale.

Registrar's Office Intern—Columbus Museum of Art (Summer 2005)
- Catalogued prints and works on paper as part of a full museum inventory and installation of the permanent collection. Researched works to be deaccessioned.

TECHNICAL KNOWLEDGE

Proficient in many remote sensing, GPS, GIS, CAD, and geophysics applications.
Data processing, database development, and related archaeological field uses, both Mac and PC.
Networking, hardware/software maintenance, repair, and troubleshooting.

Graphics/Drafting/Authoring—Photoshop, InDesign, QuarkXPress, AutoCAD, WordPress

Equipment—Scanners, CD-RW, digitizers, plotters, slide scanners

Languages—HTML, DHTML, Java, Flash, Flex, C++

DAMIAN PETERS
Web Production

415-555-8001 | damianpeters@mac.com
3 Blaine Road, Mill Valley, CA 94941

Profile

➤ **Award-Winning Content Development:** Transformed underutilized website into a vibrant, highly regarded community with more than 270,000 members. Site was selected as a Webby Awards finalist for 3 consecutive years.

➤ **Phenomenal Revenue and Profit Growth:** Grew website's annual revenues 55% in 3 years by developing multiple new revenue streams. Increased profits 45% during the same period.

➤ **On Time, On Budget Project Completion:** Applied Six Sigma project management principles to deliver "over and above" expectations, even when working to seemingly impossible deadlines.

Philosophy

❝ *I believe in asking the important questions: Is there another way…? What if…? Why can't we…? There is always opportunity for improvement, and creative professionals respond exceptionally well when given the opportunity to challenge the status quo.* **❞**

Experience

GPA MEDIA LLC, San Francisco, CA   2005–Present
EXECUTIVE PRODUCER, MEDIABUZZ.COM

Promoted to position after former employer acquired GPA. Turned around unprofitable site by leveraging content from annual Media Buzz Conference and *Media Buzz* magazine while also generating marketing leads for both organizations. Built a site that is now recognized as the industry leader.

> *"Damian is single-handedly responsible for the transformation of mediabuzz.com."*
> Jean Raymond, CEO and president, GPA Media

Value Added: Led fundamental changes that increased revenues by 55% and turned the site from a loss to a 45% profit within 3 years.

- Added revenue-generating features such as paid job postings, searchable resume database, sponsored links, banner ads, affiliate partnerships, and sponsored seminars.

- Increased site membership by 280% to 273,000. Created systems to capture key demographic information so that the membership list could be used for targeted cross-promotion to the company's other properties.

- Leveraged existing content to create new revenue streams, such as a set of recorded conference sessions that generated a 50% profit margin in its first year.

- Named one of the "Top Media Influencers of 2008" by *Technology Now* magazine.

- Conceived and planned the implementation of premium membership for the site. For a monthly fee, members will be able to access additional multimedia content, such as video footage and audio.

- Built multimillion-dollar partnerships with leading film production companies and TV networks, including NBC, ABC, HBO, and Miramax, thereby enhancing content and increasing brand exposure.

Continued

A unique feature of this resume is the Philosophy section, which allows the job seeker to speak directly to the hiring authority. Glowing testimonials (taken from his performance evaluations) highlight an Experience section rich with results.

DAMIAN PETERS
Web Production   damianpeters@mac.com   **Page 2**

Experience (Cont.)

DAVIES SLATER, INC., San Francisco, CA   1998–2005
EDITORIAL DIRECTOR, MEDIABUZZ.COM (2004–2005)

Led editorial direction for the mediabuzz.com family of websites, managing 15 freelance writers and 3 editors and working closely with site designers and programmers.

> *"Damian just doesn't give in … he is relentless when he has a great idea."*
> Peter Shaw, former producer, mediabuzz.com

Value Added: Crafted new editorial strategy that drove 343% increase in website traffic and 59% revenue growth.

- Launched annual archive of back issues on CD-ROM, generating incremental revenues of more than $44,000 per year.

- Managed major redesign of mediabuzz.com. The site had previously been managed by external developers, making it expensive and time-consuming to change content. Brought development in-house to allow daily site updates.

- Built affiliate partnerships worth more than $5 million per year in free advertising.

- Implemented a weekly email newsletter automatically generated from existing site content and sent to 60,000 subscribers.

- Revamped and communicated style guide to ensure a consistent tone across all sites.

EDITOR-IN-CHIEF, MEDIA BUZZ MAGAZINE (2002–2004)

Managed staff of 2 editors and team of freelancers, overseeing editorial content and making sure deadlines were met. Also wrote 2 monthly columns and created and maintained the magazine's website.

> *"Your impact on the magazine has been phenomenal—thank you!"*
> Peter Wallis, Editor-in-Chief, Davies Slater

Value Added: Received 11 awards for editorial excellence from the American Society of Business Press Editors between 2003 and 2004.

- Key member of launch team for mediabuzz.com, making editorial and cross-promotion decisions.

- Developed innovative product-launch campaign for mediabuzz.com that generated 50,000 page views on day one.

- Increased magazine ad revenues 30% by designing and executing "advertorial" sections.

PRODUCT REVIEW EDITOR, MEDIA BUZZ MAGAZINE (2000–2002)
PROJECT COORDINATOR, ANNUAL MEDIA BUZZ CONFERENCE (1998–2000)

Education

B.A., Economics. University of California, Berkeley, Berkeley, CA (1997)

Affiliations/Publications

Advisory Board, Media Buzz Conference, 2003–Present

Board of Directors, International Media Association, 2009–Present

Coauthor of the book *Media Marketplace* (Chrysalis Books, 2004)

Kathryn G. Oakes

4862 Greene Lane ▪ Hatfield, PA 19440 ▪ (215) 855-4863 ▪ kathryn.oakes@gmail.com

OBJECTIVE

Website Coordinator / Project Manager

SUMMARY OF QUALIFICATIONS

- Seven years of Web design experience coupled with degree in management.
- Ability to work well with people at all levels. Experience coordinating multiple functions and providing training and support.
- Strong organizational skills. Proven ability to manage multiple tasks, develop effective schedules, and deliver work on time.
- Good sense of design. Talent for conceptualizing creative solutions to achieve clients' goals.
- Solid knowledge of industry tools; monitor new trends through research.

PROFESSIONAL EXPERIENCE

BUX-MONT COLLEGE, Chalfont, PA (2004–present)
SENIOR WEBSITE DESIGNER, 2009–present
WEBSITE DESIGNER, 2006–2009
WEB ASSISTANT, 2004–2006

Design websites and manage day-to-day site maintenance. Determine design goals and specifications based on user requirements, marketing input, and comparative research. Prepare schedules and requirements documents; coordinate with marketing, content administrators, programmers, and others to deliver final product. Create mockups, final designs, templates for content developers, Flash timelines, and other special features. Test content for cross-browser compliance. Provide technical support for content providers and end users.

"I've just received a wonderful comment re the updated website from [company]—the president said that we've done more in the past six months to upgrade the site than he has seen any institution in our 'space' so evolve."

—College President

Accomplishments

- Saved six-figure fee for outside consulting by stepping in to redesign organization's primary website (http://www.buxmontcoll.edu), which was well received by customers.
- Served as designer on team that delivered project for remake of organization's main, 4,000-page website one month ahead of schedule; met deadlines on all other projects.
- Enhanced quality of sites through improvements in architecture, elimination of redundancy, and incorporation of user-friendly design; maintained quality and consistency by developing and implementing style guidelines.
- Initiated process to streamline content imports with cascading style sheets and templates.
- Improved customer service and saved time for Web staff by suggesting that first-level website support be moved to customer service group and by developing and providing training for the transition.
- Increased productivity of website support services through development of "canned procedures" for frequently asked questions.

Continued

This resume highlights management skills as well as design experience to help this Web designer advance to a management position. An impressive quote speaks to her design and project skills.

Kathryn G. Oakes

kathryn.oakes@gmail.com ▪ Page 2

PROFESSIONAL EXPERIENCE (CONTINUED)

SIGHT & SOUND, Philadelphia, PA (2001–2004)
WEBSITE DESIGNER, 2003–2004
ADMINISTRATOR / GRAPHIC ARTIST, 2001–2003
GRAPHIC ARTIST / OFFICE SUPPORT, 2001

Assisted in production of television pilot, stepping in where necessary to ensure that the desired effect was achieved. Redesigned company website; conceptualized logo animation for Tri-State Convention Center; designed signs, fliers, business cards, and other company print materials.

COMPUTER SKILLS

Adobe Dreamweaver, Photoshop, InDesign, Flash, Flex, Acrobat Reader

Microsoft Office (Word, Excel, PowerPoint, Outlook) and Visio 2010

EDUCATION

B.B.A., Villanova University, Villanova, PA (2000)
Major: General & Strategic Management
Honors: Dean's List

PROFESSIONAL DEVELOPMENT

PROJECT MANAGEMENT

Project Initiation and Planning, Penn State Abington (2010)

Franklin Covey Project Management Workshop, Franklin Covey (2007)

What Matters Most Workshop, Franklin Covey (2006)

Communication Skills, Fred Pryor Seminars, Inc. (2005)

WEBSITE DESIGN

Editing, Web Publishing, and DVD Authoring on the Avid XpressDV, Future Media Concepts (2008)

Visual Design Fundamentals, Philadelphia University (2007)

Adobe Flash, Philadelphia University (2007)

JavaScript, Berkeley Computer Training (2005)

Desktop Publishing, Montgomery County Community College (2000)

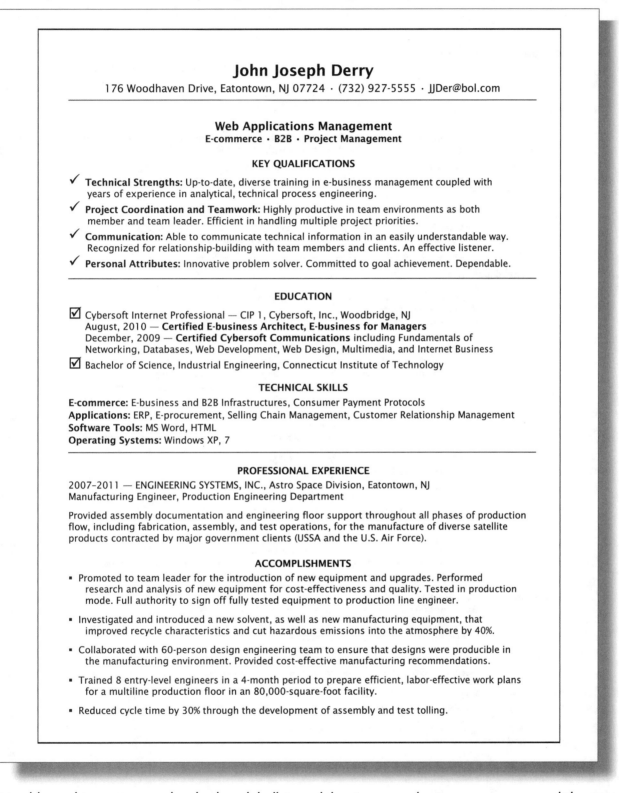

John Joseph Derry

176 Woodhaven Drive, Eatontown, NJ 07724 · (732) 927-5555 · JJDer@bol.com

Web Applications Management
E-commerce · B2B · Project Management

KEY QUALIFICATIONS

✓ **Technical Strengths:** Up-to-date, diverse training in e-business management coupled with years of experience in analytical, technical process engineering.

✓ **Project Coordination and Teamwork:** Highly productive in team environments as both member and team leader. Efficient in handling multiple project priorities.

✓ **Communication:** Able to communicate technical information in an easily understandable way. Recognized for relationship-building with team members and clients. An effective listener.

✓ **Personal Attributes:** Innovative problem solver. Committed to goal achievement. Dependable.

EDUCATION

☑ Cybersoft Internet Professional — CIP 1, Cybersoft, Inc., Woodbridge, NJ
August, 2010 — **Certified E-business Architect, E-business for Managers**
December, 2009 — **Certified Cybersoft Communications** including Fundamentals of Networking, Databases, Web Development, Web Design, Multimedia, and Internet Business

☑ Bachelor of Science, Industrial Engineering, Connecticut Institute of Technology

TECHNICAL SKILLS

E-commerce: E-business and B2B Infrastructures, Consumer Payment Protocols
Applications: ERP, E-procurement, Selling Chain Management, Customer Relationship Management
Software Tools: MS Word, HTML
Operating Systems: Windows XP, 7

PROFESSIONAL EXPERIENCE

2007–2011 — ENGINEERING SYSTEMS, INC., Astro Space Division, Eatontown, NJ
Manufacturing Engineer, Production Engineering Department

Provided assembly documentation and engineering floor support throughout all phases of production flow, including fabrication, assembly, and test operations, for the manufacture of diverse satellite products contracted by major government clients (USSA and the U.S. Air Force).

ACCOMPLISHMENTS

▪ Promoted to team leader for the introduction of new equipment and upgrades. Performed research and analysis of new equipment for cost-effectiveness and quality. Tested in production mode. Full authority to sign off fully tested equipment to production line engineer.

▪ Investigated and introduced a new solvent, as well as new manufacturing equipment, that improved recycle characteristics and cut hazardous emissions into the atmosphere by 40%.

▪ Collaborated with 60-person design engineering team to ensure that designs were producible in the manufacturing environment. Provided cost-effective manufacturing recommendations.

▪ Trained 8 entry-level engineers in a 4-month period to prepare efficient, labor-effective work plans for a multiline production floor in an 80,000-square-foot facility.

▪ Reduced cycle time by 30% through the development of assembly and test tolling.

Notable on this resume are the checkmark bullets and the strong emphasis on career accomplishments.

Jennifer C. Wallach

73 Barbizon Lane • Woodstock, VT 05412
802.885.1111 • jcwallach@hotmail.com

Qualifications Summary

- Highly motivated and accomplished **Web Page Developer/Technical Communications Professional** with strong project management and implementation abilities; resourceful design and research/documentation specialist.

- Innovative and creative initiative taker with demonstrated expertise in all facets of Web page design, desktop publishing, and computer/Internet technologies; flexible and adaptable in positively responding to changing organizational needs.

- Effective problem solver with expert communications and editorial skills.

- Highly proficient with the following Web development and graphic tools/skills: HTML, JavaScript, DHTML, and XML; Microsoft Office Suite; Adobe Photoshop, Dreamweaver, Flash, and InDesign.

Professional Experience

2007–Present   ARGON INTELLIGENCE GROUP, INC. (AIG) • Barnard, VT
Web Page Developer
- Broad range of creative/technical responsibilities includes development and ongoing product management for corporate Web site as well as sites for major clients; maintain corporate intranet and extranet with key responsibility for creation of product pages.
- Corporate/client project scope entails maintaining excellent customer relationships, managing and executing monthly updates, and coordinating/supervising contract designers.
- Successfully initiated, developed, and documented interface designs for company's first completely online HTML help system for retail systems product; implementation yielded substantial cost savings over paper production as well as enabled more timely releases/updates.
- Graphic designer for corporate marketing materials; design/author user manuals for ancillary retail systems products; provide technical consulting on as-needed basis across all disciplines.

2006   DOBSON COMMUNICATION CORPORATION • South Woodstock, VT
Marketing/Public Relations Intern
- Managed production of three monthly newsletters; oversight responsibility included story idea selection (collaborating with market coordinators), story assignments/editing, liaison to ad agency regarding layout requirements and art specifications, and final prepress approval.
- Developed and wrote internal as well as external communications including news releases, feature stories, and promotional feature pieces.
- Implemented wide range of creative design assignments, from conducting a Web page competitive analysis and implementing a company recycling program to producing a competitive event for employees of eight branch stores and executing a customer essay contest.

Education   NEW HAMPSHIRE COLLEGE • Manchester, NH
Bachelor of Arts Degree — Journalism/Public Relations (2006)
- Officer, Public Relations Student Society of America (2004–2006)
- Member, Phi Beta Lambda (Professional Business Leaders)

Continuing development includes attendance at professional seminars/conferences and meetings complemented by subscriptions to professional journals.

Affiliations   PUBLIC RELATIONS SOCIETY OF AMERICA
- Webmaster/Newsletter Editor
HTML WRITERS GUILD
SOCIETY OF TECHNICAL COMMUNICATION

This individual transferred her writing, marketing, and PR skills to a career as a Web page developer. Most of her resume focuses on communications strengths and the value she's brought to her employers.

Jim Haskins

2300 Main Drive
Apartment B
Miamisburg, OH 45342

Home: 937-555-1234
Cell: 937-555-4321
jimh@haskins.com

Web site: http://www.jimhaskins.com

Senior Web Architect

Programming • Web Development • Graphic Design

Clients

The Merry Company

County.com

Idea Imaging Group, Inc.

Marketing-Solutions Group

Blue Sky Auction Service

Prime Information Source

ChiefNet, Inc.

Smith Gallery

Typographic Services

AutoRetailing, Inc.

Jazzy Skateboards

Tech Industries/
Core Engineering

Image Photographic

Career Coaching Company

• • •

Representative Work

www.marketing-solutions.com

www.longbow.cc

www.jazzyboards.com

www.imagephotographic.com

www.careerresource.com

Additional portfolio samples available

Professional Profile

Creative Web Developer with 8 years of experience as a programmer and designer. Recognized as an innovative and solution-oriented developer of original program applications. **Experience** managing and collaborating with small and large teams of developers and designers and working in interactive and print mediums.

AREAS OF EXPERTISE

Project management • System and design integration • Web usability strategizing and testing • Diagramming information architecture and interactive design concepts • Database design • Graphic design • Strong client relations and presentation skills • Budget management

Notable Achievements

Architect of Mac OS X Internet Relay Chat (IRC) client noted for its visual design and user-friendliness. More than 3,000 downloads.

Creator and Developer of project management tool that includes real-time feedback on budgets (live tally), project status, distribution of staff effort, deadlines, and remote accessibility.

Technical Proficiencies

OPERATING SYSTEMS: Mac OS X • Linux • Solaris • AIX • Windows

DATABASES: MySQL • MS SQL • Oracle

LANGUAGES: HTML • XHTML • XML • JavaScript • CSS • Perl • PHP • C/C++

APPLICATIONS: Acrobat • Photoshop • InDesign • Flash • Dreamweaver

Continued

The left column provides links to Web sites developed by this individual. The first page of this resume could be used on its own for freelance projects; details of employment are included on page 2.

Jim Haskins • jimh@haskins.com • page 2

Professional Experience

MARKETING-SOLUTIONS GROUP, Dayton, OH
Designer, 2009–present
Strategize, design, and develop in-house and client visual communication solutions in Web, interactive, and traditional media formats. Project manager and IT system administrator.

KEY ACCOMPLISHMENTS

- Conceived and developed a project management application to boost efficiency throughout the company. Application was successfully implemented internally, and then presented as a product offering to clients, resulting in a new revenue stream for the company.

- Project manager for a complex, multimedia product launch for Prime Information Source. Assignment involved concept development, interactive CD design and programming, photo shoot direction, and design of a video wall presentation for trade show. According to Prime Information Source, this was their company's most successful new-product campaign.

INCREATION DESIGN STUDIO, Urbana, OH
Design Lead, 2008–2009
Led design team in the execution of in-house and client Web development projects. Planned and managed production processes and workflow. Key member of team that spearheaded the company's rebranding effort.

KEY ACCOMPLISHMENTS

- Successfully rebranded the company from ChiefNet to InCreation via the development of its Web site, resulting in establishing the new corporate identity with clients and staff.

CHIEFNET, INC., Urbana, OH
Web Developer, 2003–2008
Customer Service, 2002–2003
Designed and implemented new Web interfaces, graphics, and layouts.

KEY ACCOMPLISHMENTS

- Developed, designed, and managed County.com, a local community portal site that featured local events, weather, and editorial articles. The site became a showcase of ChiefNet's abilities in Web design and development.

Education

Associate of Applied Business, Clark State Community College, Springfield, OH
Graphic Art Design

Michael R. Jensen

111 East 11th Street
New York, New York 11111
(212) 222-2222
mrj@eternalspring.com

Internet Services ■ Sales ■ Consulting

Service-oriented **sales professional** offering considerable experience in **Internet consulting** and **broadband data technology**. Consistent producer, at ease dealing with high-level executives and IT professionals. Highly focused individual who enjoys working in a team environment and contributing to shared goals and objectives. Areas of expertise and strengths encompass:

◆ **Account Development**	◆ **Presentation Skills**	◆ **Account Management**
◆ **Relationship Building**	◆ **Needs Analysis**	◆ **Problem Resolution**
◆ **Strategic Alliance Building**	◆ **Negotiations / Closing**	◆ **Training and Supervision**

Professional Experience

GBX CORPORATION, New York, New York   2009–Present
Internet Consultant

- Generated $100,000 recurring revenue, year-to-date, in the marketing of data centers, T1 lines, web hosting services, colocation, and high-speed broadband data technology.
- Targeted, and successfully established relationships with, major firms, including Infoseek, *Sports Illustrated,* The Venator Group, Advanstar Communications, Elite Model Management, Infinity Interactive, 9Net Avenue, E-liance, Big Foot.com, Razor Fish, NetMix, Indignet, Star Diamond Group, Edgar Online, and Screaming Media.
- **Ranked #4 in sales** within the President's Club.
- Successfully created valuable strategic alliances by offering profit-sharing programs and special marketing agreements to various ISPs, Web developers, consultants, and telecom specialists.

MERRILL LYNCH, New York, New York   2005–2009
Senior Sales Representative

- **Cultivated $50 million in assets** and produced in excess of $400,000 in gross commissions annually.
- Raised capital for 2 Internet start-up companies that currently trade publicly.
- Consulted extensively with clients, assessing needs and providing investment guidance and recommendations.
- Provided guidance, training, and support to incoming account executives.

AT&T, New York, New York   2002–2005
Senior Sales Representative

- **Achieved 150% of quota** all 8 quarters with company.
- Targeted key accounts in lower Manhattan and provided consultative services on the use of high-end business equipment and telecommunications equipment.

Education, Training, and Skills

SYRACUSE UNIVERSITY, Syracuse, New York
Bachelor of Arts—Marketing / Economics & Political Science (double major)   2002

- PSS (Professional Selling Skills) Training
- Achieve Global (sponsored by Merrill Lynch)
- Well versed in various Internet technologies. Knowledge of Word and Excel.

This straightforward sales resume is for a man who made a career change a few years back, leaning toward Internet and information technology. His desire to continue within Internet services is emphasized.

Bernd Hieber

c/o Hermann – Koehl – Str.11
89231 NEV – VLM Germany
Telephone from USA: 0113-366-635-5278
Telephone from Europe: +33-666-355-278
Email: bernd@berndhieber.com
Web portfolio: http://www.berndhieber.com

E-business Specialist / Business Development Strategist / Marketing Executive
Creating and Driving Winning E-business Strategies for the New Economy

Dynamic planning expert offering fresh insight and a passion for innovation; proven record of contribution to high-profile, international business. Powerful strategist able to map creative budgeting, resource planning, and business development, empowering organizations with the tools, technologies, and strategies to bridge the digital business gap.

Respected leader, able to build team cohesion and inspire individuals to strive toward ever-higher levels of achievement. Exceptional relationship and management skills; relate and interface easily at the top executive levels. Complete, in-depth understanding of Web tools, trends, and business models. Solid background and qualifications in all core business functions—finance, marketing, sales, and operations.

AREAS OF EXPERTISE

- Budget Planning / Management
- Resource Management
- Personnel Training / Supervision
- Team / Group Leadership
- Strategic Planning
- Organizational Planning / Analysis
- Presentations / Public Speaking
- Multilingual: English / German / French

HIGHLIGHTS OF PROFESSIONAL ACHIEVEMENT

Inventoried existing budgetary controls, reinventing goals, strategies, and models to meet the demands of evolving digital economy. Increased competitiveness, heightened market valuation, and grew revenue.

Formatted strategies and action plans that have exceeded IPO and shareholder requirements for financial planning and reporting.

Facilitated negotiations and consensus for selection / integration of numerous development plans in company budgets.

Identified opportunities to accelerate monthly financial reporting, resulting in substantial extension of management's response options.

Pioneered and promoted award-winning Total Customer Satisfaction Project, increasing competitiveness through 8% cost reduction in packaging, 17% in storage, and 23% in shipping. Recruited to present model in final round of Motorola's worldwide project presentation competition in Toronto, Canada.

Designed and built creative Internet portal for the high-growth organization abc.org; credited with national awards and recognized by international health-care professionals as an expert in e-business marketing.

Noticed for developing highly complex and effective projecting tools for sales, costs, orders, and manpower planning requirements. Integrated marketing, product, and resource plans in budget models, now being employed as corporate-wide standard.

Continued

The resume for this internationally experienced professional is full of achievements, keywords, training, and other professional credentials. It's highly readable due to excellent organization, a clean typeface (Arial), and effective use of horizontal lines and type enhancements. Note the reference to a Web portfolio.

Confidential Résumé of Bernd Hieber   bernd@berndhieber.com   **Page 2**

PROFESSIONAL EXPERIENCE

Arrington Global Travel Distribution – Sophia-Antipolis, France, 2007–Present

Senior Officer, E-commerce Division

Senior consultant managing all Internet commerce initiatives. Direct long-term planning, budgeting, forecasting, and analysis for online sales and marketing activities in an increasingly competitive global marketplace. Provide reporting support for mergers, joint ventures, and partnership agreements. Coordinate and consolidate all company e-commerce functions, including 17 divisions, 62 departments, 158 cost centers, and 185 projects. Lead, motivate, train, and coach team comprising talented cost-control officers who produce standard and ad-hoc analysis reporting as input for crucial executive management decisions.

Motorola Multiservice Networks – Crawley, United Kingdom, and Darmstadt, Germany, 2004–2007

International Financial Assistant

International financial specialist with collaborative responsibility for the reorganization, centralization, and relocation of administration, manufacturing, and customer support for Europe, Middle East, and Africa Markets (EMEA). Key role in implementation of new tools and management systems in finance and operations. Creative participation in innovation of centralized stock and shipment management.

EDUCATION AND SPECIAL TRAINING

M.B.A., Business and Marketing
University of Tuebingen, Germany
Degree awarded 2005

Business and Marketing Studies
St. Olaf College, Minnesota, USA
2000–2001

Business and Marketing Studies
University of Tuebingen, Germany
Degree awarded 2001

Effective Presentation Training – Motorola University
Working as a Team / Six Sigma – Motorola University
Working Smarter – Leadership Development Ltd.
Six Steps to Best Quality – Motorola University
Trans-Cultural Competence – Motorola University

PROFESSIONAL AFFILIATIONS

Member, International Sales and Marketing Executives
Member, Internet Marketing Association
St. Olaf Career Advising Network

PUBLICATIONS

Standards, Certification, and Accreditation in the European Union, 2004, VDE Verlag, Berlin, Germany

Author / Coauthor of 7 scientific and nonscientific articles. Complete list of titles can be found at
www.berndhieber.com/publications.html

Supporting documentation, additional information, and references available on request.

THOMAS GEISLER

9200 Cross Oak Place
Huntersville, NC 28078

tgeisler2000@gmail.com
cell: 704.749.4403

E-COMMERCE / ONLINE MARKETING DIRECTOR

Pioneering marketing professional with 10 years of retail e-commerce experience who has achieved double- and triple-digit revenue growth for consumer products of both Fortune 500 and emerging companies. Analytical strategist with comprehensive marketing expertise, personal drive, and positive demeanor that inspires collaboration at all levels of an organization. Early adopter of technology who stays informed of new developments and trends.

- Strategic Planning & Competitive/Market Analysis
- Business Analysis
- P&L Management
- Marketing Metrics Analysis & Reporting

- Consumer Marketing & Sales
- Social Media Strategy & Implementation
- E-commerce Strategy & Website Design
- Internet Marketing / SEO / Online Advertising

PROFESSIONAL EXPERIENCE

ROCK HILL BRANDS, INC.   Charlotte, NC • 2007–Present
$10M U.S. footwear manufacturer marketing women's footwear worldwide; 40 employees.

Director of E-commerce

Create and execute online marketing strategy using SEO, pay-per-click (PPC) campaigns, comparison shopping engines (CSE), and affiliate marketing. Influence product development for seasonal product launches and promotions. Leverage limited resources into high-impact results through technical know-how and strategic partnerships. Manage $100K marketing budget. Report to Owner/CEO.

- **Revenue Growth.** Achieved explosive growth in revenue while maintaining 52% operating margin.

	FY2009	FY2010
Direct-to-Consumer Revenue	$795K (65% increase)	$1M (26% increase)
New Consumer Revenue	35% increase	39% increase
Repeat Consumer Revenue	125% increase	215% increase

- **Breakthroughs.** Delivered company's first $100,000+ month (5/09), first $200,000+ month (6/10), and first $40,000+ day (10/10) in consumer sales through online marketing, PR, and website architecture redesign.
- **Technology Advance.** Invigorated e-commerce sales by leading $50K project to replace existing technology with new platform capable of supporting marketing initiatives and growth expectations.
- **Customer Retention.** Grew customer e-mail list to 30,000+ in 18 months through opt-in campaign distinguished by improved website design, creative partnerships, viral promotions, and data mining.
- **Marketing Effectiveness.** Increased e-mail open rates by 25% and click-through rates by 47% through subject-line testing and redesigned consumer marketing e-mail template.
- **Process Improvement.** Enriched customer experience by reducing order lead times from 24 hours to real time by coordinating systems, processes, and promotions among all divisions.

GIANT BROADCASTING SYSTEMS   Charlotte, NC • 2000–2007
One of the world's largest media and entertainment companies with 60,000 employees and $20B in revenues.

Webmaster, Deals Unlimited, www.dealsunltd.com (2002–2007)

Challenged to grow online business through marketing plans and improvements to website design and merchandising. Reported to Director of Marketing.

- **Revenue Success.** Ignited annual revenue from $2.4M in FY2002 to $9.5M in FY2007 by spearheading technology and marketing efforts.
- **Customer Base Growth.** Increased active customer number from 4,500 in FY2002 to 11,700 in FY2007 through acquisition and retention campaigns.
- **Marketing Campaign.** Created and grew opt-in e-mail list to 40,000+ members by end of 2007. Segmented list to optimize results from targeted e-mail messages.
- **Technology Projects.** Partnered with department technologist on major innovations: $120K website overhaul and CRM integration; $2M Microsoft Commerce Server design and implementation; and customer service ticketing and knowledge base design, implementation, and website integration.

Page 1 of 2

Notice the words in bold that introduce each bullet point. These attention-getters are a great way to bring additional keywords into the resume.

THOMAS GEISLER — Page 2 of 2   tgeisler2000@gmail.com • (cell) 704.749.4403

GIANT BROADCASTING SYSTEM (continued)

Intranet Specialist (2001–2002)
Leveraged advanced skills in website design and marketing communication to create website graphics, content, and cross-marketing and advertising initiatives for Deals Unlimited website. Collaborated with customer service division to gain understanding of voice of the customer (VOC) to improve website experience and product selection.
- **E-mail Campaigns.** Created first e-mail marketing database and executed e-mail marketing newsletters and promotions.
- **New Product Rollout.** Teamed with marketing group to plan and launch new product rollout to maximize sales.

Employee Sales Coordinator (2000–2001)
Managed day-to-day sales operations of retail store. Assisted customers, answered phone calls, managed inventory, and completed cash register sales. Fulfilled orders for worldwide shipment.

indeezyne.com, LLC   Clemson, SC • 1998–2000
Part-time entrepreneurial Web development venture targeting small and medium businesses.
Cofounder and CEO
Teamed with partner to grow startup firm from concept to revenue generation, working evenings and weekends to complete client Web projects. Engaged in business development, including pitches to prospective buyers. Gathered project requirements and designed dynamic database applications for e-commerce sites.
- **Entrepreneurial Success.** Cultivated and grew client base, resulting in $25K annual revenues through part-time efforts.
- **B2B Expertise.** Developed multiple B2B e-commerce stores still in use today by several national firms.

PROFILE

EDUCATION
MBA in Marketing, UNIVERSITY OF NORTH CAROLINA — Charlotte, NC, 2007

BA in Political Science, *cum laude*, CLEMSON UNIVERSITY — Clemson, SC, 1999

PROFESSIONAL AFFILIATIONS
Member, American Marketing Association, 2006–Present

ROBERT ROSSTINE

Home: (407) 987-6543		17 Glenn Falls Drive
Mobile: (407) 654-9685	robross@gmail.com	Orlando, Florida 32700

E-commerce / New Business Development / Sales & Marketing

Results-oriented Management Executive with 10 years of experience leading successful start-up, turnaround, and high-growth companies. Consistently successful in identifying and capitalizing on market opportunities to drive revenue and profit growth. Strong online marketing expertise combined with traditional retail sales and marketing. Speak conversational Japanese and Spanish. Expertise includes:

- Strategic / Tactical Business Planning
- Partnership / Alliance Development
- Capital / Fund-raising
- Supply Network Development

- P&L Management
- Software Engineering / Development
- Staff Development / Management
- Investment Qualification Requirements

Recognized for E-commerce Expertise by the **Orlando Sentinel** *(October 2010),*
Inc. *Magazine (September 2009), and* **Small Business Opportunities** *(October 2008).*

PROFESSIONAL EXPERIENCE

FastServe.com, Inc., formerly TakeOut.com, Inc., Dallas, Texas   2009 to Present
A take-out food delivery operation serving 37 major markets in the U.S. and Europe.

Director, New Market Development – FastServe.com, Inc. (2010 to Present)

Led the launch of online business (TakeOut.com) specializing in a one-hour, food order delivery operation and grew it to an $800,000 operation within first year. Sold it to FastServe.com, assisted in ownership transition, and currently manage new market development.

- Engineered integration of TakeOut.com's software and data into FastServe.com's Delivery Magic system within two weeks.
- Assisted in integration of all internal and external operating systems, online marketing programs, customer tracking systems, menu guide production, and recruitment strategies.
- Conduct due diligence studies and identify new markets for penetration to meet FastServe.com's business development goals.
- Lead development of restaurant partnerships, order fulfillment/call center operations, menu guide development and production, and staff recruitment.

President/CEO – TakeOut.com, Inc., Orlando, Florida (2009 to 2010)

Built Web company from the ground up based on a newly developed unproven software program and the development of contracts with more than 95 traditional retail companies.

- Conducted due diligence studies, established company direction, developed strategic business plans, created a marketing program, instituted operating infrastructures, and recruited a management team and staff of 35.
- Raised $250,000 in operating seed capital and pioneered the startup of an online-based, one-hour, restaurant takeout and delivery service.
- Engineered solutions and worked closely with software programmers to build the nation's first Web-based restaurant delivery software that was redundant, efficient, effective, and technically sound.
- Overcame customer resistance to Web ordering through development of an online order entry system and averaged 35% of sales via the Internet, slashing labor costs and errors.
- Recorded more than $5,000 in sales in first week, growing to $1.5 million sales by 2010 with more than 30,000 unique online customers.

(continued)

Starting off with a strong summary and essential keywords and highlighting accomplishments, this resume is a powerful introduction for an e-commerce executive.

ROBERT ROSSTINE
robross@gmail.com   Page 2

PROFESSIONAL EXPERIENCE (Continued)

Delivery By Taxi, Inc., Herndon, Virginia   2008 to 2009
Corporate Manager

Recruited to interim leadership role with challenge to turn around a failing restaurant delivery business with 128 franchisees that had declined from generating $80 million to less than $50 million annually. Tasked to identify problems and implement solutions, document outcomes, build SOPs, and distribute manuals to corporate offices and franchisees.

- Developed a corporate marketing program and improved the quality of existing business unit marketing materials.
- Implemented new operating management and accounting procedures.
- Instituted database mailing programs used by all corporate stores and spearheaded a series of software improvements.
- Increased revenue 90% within six months for two of the corporate stores and 20% for the third.

Themed Diner, Maitland, Florida   2006 to 2008
District Manager

Hired to manage six privately owned and operated restaurants during a rapid growth period. Developed into a national chain with 26 locations.

- Managed the recruitment, staffing, and training initiatives for a 220-employee operation.
- Built several tracking and food control systems.

Catering & Gourmet Gifts, Inc., Orlando, Florida   2003 to 2006
Owner

Launched catering facility and upscale retail gourmet gift store with online and catalog sales.

- Achieved profitability after only 10 months.
- Produced $500,000 in sales after only two years; expanded to three locations within three years.
- Managed a catering kitchen, retail store, distribution warehouse, and 23 employees and drivers.

Earlier career included general management positions within the restaurant and retail industries.

EDUCATION / TECHNICAL TRAINING

Wright State University, Dayton, Ohio – Business Finance Concentration

RETS Technical College, Dayton, Ohio – Hotel and Restaurant Management

PROFESSIONAL DEVELOPMENT

Sales and Marketing Technologies Seminar, S&M Tech, Orlando, Florida, September 2009
(Search Engines, Effective Marketing, Redundancy, Advanced Technology)

Restaurant Delivery Service Association, Las Vegas, Nevada, May 2008
(Marketing, Operational Industry Standards, New Technology Workshops)

Internet Seminar, Nothing But Net, Orlando, Florida, April 2008
(Website Sales, Internet Business History, Networking and Partnership Building)

KEITH L. SMITH

keith@estores.com
(510) 542-4567

661 Orchard Road
Berkeley, CA 94707

INTERNET TECHNOLOGIES ENTREPRENEUR
E-commerce / Software Development / Online Merchandising

Creative, results-driven executive with **proven track record in building profitable start-up ventures,** developing strategic partnerships, and driving revenue/profit growth in e-commerce and retailing. **Decisive, visionary leader; expert at identifying and capturing online market opportunities, creating value and convenience in Web technologies, and inexpensively acquiring specialty market customers.** Expert in strategic planning, P&L management, marketing, business development, advanced technology infrastructure, and business systems.

Participative leadership style; able to build motivation, consensus, and cooperation with cross-functional teams in fast-paced environments. Effectively manage all facets of project life-cycle development, from initial feasibility and market analysis through specification, development, quality review, and implementation.

*Strategic Planning ◆ Marketing Management ◆ Strategic Financial Management
Budget Administration ◆ Risk Analysis ◆ Customer Relationship Management
Service Design/Delivery ◆ Scientific Marketing ◆ Data Mining ◆ Customer Profiling
Internet Media Buying ◆ Advertising ◆ Online Direct Marketing ◆ Venture Funding
Software Design/Development Management ◆ Business Development*

PROFESSIONAL EXPERIENCE

FOUNDER, PRESIDENT, AND CEO
I-Commerce, Provo, UT

2007–2011

Challenge: Lead start-up venture from concept through development and market launch to market leadership. **Capitalize on innovative product and service ideas** to competitively position business, build partnerships, and grow revenues.

Craft marketing strategy, distribution methods, and packaging. Acquire business-to-business and business-to-consumer relationships online.

Action: Founded company to create e-commerce sites for specialty retailers, but quickly **identified opportunity** to build unique software tool—ShopSite—to allow merchants to manage site content.

Integrated **viral marketing strategies** to promote ShopSite. **Eliminated distribution costs** by offering downloads for authorized users. Purchased cooperative advertising to pool online marketing dollars and resources.

Surveyed merchants to assess needs and rate system effectiveness. **Optimized online marketing strategies,** analyzing cost per sale per message per venue.

continued

This resume was created as part of a financing package for a start-up e-commerce company seeking venture capital. Note the effective use of the CAR strategy in describing key accomplishments.

K E I T H   L .   S M I T H   K E I T H @ E S T O R E S . C O M   Page Two

FOUNDER, PRESIDENT, AND CEO, I-Commerce, continued

Action: **Recruited talented, high-level managers** from leading technology companies. Instituted disciplined software development practices, including code management, version control, and documentation techniques.

Forged strategic alliances with key partners, including Microsoft, Adobe, Verio, and Mindspring.

Results: ◆ ShopSite user base has grown to 35,000+, making it the **most widely used small business e-commerce software worldwide.**

◆ **Pioneered method for preventing software piracy,** enabling I-Commerce to attract and forge alliances with hundreds of ISP distribution partners.

◆ Raised $1 million in venture capital. **Delivered 400% return for investors** in an average of 9 months.

◆ Utilized **disciplined budget strategies** to stretch resources and grow operations on thin cash. Never missed a payroll. Devised internal accounting system for order management, sales, and billing.

◆ **Sold company for $11 million in March 2011 to Open Market** (NASDAQ: OMKT).

GENERAL MANAGER
Electronics Education International, Irvine, CA   2004–2006

Challenge: Lead aggressive turnaround for designer, manufacturer, and distributor of educational kits and software for electronics training. Drive revenue and profit improvement for company with slow 10% annual sales growth.

Action: Streamlined operations and business practices to **achieve profit goals with only half of previous inventory and staffing levels.** Redesigned inventory and accounting processes to optimize inventory levels and reduce costs. Competitively positioned company against larger business ventures.

Results: ◆ **Doubled revenues in first year.**

◆ **Increased profits more than 80%** through innovative marketing strategies, internal efficiency planning, and revitalized business processes.

EDUCATION

B.S., Corporate Finance *(cum laude graduate),* NEW YORK UNIVERSITY, New York, NY, 2001

Victoria Lee

795 Center Street
Wellesley, MA 01801

victoria.lee@gmail.com
617.677.8189

BUSINESS EXECUTIVE, SALES LEADER & TECHNOLOGY INNOVATOR

**New Media / Broadcast Media / Internet Media & Technology / Online Product Development
Technical Ideation / Project Leadership / P&L Management / Operations Management
Sales & Marketing / New Business Development / Client Relationship Management**

Top-performing executive with a panoramic vision of business and technology, flexibility in responding to constantly changing market and economic demands, and keen understanding of customer needs and expectations. Expert in creating sustainable, profitable, and humanizing solutions that meet complex operating, financial, technical, and market challenges.

Delivered tens of millions of dollars in new revenues and millions more in cost savings through quality, productivity, and performance innovation. Creative, strategic, intelligent, and collaborative with excellent negotiation, communication, and leadership qualifications. Profoundly engaged and engaging.

EXECUTIVE BUSINESS & OPERATING LEADERSHIP

Strategic Planning & Development, Organizational Development, Multisite Operations Management, P&L Management, Team Leadership

- Appointed ad hoc **CEO for Kansas Telecom immediately following devastating Midwest tornadoes.** Kept critical communication systems online throughout Kansas, protected company assets, coordinated emergency deliveries by U.S. military, and established business continuity initiatives with industry competitors to sustain operations despite infrastructure failures.
- **Provided swift and accurate executive leadership** throughout career. Most recently, assembled cross-functional crisis team, designed improved business processes, created shared work model, and implemented real-time progress reporting to eliminate roadblocks impeding completion of 500+-page document for 9-digit bid proposal.
- Delivered **total cost savings of more than $8M** over the past 9 years to scores of companies and organizations.
- **Spearheaded successful start-up** of *Adword Magazine* covering online alliance monetization, investment, and marketing. Leadership responsibility for P&L, operations, staffing, editorial, advertising, budgeting, publication, and distribution.
- Conceived and implemented a series of **innovative employee retention programs to build sustainable workforces** across multiple businesses, customer markets, and industries.
- **Developed and deployed, within 6 hours,** a business continuity plan for regional bank and met federal audit requirements.
- Created concepts and wrote more than 40 business plans for **new ventures, mergers, acquisitions, joint ventures, strategic alliances, partnerships, turnarounds, and global expansions.**

TECHNOLOGY INNOVATION & ONLINE PRODUCT DEVELOPMENT

Thought Leadership, TV & Web Broadcast, Internet Media, New Media, Web 2.0, Project Management, Product Launch & Commercialization

- Spearheaded development of HELP, **Internet-based emergency communications system,** in response to massive communication failures following Midwest tornadoes. Awarded provisional patent and presented plan to Homeland Security, Kansas governor, and Kansas legislature. Profiled in *Telecom News* for technology innovation and success.
- Designed **content management system** for Commerce Media's **Internet news portal** that grew from concept to 6M page visits per month. Honored with Boston Chamber of Commerce's **High-Tech Award** for advances in the use and application of technology.
- Orchestrated the planning and launch of www.enews.com, a forerunner in professionally produced **Internet news broadcasts and websites.** Established new business operating model and achieved/surpassed all technology milestones.
- Designed application and managed development of **multipermission, media-publishing system** on Typo 3 infrastructure.
- Awarded provisional patent for emergency communications system and facilitated other development projects for electronic advertising technology.

Page 1 of 3

Good organization and tight writing make this three-page resume easy to skim for key facts and easy to read for detailed information. Note the functional headers on pages 1 and 2 that segment rich experience into relevant categories.

Victoria Lee Page 2 of 3

victoria.lee@gmail.com 617.677.8189

SALES, MARKETING & NEW BUSINESS DEVELOPMENT
Executive Sales Presentations & Negotiations, Brand Management, Key Account Management, New Opportunity & New Market Capture

- Contributed to **2300% revenue growth** over 4 years for Adwords Media, an international online advertising portal. Company was honored with a top **Deloitte Technology Fast 400 Award** and placement in top 20% of industry.
- Structured, negotiated, and closed **$1.9M comarketing partnership** with VeriSign to expand Adwords Media's nationwide market reach throughout new geographies and new demographic markets.
- Conceived, developed, and introduced a portfolio of marketing and sales campaigns for Blab.com, a leading Internet marketing firm serving 25% of the Fortune 500 companies. Instrumental in **doubling client base in just 11 months.**
- **Orchestrated market launch** of Epay Enterprises, a new e-commerce and merchant card processing company providing Internet commerce, ACH processing, secure gateway integration, and alternative payment solutions.
- Wrote proposals; led presentations; and negotiated, transacted, and **closed more than $10M in new revenues** over past 10 years.

CREATIVE LEADERSHIP, ADVERTISING & PUBLIC RELATIONS
Creative Concept & Ideation, Multimedia Advertising, Media Buying & Selling, Press Relations, Public Speaking, Public Outreach

- Structured and negotiated unique **advertising trade deal with prominent media group, bartering premium advertising space** in exchange for customized, Internet-based, content management system/solution.
- Won numerous **graphic design awards** from the Boston Press Association.
- Recognized as **forerunner in leveraging Internet technology** for political campaign outreach, producing favorable election results.
- Managed hundreds of **high-profile, high-impact local, regional, national, and international public relations, marketing, and product confidence campaigns** for several Midwest companies immediately following severe tornado damage.

PROFESSIONAL EXPERIENCE

Senior Program Manager—Online & Print Media, XYZ Corp., Boston, MA 2006 to Present
Member of senior operating management team with broad-reaching responsibilities for project leadership, online technology development and solutions, client relationship management, and publications management. Revitalized entire business group, renewed spirit of collaboration, and introduced performance-driven project management methodologies and metrics. Delivered flagship 300-page annual technical manual on schedule for the first time in an estimated 15 years.

Executive Consultant—Business Development, Product Development & Technology, KS & MA 2002 to 2006
Provided executive leadership to presidents, CEOs, COOs, CFOs, CMOs, CIOs, boards of directors, owner and investor groups, shareholders, and others of more than 100 companies—start-ups, emerging enterprises, turnaround companies, and high-growth corporations. Experience spans more than 25 different industries, from brick-and-mortar businesses to national government agencies to global technology ventures. Built reputation as a trusted and valued confidante and advisor.

Business Development Manager, Commerce Media, Topeka, KS 2000 to 2002
Member of 4-person executive management team that negotiated complex acquisition of Midwest Broadband through bankruptcy courts to create Commerce Media, a service-based Internet advertising company generating $14M annually. Directed marketing, creative design, business development, legal affairs, teams, and customer service/support.

Managing Editor, KKAN News/Online Broadcasting, Topeka, KS 2000
Pioneered the convergence of broadcast news with Internet technology within local region and created online news portal that captured 250K viewers in first 3 months. Directed editorial, broadcasting, advertising, sales, HR, and training for Web station.

Previous Professional Experience: Fast-track promotion through a series of increasingly responsible positions as a **Editor** and **Computer Graphics Designer** in the healthcare industry. Transitioned into print media as a **Reporter** and **Section Editor.**

Victoria Lee   Page 3 of 3

victoria.lee@gmail.com   617.677.8189

EDUCATION & TECHNICAL TRAINING/CERTIFICATION

Online Accessibility Training Conference, Boston University, 2009

MS Project Orange Belt Certification, International Institute for Learning, Inc., 2007
(Awarded 21 professional development credits toward **Project Management Professional – PMP – Certification**)

Graduate Studies in Newspaper Management, Markets & Economics, Northeastern University, 1995 to 1996
(Winner/Presenter, "The Future of Journalism," Northeast U.S. Journalism Conference/Brown University, 1996)

J.D. Candidate, Topeka Law School, Topeka, KS, 2004 to 2005
(Attending second year of 4-year program when studies were interrupted by tornadoes)

B.S., Communications, The Ohio State University, Columbus, OH, 1999

Professional Media Studies, Broad Institute, Chicago, IL, 1993

TECHNICAL PORTFOLIO

Software & Languages: MS Office Suite, MS Project, Dreamweaver, Photoshop, QuarkXPress, NewsMaker, Keynote, Pages, Acrobat Pro with Electronic Markup, OmniGraffle, InDesign, Illustrator, Freehand, Flash, Final Cut Pro, Aperture, Visio, Quickbooks, PHP, HTML, MySQL

Web Interfaces: Google Adwords, Typo3 CMS, Joomla CMS, VTiger CRM, PhPadsNew

PRESENTATIONS

- Keynote Presenter, "The Future of Online Advertising," *Adword Magazine* Conference, 2009
- Conference Presenter, "Technology Advancements in Advertising," Northeast Advertising Council, 2008
- Panelist, "The Media and Online Advertising," Tech Future Conference, 2007
- Testimony Presenter, "Benefits of Emergency Communications Systems" (following tornadoes), Kansas State Legislature, House of Representatives, Committee on Judiciary, 2006

PUBLICATIONS

Author of 200+ articles on a broad cross-section of topics, from media, broadcasting, and online technologies to health care, genetics, job search, economics, history, environment, public works projects, the courts and judicial system, and local city government. Published extensively in *Adword News, The Topeka Post,* and the *Boston Business Journal.*

CHAPTER 9

Resumes for Project Managers and Technology Consultants

- Technology Project Managers
- IT Project Managers
- Systems Analysts
- Telecommunications Managers
- Technology Leaders
- Project Management Executives
- Technology Consultants

Charles Farrow

27 Central Avenue, Toms River, NJ 08754
(732) 929-5555 Home • (732) 929-8888 Mobile • cfarrow@ole.com

Project Management
IT Systems Installation and Technology Integration

Results-driven leader with information systems installation and integration experience. Expert in full-cycle project planning and implementation, working closely with end users during the design, development, and training stages. Energetic and decisive business leader able to merge disparate personnel into group-centered project teams. Core competencies include:

✓ Strategic Business Planning	✓ Reengineering	✓ Project Management
✓ Interdepartmental Coordination	✓ Change Management	✓ Resource Management
✓ Management & Administration	✓ Technology Transfer	✓ Client Relations

Strong abilities in applications analysis and back-office operations. Demonstrated business acumen and ability to meet fiscal and deadline commitments. Team-building, relationship-building, and communications skills.

PROFESSIONAL EXPERIENCE

CCS Systems (software vendor/ASP to Fortune 500 companies), Toms River, NJ   2000–2011

Director (2004–2011), **Training Director** (2000–2004)
Managed multimillion-dollar IT projects for large-scale corporate home office applications. Fully responsible for project P&L. Clients included Westney, Cal-Mart, James, Home Store, Jill Jones, D-Mart, and River Royal. Maintained direct and ongoing client contact to ensure smooth operations.

Accomplishments

☑ Achieved productivity gains of up to 50% through the development and implementation of projects on time, to specifications, and within budget. Consistently met or exceeded performance criteria.

☑ Vital member of steering committee that identified user needs and developed customized solutions for more than 150 clients. Personable, direct approach contributed to client loyalty.

☑ Led projects through entire project development cycle to develop application-specific systems capable of meeting current and long-range corporate information management requirements. Produced and managed deliverables through formal project plans.

☑ Matrix-managed 20-member, cross-functional team (hardware, software, quality control, technical support, and training), assigning team responsibilities and overseeing tasks and timelines. Often called on to use personal judgment, diplomacy, and analytical sense to troubleshoot problems.

☑ Pioneered innovative team-building and cross-functional project management techniques to expedite workflow, simplify processes, and reduce operating costs.

☑ Designed and implemented user setup, end-user training materials, and testing procedures.

River Royal (Division of Royal, Inc.), New York, NY   1993–2000

Divisional Planner (1997–2000), promoted from **Planner** and **Senior Planner** (1993–1997)

EDUCATION
B.S., Marketing, 1991: McGill University, Ontario, Canada

COMPUTER SKILLS
Microsoft Office (Word, Excel, PowerPoint, Outlook)

With most of his professional experience at one company, this individual was able to construct a concise, one-page resume that effectively highlights his project accomplishments.

RESUME 75: BY MARJORIE SUSSMAN, MRW, ACRW, CPRW

PAMELA FRENCH

STRATEGIC PLANNING ♦ TECHNOLOGY ♦ CUSTOMER RELATIONS

22 SE Sixth Terrace, Gainesville, FL 32654
352-789-9766 ♦ pamelafrench@aol.com

PROJECT MANAGER

Solving problems and delivering software solutions for healthcare companies.

♦ **Hands-on Management Experience:** Senior manager of remote monitoring and technical support teams servicing thousands of medical end users. Scheduled for PMP certification testing, July 2011.

♦ **Professional Services Background:** Project manager and product coordinator with Leffert Healthcare R&D and WebMD, supporting local and national clients.

♦ **Process Documentation and Metrics Focus:** Proactively documented and enforced processes; expert at preparing reports on short notice; skilled in making smart, timely decisions in managing crisis situations.

♦ **Fast-Track Success:** From customer service representative to product coordinator, software educator, and senior manager during 14 years of dedicated service in an atmosphere of frequent organizational change.

♦ **People, Process, and Operational Expertise:** Recruit right-fit employees; build sound and sustaining teams; and create order amid the chaos of dynamic, high-volume environments.

PROFESSIONAL EXPERIENCE

LEFFERT HEALTHCARE R&D, Tampa, FL   1996 to 2011

Subsidiary of UK-based software developer The Leffert Group, providing business management applications for small and midsized companies in diverse industries throughout the world; annual revenue $425M.

Overview: *Challenging roles during 14 years of frequent organizational change—2 mergers and 3 administrations (Medical Manager Corporation, WebMD, Leffert Software). Fast-tracked through customer service, product development, and program management to senior management.*

Senior Manager, Development Support (2006–2011)

Planned, managed, and staffed day-to-day operations of division, combining level 3 development support and remote monitoring systems teams. Oversaw all personnel hiring, promotions, disciplinary actions, and releases. Supervised 15 direct reports (senior technical support engineers) responsible for providing support to 2 national groups of more than 150 level 2/enterprise site technical support staff members servicing 2,000+ customers with practice management and electronic medical records systems.

Operations & Staff Management

♦ Ensured team stayed current on all new product functionalities; standardized and streamlined workflow to ensure seamless operations for prompt resolution of customer issues.

♦ Created collaborative culture of cross-functional teamwork that was instrumental in meeting aggressive deadlines and resolving customer crises.

♦ Provided resources and managed tasks associated with noncrisis software implementations, upgrades and conversions, and database migrations associated with operating system platform changes.

Customer Support

♦ Managed several projects at any given time—established goals and timelines, acquired cooperation of multifunctional teams, and juggled company resources to meet project needs.

♦ Personally worked with software developers, support managers, field services managers, and implementation managers to manage escalations.

♦ Provided long-term solutions to customers via routine software upgrades, service packs, and hot fixes.

Projects

♦ **O/S Platform Migrations for Targeted Sites:** Provided oversight and resources for portion of the project that included negotiations with third-party consultants for data migrations over the course of 28 months.

♦ **Hot Fix Pilot Process Development:** Project leader for 4-month project to improve delivery of software hot fixes to specific sites. Identified and communicated with all stakeholders to successfully create and document seamless processes and workflow among multiple cross-functional teams.

♦ Supervised staff in providing more than 10 hot fixes (containing dozens of fixes) via new cost-saving, automated delivery system while triaging at least 30 issues each week across multiple product lines.

Continued

The Overview section explains the chronology of the company, which has gone through multiple ownership changes. Headings break up a lengthy list of accomplishments and help readers move quickly through the resume.

PAMELA FRENCH   352-789-9766 ♦ pamelafrench@aol.com

Software Defect Manager, Intergy Practice Management Software (2003–2006)

Created and managed a technical team specializing in product support to effectively eliminate backlog of defect reports from customers. Formed from the existing research phone team, the subteam was ultimately merged to become the development support team.

♦ Accelerated flow of service packs to customers by training phone team to move defect reports more efficiently to developers in a format that facilitated rapid delivery of solutions.

♦ Reduced backlog of customer defect reports 50% in 5 months; completely eliminated backlog in 12 months.

♦ Worked 2,271 issues across 8 products that required programming solutions and were included in service packs and new version releases.

♦ Resolved approximately 2,000 issues requiring no development intervention.

Product Coordinator, Intergy Practice Management Software (2001–2003)

Coached and supervised research phone team in conducting information-gathering interviews with users of the practice management software. Provided feedback to the CEO and development directors for use in product design and development.

♦ Participated as key member of project team, customizing and implementing call-tracking software.

♦ Produced 150+ conversational-style interview scripts and, using qualitative research software, stored each interview in a format allowing keyword searches and trend report generation.

Software Support Technician, Intergy Software Beta Program (2000–2001)

Provided support for 20 beta sites via remote connection and on-site visits. Conducted intensive training for regional staff on implementing the software.

♦ Developed informal method to track feedback from the sites and track all development code delivered.

♦ Provided rapid delivery and implementation to sites, significantly increasing customer satisfaction and leading to increased product endorsements and sales.

Customer Service Representative, Medical Manager Software (1996–1999)

Developed and conducted train-the-trainer sessions on Medical Manager software at local businesses and colleges in response to the software's growing popularity. Met the increasing demand for trained office workers to heighten customer satisfaction and expand brand recognition.

Earlier experience: Taught *Medical Manager Practice Management Software, Introduction to Computers,* and *Business English* at Career City College and Webster College, Gainesville, FL.

EDUCATION & PROFESSIONAL TRAINING

PMI Project Management Professional (PMP)
July 2011 scheduled testing

University of Florida Leadership Development Institute
Project Leadership & Communications, 2005
Project Management Tools & Techniques, 2005

University of Florida at Gainesville
Ph.D. in Counselor Education, 1998
B.S. in Business Education, 1979

Proficient in Siebel; Work Management System; MS Word, Excel, Project, PowerPoint, Access.

ALICIA NAVARRO

7600 Muir Drive #207 • San Jose, CA 95101

(cell) 408-912-6209
alinavarro@gmail.com

PROJECT MANAGER

Combining fresh ideas and leadership abilities to deliver world-class technical projects.

Senior Project Management Professional with 12 years of global IT and business analysis experience in complex corporate environments, focusing on application and infrastructure installations, telecommunication system upgrades, and software development. Skilled in managing project stakeholders and teams to define and achieve project goals while controlling costs. Excel in constructing and implementing changes that enhance the performance, reliability, and functionality of software applications. Bilingual English/Spanish.

Project Management Methodologies • Business Plans • Change Management • Team Leadership
Business Analysis • Systems Analysis • Operational Streamlining • Process Reengineering
IT Standards Development • Security & Disaster Recovery • Technology Evaluation

PROFESSIONAL EXPERIENCE

APOLLOS SAFETY SYSTEMS — Palo Alto, CA   2009–2011
$120M manufacturer of detection/prevention systems for aerospace and defense; 375 staff.
IT Manager
Succeeded in multiproject environment to deliver strategic and tactical leadership for mission-critical IT improvements. Defined, planned, and executed implementations of ERP and business applications, telecommunications/infrastructure systems, and Web technologies. Managed data center, help desk, $2.5M budget, and team of 6 staff and consultants. Led company's first IT steering committee.

- **Achieved performance objectives** by rebuilding IT organization with new service model that addressed previous support gaps. Restructured roles and responsibilities and evaluated processes to identify opportunities to simplify operations.

- **Satisfied business requirements** by improving ERP systems, resulting in increased user knowledge, credible data quality, improved business intelligence, and standardized reporting.

- **Advanced IT staff skills,** training in PMP and customer service delivery to fully support core ERP applications. Saved $300K in annual consulting fees.

- **Conceptualized and implemented risk-mitigation strategy** that included server and network security, wireless network protection, new backup tape library, server consolidation, virtualization and SAN technology, and upgraded switch and firewall.

- **Created high-performance IT team** with new structure, process, and training for IT service and project success. Developed policies and procedures for ticket management, troubleshooting, and service, including SLAs for help desk.

- **Transformed IT group's role** into an integral business partner by leading IT steering committee to partner with business unit representatives in developing standards and prioritization for all IT projects, resulting in outcomes that were on time and within budget every time.

GOLDEN HEALTH SOLUTIONS, LLC — Los Angeles, CA   2007–2009
$120M global leader in dietary supplement industry; 850 employees.
Project Manager
Led systems implementations by developing business specifications, orchestrating testing activities, and directing documentation of systems and operations. Spearheaded project management and led team in module development. Served as liaison between IT and business units and communicated implementation activities to user communities.

- **Appointed SME** of warehouse and distribution system by quickly mastering user interviews, defining current operations and future requirements, and identifying business and user issues.

- **Performed rigorous testing** that ensured warehouse, inventory, and transportation modules met all requirements, winning high acclaim from implementation team.

Page 1 of 2

Strong and specific accomplishment statements provide credible evidence of this project manager's skills and expertise. Notice the branding statement just below the headline.

RESUME 76, CONTINUED

GOLDEN HEALTH SOLUTIONS, LLC (continued)

- **Guided integration of business processes and data flows as SME** after taking initiative to understand impact of modules and systems on each other.

- **Managed equipment implementation project** after building business case for upgrading outdated scanners and barcode system. Won approval after concluding that equipment would fail under new JDE warehouse module.

CENTENNIAL CABLE NETWORKS — Los Angeles, CA   2006–2007
Cable TV entertainment and news network.
Project Manager Consultant
Directed major project to upgrade JDE ERP from World to Enterprise One application suite. Implemented upgrade for cable, broadcast, and TV companies, leading all project planning, initiation, resource management, execution, communication, testing, going live, and closure.

- **Stepped in to take over project** from previous consultant, quickly grasping business requirements and challenges. Saved client hundreds of thousands of dollars by persuading change in implementation approach and implementation partner.

- **Accelerated project completion by 6 months** by eliminating duplication of effort through phased implementation by company that also provided users with a smooth transition.

- **Credited for creating successful implementation team** consisting of the newly collaborative financial groups of all 3 companies. The team developed a first-ever unified chart of accounts that still allowed transaction tracking by individual company.

- **Acquired new role as development group leader** to manage life-cycle development for legacy conversions, interfaces, and custom JDE development.

BACA MEXICO, S.A., de C.V. — Mexico City, Mexico   1999–2006
200-employee distribution company of $3.5B beauty products manufacturer.
Director of Information Systems
Launched the IT department from the ground up, implementing JDE process improvements, redesign of Hyperion database, and migration to Lotus Notes email. Emphasized project management approach to optimize resources across all activities. Developed all IT standards, policies, processes, and procedures. Managed 4 staff, 6 contractors, and $2M budget.

- **Created company's first IT strategy** that provided a platform for budgeting, resource allocation, and timeline management.

- **Increased IT department uptime productivity 50%** by introducing on-site support, new help desk processes, and extensive training for end users.

- **Improved functionality** of finance, distribution, and warehouse functions by reimplementing JD Edwards. Boosted on-time delivery by reducing errors through training.

- **Implemented state-of-the-art EDI system** with zero downtime, resulting in enhanced activity with trading partners by meeting all their EDI requirements.

EDUCATION & CREDENTIALS

Master of Business Administration (MBA) — Concentration: Strategic Management
PEPPERDINE UNIVERSITY — Malibu, CA

Bachelor of Science in Business Administration
Major: Business Administration; Minor: Computer Applications and Systems
CALIFORNIA STATE UNIVERSITY — Fresno, CA

Technical Skills
- Microsoft Project • Visio • PowerPoint • Access • SharePoint • Office
- AS/400 • Oracle • DB2 • SQL • JD Edwards • PeopleSoft • Hyperion • Cognos
- SDLC • Agile • Waterfall • RAD
- Networks • Servers • LANs • WANs • VLAN • VPN • Firewalls • Wireless • VM Ware • SAN
- SOX • SSA • Export Compliance • ITIL • IT Governance Standards

STANLEY KRAWCHEK, PMP

914.505.2004 • stankay@optonline.net
79 Palisades Court, White Plains, NY 10601

TECHNOLOGY PROJECT MANAGER

Business Transformation • Merger Integration • Enterprise Project Leadership

Strategic, growth-focused technology leader who approaches IT from a business mindset and uses decisive leadership skills to drive critical initiatives through complex, dispersed organizations. Expert in devising business process solutions that support stringent reporting, compliance, security, and government certification requirements.

- Spearheaded business integration of 2 merged billion-dollar-plus companies, devising and executing $10M project plan that projects positive ROI in just over 2 years.

- Led $28M SAP implementation for Channel Communications, on schedule and 17% under budget.

- Created blueprint for successful ERP implementation across Channel's nationwide radio division.

Technology expertise includes applications; infrastructure; desktop support; Java- and Web-based systems; client-server environments; communication technologies; SQL databases; SAP/enterprise systems; and all Microsoft systems, platforms, and applications.

EXPERIENCE AND ACHIEVEMENTS

CHANNEL COMMUNICATIONS   New York, NY, 2005–Present
Project Manager: EZ Communications Acquisition Integration, 2010–Present

Handpicked to drive business transition for $2.7B spin-off of Channel's radio division to EZ Communications. Orchestrating complex, business-wide initiative to build new operational infrastructure for the merged entity that doubled the size of Channel Radio and created the third-largest radio broadcaster in the U.S.

As senior IT executive reporting to the VP of finance, manage $10M budget and a team of 25 business and technology professionals dispersed nationwide. Project scope encompasses business policies and procedures, business management systems, HR and payroll systems, IT infrastructure, and broadcast and engineering systems/facilities.

- Developed comprehensive business plan—selecting optimum systems, designing new operational procedures, and streamlining business processes to deliver measurable bottom-line benefits:
  – 10% head count reduction
  – Rapid (2 years) payback on $10M project investment

- On schedule, within budget to complete project by third quarter 2011.

Project Manager: Channel Radio SAP Integration, 2008–2010

Drove successful implementation of SAP for 23 North American media outlets. Led project for the division and collaborated with additional 18 project managers across the entire Channel enterprise on $500M, multiyear implementation. Rolled out multiple project initiatives related to software configuration and deployment, business process reengineering, and process migration. Built and led dispersed site rollout team, managing $28M budget with full accountability for quality, timeliness, and completion of all project deliverables.

- Successfully delivered project on aggressive schedule and 17% under budget.

- Devised and led an extensive communication and education program, building widespread acceptance and support for significant change affecting every aspect of daily business life for 5,000-employee division.

Continued

Each job description leads off with a bold phrase or sentence summarizing the most notable achievement in that role. Key accomplishments are also highlighted in brief bullet points as part of the summary.

STANLEY KRAWCHEK, PMP   914.505.2004 • stankay@optonline.net
                                                                    Page 2

CHANNEL COMMUNICATIONS, continued
IT Project Manager: Radio Division, 2005–2008

Brought on board to rescue a faltering ERP implementation. Hit the ground running, rapidly resolved software and hardware problems, and completely stabilized the system in 30 days. Subsequently led additional critical projects for the nationwide business units. Managed contract vendor relationships.

- Created and managed annual operating plan for financial business systems.

- Drove the development of intranet/extranet for all ABC business units.

- Served as business unit lead for the functional and technical integration of e-procurement initiatives.

METRO TECHNICAL SOLUTIONS—Professional Services   Newark, NJ, 2004–2005
IT Project Manager

Hired for combined insurance/business/technical expertise; quickly resolved urgent problems with a key client project and remained as contract employee to manage full life-cycle implementation of policy and claims administration software for property and casualty insurance companies.

- Performed detailed requirements analysis of clients' business processes for integration with new software.

- Closely mapped data conversion processes and executed detailed testing scenarios to ensure data integrity.

HI-TECH ASSOCIATES—Professional Services   White Plains, NY, 2003–2004
Senior Implementation Consultant

Brought deep business/systems knowledge to hands-on technology role. Managed full life-cycle implementation of general ledger and accounts payable software and provided end-user training on all applications.

ERNST & YOUNG—Financial Solutions   Hartford, CT, 2001–2003
Business Systems Analyst, 2002–2003

Defined and developed best business practices in support of major project to develop and implement a proprietary reinsurance business process system in a client-server environment. Led a team of application testers in meeting strict project deadlines for testing and documentation processes.

Insurance Accountant, 2001–2002

Provided specialized insurance accounting services for a $50M book of business. Analyzed and reconciled transactions; prepared month-end adjustments; served on project team for statutory annual statements.

EDUCATION AND PROFESSIONAL CREDENTIALS

Bachelor of Science in Business Administration: University of Connecticut, Storrs, CT, 2000

PMP (Project Management Professional): Project Management Institute, 2010
MCSE (Microsoft Certified System Engineer): Microsoft Corporation, 2007
CCA (Citrix Certified Administrator): Citrix Systems, Inc., 2005

CRAIG LAND

699 River Drive		Home: (610) 677-5733
Narberth, PA 19072	craigland@gmail.com	Cell: (484) 626-1005

Executive Summary

Senior-Level IT Project Manager/Business Analyst/Integration Specialist with history of achieving cost savings and enhancing system functionality. Track record of tackling—and solving—tough business and technical problems for companies in transition. Strong leader with demonstrated ability to work effectively with people at all levels and in all functional areas.

Experience encompasses full system development life cycle, from requirements gathering to final implementation and customer training, in mainframe, client-server, and Web environments. Solid knowledge of IT tools, methods, and standards, as well as financial, sales, and manufacturing systems.

Professional Experience

Project Manager, 2010–present
TANDY BAKERY, Wayne, PA; Computer Consultants, Inc. (agency), Philadelphia, PA
The number-one dessert bakery in the Northeast, with 24-hour data processing at 15 locations.

Tasked with integrating accounts receivable and production applications to Web-based client-server system following company acquisition. Served as liaison between business and technology groups at different locations, gathering requirements, overseeing definition of specifications, coordinating implementation, and verifying integration test results against requirements. Currently managing final report-building phase and training users on new system.

Accomplishments

- Achieved on-schedule integration into one Oracle data warehouse and one application with customized reports for 15 locations.
- Delivered substantial cost savings with integrated system: IT workforce reduced by 80%; accounting and production staff reductions estimated at 50% on project completion.
- Retained all required business functionality on new system.
- Received exceptional reviews on quality of training and accompanying documentation.

Project Manager, 2008–2010
NETLEARN CORPORATION, King of Prussia, PA
A Web-based provider of digital learning resources for the K–12 market.

Oversaw integration of sales and accounting applications with Oracle database for one-year-old company in data warehouse environment. Met with department managers to determine business needs, developed high-level design requirements and specifications, and created project plan. Directed third-party company in rebuilding database to support requirements. Managed in-house implementation, working with executive management; IT specialists; and data warehouse, operations, sales, and accounting staff.

Accomplishments

- Successfully completed project on schedule and in accordance with requirements.
- Automated numerous sales and accounting functions.
- Empowered sales and marketing staff with system that generated 20 critical reports required for tracking state of business and increasing sales.

Continued

This resume emphasizes business skills and accomplishments to give this individual a competitive edge over other candidates with equally strong technical capabilities.

CRAIG LAND

craigland@gmail.com ■ Page 2

Information System Integrator/Business Analyst, 2006–2008
CAR-TOUCH ENTERPRISES, Horsham, PA
An auto detailing franchise with 300 locations throughout the United States and Canada.

Led team in migrating AS/400 legacy systems to client-server environment. Gathered requirements, investigated existing hardware and software, and researched third-party solutions. Designed and developed Visual Basic GUI application with Oracle back end, which performed inventory control, purchasing, sales and marketing, vendor development, and R&D financial management. Implemented remote service enabling franchises to access central database, as well as a telephone system enabling customers to reach any franchise via a single number.

Accomplishments

■ Saved $50,000 annually and improved quality of reports with updates to telephone application.
■ Proposed system conversions and application updates potentially yielding savings of up to $1 million and improving operations with automated, on-demand, up-to-date reports.

Project Manager, 2005–2006
FORD CONSULTANTS, Princeton, NJ
An IT consulting firm providing solutions for Global 1000 corporations.

Managed development of client-server applications in three areas: construction, project evaluation and facilitation, and employee/financial/purchasing reports.

Project Manager/Programming Manager, 1998–2005
GRANGE MARKETING, Philadelphia, PA
One of the largest direct-marketing companies in the metropolitan Philadelphia area.

Led multiple short-term direct-marketing projects from beginning to end in fast-paced environment. Developed project proposals, obtained customer approval, and oversaw development and support. Simultaneously managed long-term accounts with insurance companies and federal agencies, supplying payroll and other data services. Supervised staff of 15 in IT, operations, customer service, and marketing.

Accomplishments

■ Consistently increased sales and achieved profits in line with objectives—15%–20% per project.
■ Successfully managed government accounts with strict time frames and security requirements.

Education, Certification

B.S., Accounting, Temple University, Philadelphia, PA

Project Management Certificate, Penn State Great Valley, Malvern, PA

Computer Programming Certificate, Philadelphia Training, Philadelphia, PA

Additional IT Courses, Drexel University, Philadelphia, PA
Windows NT/Server, PL/SQL, Oracle, C++, Power Builder, Visual Basic

RESUME 79: BY ALICE HANSON, CPRW

Jackie Cardiff

(206) 523-1090   10007 Shoreline Avenue NW ▪ Seattle, WA 98000   jackie.cardiff@mac.com

Senior Business Systems Analyst / Documentation Lead

Experienced IT solutions analyst and matrix-team tech leader with strong IT / analysis / tech writing / documentation / user training skills and 10+-year success record on private & public sector COTS projects.

QUALIFICATIONS

Experience	More than 10 years of experience in IT consulting in public and private sector environments, 2 years in technical writing, and 8 years in systems analysis of complex business systems, including documenting business and system process flows, creating logical data models, and writing user and functional requirements.
Business & Systems Analysis	Currently work with business users at IKON to create business and system requirements for Puget DOT. Worked with 47 business experts representing 18 businesses in 5 divisions to establish business and system requirements for purchase of FDM software by Puget Fire Department.
User Training	Created training plan and curriculum materials including system user guides, job aids, seminar outlines, and oral presentations to accommodate diverse audiences at McCaw Wireless.
COTS Implementation	Worked with Puget Fire Department to plan integration of commercial off-the-shelf (COTS) FDM software enterprise-wide.
Vendor Evaluation	Evaluated FDM software for Puget Fire Department for their 8 lines of business.
Software Testing	Managed test teams that performed systems and user acceptance testing.
Documentation	Excel at synthesizing complex information into high-quality, highly usable documents that fit the needs of the target audience, utilizing proven writing, editing, layout, and organizational skills.
Vertical & Horizontal Communication	Ten-year success record working at all levels, internally and with multiple vendors/agencies, to drive positive change, gain acceptance, meet deadlines, and resolve problems in a timely manner. Excel at motivating matrixed teams to embrace value of business process improvement.

EXPERIENCE

VULCAN TECHNOLOGY PARTNERS,
2003 to Present

Areas of Achievement:

Business Requirements

Business Process Redesign

System Automation

End-User Guide Development

Application Integration

Enterprise-Wide Business Analysis

Creation of Business Process Models

Content & Business Rules

COTS Implementation

SENIOR BUSINESS ANALYST / CORPORATE TRAINER
Manage multiple concurrent assignments on-site for technology consulting firm's clients. Create change management plans, executive summaries, and training curricula. Train staff in change management methodologies through group and individual training, job aids, and quick user guides. Develop corporate standards and reengineer systems to comply with industry standards.

Select Business & Systems Analysis Projects:

- **Puget Department of Transportation (IKON):** Current project—Working to collect business requirements for permits and inspections for use of right of way (ROW).

  Previous Project (2008–2009)—Business process redesign and system automation that improved availability of street design information from 8 months to 10 days. Developed and delivered end-user guide and training materials for city's street network database and GIS.

- **Puget Fire Department:** Established strategic threshold for application integration and laid foundation for future integrated IT development. Planned and conducted enterprise-wide business analysis across 8 lines of business for potential integration of more than 78 stand-alone applications into central repository. Facilitated joint requirements planning sessions with 47 business experts representing 18 units across 5 divisions. Created business process models integrating 8 lines of business. Identified information exchanges defining content/business rules.

The hybrid format of this resume emphasizes both functional skills areas (in the left column) and business performance and results. It helped this candidate secure an interview from among 350 applicants for a job with the City of Seattle.

Systems Analyst
(206) 523-1090   Page 2   **Jackie Cardiff**
jackie.cardiff@mac.com

VULCAN TECHNOLOGY PARTNERS, continued

Bus. / Fee Requirements
Screen Layouts
Application Logic
Business / System Process
Documentation
Change Control Processes
Service Quality
Improvements
Market Analysis
High-Level Presentations
IT & Business Solutions
Change Management
Plans
Fit & Gap Analysis
Interviewing
Facilitating Multilevel
Meetings

- **Puget County Department of Development and Environmental Services:** Implemented COTS (Permits Plus), a specialized client-server construction and land-use permit-management system for PC networks. Defined business and fee requirements to track billing. Designed screen layouts/fee computations. Built application logic. Fulfilled critical deadlines.

- **McCaw Wireless:** Analyzed and synthesized business and system process documentation for customer-care database to increase development productivity by 80%. Developed and implemented change-control processes and facilitated cross-functional change control boards.

- **Vulcan Technology Partners:** Led strategic marketing initiative to improve quality of product delivery and reduce time to market from 3 months to 6 weeks. Enhanced attractiveness of consulting team in highly competitive market. Performed market research and analysis, interviewed 34 business experts, developed business strategy, prepared and delivered presentations supporting business case, wrote executive summary, and conceived software solution.

- **Puget County Superior Court:** Avoided $3 million in system development costs by writing change-management plan based on operational, technical, and economic feasibility. Conducted fit and gap analysis comparing juvenile-justice information-management system to proposed state system. Interviewed individual business experts and facilitated cross-functional meetings to identify critical business process in 6 juvenile-justice practice areas.

- *The Snohomish Ledger:* Planned, defined, and tracked all tasks and milestones. Estimated time and completion costs for converting from evening to morning distribution. Met all critical deadlines and delivered enhanced system to support product for home delivery.

**OTHER
EXPERIENCE**

Areas of Achievement:
Technical / Procedural
Documentation
End-User Documentation
Online Help Systems
Organizational &
Personnel Management
Leadership, Mentoring &
Supervision
Budgets & Financial
Administration
Matrixed Team Leadership

Business Systems Analyst — King City Light, Seattle (1998–2003)
Program Coordinator — Puget County Department of Public Health, Seattle (1994–1998)

Held increasingly responsible management positions with an emphasis on organizational development, business analysis, customer service, and program management. *Highlights:*

- Developed end-user documentation and online help systems for new software. Analyzed customer service and wrote new customer-service procedure manuals.

- Evaluated and defined processes, tools, methods, and critical success factors impacting processes. Calculated ROIs. Hired, trained, and supervised 16 union-represented employees. Analyzed, developed, and standardized job procedures. Liaison with high-level executives in other agencies.

- Recommended and prepared justifications for $2.2 million budget. Reconciled annual $6 million cash intake by branch office. Supervised financial reports for city treasurer's office. Managed $500,000 annual cash flow for commercial real estate firm.

- Pioneering leader on team of 5 multi-county administrators credited with planning and building business foundation that became nationally recognized program for public education and service to the AIDS population.

EDUCATION & CREDENTIALS

B.S., *summa cum laude*, Stanford University

Certificate in Dependable Strengths Articulation

BRIAN D. DE BOER

123 Pheasant Court
Liberty, Missouri 64068
816-555-5555 • bdeboer@aol.com

CAREER PROFILE

Telecommunications professional with 20+ years of experience in Project Management, Sales, Service, and Purchasing/Billing. Indispensable in financial turnaround of major telecommunication company's cabling business from negative revenues to **million-dollar-per-year profits.** Concurrent responsibilities in sales force instruction and collaboration, motivating others to act on technical and customer-related initiatives. History of strategic technology deployment to streamline processes, slash expenses, and drive profits. Highly effective in communicating and monitoring expectations.

➤ Project Management	➤ Sales and Marketing / Presentations
➤ Purchasing / Inventory Management	➤ Custom Wiring / Cable Contracting
➤ Contractor Management	➤ Customer Relationship Management

CAREER ACHIEVEMENTS

Project Management

- Spearheaded ground-up construction of a large contractor database (40+ contractors) over 4 states. **Results:**
  - ➤ **95% contractor-membership** in the ABC Technologies authorized service program.
  - ➤ **35% climb** in company's **cabling margin,** primarily through analysis/reduction of expenditures.
- Boosted sales force productivity by training team on key customer questions and methods to identify sales opportunities. **Result:** 50% increase in new business lead generation.
- Streamlined job bid turnaround time from 1 week to 2–3 days by maximizing technology use.
- **Slashed** time spent on accounts receivable **paperwork** by approximately 8 hours weekly through successfully implementing direct billing method.
- **Engineered a contract** with a major **17-location account,** culminating in accountability as national account contact for all Systimax cabling. **Results:**
  - ➤ Upgraded all production/box plants nationwide.
  - ➤ Project-managed all locations and sourced nationwide to attain a single point of contact.
  - ➤ Delivered finished product that exceeded client expectations and increased future business.
- Nominated by account executives (based on outstanding accomplishments) to attend first XYZ Communications Elite meeting.
- **Increased profit** margin **25+%;** tagged by ABC Technologies to present success strategies (on generating a profitable cabling business) at wiring conference.

Sales

- **Exceeded sales quota 175%,** 2 years (Millionaires Club).
- **Achieved 150% of sales quota,** 2 years (Superachievers Club).
- Recruited to ABC Technologies Network Systems National Task Force that originated a pricing structure for Global Emerging Market organization.

Continued…

This resume is in a primarily functional format, showcasing achievements under key subheadings and placing details of work experience on page 2.

BRIAN D. DE BOER

816-555-5555 • bdeboer@aol.com
Page Two

CAREER PROGRESSION

Steady telecommunications career progression. Initiated career with National Communications and presently perform project management at XYZ Communications. Each transition generated from company/divisional "spin-offs" (mergers, acquisitions, purchases, and so on).

XYZ COMMUNICATIONS (ACQUIRED A DIVISION OF **ABC TECHNOLOGIES**), Olathe, Kansas, 2010–Present
Regional Wiring Coordinator • Contractor Manager • Provisioning Coordinator
Charged with supervising 40 contractors in 4 states. Project-plan and execute custom cabling jobs from order to installation to billing to customer satisfaction. Participate in design meetings at customer sites. Negotiate with suppliers for optimum material prices and continually streamline processes/procedures, resulting in declining expenses and climbing profits. Manage purchasing and inventory.

ABC TECHNOLOGIES (ACQUIRED A DIVISION OF **MIDWEST TELEPHONE**), Olathe, Kansas, 2006–2010
Provisioning Coordinator • Contract Manager • Wire Design Specialist/Account Executive
Similar to prior Account Executive position at Midwest Telephone.

MIDWEST TELEPHONE (A SPIN-OFF FROM **NATIONAL COMMUNICATIONS**), Lenexa, Kansas, 1994–2006
Account Executive • Systems Technician
Consistently exceeded sales quotas, earning placement in Millionaires and Superachievers clubs. Originated a profitable cabling business from ground up to 40 contractors in 4 states by effectively networking, accruing leads, generating proposals, and closing sales.

NATIONAL COMMUNICATIONS, Lenexa, Kansas, 1992–1994
System Technician • Repair Technician • Installer

COMMUNICATIONS EDUCATION / KNOWLEDGE

Bachelor of Science in Telecommunications, University of Missouri, Columbia, Missouri

- ➤ Graduate, **ABC Technologies Career Path Program,** 2008
- ➤ **Certifications:** Panduit; Mohawk; Bertek; Belden and ABC Technologies Fiber Optics; ABC Technologies Systimax Certification in Installation, Sales, and Design/Engineering
- ➤ **Training:** LAN and WAN environments, networks, DSU/CSU
- ➤ **Installation/Repair:** Tier 1/Tier 2 Levels
- ➤ **Other:** All Comkey products; all other AT&T vintage PBX switches; UNIX language; advanced electronics

PROFESSIONAL AFFILIATION

- ➤ **Member,** BICSI, 2005–Present

19522 Antioch Road Overland Park, Kansas 66211	**KATE C. BALDWIN** kcb@everestkc.net	H: 913.555.3467 C: 913.555.2925

UTILITIES / PUBLIC WORKS / TELECOMMUNICATIONS INDUSTRIES
Engineer ■ Project / Program Manager ■ Contract Negotiator

Detail-oriented and quality-focused professional with 15+ solid years in the utility industry. **Instrumental leader in Secure Communication Services' 17-year history of success** in project management, maintaining a stellar track record of client satisfaction, follow-on work sold, and assignment completion on time and **under budget as much as 25%.** Focus is improving service for residential and commercial customers in diverse carrier service areas. Exceptional critical-thinking abilities positively impact technically complex projects.

—Areas of Knowledge and Experience—

- Engineering Design
- Quality Assurance
- Contractor / Supplier Negotiation
- Contract Preparation / Execution

- Easement Research / Procurement
- Written / Oral Communication Skills
- Interpretation of Building Plans / Specs
- Construction Cost Estimates

- Requests for Proposal / Quotation
- Complex Project Management
- Resource Management / Utilization
- Cross-Functional Team Management

PROFESSIONAL EXPERIENCE

SECURE COMMUNICATION SERVICES, INC., Leawood, Kansas   2001 to 2011
DESIGN ENGINEER / PROJECT MANAGER

Performed hands-on management of this **design engineering, construction estimating, and project management** enterprise serving the telecommunication industry. Key clients: Sprint, Everest Communications, and local school districts.

Marketed contract service to local providers, secured provisioning contracts, and managed the ensuing projects, ranging from nine months to one year per project. Recruited and managed public/independent contractors on clients' diverse job sites. Detailed engineering specifications; ordered material; and prepared drawings, installation notes, and cost estimates. Negotiated permanent easements with property owners. Collaborated weekly with customers to maintain project integrity.

—Achievements in Negotiation—

- **Negotiated *all* project contracts** with Sprint, Everest Communications, Kansas University, local school districts, and other clients.
- **Achieved 100% success in negotiating** hundreds of permanent utility easements with property owners.
  - Applied knowledge of procurement practices, including legal aspects: researched ownership, accessed current warranty deed, performed chain-of-title search, and located existing easements.
  - Negotiated a diversity of easements, including cell sites that sometimes involved enlarging existing sites to accommodate the (larger) cell sites.

—Achievements in Budget Management—

- **Continually ran 98% of budget** on Sprint jobs, exceeding contract expectations.
- **Led major, $125M project** that involved linking seven central office locations via fiber-optic cable.
  - Managed complicated project from initial engineering specifications to final construction inspection.
  - Faced with and successfully overcame numerous challenges, including identifying appropriate location in bedrock to place cable, crossing rivers, and working around oil company pipelines.
  - Collaborated with inspector, city, and highway department to ensure cable was placed at proper depth; met with Corps of Engineers; interfaced with companies for proper specifications for crossing their easements; and orchestrated a number of other details to ensure project was built on time and as designed.
  - Achieved project outcome **within 2% of forecasted budget.**
- **Consistently remained 18% to 25% under project budget** on all other projects.
- **Developed quality checklist** and then achieved buy-in, improving efficiency of engineering projects that eventually led to **35% reduction in bid prices.**

Continued

Subheadings are used to call out achievements in specific areas that will be of interest to hiring authorities. The format makes it easy to quickly skim the resume for key information.

Kate C. Baldwin, Page Two   H: 913.555.3467 ■ C: 913.555.2925

—**Achievements in Personnel / Project Planning and Management**—

- **Successfully recruited/directed project managers, engineers,** transmission engineers, construction inspectors, and CAD drafters for varied assignments across four states, cultivating a solid network of contractors and referrals.
  - Managed human resources details for up to 20 employees, including health care and regulatory requirements and performance evaluations.

- **Saved future relocation costs** by identifying clearance problems, then planning reroute of entire communication systems, initially adding to project cost, but dramatically curbing long-term spending.

—**Other Achievements: Service Delivery, Presentations, Awards**—

- **Optimized service delivery and specifications** by contributing to new engineering, estimating, and construction procedures for long-distance fiber routes.

- **Delivered presentations to local service providers/employees** on Long-Range Outside Plant Planning (LROP), easement procurement, and fiber routes from central office to central office.

- **Awards: Young Engineer of the Year,** Midwestern Society of Telephone Engineers; **Small Business of the Year,** Leawood Chamber of Commerce.

BLUE DESIGNS, Lenexa, Kansas   1994 to 2001
TELECOM ENGINEERING SUPERVISOR

- **Created and implemented internal staffing processes** for LROP for telecommunications projects.

- **Managed outside plant engineering projects** from routine work orders to customized estimates.

- **Applied engineering concepts** such as resistance design, loading, pressurization, dedicated plant, underground cable, buried cable, aerial cable, pair gain, pole lines, fiber cable, and outside plant mechanized computer programs.

U.S. ELECTRIC, Topeka, Kansas   1991 to 1994
TECHNICAL WRITER ASSOCIATE

- **Challenged with concept-to-completion** engineering projects: captured all field notes, secured right-of-way easements, and monitored the proper specification of drafts.

- **Promoted to satellite office manager** at remote location.

PROFESSIONAL DEVELOPMENT

- **Bachelor of Science in Telecommunications,** DeVry University, Kansas City, Missouri

- Outside Plant Engineering course, Western Electric

- Multiple Right-of-Way courses

- **Selected Technical Knowledge:** Microsoft Word, Excel, PowerPoint, Outlook Express; T1 Integrator; T1 Complete; T1 Mighty Mouth; SDSL Endeavor

LEE CARRION

816-937-1141   58172 Georgia Hwy. 736 ◆ Townsend, Georgia 31714   lee.carrion@verizon.net

VISIONARY TECHNOLOGY LEADER

Project Management ◆ *Research & Development* ◆ *Strategic Planning & Analysis* ◆ *IT Consulting*
Team Leadership ◆ *Product Development* ◆ *Staff Training*

Focused, dedicated, and highly motivated professional offering 11+ years of solid contributions and blended background in technology management and accounting. Exceptional dedication to growing with cutting-edge technologies and seeking to achieve beyond expectations in every endeavor. Motivational leader and communicator, capable of building cohesion and project engagement across all levels of staff, management, vendors, and customers.

Proven expertise in life-cycle project management from conception to completion, driving process improvements at all levels with forward-thinking, strategic-planning attitude to surpass expectations and goals. Accomplished trainer, developing online classes and delivering diversified training to more than 600 professionals. Strong belief in training and education as path to success and positive change.

Areas of Strength & Expertise

◆ Technology Management	◆ Strategic Planning	◆ New Product Development
◆ Networking & Infrastructures	◆ Technology Training	◆ Budgeting
◆ Change Management	◆ Security Policies	◆ Team Building
◆ Virtual Team Leadership	◆ Regulatory Issues	◆ Media, Firewalls & Servers
◆ Customer Service	◆ Evaluation & Testing	◆ Hardware & Software

TECHNICAL SKILLS

Knowledge: Highly skilled in troubleshooting, resource capitalization, documentation, policies and procedures, and new technology launch.

Software: Windows Server 2008, MS Office 2010

Hardware: Routers, Servers, PCs, Media

PROFESSIONAL EXPERIENCE

Southeast Technical Institute   2008–Present

TECHNOLOGY SPECIALIST

Drive new technologies, coordinating networks in multiple locations. Manage media, firewall, servers, and computer labs. Direct projects through virtual teams; supervise and train IT staff. Provide internal customer service, computer troubleshooting for instructors and executive personnel, and external customer service, supporting and training local business community on software and hardware. Collaborate with campus executives and staff to track project progress and ensure fulfillment of IT goals. Develop budgets.

Achievement Highlights:

- Cultivated campus network to support 400–500 students, setting up labs, servers, firewall, routers, and Internet access. Designed media labeling for patch panels, implemented policies and procedures, instituted test centers, ordered all technical supplies, and trained IT staff.
- Initiated technology and process improvement measures, including scanning forms for campuswide accessibility, designing online shortcut learning, and directing installations and upgrades.
- Consolidated operating systems to Windows Server 2008, facilitating tech support efforts.

Continued

The headline and subheading that lead off the resume demonstrate an effective placement of keywords, further supplemented by the Areas of Strength & Expertise list at the end of the profile.

LEE CARRION — lee.carrion@verizon.net — Page 2

PROFESSIONAL EXPERIENCE, continued

Atlanta Sports Therapies   2004–2008

ACCOUNTANT

Trained and supported companies on planning and setting up accounting software, maintained spreadsheets, performed audits on equipment, and set goals to decrease debt ratios, constantly updating on accounting regulations and technology improvements. Managed purchases, sales, and rental of property and coordination of international trips. Created 3D images for presentations and maintained digital camera images and scanned images on PC.

Charlois, Shepard, Pruyn & Black, CPA Firm   2000–2004

JUNIOR ACCOUNTANT

Supported clients in accounting, training clients and staff on accounting software, ensuring proper use of software, planning budgets, and managing accounting books for several companies. Maintained complex spreadsheets, coordinated loan application forecasts and projections, completed tax returns, performed audit procedures on nonprofit organizations, and supervised bookkeepers.

EDUCATION & TRAINING

Bachelor of Science in Accounting — Valdosta State University
Associate of Business Administration — Abraham Baldwin College

Technical Training: NetWorld Interop Conference, Windows Server 2008, TCP/IP, Cisco Basic Routing, Checkpoint Firewall-1, MS Office, NetMeeting, Basic Oracle—Introduction Class, Basic Linux—Introduction Class, Mastering the Secrets of VPNs, Voice over IP

Management Training: Zig Ziglar's Over the Top, Becoming a Team Leader, Business and Personnel Management; Dale Carnegie's How to Handle Difficult People, How to Be a Supervisor in a Competitive World

Pending Certifications: MCSE & CCNA

PROFESSIONAL AFFILIATIONS / PRESENTATIONS

Member: CPA Association, Chamber of Commerce, Toastmasters, Kiwanis

Presentations: Technology Mission—2008, Becoming a Leader—2006, Telephone Techniques—2005

KAULANI MAKINO

507 Bedford Drive, Camarillo, CA 93010
Home: (805) 555-1212 | makinopc@hotmail.com

**Systems Engineer / Network Administrator / Analyst with 10+ years of experience in
wired and wireless secure networks. Computer degree and multiple certifications.**

PROFESSIONAL EXPERIENCE

SYSTEMS ENGINEER / NETWORK SECURITY CONSULTANT   2005–2011
COMPUTER SCIENCES CORPORATION, INDUSTRY SERVICES GROUP, El Segundo, CA

Key technology advisor to health-industry clients during their wireless LAN migrations. Produced life-cycle cost
and security analyses involving system requirements determination, modeling, and trade-off studies; baseline
configuration; and test plan, criteria, and procedures development.

➢ Collaboratively designed and set up a secure IP broadband-based satellite system that delivered global
communications and positioning (GPS) to more than 50 corporate enterprise partners and 10,000 employees.

NETWORK ADMINISTRATOR / ANALYST   2002–2005
CONCURRENT COMPUTER CORPORATION, Laguna Hills, CA

Charged with providing secure networking solutions and technical support to industries including academic,
aerospace, and scientific. Performed advanced analysis and optimization of network, server, and workstation
performance.

➢ Reengineered the company's archaic backup system, replacing it with supersized shared-disk arrays and
pooled devices connected within a secure storage-area network (SAN). The results were reduced backup
costs, zero data loss, and a 30% cut in overtime labor.

SYSTEMS ENGINEER I   2001–2002
ELECTRONIC DATA SYSTEMS CORPORATION (EDS), Folsom, CA

Performed wireless network feasibility studies for government-specific applications.

➢ Baselined a local prison's wired/wireless network infrastructure. This baseline became the backbone of a bid
for a multiyear, multimillion-dollar state prison communications network.

TECHNICAL SKILLS SUMMARY

CORE STRENGTHS: Project planning and management for wired/wireless connectivity (e-mail/groupware/
Internet/intranet); hardware/software configuration; RSA-compliant security/firewalls

PLATFORMS: Windows and Mac OS, Exchange, Active Directory, Linux, UNIX, Cisco, Novell NetWare

SECURITY SOLUTIONS: Norton Internet Security Corporate, McAfee Enterprise, Sun Identity Server, Oracle
Application Server, Citrix Metaframe Password Manager, Datakey CIP, IBM Client Security, Cisco Secure Access
Control

EDUCATION and CERTIFICATIONS

Bachelor of Science in Computer Science (BSCS), University of California at Los Angeles	1998
Microsoft Certified Systems Engineer (MCSE)	2005
Cisco Certified Internetwork Engineer (CCIE), Security+	2008
Certified Information Systems Security Professional (CISSP)	2009

*A brief headline-style introduction immediately communicates this job seeker's focus and key qualifica-
tions. One key project or achievement is highlighted for each position.*

MICHAEL SAWYER, MBA, PMP

2525 Horseman Drive, Plano, TX 75025 ♦ m_sawyer@hotmail.com ♦ (972) 390-9067

PROJECT MANAGEMENT EXECUTIVE

~ Delivering Proven, Accomplished PMO Leadership with a History of Success:
Overseeing Multimillion-Dollar Initiatives, Capturing Multimillion-Dollar Savings & Exceeding Expectations ~

High-energy, detail-oriented senior-level professional offering 17+ years of PMO experience, advanced financial modeling knowledge, and superior strategic planning skills. Known for uncompromising integrity; collaborative style; and ability to formulate broad, enterprise-wide solutions.

Extensive experience leading matrix, cross-functional teams and working with customers on requirements, planning, risk management, project issue resolution, and corrective action plans. Superior skills coaching project managers in best practices, including estimating, budgeting, planning, executing, and reporting.

CORE COMPETENCIES

♦ Project Portfolio Governance & Oversight	♦ Strategic Planning & Execution	♦ Risk Assessment & Mitigation
♦ IT Governance & Value Delivery	♦ PMO Design & Implementation	♦ Project Prioritization & Alignment
♦ Project Audit, Rescue & Recovery	♦ Policy & Process Improvement	♦ Resource Capacity Planning
♦ Strategic Change & Transformation	♦ Budget Creation & Control	♦ Demand Management

CAREER CHRONOLOGY

<u>Castle Network Communications, Inc.</u>, Richardson, TX   2008 to Present
SENIOR MANAGER, PROGRAM MANAGEMENT, Services and Solutions

Establish project management methodology, processes, and reporting for services and solutions practice areas. Devise and implement business management controls and collaboration tools to achieve planned financial and operational performance. Coach program / project managers on best practices, including project planning / scheduling, issue / risk management, and quality reporting / metrics.

♦ Strengthened services project management with the establishment of a Program Management Office (PMO) to provide oversight, methodology, process, tools, and transparency for a $14.3 million project portfolio.

♦ Increased team utilization from 65% to 88% by streamlining methodology, tools, and processes to align with project size and risk. Instituted resource capacity / demand model to improve staffing decisions.

♦ Increased revenue forecast accuracy 190% by improving project controls and deploying scorecard and status-reporting process.

♦ Captured 9% of revenue through an improved, emphasized change / scope management approach.

♦ Received 7 Kaizen Awards for implementing process and tool improvements, capturing $97,000 in year-to-year savings.

<u>Allied Computer Management Services (ACMS), Inc.</u>, Dallas, TX   2006 to 2008
SENIOR MANAGER, TRANSITION and PROGRAM MANAGEMENT, Operations Advisory Services

Recruited to work closely with senior-level leadership to conduct in-flight quality program reviews, risk management reviews, project recovery, and tollgate reviews. Developed and performed content review of ACMS program / project management methodology, SharePoint collaboration / reporting site, and enterprise project management environment. Consulted and provided guidance / direction to practice leads on establishing PMO organization and implementation of methodology.

♦ Recovered $70 million, 7-year finance and accounting outsourcing program, including customized accounts payable software solution, by removing obstacles and deriving go-live schedule that previously had no project work plans to support go-live date.

♦ Rescued $10 million global SAP implementation program by implementing PMO and developing predictive, integrated project work plans.

♦ Created workable project schedule and go-live strategy for $55 million software product, conducting project-controls assessment and in-flight project quality review.

♦ Strengthened PMO by leading assessment and program oversight for $1.4 million total benefits outsourcing program.

♦ Improved project controls by completing project review for $13.1 million Medicaid-recognized revenue enhancement program.

Continued

Good design and tight writing keep this resume very readable despite including a wealth of detail in the technically complex arena of program management.

MICHAEL SAWYER	Page 2	(972) 390-9067

McKinsey & Company, Dallas, TX   2000 to 2006

MANAGER, GLOBAL PORTFOLIO MANAGEMENT OFFICE (PMO), ATIS Network Services (2004 to 2006)

Engineered global PMO for 246-member team charged with prioritizing, planning, and controlling project portfolio with 75+ IT outsourced programs / projects totaling $18.1 million for FY06 and $6.9 million for FY05. Planned and approved business cases and measured cost savings of multiple IT and ITO project initiatives.

♦ Devised strategic plan and model to align the PMO to the CIO IT governance process.

♦ Captured, optimized, and realized portfolio value based on IT strategy, project priority, and resource capacity.

♦ Improved resource utilization and optimization by leading oversight of resource capacity versus project demand / priority management.

♦ Formulated Mercury ITG (HP PPM) migration strategy for demand, project, and resource management from Microsoft Project Server.

♦ Enhanced successful project delivery by instituting project tollgate review process for methodology and deliverable quality.

SENIOR CONSULTANT, GLOBAL PROGRAM MANAGEMENT OFFICE (PMO), ATIS Network Services (2002 to 2004)

Directed Global PMO for 227-member team to grow and strengthen project management through effective planning, execution, and coaching of matrix organization. Achieved financial and schedule targets by conducting quality reviews and driving strategic change initiatives.

♦ Spearheaded deployment of an Enterprise Project Management solution using Microsoft Project and Microsoft Project Server. Leveraged portfolio analyzer to report on key performance indicators.

♦ Secured 48% increase in reporting compliance and 65% increase in tracked projects with implementation of workforce-optimization solution that enabled more-efficient control of resource utilization.

♦ Achieved 100% process-improvement savings by designing an integrated dashboard Web site to control and report on all projects.

♦ Reduced aggregate completion of PMO projects 3+ months ahead of schedule by tracking, measuring, coaching, and improving project management practices, utilizing software tools and scorecard reporting.

CONSULTANT, PROJECT MANAGEMENT OFFICE (PMO), CIO Network Services (2000 to 2002)

Developed PMO for 176-member global team to oversee and control programs / projects. Defined and implemented PMO to track and manage issues, risks, dependencies, and deliverables for all projects. Developed and executed processes and methodologies for continuous project management improvement activities, including earned-value analysis and risk management.

♦ Produced $4.7 million cost savings by leading $2.5 million "Centralization of Services" program.

♦ Captured $7 million global cost savings by spearheading $4.5 million "Leveraging the Internet" program.

Affiliated Management Systems (AMS), Inc., Baltimore, MD   1998 to 2000

CONSULTANT, PROJECT MANAGEMENT OFFICE (PMO), Government & Education Management Systems (1999 to 2000)

Directed PMO for Integrated Revenue Management System software design and implementation program valued at $141 million. Instituted engagement management framework and program processes for 234-member project team. Developed and maintained recognized revenue financial model.

ANALYST, PROGRAM MANAGEMENT OFFICE (PMO), Government & Education Management Systems (1998 to 1999)

Led PMO for Integrated Revenue Management System software design and implementation program valued at $57 million for 114-member project team. Completed cost analysis for contract extension and modification. Conducted engagement and contract closeout by reassigning resources and ensuring all deliverables were complete.

Other Experience:

PRACTICE ADMINISTRATOR, The Heart Place (1998)
PRACTICE MANAGER, Innova Medical Group (1992 to 1998)
MENTOR / REVIEWER, National Math Foundation's SBIR / STTR Commercialization Program Grant Program (2007 to 2010)

EDUCATION

Master of Management, Strategic Leadership, University of Texas at Dallas, 2006

Master of Business Administration (MBA), Finance, Illinois State University, 1997

Bachelor of Business, Finance & Operations Management, Illinois State University, 1992

Project Management Professional (PMP) Certification, Project Management Institute, 2002

Foundation Certificate in IT Service Management, Information Technology Infrastructure Library (ITIL), 2005

♦ ♦ ♦ ♦ ♦

PATRICK McLAUGHLIN

18 Lake Court ◆ Chicago, IL 60610
312-449-2325 Home ◆ 312-232-7869 Cell ◆ pmclaughlin@gmail.com

SENIOR-LEVEL CONSULTANT – DESKTOP INFORMATION SYSTEMS

Database Applications ◆ Data Conversion Projects
Systems Analysis ◆ Design & Development ◆ Project Management ◆ Training & Support

Developing data solutions that set the standard for ease-of-use, robustness, and value delivered.

High-energy consultant with a wealth of experience designing and delivering feature-rich data management solutions for broad range of business applications. Innovative designer; a visionary thinker with a stellar record in recognizing unknown needs and developing intuitive, user-friendly solutions that surpass expectations.

<u>Core Expertise:</u>

- ✓ Developing well-conceived desktop information systems that take data and turn it into information.

- ✓ Building applications with a mind toward the future, delivering flexible, robust solutions—comprehensive data management systems—that can be adapted to meet unanticipated needs.

- ✓ Designing easy-to-use graphical user interfaces so intuitive they virtually eliminate the need for training.

- ✓ Overseeing database design projects, serving as liaison between end users and technical teams to facilitate identification and dissemination of business requirements.

SELECT CAREER HIGHLIGHTS

- **Accumulated extensive expertise in building data management solutions, designing and delivering well-received systems for notable clients such as UPS, Kraft, and the State of Illinois. Among successes:**

  - ✓ Hired by UPS for 3-week assignment, kept on board for 7 years, handling key conversion project covering 2 legacy systems. Achievements included creating an extracting tool with graphical user interface that worked like clockwork, facilitating nightly downloads while ensuring accuracy of data in high-pressure situation.

  - ✓ Developed weekly hot-list generation system, developing tool to pull order, inventory, and scheduling data from SAP to be used by logistics group to predict backlogs and back orders.

  - ✓ Created product evaluation application for Abbott Labs that shortened intensive 3-week data evaluation process to just minutes. Key feature was system for archiving images of products for easy retrieval and review, providing quick visual corroboration and incorporating then-groundbreaking bar-coding technology.

  - ✓ Developed data management system for clinical application, a system capable of evaluating results of thousands of tests across hundreds of dialysis patients, calculating measurements, and producing reports. Replacing mostly manual system with no reporting capability, application was a huge time-saver.

  - ✓ Built feature-rich production scheduling system for steel rack manufacturing company. Comprehensive all-in-one system included cost/commission calculators, form downloads, and customer communication tools.

- **Led major system projects for clients, effectively developing project plans, directing teams, and managing budgets to deliver results that met, if not exceeded, expectations:**

  - ✓ Managed large-scale systems analysis/assessment projects for various clients, identifying and documenting needs and vulnerabilities across multiple locations and recommending action and remediation plans.

  - ✓ Rescued failing attempt to install System Management Server (SMS) in 4 locations, designing and implementing solution that featured enhancements such as a user security module and "back door" inventory reporting system.

Continued

Projects are grouped under powerful introductory statements that communicate value. Notice how consulting and contract employment are presented in one listing on page 2, rather than delineating specific assignments with different companies.

PATRICK MCLAUGHLIN	PMCLAUGHLIN@GMAIL.COM	PAGE 2

- **Developed and delivered individual and group computer training seminars for a variety of audiences (Fortune 500 firms, computer training outfits, and schools/colleges), earning rave reviews for ability to relate to student needs and deliver highly relevant content:**
  - ✓ Provided one-on-one tutorials for executives at UPS, Kraft, Baxter International, and Motorola.
  - ✓ Conducted training courses for IT professionals, enriching content with real-world experience.

PROFESSIONAL EXPERIENCE

CONTRACT EMPLOYMENT   1994 to present
Independent Consultant Systems Analyst/Systems Developer/Project Manager

Design and develop systems/database applications for well-known clients across the financial, pharmaceutical, government, and healthcare industries, creating solutions to meet a broad range of business needs.

- Have enjoyed long-term engagement with UPS, repeat assignments with Kraft and Abbott Laboratories, and individual stints with numerous other companies, building long list of highly satisfied clients.

CHEMICAL BANK   1988 to 1994
Technology Manager/Applications Development Manager

Oversaw technology initiatives for major global department with worldwide offices and branches. Assessed needs, recommended solutions, and managed implementation of best-choice options.

- Led team in designing robust, user-friendly applications that improved efficiency. Among successes, implemented accounting system that increased departmental throughput by 300%. Also, saved more than $2.5 million through strategic consolidation/conversion of applications.

TECHNOLOGIES

Software:	Access, Excel, Word, Project, PowerPoint, Crystal Reports, Paradox, SMS, Dreamweaver, Publisher, ReportSmith
Languages:	VBA, VB, SQL, PAL, ObjectPAL, HTML, Fortran, COBOL
Databases:	Access, SQL Server, Paradox, Sybase, Oracle
Design Tools:	ERwin, InfoModeler, Visio

PROJECT SUMMARY

Range of Applications Developed

◆ Product Evaluation	◆ Component Catalog	◆ Lead Generation/Tracking
◆ Quality Assurance	◆ Production Scheduling	◆ Market Segment Tracking
◆ Defect Tracking	◆ Vendor/Contract Management	◆ Rates and Booking
◆ Clinical Testing	◆ Timesheet/Expense Accounting	◆ Employee Skills Inventory
◆ Notification Reporting	◆ Facilities Relocation	◆ Training/Certification Tracking

Partial List of Clients

◆ Kraft	◆ Baxter International	◆ Abbott Laboratories
◆ UPS	◆ McGraw-Hill	◆ Hewitt Associates
◆ ConAgra	◆ Sara Lee Corporation	◆ University of Illinois
◆ Solo Cup Corporation	◆ Nalco	◆ DePaul University
◆ Motorola	◆ Northwestern Hospital	◆ State of Illinois

RICHARD F. AMIRPOUR

19345 Miller Way • Austin, TX 73301
(mobile) 512-242-6691 • (home) 512-528-3571
amirpour@gmail.com

TECHNOLOGY CONSULTANT

Market-Driven Technology Innovations • Project Leadership • Application Development

Creative and forward-thinking IT professional with more than 20 years of experience leading the development and implementation of client-focused software solutions. Technology strategist who excels in solving challenging problems through business acumen and expertise in multiple technologies. Engaging communicator talented in leading teams for high-performance outcomes and in building productive client relationships.

Strategic Planning • Entrepreneurship • Process Reengineering • IT Strategies • Software Development
System Design • System Integration • Technology Deployment • Technology Evaluation
Data Mining • Outsourcing • IT Consulting

PROFESSIONAL EXPERIENCE

NEXT CENTURY IT, INC. — Austin, TX   1995–Present
Privately held software solutions provider helping clients retain customers and maximize revenues.
Founder • President
Deliver strategic and tactical IT leadership for customized software solution development to meet client business needs. Gather requirements and translate them into functional specifications. Manage major business functions including administration, vendor relations, business development, and finance. Direct 8 technical staff.

PROJECT AND PERFORMANCE HIGHLIGHTS:

Data Processing Automation Project for Canadian Exporters
- Challenged to create software system to automate data submissions from Canadian exporters to U.S. Customs and Border Protection Agency.
- <u>Result:</u> Achieved savings of $12M/year for largest privately held customs broker by automating 23% of manual process. Secured customer satisfaction by accelerating data processing and minimizing border delays, resulting in broker's competitive advantage and increased customer base.

E-commerce Business for Women's Apparel and Linens Brand
- Envisioned, developed, and implemented new e-commerce store for Web-based consumer sales.
- Propelled client's business by providing e-commerce store with rapid order management, including merchant services for immediate payment processing, warehouse integration for same-day order processing and inventory management, and shipment notification and tracking to customers.
- <u>Result:</u> Store generated sales of $2.25M in first 2 years of operation.

E-commerce Site and Online Inventory Management System for Retailer
- Created e-commerce site for retailer with 95 physical locations nationwide, designed to save shipping charges by fulfilling orders from nearest store to customer.
- System identified closest store with inventory, created and faxed picking and packing slips, and provided up-to-date information for customer service staff.
- <u>Result:</u> Site increased sales from $800K to $1.5M while requiring low operational expenses.

Data Warehouse and Data Mining Tools for Customs Broker Firm
- Created and implemented data warehouse and data mining tools for largest U.S. customs broker.
- Extracted and converted data from nonrelational legacy database to relational database.
- <u>Result:</u> Jumpstarted marketing, sales, and operations activities by providing near-live detailed reports on customer activity and branch performance, compelling sound decision-making.

continued

Significant consulting projects are spelled in out some detail, with results emphasized using underlining. The Technical Skills summary section on page 2 provides a comprehensive listing and eliminates the need to get too technically specific in the narrative sections of the resume.

INDEPENDENT CONSULTING — London, UK   1992–1995
Project Manager • Software Developer
Met unique challenges from clients requiring software innovations. Provided technical expertise to development projects, serving as liaison with software vendors to bridge corporate and technology goals.

- Integrated branding strategy with software development to create electronic corporate identity management system for Fortune 500 client that preserved corporate logo standards for color, size, and correct use, eliminating need for expensive custom manuals. Developed Web-based versions for intranet and extranet used by vendors.
- Partnered with Fortune 500 client representatives to obtain worldwide patent for software.
- Improved reliability of largest U.K. grocery chain's VM system configuration and vendor application. Produced 250% system performance improvements and reduced daily operational bottlenecks by recommending changes to memory storage capacity, user procedures, and software components.

CTS SOLUTIONS — Boston, MA   1990–1992
$50M technology and software solution company servicing Fortune 500 companies, with more than 500 employees.
Senior Consultant
Aligned client's operational software with strategic business objectives. Identified and addressed accounting and sales system weaknesses for client's 10 European subsidiaries.

- Designed and developed bill-of-material system that increased client's revenues through new ability to create customized marketing packages for prospective customers.
- Strengthened client satisfaction by analyzing, designing, and developing automated sales reconciliation system that addressed inventory discrepancies and slashed month-end reconciliation from days to hours.
- Enriched client's ability to maximize use of reconciliation system by conducting user training classes for representatives of 10 European countries and by writing system and user documentation.

EDUCATION & CREDENTIALS

B.S. in Computer Science — TEXAS A&M UNIVERSITY — College Station, TX

TECHNICAL SKILLS:

- Microsoft .NET Development Platform, ASP .NET, VB .NET, C#
- Microsoft SQL Server 2005, 2008
- Microsoft BizTalk Server 2006 R2
- Microsoft Commerce Server 2007, 2009

- Microsoft SharePoint Server 2007
- Business Object Crystal Reports
- Prime Information, UniVerse, PICK
- Microsoft Visio
- Microsoft Project

Justin Filmore

Midland, MI • 989.587.4499 • JFilmore@aol.com

HEALTHCARE MANAGEMENT/INFORMATICS

Sixteen years of professional experience in healthcare. Expertise in data warehouses, data management, and web portals. Combination of strategic and tactical skills and innovation resulting in landmark clinical operations technology models. Advanced skills in organizational change and project leadership. Great success as interdepartmental liaison through ability to articulate the business and technology "vision" to all audiences. Master's degree, PMP, Six Sigma, and business process and requirements management skills.

AREAS OF EXPERTISE

Change Leadership	**Project Management**	**Data Management**
IT–Business Integration	**Health/Medical Informatics**	**Strategic Business Planning**
Team Building & Leadership	**HIPAA Compliance**	**Content Management**

PROFESSIONAL PROFILE

MEDICAL SOLUTIONS CORP., Novi, MI   2006–Present

Profile: Physician organization dedicated to healthcare delivery and finance; $7M in annual revenue, 35+ employees. Focus is on lowering costs for insurance companies and self-insured employers and improving the health of their members.

VICE PRESIDENT, INFORMATION TECHNOLOGY DIVISION

Leveraged Lean Six Sigma principles to design tools, programs, and processes that decreased costs, increased revenues, and positioned the company for ongoing improvement and future market expansion.

- Created a novel hardware/database management and business intelligence platform that channels 100% of revenues and positioned company to increase revenue streams across all business lines.
- Among select projects, converted to ASP Web Application Environment; this amplified capabilities and reduced operating expenses. Leveraged clinical resources to expand revenues $4M per year.

ACTON MORRIS, Columbus, OH   1999–2006

Profile: One of the world's largest reinsurance companies. HQ in Zurich; $57B annual revenue; 1,500 U.S. employees.

ASSISTANT VICE PRESIDENT, PROJECT MANAGEMENT (2002–2006)

Designed the new enterprise project management office model. This included all policies, procedures, and best practices. Performed corporate manager role in support of internal clients—for example, strategic business units and corporate shared service units.

- Led teams in process redesign projects that involved HR. Transitioned all elements of HR's organizational model (Operations, Staffing, IT) and migration to SAP. Reduced staff overhead, improved workflows, and eliminated redundant processes.
- Prepared departments for Global HR SAP implementation.
- Managed cross-functional teams of 4–50 supporting domestic and global projects worth $200M.
- Avoided $30M in expenses and solidified reputation for excellence in fiscal leadership.

DIRECTOR OF INFORMATION MANAGEMENT, PARKE HEALTH DIVISION (1999–2002)

Profile: The Parke Health brand combines Acton Morris' global insurance, reinsurance, and risk-management expertise in the field of healthcare with more than 6,000 experts in 22 locations worldwide.

- Supported the U.S. branch: 40 employees, $100M in annual revenue. Business unit sells financial reinsurance products to U.S.-based healthcare markets: HMOs, group health plans, self-insured employer groups, and TPAs.
- Supported IT, finance, HR, and legal departments. Ensured that IT and business development strategies were in complement.
- Surveyed/assimilated emerging best-in-class population management products and technologies—many of which went on to become major assets—for example, Medical Solutions was later purchased by Aetna.
- Furthered leadership skills; led teams of 2–10 associates in high-visibility projects.

Continued

Extensive experience in health-care technology consulting is showcased in this well-designed resume. Notice the section at the end consolidating education, training, and a relevant internship.

989.587.4499 **Justin Filmore** JFilmore@aol.com

MEDICAL RESOURCE NETWORK, Cane, NY 1998–1999
Profile: A new division of Lattes HealthCare; focus on the Capitated Home Health Care market.
REGIONAL IT DIRECTOR / SENIOR PROJECT MANAGER
Helped CIO design and launch a new $200M, 200-person call center.

- Managed information systems in support of risk capitation contracts with major health insurers (e.g., Aetna) that covered 3.7 million customers. Supported clinical operations, claims management, and provider networking.
- Provided change leadership as the division grew to 400 employees, with revenues of $100M per year.
- Developed best practices for EDI/performance reporting and business process management. Managed all aspects of HIPAA planning and compliance.

ST. MARK MEDICAL CENTER, Newark, NJ 1996–1998
Profile: One of the largest acute-care hospitals in NJ; 400+ beds, 2,450+ employees.
DIRECTOR OF MANAGED CARE ADMINISTRATION
Originally hired as a management analyst and quickly promoted to director of managed care administration with 7 reports and primary focus to build the managed care business: PSO and ERISA business lines.

- Led and mentored team that managed main source of revenues: risk-sharing contracts with 7 HMOs.
- Revitalized database management tools and business processes to retain credentialing and care management functions, which reduced costs and replaced antiquated processes.
- Designed SOPs for provider relations and capitation administration.
- Reengineered operations to support corporate requirements.

WAYNE GENERAL HOSPITAL, Wayne, NY 1994–1995
Profile: An acute-care hospital serving mostly Jackson County; 250+ beds, 700+ employees.
PLANNING ANALYST
Managed IT projects that produced measurable improvements in hospital performance and patient care. Findings and recommendations supported enhanced community support and hospital standing. Reported to the director of operations management, who reported to the CEO.

- Conducted in-house studies and designed improved reporting tools that became a best practice and supported Joint Commission Accreditation.
- Worked on numerous high-visibility strategic planning and analysis projects.
- Established reputation as a gifted interdepartmental liaison, able to design and promote effective new IT solutions within the entire healthcare business model.

EDUCATION, CERTIFICATIONS & INTERNSHIP

RUTGERS UNIVERSITY, New Brunswick, NJ—**Master's degree, with honors**—Healthcare specialty
OHIO STATE UNIVERSITY, Columbus, OH—**Bachelor of Arts**—English

Certifications include: Project Management Professional (PMP), Advanced Project Management Certification (APMC), and Microsoft Project Server Master's Certificate

Training: SQL Server/Visual Studio 2008; MS Office Suite (advanced—programmer level); VB.NET, ASP.NET, TSQL, and VBA; IBM AS400; MS Visual Studio, Windows Server 2003/8, Exchange 2003/7 and ISA; extensive experience in relational database and object-oriented programming, business process modeling, business requirements management, and technical specifications

Internship: Worked with the CEO of Veteran's Memorial Home (Granville, OH) and the director of gerontology at Bergen Regional Medical Center (Bedford, NJ), gaining invaluable insight to the healthcare industry.

Roy G. Grossberg

40 Cypress Street, Laguna Beach, CA 92603 • (949) 342-4305 • royg@royggrossberg.com

Technology Entrepreneur and Consultant
Healthcare • Banking • Real Estate • Telecommunications

Prolific inventor and successful entrepreneur with a "golden touch" for pinpointing lucrative market niches. Created and grew several successful technology companies. Expert in international business and fluent in English, Hebrew, and Spanish; competent in Italian and French.

- Credited as inventor of numerous methods and devices in telecom, banking, and software sectors.
  - Recently filed 2 patents: a new type of centralized database, and a device that enables intercarrier routing for VoIP (Voice over Internet Protocol).
  - Invented one of the world's first trading-floor systems for stock exchanges (1980) and OUTERBANK, arguably the world's first online banking system (1978).
- Creative problem solver who thrives on technical challenge and quickly devises a solution for any technical obstacle.
- Adept at all phases of business creation, including R&D, product development, marketing, sales, financing, outsourcing, HR, and company administration. Exceptional ability to recruit top talent and assemble winning teams.

─────PROFESSIONAL EXPERIENCE─────

UNITEL LLC, Costa Mesa, CA   2005–2011
Telecom startup company, facilitates routing between carriers for Voice and Video over IP.
Founder | Chief Operating Officer | Chief Technology Officer

Created a successful company, starting from scratch, based on a technical breakthrough (IPexchange™) that facilitates telecom over IP. Outsourced software development, lined up numerous service providers, and took charge as overall project manager.

- Developed and brought to market a proprietary technology (patents pending).
  - Designed a new type of centralized database that lets carriers and IP domains directly route VoIP calls and other IP communications.
  - Collaborated with prospective clients. Pitched investors and touted Unitel in the business media. Won support by promoting benefits such as value-added services and major savings in hardware, software, and operational overhead.
  - Personally solved a critical technical obstacle that stumped outside technical teams. Stepped in, spent nights researching the problem, and devised a solution that leveraged personal expertise in SIP, TCP/IP, and UDP.
- Recruited top technical talent and developer firms by communicating compelling vision for Unitel.
- Completed the project, brought it to market, relinquished involvement in daily business operations, and ensured a seamless transition for new management.

PRUDENTIAL DOUGLAS ELLMAN (PDE) INC, New York, NY   1993–2010
Leading commercial real estate brokerage and management company.
Promoted to CTO (2000–2010)
President of joint venture, RE Tracking Systems LLC (1998–2005)
Promoted to Director of IT (1998–2000)
Systems Analyst (1993–1998)

continued

This technology consultant's notable and industry-changing inventions are highlighted in the summary as well as the position descriptions. Note the final bullet in his current job that clearly communicates that he is no longer involved in the day-to-day business and can take on a new challenge.

Roy G. Grossberg_____ (949) 342-4305 _____ royg@royggrossberg.com _____ Page 2

Created IT infrastructure that paved the way for 12 years of steady revenue and profit growth for PDE. Continually upgraded systems and established PDE's Web presence. Applied new technology that improved internal controls and accelerated business processes.

- Invented a software application, Real Estate Tracking System, that streamlined brokerage processes for PDE as well as the entire commercial real estate industry.
  - RE Tracking System led to major contracts, valued at nearly $10 million over a 5-year period, with a Fortune 100 company.
  - Set up a new company — RE Tracking Systems LLC, a joint venture with PDE — to market the software to other real estate companies. Managed the joint venture as president.
- Reduced annual operating costs 60% by cutting head count, increasing productivity, and consolidating operations. Introduced work-from-home capabilities that conserved office space and reduced capital expenditures.
- Invented and marketed RealtorPro™, commission-management software for commercial real estate.
  - Saved PDE more than $9 million in lost revenue over a 7-year period.
  - Eliminated human error, improved expense forecasts, and tightened controls on revenue.

COMPUTER ONE INTERNATIONAL, Brooklyn, NY   **1989–1993**
Value added reseller (VAR) for computer hardware and software (part of Anixter Group).
Technical Department Manager | Systems Engineer | Software Architect
Managed technical support; improved client services; and developed custom, on-demand applications for many customers. Strengthened and simplified the guarantee process.

- Created a dispatch system that revolutionized NYC's technical-support industry by cutting response time from days to 2 hours or less.
- Successfully sold more than $5 million in service contracts to major financial firms in NYC.

————ADDITIONAL SOFTWARE SUCCESSES (1978–1989)————

RGG SOFTWARE SOLUTIONS LTD, Tel-Aviv, Israel (1987–1989): President

- Developed statistical software for daily P&L reporting for Israel Discount Bank.
- Developed POS computing and an SEC-compliant reporting system that processed bills-of-materials and reverse bills-of-materials for a jewelry manufacturer (1985).

TEL AVIV DISCOUNT BANK LTD, Tel-Aviv, Israel (1978–1987): Senior Systems Analyst

- Created OUTERBANK, arguably the world's first direct-to-customer, online banking system (1978).
- Invented world's first trading-floor software, which established real-time and online communication between banks and stock exchanges (1980).
- Developed telecom emulators between Burroughs and IBM mainframes (1978).

————————EDUCATION————————

Technion, Israel Institute of Technology, Haifa, Israel (1976–1978)
Three years as electronic engineering major. Left the university to start a business and pursue independent research in software.

CHAPTER 10

Resumes for Technology Managers and Executives

- Technology and Business Executives
- Information Technology Executives
- Technology Operations Managers and Executives
- Information Security Officers
- Telecommunications Industry Executives
- CIOs, Vice Presidents, and Directors of Technology

Michael D. Sierra, MBA

1610 Spanish Ridge Ave. | Las Vegas, NV 89148
C 702.399.7285 | michael.d.sierra@yahoo.com

EXECUTIVE DIRECTOR OF BUSINESS INTELLIGENCE
Positioned to lead next-generation business intelligence.

Interconnect information management disciplines to deliver valued-based programs with commitment, shared purpose, and achievement of enterprise goals in

- Business Analytics
- Data Governance
- Business Intelligence (BI)
- Metadata Management
- Performance Management
- Data Quality
- Enterprise Information Management
- Master Data Management
- Data Integration

Insight: Established data-driven and highly informed decision-making capabilities for the executive office, including analysis of and insight into complementary services costing hundreds of millions.

Foresight: Developed metrics for executive management team to gain foresight into market conditions and trends, providing capabilities to answer difficult "what if" questions.

Understanding: Increased understanding of financial performance through use of metrics, data visualization, and executive scorecards.

Efficiency: Achieved multimillion-dollar cost savings in operations management through measurement, analysis, and process improvements.

Effectiveness: Energized and led implementation of enterprise-wide budgeting system that dramatically reduced time and effort to access information critical to decision making.

> *"Business intelligence is the ability of an organization or business to reason, plan, predict, solve problems, understand, innovate, and learn in ways that increase organizational knowledge, inform decision processes, enable effective actions, and help to establish and achieve business goals."*—Dave Wells, BI industry expert

PROFESSIONAL EXPERIENCE

MTM ILLUSION, Las Vegas, NV   2007–Present
Executive Director of Financial Services
Recruited to restructure a failing project with $1M in development costs and few results. Entrusted to turn around people, processes, and technology to realize the CFO vision of standardizing and transforming the collection, organization, and distribution of accounting data to support board of directors' and executive management's decision making.

Highlights of Achievements:

- Orchestrated implementation of an enterprise-wide budgeting system for 14 properties and 450 users, delivering within 2 years. Achieved a first-ever consolidated view of corporate and property budgets that dramatically reduced time and effort to access information critical to decision making.
  - Exceeded CFO expectations for year one by including 3 more properties than original estimate.
  - Deployed further improvements in performance, training, and maintenance in year two to include all properties, without increased staffing.
  - Incorporated forecasting capabilities for enterprise planning, completely independent of troublesome one-off manual spreadmarts.
  - Enabled analysis of actual versus budget reports with quick access to drill-down details.
- Realized annualized cost savings of $4.9M by developing an enterprise-wide financial data warehouse to integrate data from multiple point-of-sale, property management, and player tracking systems.
- Implemented a chart of accounts conversion to produce dramatic improvements in consistency and transparency, reducing the number of accounts by more than 75%.
- Achieved 100% user acceptance after redesigning financial reporting system to reduce hundreds of report variations into a single set of standard reports.
- Enabled fact-based decision making by executive office, providing multidimensional, cross-property analysis of complimentary player services costing hundreds of millions.

Continued

In addition to its strong content, this resume is distinguished by a relevant industry quote and the eye-catching format of the name at the top of both pages of the resume.

MICHAEL D. SIERRA, MBA

C 702.399.7285
michael.d.sierra@yahoo.com

CASINO ENTERTAINMENT, INC., Las Vegas, NV   1998–2007
Director of Business Intelligence (2005–2007)

Retained as Director of Business Intelligence after the largest merger in the history of the gaming industry. Valued for past achievements in delivering enterprise-wide financial systems and for possessing the vision and direction needed to integrate a complex array of systems and people. Set as a first task to assemble a cross-functional team of 18 corporate and property leaders to evaluate the current and future state of the business. Through ongoing discussions and negotiations, developed the financial analysis, reporting, and planning capabilities for the new organization, adding a large amount of "intelligent" functionality to the financial systems.

Highlights of Achievements:

- All 40 business units successfully completed the 2007 budget on new system that was redesigned through the collaborative efforts of internal partnerships.

- Saved $700K and nearly halved the number of required seats by resolving technical challenges that reduced licenses from 354 to 157.

- Served as a strategic change manager to deliver an executive revenue reporting system; consolidated data from 40 casino resorts and standardized the practices of 270 data-entry operators to improve data quality.

- Received 100% buy-in on an executive scorecard that was designed with an easy-to-use Excel front end and linked to Cognos Finance on the back end.

EMPEROR'S ENTERTAINMENT, INC., Las Vegas, NV (acquired by Casino Entertainment for $9.3B)
Director of Business Intelligence (1998–2005)

Spearheaded the charge to implement multidimensional analytic applications and reporting tools to enable cross-property comparisons in GL, DOR, and budgeting systems. Created a training program, including customized training material, to transition more than 200 users to more-advanced technology and increased functionality.

Highlights of Achievements:

- Designed and built an enterprise-wide system to collect, consolidate, and report the daily operating statistics from 18 properties to the board of directors and executive management team.

- Realized $100M in cost savings by implementing a centralized reporting and analysis system that reduced the time, effort, and resources needed to analyze and manage company operations.

- Replaced a time-intensive and error-prone budgeting system with right-time access to accurate information for 8 casino resorts. Initiated collaborative efforts enterprise-wide to provide consistency and comparability across properties, delivering system on time and below budget.

- Received enthusiastic C-level sign-off of enterprise-wide capital budgeting system that consolidated information in easy-to-use formatted Excel spreadsheets. Link to enterprise planning system enabled real-time analysis of capital decision impacts made quarter by quarter and year end.

- Developed metrics reporting system for executive management team to analyze market conditions over time, incorporating such measures as market capture percentage and market penetration.

EDUCATION AND PROFESSIONAL DEVELOPMENT

MBA, Emphasis: Information Technology, University of Nevada, Las Vegas

MS, Exercise and Sports Science, University of Arizona

BS, Health and Human Performance, University of Montana

PMP, Certified Project Management Professional

The Data Warehousing Institute (TDWI), numerous courses in business intelligence, business analytics, data mining, spatial analysis, data integration, and program and project management.

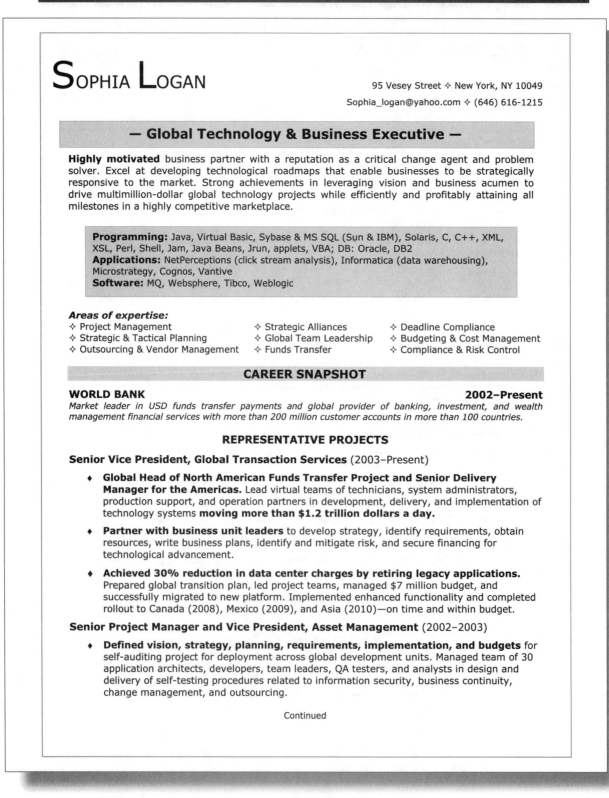

Sophia Logan

95 Vesey Street ✧ New York, NY 10049
Sophia_logan@yahoo.com ✧ (646) 616-1215

— Global Technology & Business Executive —

Highly motivated business partner with a reputation as a critical change agent and problem solver. Excel at developing technological roadmaps that enable businesses to be strategically responsive to the market. Strong achievements in leveraging vision and business acumen to drive multimillion-dollar global technology projects while efficiently and profitably attaining all milestones in a highly competitive marketplace.

Programming: Java, Virtual Basic, Sybase & MS SQL (Sun & IBM), Solaris, C, C++, XML, XSL, Perl, Shell, Jam, Java Beans, Jrun, applets, VBA; DB: Oracle, DB2
Applications: NetPerceptions (click stream analysis), Informatica (data warehousing), Microstrategy, Cognos, Vantive
Software: MQ, Websphere, Tibco, Weblogic

Areas of expertise:
- ✧ Project Management
- ✧ Strategic & Tactical Planning
- ✧ Outsourcing & Vendor Management
- ✧ Strategic Alliances
- ✧ Global Team Leadership
- ✧ Funds Transfer
- ✧ Deadline Compliance
- ✧ Budgeting & Cost Management
- ✧ Compliance & Risk Control

CAREER SNAPSHOT

WORLD BANK   **2002–Present**
Market leader in USD funds transfer payments and global provider of banking, investment, and wealth management financial services with more than 200 million customer accounts in more than 100 countries.

REPRESENTATIVE PROJECTS

Senior Vice President, Global Transaction Services (2003–Present)

- ♦ **Global Head of North American Funds Transfer Project and Senior Delivery Manager for the Americas.** Lead virtual teams of technicians, system administrators, production support, and operation partners in development, delivery, and implementation of technology systems **moving more than $1.2 trillion dollars a day.**

- ♦ **Partner with business unit leaders** to develop strategy, identify requirements, obtain resources, write business plans, identify and mitigate risk, and secure financing for technological advancement.

- ♦ **Achieved 30% reduction in data center charges by retiring legacy applications.** Prepared global transition plan, led project teams, managed $7 million budget, and successfully migrated to new platform. Implemented enhanced functionality and completed rollout to Canada (2008), Mexico (2009), and Asia (2010)—on time and within budget.

Senior Project Manager and Vice President, Asset Management (2002–2003)

- ♦ **Defined vision, strategy, planning, requirements, implementation, and budgets** for self-auditing project for deployment across global development units. Managed team of 30 application architects, developers, team leaders, QA testers, and analysts in design and delivery of self-testing procedures related to information security, business continuity, change management, and outsourcing.

Continued

Crisp and clean, this resume focuses on the most essential information to maximize its impact. The appearance is spiced up with a touch of appropriate gray shading.

SOPHIA LOGAN

95 Vesey Street ✦ New York, NY 10049
Sophia_logan@yahoo.com ✦ (646) 616-1215

JB SUMMIT MUTUAL   **1992–2001**
A global financial services firm with assets of $2.1 trillion and operations in more than 60 countries.

Senior Program Manager/Vice President, E-commerce Merger & Acquisitions Division (2001)

♦ **Led application portal team of 24 cross-functional vice presidents, officers, and consultants** that delivered an integrated "banker's desktop" with Web interface, supporting all global platforms of the bank. Spearheaded brainstorming sessions, defined and developed vision and strategy, set goals and budgets, and, in collaboration with LabSummit, developed a wireless platform that delivered portal content.

Client Knowledge Engine (CKE), LabSummit (2000–2001)

♦ **Transformed JB Summit business model,** enabling bank to capitalize on revolutionary technological possibilities brought on by the advancement of Internet technology. Drove global application development, analysis, customization, and integration of all client accounts and activities.

♦ **Built client data warehouse and designed analytical tools of inquiry** to examine data, identify behaviors, and personalize service. Resulted in major expansion of cross-selling opportunities across the global bank.
(Covered by and quoted in CIO Magazine, April 15, 2001)

Asset Management Services (AMS) (1997–2000)
Global Markets (1992–1997)

♦ **Assumed responsibility for failing project and turned it into a major success story for the bank.** Collaborated with business teams across all institutional markets and successfully migrated banking operations from "silos" to "horizontal" levels of knowing, understanding, and serving clients. Ranked among first banking pioneers to implement a Client Relationship Management (CRM) tool that provided profiling, calendar, and contact management functions.

♦ **Spearheaded Y2K effort for private bank.** Led teams and managed budgets for 70+ professionals, supporting critical production applications across lines of business. Met all goals and deadlines; achieved seamless transition.

Previous project management achievements:
At **National Bank,** led initiatives on global custody and corporate security relating to domestic and international technology feeds. At **Pinkerton,** developed financial mainframe systems for Federal Home Loan Bank, Manufacturers Hanover Trust, and Harcourt Brace Jovanovich.

EDUCATION

Bachelor of Science, University of Pennsylvania

Management, Technology & Leadership Training, New York Institute of Science

RESUME 91: BY MARJORIE SUSSMAN, ACRW, MRW, CPRW

SAMUEL LEHMAN

lehman@gmail.com   467 West 55th Street, Apt. 3D • New York, NY 10024   212-996-5757

SENIOR LEADERSHIP—GLOBAL MARKET
INFORMATION TECHNOLOGY | VIRTUALIZATION | PRODUCT DEVELOPMENT

Astute technology and business strategist, marshaling resources to support and achieve extraordinary goals.

Growth driver with **12 years of success in data-intensive environments** of GSS and a **$2B global technology, media, and telecommunications** hedge fund. Provide the technology vision, planning, and leadership for groundbreaking success. Build nimble, solutions-driven teams to deliver sophisticated systems that drive business performance. Achieve competitive edge and substantial cost savings through rapid and expert implementation of advanced technologies.

Expertise:

Strategic Planning & Leadership	Cutting-Edge Product Delivery
Productivity & Efficiency Improvement	Budget Management
Organizational Change Management & Development	Team Building & Team Motivation
Best Practices Assessment & Implementation	Consensus Building
Systems & Communications Breakthroughs	Client Satisfaction & Support

EXPERIENCE & ACHIEVEMENTS

TAILLE MANAGEMENT LLC—New York, NY (2006–Present)

Top 100 privately held global technology, media, and telecommunications hedge fund with $2B in assets under management.

Repeatedly being challenged to take on complex issues and repeatedly delivering stellar results—transitioning through evolving roles, wearing many hats, and succeeding at every turn. *Highlights include:*

Director of Software Solutions / Site Executive (2009–Present)

Handpicked by CEO to design, launch, and oversee the Software Development Division, which focuses on solving business process issues. Crafted the division's overall mission and objectives, including recruiting a 15-member development team, identifying and leading construction of the physical location, defining the product, and building the software. Acting as a **C-level executive,** started up the new division in 6 months, acting quickly to transform a prototype system into a robust product set for controlling operational functions, from research and portfolio management through vendor negotiations, strategic and investor relationships, productivity, and human resources. **Budget: ~$3M.**

- **Oversee complete life cycle** of product development—technology selection, architecture, quality assurance, competitive analysis of third-party vendors, and licensing of third-party software.
- **Managed a cross-functional team** of developers, business analysts, and quality assurance experts in developing the application.
- **Generated considerable cost savings** through displacing multiple third-party software products, improving the management and performance of the company's portfolio, and enhancing overall research capabilities.
- Currently in early stages of **commercializing the product suite** with the potential for establishing partnership with an existing financial software vendor to improve its offerings.

Systems Architect / Research Technologist / Media Lab Manager (2006–2009)

Reporting to the COO, provided strategic and technical leadership to enhance the research and evaluation process of new products in the technology, media, and telecommunications (TMT) sector as the company grew and expanded its presence in the global market. Implemented software systems to improve the identification of potential investments and the portfolio management system. Built and maintained the Internet media lab **(Budget: $30K)** used by analysts to perform firsthand product assessments.

- **Developed software tool** that calculated the revenue of an Internet company and significantly improved fund marketing. The tool was used during a year with **60%** total fund returns.
- Implemented **stock screening** for research and marketing materials ideas to attract new investors.
- Refined the **research process** to continuously identify opportunities for new technology tools and ensure the efficient execution of the research processes.

Continued

Standout elements of this resume include a branding statement below the headline, a brief overview below each company listing, and a consolidated section at the end that includes much distinguishing information.

SAMUEL LEHMAN   lehman@gmail.com • 212-996-5757

GLOBAL SOFTWARE SOLUTIONS (GSS)—New York, NY (1998–2006)

Fortune 15 global software solutions provider with $1.2B annual revenue from its enterprise-database software product.

Career-track progression from DB2 Customer Advocate/Staff Engineer to Solutions Architect, Design Center for E-transaction Processing, and ultimately to **Solutions Architect/Senior Software Engineer** with the GSS Software Group—Information Management Division. *Highlights include:*

Solutions Architect (DB2 Development) / Senior Software Engineer (2002–2006)

Resident DB2 expert for time-critical projects, with full responsibility for architecture, high-availability design, and performance of all data-intensive management products. Provided quick response and on-site global support for countless clients, including UBS Paine Webber and Samsung (Korea).

Participated as **Architect/Database Technical Lead for the New York Stock Exchange TradeWorks Initiative, establishing GSS's presence on the floor of the NYSE.** Fine-tuned end-to-end performance, high availability architecture, quality assurance, failure/recovery procedures, and disaster recovery architecture for the groundbreaking project and solid customer reference for future business ventures.

- Delivered frequent presentations to user groups and trade conferences as **evangelist** for the DB2 product line.
- Gained reputation as **technology deal closer,** ensuring GSS products/solutions fulfilled all customer needs.
- Forged a strong success rate in creating a **loyal client base** that never used competitor products.
- Member, **Joint GSS/NYSE Continuous Availability Task Force.**
- Member, **DB2 Product Architecture Review Board,** defining and prioritizing next-generation line items**.**
- Named **"Future GSS Technical/Executive Leader"** on the GSS Technical Resource List.

Solutions Architect—GSS Design Center for E-transaction Processing / Advisory Software Engineer (2000–2002)

Promoted to GSS's Design Center team of experts representing each of GSS's hardware and software divisions.

- Delivered formal DB2 trends and directions briefings to more than 50 **Fortune 500** CIOs and CTOs.
- Led or participated in more than **30 design workshops,** addressing end-to-end e-business architecture topics, including security, auditing, performance, high availability, application integration, and application migration.

DB2 Customer Advocate / Staff Software Engineer (1998–2000)

Recruited while still in college to GSS's 6-month training course on S/390-based technology and GSS sales and management techniques. Provided sales support and DB2 on-site customer support in the implementation of new product functions and best practices.

PROFILE

EDUCATION	BS in Computer Sciences–Binghamton University, Binghamton, NY, 1998
	GSS E-business University (hardware and software training)
AWARDS	GSS Invention Achievement Award (patent submission, "Method for Identifying User Authorization Based on Physical Access"), GSS Software Group Star Award, GSS Bravo Award
PRESENTATIONS	Speaker, SHARE Conference (2001–2005)
	International DB2 User Group (2001–2005)
	WebSphere Technical Exchange (2001–2003)
PUBLICATIONS	Coauthor, *GSS Redbook,* "WebSphere and DB2 for z/OS: The Perfect Couple"
	Coauthor, *GSS Redbook,* "GSS WebSphere and VisualAge for Java Database Integration with DB2, Oracle, and SQL Server"
	Coauthor, *GSS WebSphere Application Server for z/OS V4 Certification Exam*
	Author, *GSS White Paper: SQLJ Development and Deployment*
	Author, *GSS White Paper: Implementing the WebSphere Application Server for AIX Administrative Repository and Session*

PETRA BRANDT

183 VALLEYVIEW DRIVE, BELLE VERNON, PA 15012 ~ 724.872.9030 ~ petra@home.com

Senior Director, Information Technology

Set standards in information services and end user and supervisor training and improve customer satisfaction. Experienced in planning, managing, and rolling out high-profile projects—all on time and within budget.

~ Cost Control ~ Budgetary ~ Productivity Enhancement ~ Custom Applications Programming ~ Process Automation ~ Program Planning/Evaluation ~ Resource Planning ~ Quality Assurance/Quality Control (QA/QC) ~ ISO 9001 Certification ~ Marketing Program Development ~ Sales/Marketing Training ~ User Training ~ Client Connectivity ~ Internal/External Clients ~ Vendor Selection and Negotiation ~ Multidisciplined Team Leadership ~ Clinical Research ~ Clinical Testing ~ Clinical Trials ~ Health Care, Oil Industry Experience ~

Quality Improvements, Process Automation, Project Management Success

STEWART COMPANY, BELLE VERNON, PA   2006 to Present
Leading U.S. provider of esoteric and routine clinical testing and clinical trials.

Senior Director, Information Technology (2008 to Present)
$200M Division ~ 7 Direct Reports, 65 Indirect ~ $13M Annual Budget Always Met ~ Boosted Morale ~ Direct Report, Regional Information Technology Director

- **RETAINED STAFF:** Reduced IT employee turnover from 36% to less than 7% in first year.

- **INITIATED LONG-TERM STRATEGY:** Selected a vendor who authored short-term and long-term LAN improvement/expansion strategies, which were nonexistent prior to my involvement.

- **ESTABLISHED STANDARDS:** Led 10-person team in defining software life cycle development SOPs and secured ISO 9001 certification for laboratory with no carry-overs. Involved lab staff in design reviews, defined timelines and software requirements up front, and standardized documentation/validation.

- **EXPANDED TRAINING:** First person in IT to conduct team-building workshops. With minimal budget, launched a team agreement incorporated as a model for IT that improved customer and staff satisfaction. Developed sales training in 1 month that streamlined technology and got 500+ IT, sales/marketing, and business administration decision makers up to speed seamlessly.

- **IMPROVED QUALITY:** Served as 1 of the 8 senior leaders on Quality Management System Steering Committee—results improved customer satisfaction and quality.

- **CUT THE EXCESS:** Shaved $60K while negotiating telecommunications, PC support, and customer and laboratory systems support contracts.

- **ENHANCED COMMUNICATION WITH CLIENTS:** Adept at translating technical aspects of connectivity options, regularly requested by sales/marketing team to explain features to clients' nontechnical staffs.

Director, Customer Systems (2006 to 2008)
Staff of 22, 4 Managers ~ $4M Budget ~ Improved Customer Assistance ~ Reported to Senior IT Director

- **SET COMPANY STANDARD:** Rolled out Web-based system generating 90% ROI in first year—saved $200K+ annually. Directed 7 team members who replaced outdated systems and created mechanism guaranteeing 3-month upgrade at customer site. Negotiated $45K savings on original bid. Product adopted as corporate standard for hospital customer systems—400+ systems in use today.

- **INITIATED EXTERNAL 24/7 CUSTOMER HELP DESK:** Created single point of contact for customer connectivity issues and led implementation for round-the-clock technical support.

(continued)

Highly relevant results are highlighted at the beginning of each accomplishment statement, making this a hard-hitting, easily skimmed resume. Note the original heading that replaces the traditional "Professional Experience" wording.

Chapter 10: Resumes for Technology Managers and Executives

| 724.872.9030 | **PETRA BRANDT – 2 of 2** | petra@home.com |

STEIN LABS, PITTSBURGH, PA   2001 to 2006
Esoteric testing laboratory and diagnostics manufacturing company.
Director, Information Systems
Staff of 5 ~ Direct Report to CEO ~ Implemented First CPU Interfaces and Customer Connectivity ~ Highly Visible Role with Clients

- **RESUSCITATED CONVERSION:** Because a consultant fell short of expectations, took over project and had it in place in 4 months. Managed 2 programmer analysts who converted 2 CPT/UNIX systems into a MUMPS-based system, expediting customer processing.

- **ENHANCED COMPETITIVE EDGE:** Brought in customer inquiry/reporting system on time, on budget. Created first online access to test criteria and automated patient report printing, keeping Stein "cutting edge."

- **OFFERED INNOVATIVE SERVICES:** Led implementation of first bidirectional customer interface and rolled it out with a targeted marketing program. Successfully introduced online database of antibiotic-resistant organisms, enabling end users to upload, track, and trend data against entire U.S.

HILL ARCHITECTS, PITTSBURGH, PA   1999 to 2001
Software vendor for turnkey distribution systems.
    Project Manager—Successfully facilitated DEC system conversions for multibillion-dollar, Fortune 500 clientele in domestic locations. Led IS project teams of up to 16 members. All projects were completed on time.

THE CANCER CENTER, BELLE VERNON, PA   1998 to 1999
World-renowned cancer research center.
    Programmer/Analyst—Worked in the section for infectious disease. Designed MUMPS medical research database for clinical trials, replacing outdated cataloging methods. Wrote laboratory tracking system, maximizing storage and improving the tracking of specimens and cultures. Trained end users at all levels, from technicians through pharmacists, secretaries, and physicians.

SIGMA OIL COMPANY, DHAHRAN, SAUDI ARABIA, and EL PASO, TX   5 years
Number-one oil producer worldwide.
    Programmer—Improved real-time electrical power system control efficiency. Instrumental in developing a purchasing/traffic system to expedite shipments to Saudi Arabia.

Education

UNIVERSITY OF PITTSBURGH, PITTSBURGH, PA
Bachelor of Science in Business Computer Information Systems

CONTINUING EDUCATION—STEWART COMPANY: Project Management, 2009; Supervisory Skills Certificate Process, 2007; Leading Your Team, 2006; Innovation Process, 2006

Publications

Brandt, Petra. "Human/Computer Interfaces: A Randomized Trial of Data Entry and Editing Formats," SCAMC Proceedings, The Computer Society of the IEEE, Washington, DC, August 1999.

Brandt, Petra. "A Database for Clinical Research in Infectious Diseases," Proceedings Quarterly of the MUMPS Users Group, New Orleans, LA, June 1999.

Brandt, Petra. "User-Interface Design: A Study in Data-Entry Methods," AAMSI Congress Proceedings, San Francisco, CA, May 1999.

229

Michael Roland

52 North Lake Drive
Chicago, IL 60642

mroland@chicago.us.mensa.org

773.715.4567

Senior Technology Officer

Global Vision | Start-Ups | High-Growth Organizations | E-commerce

*Leveraging technology resources to support business priorities and
achieve extraordinary goals that impact bottom-line success.*

Builder and leader of innovative strategies and solutions-driven teams, delivering leading-edge technology systems that drive business performance and efficiency. Provide vision, planning, and leadership for notable success stories in the technology industry. Achieve a competitive edge and substantial cost savings through rapid and expert implementation of advanced technologies. Lead lean, focused organizations to deliver outstanding results with limited resources.

Technology: Extensive technical background includes infrastructure design and implementation and a thorough knowledge of ISO-9000 and SAS-70 certification, Sarbanes-Oxley compliance, Six Sigma, Agile, and business process engineering. Clearly communicate technologies and their relevance to the business process to drive sales growth.

Management: Key roles in strategic business planning, technical and operational management, multimillion-dollar budgets and financial accountability, and the pursuit of new business opportunities. Known as a creative problem-solver and "go-to" person for diverse business challenges. Consistent success in cost controls, productivity, logistics, and globalization.

Career Highlights

Quill...................................... **Personally guided Quill and an enterprise client toward a mutually beneficial product.** Broadened the carrier's industry and competitive landscape understanding to leverage new features while propelling Quill's products through a major release with a number of competitive enhancements that drove profitability and impacted the bottom line.

NewTech.............................. **Independently built an enterprise-level, industrial-grade commercial shipping application** into a highly competitive product that outshone the competition and positioned the company for a $10M acquisition.

Constellation Engineering.... **Within 24 hours, developed and implemented a plan of action** that restored a bank's data system and successfully avoided a large-scale financial disaster.

Career Track

QUILL, Marlborough, MA

2004–Present

London-based international producer/provider of software supporting supply chains, imports/exports, and shipping with annual revenue of £24M and £60M market cap.

<u>**Vice President, Technology and Enterprise Architecture:**</u> **Recruited with the acquisition of NewTech,** based on expertise in NewTech's enterprise shipping software and to maintain continuity in the software's development and maintenance. Member of the senior management team, tasked with providing expertise in the company's expansion into India. Day-to-day tasks ranged from technical design and architecture of software products to active involvement in the entire sales cycle from up-front designs and explanations of architectures to implementation design, hands-on technical leadership, and customer support.

☑ **Implemented a record-breaking $4M+ contract** with Purolator. Designed and built the complete solution, aligning customer goals with future product enhancements and designing a deployment architecture that would enable them to roll out 5,000 instances of Quill's application under control and up-to-date.

☑ **Designed and helped build integration with Axapta** to gain access to the Dynamics AX market.

☑ **Structured Oracle integrations** currently being built into standard integrations from Oracle's ERP.

☑ **Implemented Agile methodology** to improve code quality and delivery time.

continued

A strong Career Highlights section, set off by double lines, provides a quick snapshot of notable career successes that are further explained later in the resume.

Michael Roland   page 2   mroland@chicago.us.mensa.org | 773.334.5896

NEWTECH, Chicago, IL   2000–2004
Top enterprise shipping software manufacturer/designer that was acquired by Quill in 2004.

> <u>Chief Technology Officer:</u> **Succeeded in developing a mediocre middleware application into a sellable product licensed at the $250K level.** The highly competitive enterprise shipping solution won business from companies such as Neiman Marcus, Stuller, and Anixter. Oversaw all aspects of internal IT/software product development and customization for customers.

> ☑ **Transformed start-up into the top enterprise shipping software manufacturer** by overseeing the planning and building all of its systems, infrastructure, products, and teams.

> ☑ **Positioned company for $10M acquisition** in less than 4 years.

> ☑ **Built a SAS-70–compliant data center** to host Office Max's shipping solution.

RAP, Dale, IL   1996–2000
Billion-dollar manufacturer of airplane parts for commercial jets.

> <u>Vice President, E-commerce:</u> **Designed strategic business plan and technology to launch a joint venture dot-com company,** spun off as an independent entity that generated $3M in the first year alone. Led all customer-facing activities (website, EDI, order-taking, etc.) and internal infrastructure and architecture for the company's e-commerce.

> ☑ **Hired and led a 60-member IT team to build the business into a $1B operation;** oversaw 120 additional employees on the operational side.

> ☑ **Stabilized systems from 90% uptime to 99.99%.**

> ☑ **Implemented flawless data center move** with no downtime.

> ☑ **Migrated outdated legacy system to Oracle ERP** on time and under budget.

> ☑ **Initiated business opportunities with the military** by building a website portal.

> ☑ **Drove infrastructure integrations after acquisitions.**

CONSTELLATION ENGINEERING, Chicago, IL   1990–1996
General consulting firm specializing in Oracle, Novell, and IT management.

> <u>Vice President, Technical Services:</u> **Personally engaged to act as interim CIO or CTO** for customers in transition. Clients included the Illinois Regional Transit Authority/Chicago Transit Authority, Wright Patterson AFB, international banks, and Fortune 500 companies. In addition to Oracle DBA and Oracle Developer, Novell, and UNIX administration, performed IT analysis.

> ☑ **Repeatedly recognized** for ability to solve high-level IT problems.

> ☑ **Overhauled at least a dozen IT departments** by analyzing failures in business operations, processes, and procedures and successfully implementing changes in either a managerial or consulting role.

> ☑ **Winner of Oracle's first programming competition.**

Prior: Senior Software Engineer for **APPLIED SYSTEMS INSTITUTE,** Washington, DC.

Professional Profile

EDUCATION	**MBA,** University of Phoenix, San Francisco, CA, 1992
	BS, Computer Science & Psychology, Antioch College, Yellow Springs, OH, 1990
COURSES TAUGHT	C, C++, Oracle Administration, PL/SQL, Relational Algebra, Networking Theory, Routing, Supply Chain Logistics, Oracle Developer (forms, reports, graphics)
PUBLISHED WORKS	<u>The Oracle Developer/2000 Handbook</u>, Prentice Hall Technical Reference, 1999
	Technical Editor, Baman Motivala's <u>Oracle Forms Interactive Workbook</u>, Techno Publishing, 2000
LANGUAGES	Include C, C++, C#, Java, Perl, Python, SQL, PL/SQL, PHP, ADA, Prolog, shell scripting

Richard A. Van Houten

Cell: (404) 461-2219   380 Peachtree Drive • Buckhead, GA 30339   ravanhouten@yahoo.com

Chief Information Security Officer (CISO)

Retail • Construction • Aerospace • Defense

Master IT Strategist and Implementer Who Built a Global IT System from the Ground Up

Take-charge IT executive and natural leader with special expertise managing information security and global data centers for extremely large and complex enterprises. Relentlessly tighten security, improve business processes, and cut overhead. Known for exceptional strength in three areas:

- **Versatility:** Wear many hats. Repeatedly tasked to orchestrate large-scale IT initiatives that encompass infrastructure, facilities and building construction, organizational restructuring, and negotiation with local governments, property owners, and unions.

- **Leadership:** Steadily promoted through the IT ranks by the USA's second-largest retail company. Acquired hands-on leadership skills and training as civilian executive and noncommissioned officer in the U.S. Army.

- **Initiative:** Expert at taking a vague idea and transforming it into a functioning department or new business process.

Executive Performance and Achievements

THE HOME DEPOT (THD)   Atlanta, GA, 1987–Present

Second-largest retailer in the USA with 2,200 stores, $72 billion annual revenues, and 323,000 employees. Sells construction products and services worldwide.

Promoted 5 times and commended with more than 18 awards and honors. Currently managing 260 people with dual reporting to the Vice President of Computing Services and the Corporate CIO.

CAREER PROGRESSION, THE HOME DEPOT

Chief Information Security Officer, CISO (2004–Present)

Director, IS (2003–2004)

Strategy Manager, IS (2002–2003)

Strategic Applications Manager, Information Security (1997–2002)

Data Center Manager (1994–1997)

Various Development and Engineering Roles (1987–1994)

CAREER HIGHLIGHTS, THE HOME DEPOT (1996–Present)

- Established THD's IT compliance strategy ("TotalMatrix") to ensure enterprise IT compliance with SOX, PCI, HIPPA, and privacy laws.
    - TotalMatrix led to Comprehensive Security Risk and Compliance Review, which was adopted throughout Home Depot.
    - Improved CoBIT rating 15% (from 2.8 to 3.2).

- Achieved PCI (payment card industry) certification within 9 months by implementing a $54 million remediation initiative. Led team that designed and patented 2 retail-encryption tools for credit card data.

- Created a forensic-investigation unit that supports the legal department during proceedings. New unit processed 495 requests and saved $15 million in first year by eliminating outside services. Currently processes 1,000 requests and saves THD $42 million annually.

- Originated THD Information Security (IS) team, which consolidated IT security operations. Grew initial team (1996) from 6 people and $3.5 million budget to 120 certified security professionals and $74 million budget.

Continued

By combining all roles with one company into one section and using headings to segment key accomplishments, this resume sharply focuses the reader's attention on the candidate's expertise in the field of data security.

(404) 461-2219   Richard A. Van Houten   ravanhouten@yahoo.com

SELECTED PROJECTS (2005–Present)

- Selected by the CIO to create a new department, improve performance of IT field implementation teams, and consolidate strategy for disaster recovery and continuity of business.

- Created enterprise business continuity team—initial investment $4.2 million—that delivered enterprise IT pandemic plan, business continuity strategy, global data center strategy, business risk analysis, and a global risk categorization model (all implemented within 1 year).

- Achieved additional spending reductions, including:

  - Cut labor spending $8 million by optimizing performance of field implementation teams.

  - Negotiated labor and technology agreements on $998 million total budget, cutting store implementation costs by 12% per site.

  - Reduced telecom expenses $4 million as part of postaudit process during FY2010 (and expecting an additional $7 million savings in FY2011).

  - Slashed cabling expenses 50%—from $16 million to $8 million—by liquidating department, reducing workforce, and outsourcing work to third parties.

- Implemented a cost-reduction project that cost $170,000 to implement but saved $1.1 million in labor, inventory, and fuel consumption for store-expansion projects.

- Achieved 85% improvement in energy efficiency during data-center expansion—from 65 to 120 watts per square foot—and extended the life of the data centers by an additional 2 years.

MAJOR INFRASTRUCTURE PROJECTS (1997–2003)

Handpicked by Home Depot CEO and CIO to transform the IT organization to keep pace with THD's explosive growth. The 6-year project included additional buildings, personnel, and data centers—and ultimately required a $346 million investment and 330 acres of commercial office property.

- Project-managed creation of new offices for 3,500+ personnel that cost $61 million in land and construction.

- Consolidated data centers into a single, low-cost operation 14 miles from Home Depot's HQ—a $67 million land and construction investment—that paid for itself within 3 years. Both data centers are Tier IV protected (among a handful of nonmilitary data centers that can operate without battery backup).

- Built an IT distribution center that consolidated technology projects ("ORB Complex"), a $7 million project located with a new data center. Also built a $5 million backup disaster recovery facility. Construction involved extensive negotiation with utilities, owners of private property, and local governments for road widening and approvals for easements.

Distinguished Military Service

ARMY NATIONAL GUARD: Awarded Bronze Star, Kuwaiti Liberation Medal, and other military honors during combat deployment as Battalion Fire Direction Chief in Operations Desert Shield, Desert Storm, and Desert Watch (1990–1992). Trained extensively in practical leadership skills as noncommissioned officer (honor graduate, U.S. Army Primary Leadership Development Course).

Education and Professional Development

B.S., Organizational Management and Ethics, John Brown University, Siloam Springs, AR (1998)

Certified Information Systems Security Professional (CISSP)

Certified Information Security Manager (CISM)

Extensive training in CoBIT, ITIL, and HIPPA

Allison Brown

2345 Marcus Avenue, Apt 611

Phone: 305-123-1234   Miami Beach, FL 33140   Abrown59@aol.com

INFORMATION TECHNOLOGY / BUSINESS SYSTEMS EXECUTIVE

Aligning information technology with business to create solutions and opportunities that drive change

Dynamic, innovative professional with proven track record designing, developing, and delivering successful **cost-effective, high-performance technology and information systems solutions.** Results-driven, analytical problem solver with extensive experience in identifying opportunities and developing new business strategies and implementation framework to meet challenging multinational business demands. **MBA, fluent in Spanish,** conversant in French. **Particular areas of expertise** include **strategic planning, staff motivation,** and

- Financial Services
- Risk Management
- Change Management
- Project Management
- Customer Service
- Systems Administration
- Budget/P&L Management
- Negotiation & Presentation
- Crisis Management

PROFESSIONAL EXPERIENCE & SELECTED ACCOMPLISHMENTS

VISA INTERNATIONAL, Miami, FL   **2008–Present**

Vice President, Information Systems, **Latin America & Caribbean Region**

Provide day-to-day leadership and direction in all aspects of technology for a region of Visa known for its innovation and change management. Technology unit supports more than 450 users and 5 remote sites in Latin America and provides project management, consulting, programming and development, infrastructure (LAN and servers), desktop, and help desk support. Manage 20 employees and 5–10 consultants.

- Redirected, restructured, and turned around underperforming internal technology division into strong, successful, customer-focused, results-oriented strategic unit.
- Identified problems, provided viable solutions, persuaded senior management to accept proposals, and improved employee morale and involvement, which increased internal customer satisfaction by 55%.
- Initiated, created, and spearheaded several large-scale, high-profile enterprise projects:
  - **Data Warehousing:** Created central source to access regional transaction-level data.
  - **Paperless Office:** Strategized, planned, and implemented pilot to reduce paper flow and storage.
  - **Customer Resource Management:** Evaluated and piloted tools, selected instrument, and implemented.
- Developed processes, procedures, and guidelines for project documentation, process flows, RFPs, pilot programs, hardware and software licenses, and purchases; reduced costs by $500,000.
- Member of several high-profile technical and change management teams working to improve global systems.

FEDERAL FARM CREDIT BANKS FUNDING CORPORATION, Jersey City, NJ   **1997–2008**

Director and Vice President, **Information Systems & Securities Operations** (2000–2008)

Recruited to turn around troubled securities processing unit and create a technology department. Managed 12 professionals: securities processing analysts, programmer/systems analysts, and systems administrators.

- Founded and developed high-performing technology group that identified business problems, recommended technical solutions, assessed business/technical risks, worked with users to instill ownership, and delivered projects on schedule and within budget.
- Updated corporate Internet plan, created security policy, upgraded firewall, and ensured uninterrupted connectivity.

Continued

The branding statement beneath the headline is an eye-catching, concise, effective summary of this individual's executive philosophy.

ALLISON BROWN   ABROWN59@AOL.COM   PAGE 2

Assistant Vice President (1998–2000)

- Formulated and directed long-range plan to change corporate architecture from proprietary minicomputer environment to company-wide client/server model, which reduced support costs by 50%, improved service quality by 75%, increased access to critical information by 100%, and ensured future adaptability.
- Created training program for technical staff to develop account management and consulting skills; reduced project delays by 30% and increased cross-functional awareness.
- Managed major systems projects through entire life cycle, including:
  - Implementation of online allocation database handling monthly bond auctions.
  - Origination and design of debt-tracking and payment system that provided online historical information on all outstanding fixed-income securities, which totaled more than $63 billion.

Manager (1997–1998)

- Reorganized and redirected underperforming operations unit, saving more than $200,000.

CITICORP, N.A., Domestic Funding Services (DFS), New York, NY   **1990–1994**
Manager, 1994; *Assistant Manager,* 1992–1994; *Management Associate,* 1990–1992

- Managed daily operations for Citicorp and three subsidiaries, serving as liaison between Citicorp traders/Citibank operations and Chief Financial Officer/investors. Managed and trained 10 employees.
- Played a key role in development of new DFS Self-Audit Business Unit, which identified and solved broad range of financial/accounting problems, increasing departmental efficiencies between 50% and 70%.
- Turned around problem-ridden subsidiary, resulting in first acceptable audit in three years.
- Sent to Aruba to start up foreign exchange and cash management unit for overseas subsidiary.
- Managed Citicorp cash management function totaling $2 billion daily.

PROFESSIONAL AFFILIATIONS

Association for Women in Computing (AWC)
National Association for Female Executives (NAFE)
Kellogg Alumni Association

EDUCATION

MBA, Finance & International Economics, **J.L. Kellogg Graduate School of Management,** Northwestern University, 1996
BA, Economics and French, **Fordham University,** 1990

Denny G. Wong

11650 W. Shepherd ▪ Houston, Texas 77088 ▪ (281) 966-7276
email: denny@flex.net

INTERNATIONAL TELECOMMUNICATIONS & INFORMATION TECHNOLOGY

New Business Development & Advanced Technology Networks / General Management
VoIP / System Design & Integration / E-commerce Solutions
Start-up, Turnaround & High-Growth Operations

Trilingual (Vietnamese/Chinese/English) IT management professional with extensive experience building and leading domestic and international business development initiatives within the telecommunications industry. Consistently successful in identifying and capturing market opportunities to accelerate expansion, increase revenues, and improve profit contributions. Extensive experience developing partnering alliances throughout Asia and the Pacific Rim. Core management qualifications include:

➢ Strategic Sales & Market Planning	➢ Market Research & Analysis
➢ Staff Training & Development	➢ Product & Market Positioning
➢ Key Account Relationship Management	➢ Sales Forecasting & Reporting
➢ International Market Development	➢ Budget Development & Control
➢ New Product & Service Launch	➢ Global Commercialization

Led the startup and development of two international telecommunications companies,
and spearheaded their launch in the United States, Thailand, the Philippines, and
Mexico.

Equally strong technical expertise in the design, development, and delivery of cost-effective, high-performance technology solutions to meet challenging business demands. Heavy design and programming experience with Windows, UNIX, Linux, HTML, ASP, Java, FTP, SAS, and Visual Basic. Software and database proficiency in MS Office, Access, Lotus SmartSuite, Lotus Notes, SQL, and Oracle. Voice over IP Telephony experience includes gateways, gatekeepers, billing solutions and unified messaging. Experience with protocols including PSTN networks, ISDN, BRI/PRI, T1/T3, E1/R2, SS7, TCP/IP, H323, SIP, HTTP, MGCP, and RTP.

PROFESSIONAL EXPERIENCE

WONG.COM, INC., Houston, Texas   2010–Present
Cofounder / Vice President of New Business Development / Chief Technology Officer
Partnered with two other entrepreneurs in the development of a telecommunications company designing Web-based technologies to support global communication networks. Assumed leadership role in international business development, marketing, sales, systems engineering, and operations. Identified and secured seed funding through venture capital and private investor groups. Designed internal and external technology infrastructures to ensure affordability, reliability, and durability. **Developed and built strategic partnering alliances with Cisco, Vocaltec, AT&T, international telecommunications companies, broadband providers, ITSPs, and ISPs.**

Continued

For a multilingual executive with extensive global experience, the resume leads off with a lengthy summary encompassing both executive and technical skills. Then it highlights key accomplishments in the Professional Experience section in bold type.

Denny G. Wong	denny@flex.net	Page Two

PROFESSIONAL EXPERIENCE
(Continued)

QUESTEL COMMUNICATIONS, INC., Houston, Texas   2009–2010
Cofounder / Vice President of Network Engineering
Established and built a global Voice over IP network services company from inception. Full responsibility for strategic business planning, engineering, network architecture, risk management, and capacity planning. **Spearheaded VoIP expansion and deployment throughout Asia Pacific. Opened and managed operations in the United States, Thailand, the Philippines, and Mexico.** Designed and implemented Cisco-powered Voice over IP global communication networks.

INFORMATION SCIENCE CORPORATION, Houston, Texas   2008–2009
IT Consultant
Assigned exclusively to DuPont to expand its global business operations. Created extensive WAN network using T1 and Frame Relay technology to connect all company locations, and developed its Internet e-mail systems.

H.T.I.S. TELECOMMUNICATIONS, INC., Houston, Texas   2006–2008
Manager of Systems Engineering
Assumed full responsibility for the design and installation of LAN/WAN technologies, client/server architecture, Windows Server and Novell operating systems, and applications software. Proposed integrating voice processing servers and telephony gateway equipment to customer specifications.

RELIANT ENERGY, Houston, Texas   2004–2006
Corporate Information Network Specialist
Recruited to assist IT director in upgrading and enhancing LAN/WAN technologies. Prepared budgets and made appropriate recommendations on hardware and software equipment. Configured Cisco, 3Com, Asanta, WellFleet, and SynOptics networking systems.

WILLIAMS COMMUNICATIONS, The Woodlands, Texas   2003–2004
Corporate Operations Analyst
Established workstations and file and print servers and installed Windows applications. Configured Northern Telecom (PBX) and Octel telephone systems. **Recipient of Williams Communications Systems Team Service Award.**

EDUCATION

Sam Houston State University, Huntsville, Texas: **BS, Engineering,** 2002
Specialization in Computer Science

PROFESSIONAL AFFILIATIONS

Association of Communications Enterprises
International Engineering Consortium

MARTHA JACKSON

25003 Citadella Place, Wallingford, CT 06492 ▫ Cell: 203-254-8874 ▫ Email: mjackson@aol.com

SENIOR TECHNOLOGY EXECUTIVE

Chief Technology Officer ▸ Chief Information Officer ▸ Senior Vice President
Astute Technology Vision / Pragmatic Leadership Style / Turnaround Strategies

Leveraging Emerging Technology to Minimize Business Risk, Contain Escalating Costs,
and Improve Operational Sustainability

Forward-thinking executive able to transform business operations, fuel company growth, and drive revenue performance through comprehensive, innovative technology solutions. Articulate, compassionate communicator with natural talent for leading teams through politically charged, unpredictable corporate environments. Primary architect and pioneer of groundbreaking, "first-of-their-kind" technology initiatives that reposition companies for long-term growth and continued financial success. Core competencies include

Technology Planning & Direction | IT Policy & Procedure Formulation | Profit & Revenue Maximization
Strategic Alliances & Partnerships | New Technology Development | Global IT Service Delivery
Technology Outsourcing Solutions | Process Redesign & Automation | E-commerce & B2B Solutions

TECHNOLOGY MANAGEMENT & LEADERSHIP EXPERIENCE

HEAD OF ENTERPRISE IT SERVICES, *The Hyland Insurance Group*, Worcester, MA (2006 to present)

Challenged to turn around and stabilize operations with growing project backlog, declining employee morale, and mounting technology costs.

Develop IT strategy to promote long-term business growth and realign processes/systems that support business needs. Direct cross-functional team with up to 55 employees and manage $15 million budget. Report to CTO.

Performance Milestones:

▫ **Technology Planning & Direction:** Formulated a comprehensive IT strategy and introduced a $20 million, 3-year roadmap to align emerging technologies with long-range business objectives.

▫ **Profitability Enhancement:** Decreased project management and process methodology costs 40% by eliminating process overhead and integrating iterative software development practices.

▫ **Cost Reduction:** Eliminated approximately $5 million in system maintenance costs and reduced lost productivity by restructuring more than 33,000 database applications, reports, and reporting tools.

▫ **Process Improvement:** Increased work productivity 30% and generated $2 million in annual savings by partnering with offshore company for application development services.

▫ **Policies & Procedures:** Instituted standard policies/procedures and streamlined selection processes for reporting tools that helped company avoid $700,000 in annual costs.

DIRECTOR OF ARCHITECTURE & STRATEGY, *The Bell Insurance Group*, Hartford, CT (2004 to 2006)

Implemented technology solutions and drove technology-based initiatives set to double annual revenues by the year 2010.

Selected as one of top 100 executives to serve on company's business strategy group. Tasked with application and information infrastructure evaluations and enterprise IT strategy development. Reported to the CIO and business unit COO.

Performance Milestones:

▫ **Capacity Planning:** Assembled and chaired an Enterprise IT governance program that decreased IT development costs 15% and eliminated redundant capabilities in just 8 months.

Continued

The primary challenge/accomplishment of each position is called out in bold, bordered sections that draw attention to this distinguishing information.

MARTHA JACKSON   mjackson@aol.com   **PAGE TWO**

DIRECTOR OF ARCHITECTURE & STRATEGY continued

- **Cost Reduction:** Slashed application development costs 40% by pioneering cosourcing and offshore outsourcing strategies.

- **IT Direction & Initiatives:** Secured $10 million in technology funds to formulate a 3-year business strategy program for the company. Devised a 5-year, $40 million strategic IT roadmap and execution plan.

HEAD OF INFORMATION MANAGEMENT SERVICES, *Concord Group*, Hartford, CT (2001 to 2004)

Recruited to identify possible synergies and implement technology standardization for a global development company challenged with internal redundancies resulting from multiple business acquisitions.

Provided solutions for corporate-wide initiatives, including IT planning, business intelligence, business continuity, service delivery, CMMI implementation, and outsourcing. Directed 125-member team across 5 countries and managed $30 million budget. Reported to CTO.

Performance Milestones:

- **Talent Development:** Pioneered and drove a successful, corporate-wide talent development initiative, "Invest in Our People," that significantly increased employee morale and overall team performance.

- **Contract Negotiations:** Diminished escalating costs and reduced inefficiencies by aggressively negotiating a $50 million, 5-year infrastructure outsourcing contract.

- **Cost Reduction:** Established a multiyear enterprise data architecture and data transformation program that lowered operating costs 20%, eliminated redundancies, consolidated applications, improved data accessibility, and increased data value.

- **Operational Effectiveness:** Boosted cost effectiveness 15% and increased operational efficiency 30% by executing an enterprise information-management service.

EXECUTIVE DIRECTOR OF INFORMATION MANAGEMENT, *Cyberian Technology*, Kent, CT (1998 to 2001)

Joined startup firm in executive leadership and technology management role. Tasked with managing new business development, market segmentation, technology partnerships/alliances, and overall technology operations. Teamed with executive management team and board of directors to strategize on long-term/short-term IT initiatives. Reported to the CTO.

Performance Milestones:

- **Revenue Growth:** Orchestrated rapid company growth from $10 million to $125 million in annual revenues; consequently expanded professional staff from 40 to 200 employees.

    - Added $1 million in new revenue stream by transforming IT department from traditional cost center into revenue-generating unit.

- **Technology Integration:** Grew annual revenues by $4 million in less than 12 months by designing and implementing a Web-based, Enterprise Customer Relationship Management (eCRM) system.

TECHNICAL MANAGER OF IT OPERATIONS, *Virtual Software Pvt. Ltd.*, Toronto, Canada (1995 to 1998)

SENIOR SYSTEM ANALYST, *System Transport Corporation*, Hartford, CT (1991 to 1995)

EDUCATION

University of Connecticut, Hartford, CT
MBA in Finance
BA in Business Management

PAUL HARDING, CPIM

pharding@netscape.com

716 Pine Run ◇ Scranton, PA 15238 ◇ 412.558.4589

Information Technology Executive

Supply Chain, Logistics, Government

Technology Leader focused on development and deployment of cutting-edge products that optimize performance, drive growth, and increase profitability. More than 20 years in leadership roles with consistent record of exceeding expectations. Subject Matter Expert who excels at transforming processes and building and leading cross-functional teams to achieve objectives. Able to communicate the vision, build rapport, and create consensus at all levels of an organization. Respond to challenges with confidence, determination, and focus.

Core Competencies

• C-level Relationships	• Change Management
• IT Leadership	• Performance Improvement/Metrics
• Lean Methodologies	• Cross-Functional Collaborations
• New Product Development	• Military/Government/Domestic Systems

EXECUTIVE PERFORMANCE

DALCO Supply Chain Solutions, Pittsburg, PA   2007–2011
Global Top 50 third-party logistics solutions supplier.

Project Manager
Promoted from Operations Consultant to Project Manager to lead project teams for on-site client initiatives and turn around multiple high-value upgrade projects.

- Volunteered to live overseas and spearhead 8-month assignment to manage on-time delivery of first fully automated European transportation client that included securing compliance with IATA and UN regulations for transporting dangerous goods.
- Managed $2M supply chain implementation for "Big Box" retailer after PM quit abruptly. Led 20+-member team, replacing multiple systems of competitor's IT solution and modifying processes that provided real-time view to facilitate last-minute decision making.
- Accepted PM role at Director's request to take over stalled project for entertainment industry giant that became the company's first live and operational customer after upgrade to new platform.

Metropolitan Engineering, Rockville, MD   2005–2007
Premier strategy and technology consulting firm, helping government, institutions, and infrastructure organizations solve mission-critical problems.

Associate
Prospected for RFPs and RFIs and provided vision and leadership for multiple project teams, implementing supply-chain best practice for wide range of clients.

- Led 20+-member cross-functional team and coordinated multiple agencies to implement new facility for the U.S. government that lowered costs while improving security and employee safety.
- Recruited 3-member team for 1-year project to provide analysis of proposed IT and supply-chain solutions for Federal Agency and present results to (50+) internal project team.
- Played key role as IT Specialist providing and supporting IT solutions for $1M+ service contract for build-out of customized warehouse solution for company providing classified products to the military.

Custom Developers, Norman, OK   2004–2005
Provider of wide variety of integrated business applications to assist in day-to-day execution and operation of financials, CRM, HR, and business processes.

Senior Product Marketing Manager
Marketed integrated suite of transportation, warehousing, inventory, RFID, and asset management solutions.

- Grew transportation license revenue 34% and increased year-over-year contract closings 10% by attending conferences and giving presentations on transportation-related subjects.
- Established unique brand by creating marketing campaign focused on applying RFID outside traditional logistics and launching first customer that used RFID to manage IT assets.

Page 1 of 2

Showcasing expertise in the supply chain and logistics arena, this resume includes keywords in every position as well as the summary. It is crisply written and loaded with results.

PAUL HARDING	pharding@netscape.com	**Page 2 of 2**

SJM Freight Management, Alexandria, VA   2002–2004
3PL, consulting, and freight management company for retailers, wholesalers, and manufacturers.

Vice President
Provided day-to-day leadership for company that generated $2M+ in annual top-line revenue.
- Presented recommendations that enabled McDonald's to reduce freight costs $5M.
- Generated $600K+ annual savings for "Big Box" retailer by reducing empty backhaul miles 10%.
- Saved SJM $200K+ by recommending application of continuous moves within carrier base.

Accurate Data Synchronization, McLean, VA   2001–2002
Provider of sourcing, supply chain, data synchronization, and product life-cycle management solutions for the retail consumer goods industry.

Product Manager
Recruited to re-energize organization by developing and marketing new line of supply chain products.
- Received executive buy-in to collaborate in development of visibility, transportation management, global trade compliance, and landed cost analyzer products.
- Researched, negotiated, and managed relationships with and deliverables from partner IT vendors.

World Trade Solutions, McLean, VA   2000–2001
Privately held developer of information management systems that automate regulatory hurdles faced by international import/export shipping operations.

Director of Global Professional Services
Brought on board to build divisions for consulting, product support, education, and release management.
- Achieved $1.4M services revenue goal despite software sales making only 40% of license revenue goal.
- Generated 300% increase in additional services sales from the implemented customer base.
- Reduced Day Sales Outstanding (DSO) from more than 130 days to 79 days.

Pinnacle Consulting, Roanoke Rapids, NC   1999–2000
Management, technology, and ERP consulting company in the consumer products and life sciences industries.

Senior Practice Project Manager
Recruited to launch new supply chain practice.
- Achieved $1M first-year revenue goal by closing deal to upgrade the IT for all distribution centers of North American retailer and selling network optimization plan to midsized aircraft parts supplier.
- Delivered highest margins in company by designing deals and wording contracts that easily captured higher margin "out-of-scope" revenue.

Mattingly, Inc., Alexandria, VA   1986–1999
Transportation Consultant, Sr. Transportation Consultant, Project Manager, Support Manager
Recruited as founding logistics employee. Designed IT products and solutions that achieved dominance within retail and foodservice verticals, facilitated revenue growth from $8M to $150M+ and enabled company to go public at $10/share and grow to $120/share in 6 years.

EDUCATION / CERTIFICATION / AFFILIATIONS

B.S., *Business Administration,* Marketing Major, Indiana University, Bloomington, IN

CPIM *(Certified in Production and Inventory Management),* APICS, Chicago, IL

Member: **APICS, CSCMP, PMI**

PATRICK WILLIAMS

415-229-1210   2971 Damian Drive | Walnut Creek, CA 94957   p.williams@mac.com

VICE PRESIDENT OF TECHNOLOGY / CHIEF TECHNOLOGY OFFICER

SHOESOURCE | TECHSTUFF | E-AUCTION.COM

Provided technological leadership, innovation, and talent to transition each company from concept into a highly valued, highly respected, and remarkably profitable corporation, each #1 in its market space.

Chief technology executive with strong record of success in developing innovative technologies for Internet companies, including some of the most successful in the past 15 years. True business partner to executive teams, VC and private equity firms, investors, and other shareholders to lead start-up and early-stage ventures from concept through IPO. Unique, collaborative leadership, communication, and team-building style that propels performance and sustains accelerated growth. Consistent achievement in guiding executives to business and financial success, leading colleagues to technological excellence, and supporting users with best-in-class applications and solutions. Stanford MBA.

Technology & Organizational Leadership Expertise

Technology Leadership & Innovation	Strategic Planning & Global Business Development
New Product Development & Launch	Customer Relationship Management & User Experience
Next-Generation Technology Ventures & Enterprises	B2B & B2C Technology Solutions & Enterprise-Wide Systems
Executive Leadership & Business Management	Java, ASP/COM, XML, VB/C++, Oracle, SQL Server, MySQL, CRM

PROFESSIONAL EXPERIENCE

SHOESOURCE, San Francisco, CA   2007 to Present

Vice President – Technology, Product & Customer Care

Drove development of complex technology suite and infrastructure at foundation of company's transition from start-up to $80M+ in annual revenue and #1 rating in online apparel sales.

Member of 6-person senior executive team and key contributor to strategic planning and direction, market positioning, organic growth, and product and service development. Lead presentations to the board of directors and other stakeholders.

As senior technology executive, direct software and systems development, network engineering and operations, business intelligence, internal IT network, data center, and all technology evaluation and acquisition efforts. Leverage expertise to drive product development and enhance user experience. Direct a staff of 120 and $18M annual budget.

- Positioned company and technology for 50%–80% continued growth in revenue over next 3–5 years.
- Fostered collaborative innovation with technology and product teams to deliver first-ever apparel applications to the iPhone and other smart phones.
- Maintained 99.99% uptime for 4+ years, even during major advertising campaigns that spiked traffic 30x.
- Orchestrated successful and profitable expansion into European market. Oversaw U.K. technology development team and continue to provide strategic leadership. Currently facilitating 2011 expansion into Brazil and Australia.
- Led credit card task force through implementation of key technologies to accelerate transaction processing and reduce failure rate, resulting in potential gain of $4M in additional annual revenue.
- Architected failover and redundancy throughout all levels of the system. Rebuilt production site in hosting facilities with state-of-the-art infrastructure including virtualized production servers and 3PAR SAN to enhance integrity.

TECHSTUFF, San Jose, CA   2004 to 2007

Executive Consultant – IT Development & Operations

Retained by VC firm to evaluate proposed investment in TechStuff.com through technology due diligence. Following recommendation to proceed with acquisition, given full autonomy for revitalizing, expanding, and strengthening all internal IT resources. Partnered with CEO and other key executives to identify emerging market opportunities and develop technologies responsive to changing consumer purchasing patterns and dynamics.

- Managed nationwide recruitment effort to source and hire new VP of Engineering and CTO.
- Built sophisticated pricing matrix and engine to control inventory and product pricing.
- Consulted with VC board on other proposed investments to evaluate technology innovation and potential.

Continued

Showcasing more than a decade of groundbreaking technological leadership for Internet companies, this resume is clean and crisp, with just enough detail to explain the impressive results.

415-229-1210 **PATRICK WILLIAMS** p.williams@mac.com

E-AUCTION.COM, Seattle, WA 1997 to 2004

Member of the original technology team that drove IT vision and created solutions that propelled E-Auction's growth from 700K customers, 50 employees, and $35M in revenue to 10M+ customers, 700 employees worldwide, and $1.2B in revenue. Positioned company as 1 of only 3 dotcoms to emerge from dotcom era with $1B+ in revenue.

Vice President of Development – International Systems (2000 to 2004)

Orchestrated launch of E-Auction throughout Europe and Asia to penetrate global market. Led entire project, from concept through delivery of end-to-end system involving international Web site, Oracle database with middleware, multiple back-end CRS supplier interfaces, customer service and CIS systems, and back-office accounting. Managed $30M+ in budgets across multiple international business units and joint ventures.

- Advised business unit presidents, executives, and steering committee on key project milestones and opportunities.
- Managed 8 project directors and 100+ team members, with development groups on 4 continents. Centralized and prioritized project requirements across multiple business units and locations and consistently exceeded goals.
- Outsourced projects to offshore team, reduced contractor burn rate 75%, and captured $10M in annual savings.

Vice President of Development – CRM Systems (1997 to 1999)

Built E-Auction's customer technology—3 infrastructure systems and underlying e-commerce architecture still in use today: customer transaction and tracking database, campaign management system, Web-based customer service system. Led technology recruitment to support fast-track company growth. Directed teams of up to 160.

- Led 6-month project to reengineer database, middleware, and front-end components and design/implement redundant and scalable architecture to seamlessly manage transactions for 10M customers with no downtime.
- Developed Web-based customer self-service and email applications using existing technology architecture. Scaled up from 1 call center with 100 agents to 12 call centers with 1,000 agents to sustain >1,000% growth in 18 months.
- Launched IT-sponsored project that captured $73M new revenue in first year by strengthening user experience.
- Conceived and developed adaptive marketing programs that delivered $4M+ in gross profits in first year.
- Delivered new technology product 3 months ahead of schedule, earning E-Auction a $1M contract bonus.

TECH SERVICES CORPORATION, San Francisco, CA 1994 to 1996

Technology Consultant

Spearheaded development of several of Tech Services' systems and solutions at onset of technology revolution. Developed proprietary Web browser, early-stage Internet HTML, proprietary workstation, and text-processing software. Led technical design for multimedia interactive cable product.

Advanced rapidly through first 4 years of career as **Technology Developer** with Intel and Aldus (now Adobe).

EDUCATION & PROFESSIONAL ACTIVITIES

MBA, STANFORD UNIVERSITY, 1996 | **BS, Mathematics, UNIVERSITY OF CALIFORNIA, Berkeley,** 1989
Finance for Non-Finance Executives, COLUMBIA BUSINESS SCHOOL, 2008

LILY MICHALEK

354 Anoka St • Stillwater, MN 55082
(cell) 651-317-8293 • lilym@hotmail.com

SENIOR EXECUTIVE: INFORMATION TECHNOLOGY

Strategic Enterprise Solutions • Emerging Technologies

Innovative IT strategist with global business acumen and expansive breadth of expertise in enterprise application design, development, and implementation. Experienced in both Big Five consulting and Fortune 500 technology environments. Analytical problem solver and polished communicator practiced in leading project teams through change management initiatives to attain market dominance. Prolific author of technology white papers.

Global Implementation Projects • Enterprise Data Management • Business Intelligence
Performance Management • Business Process Improvement • Client Relationship Management

Carlson School of Business Executive MBA

PROFESSIONAL EXPERIENCE

BLUE MOON CONSULTING, INC. — Minneapolis, MN   2006–Present
International management and technology consulting firm.
Senior Architect • Director, Oracle National Practice
Key driving force behind vision and implementation of major client projects ranging from $1M to $10M. Build business development through client presentations that produce $1.5M/year in new deals. Direct 10–20 member project teams and hold project P&L accountability. Represent company at industry events as conference speaker and white paper author. Boost internal productivity and communications through leadership of division's improvement team.

Project and Performance Highlights:

- **Integration of Acquisitions into Centralized IT Operations.** Mapped future of international healthcare software company by creating 5-year IT plan that optimized systems of multiple acquisitions. Delivered effective and scalable combination of platforms, technologies, tools, processes, and best practices.

- **Comprehensive Data Management Strategy.** Improved executive and tactical decision making of large, regional healthcare services corporation by creating and deploying EDM and BI roadmap that boosted data quality through consistent data governance and by coordinating architecture.

- **EDM and SOA Strategy.** Designed EDM and SOA plan to meet changing business forces with agile and proactive solutions for prioritization, resourcing, and enterprise application development.

PETERSON COMPANIES — Plymouth, MN   2004–2006
Leading management and technology consulting firm serving Global 2000 clients.
Senior Manager, Communications & Content National Practice
Delivered strategic and tactical IT leadership for client projects in challenging international environments. Balanced resources, ROI, and risk to profitably manage IT project portfolio. Accountable for project budgets up to $10M. Mentored 4 IT managers.

Project and Performance Highlights:

- **Business Process Engineering and Data Warehouse.** Transformed Canadian public health agency from manual system to data warehouse capable of supporting rapid public health emergency efforts.

- **State-of-the-Art Communications and IT Security.** Partnered with Egyptian Tourism Ministry to develop plan for enhancing tourism activities through emerging technologies. Acquired second project to improve IT operations of Egyptian Customs Processing Agency by planning enterprise, IT, and security architecture.

- **Company Spin-Off.** Delivered flawless technology separation of Verizon's 24/7 wireless operations to Hawaiian Telecom, orchestrating server move, new technology installation, and disaster recovery plan.

Page 1 of 2

Each Project and Performance Highlights section is introduced with bold type to instantly communicate key areas of expertise and accomplishment.

LILY MICHALEK — **Page 2 of 2** • (cell) 651-317-8293 • lilym@hotmail.com

TECH DESIGN & LOGISTIX — Stillwater, MN   2002–2004
Privately held technology consulting firm.
Chief Consultant, President
Propelled start-up firm from concept to revenue generation, leveraging initial investment into thriving business.

- **HIPAA-Compliant Architecture Design and System Implementation.** Met patient data regulatory requirements for Blue Cross Blue Shield organization's enterprise applications, middleware, and data warehouse projects.
- **Project Rescue.** Achieved "impossible" deadline, attaining HIPAA-compliant transactions system for international health insurance company within 8 months by directing 225-member project team to implement systems and middleware and to perform business process engineering and IT reorganization.

DIGITAL FORT — White Bear Lake, MN   2000–2002
Technology consulting company.
Chief Technology Officer
Led technology operations through period of acquisitions and business upheavals. Advanced Microsoft and Java consulting and product development arms, directing 30 staff and managing $40M P&L and $25M in client projects.

- **IT Reorganization.** Launched meta product group to give product development team members sense of ownership and pride in contributions generating 70% of company revenues.
- **Cost Management.** Saved time and resources by directing staff to develop reusable solution frameworks and components for future client projects.

THOMPSON GROUP WORLDWIDE — St. Paul, MN   1997–2000
Senior Manager, Communications, Content & Commerce Practice
Advanced Fortune 500 client goals by serving as architect for large-scale telecom software development and system integrations / implementations for multinational consulting firm. Forged corporate technology innovation strategy and carried out international outsourcing goals. Strengthened relationships with major clients that included Quest and AT&T.

STL TECHSYSTEMS, INC. — Minneapolis, MN   1995–1997
Senior Manager of Information Systems Development & Integration
Achieved breakthrough results for telecom billing and customer care projects in Sweden and the U.K. for a $300M technology consulting company. Directed software and system design and implementation, business process engineering, and enterprise data migration.

3M — Maplewood, MN   1987–1995
Software Development Manager • Systems Architect
Directed software development for network applications, including configuration management and product enhancements. Held P&L accountability for department and supervised 25 cross-functional team members.

Career Note: Also served in U.S. Air National Guard as Communications Systems Specialist with Secret security clearance.

EDUCATION

M.S. in Computer Information Systems GPA: 3.9/4.0	UNIVERSITY OF ST. THOMAS, St. Paul, MN
Executive MBA—Technology Management GPA: 3.9/4.0	UNIVERSITY OF MINNESOTA, Minneapolis, MN
B.S. in Computer Science	MACALESTER COLLEGE, St. Paul, MN

LUCILLE JANZEN

ljanzen@gmail.com

73 Granite Links Drive
Quincy, MA 02171

Mobile: 617.247.9818
Home: 508.771.4091

SENIOR EXECUTIVE – INFORMATION SYSTEMS, TECHNOLOGIES & SOLUTIONS
Chief Information Officer / Chief Technology Officer / MBA & MS Degrees

Sixteen-year career championing technology innovations across multiple industries and business markets. Expert in leveraging IT to support successful start-ups, turnarounds, and high-growth companies. Manage from the intersection of business and technology to deliver measurable gains in revenues, profits, and performance. Dedicated mentor who builds collaboration and instills trust and confidence.

Strategic Business Planning	Process Redesign & Optimization	Technical Ideation
Organizational Transformation	New Business Development & Capture	E-commerce Applications
Customer Relationship Management	Outsourcing & Vendor Negotiations	Multisite Operations
Revenue & Profit Growth	Cost Reduction & Elimination	Technical Staffing & Recruitment

PROFESSIONAL EXPERIENCE

CHIEF TECHNOLOGY OFFICER – Interim   2008 to Present
Consultant to C-level executives, company owners, and investors on business and technology issues including strategic planning, technology adoption and implementation, IT and data security, business processes, and best practices. Notable engagements:

- Interim IT Director / CIO working in partnership with Corporate Director of Client Services of $40M company to create first-ever corporate IT security program. Authored formal policies and procedures for systems and data security and developed risk assessment tools and roadmap for future technology planning, acquisition, and integration.
- Masterminded consolidation of multitiered technology infrastructure and resources as regional automotive group downsized in response to economic constraints. Created corporate plan for technology expansion and integration following market recovery.
- Spearheaded selection and implementation of Oracle ERP system for 75-year-old, multisite retail company.

CHIEF INFORMATION OFFICER / SENIOR VICE PRESIDENT   2002 to 2007
BEACON FINANCIAL, Boston, MA
Recruited to resolve critical regulatory compliance issues resulting from inadequate IT resources, processes, and personnel while managing the expansion of internal technology capabilities to support company's fast-track growth. Eliminated roadblocks impacting IT functionality, stability, and security by integrating innovative systems, applications, solutions, architectures, and business continuity and disaster recovery plans. Managed a staff that grew from 30 to 120+. Promoted from VP to SVP within first year of hire.

- Won funding and approval from top executives for comprehensive re-architecture of enterprise-wide technology. Authored Strategic Technology Plan to support both corporate and line-of-business operating and financial objectives.
- Increased systems availability to 99.99% through pioneering efforts in virtualization, colocation, and standardization.
- Designed customized billing system in C#.NET, resulting in $300M in new revenues through improved staff utilization.
- Introduced Business Intelligence and CRM systems through an integrated portal and captured $100M+ in new revenue growth.
- Reduced IT operating costs 20% by streamlining processes with SOA, SaaS, a formal vendor engagement process, and strict enforcement of business case development and risk management methodologies.
- Chaired technology oversight committee to ensure strict and consistent compliance with both U.S. and international standards (SOX, GLBA, SAS70, FFIEC, SEC, OCC, FINRA, OBRE).

REGIONAL INFORMATION TECHNOLOGY DIRECTOR / ASSISTANT VICE PRESIDENT   1999 to 2001
XYZ INVESTMENTS, INC., Boston, MA
Recruited to plan and orchestrate start-up of new technology division to support company's expansion into e-commerce market. Built 24x7x365 combined call center/data center and high-transaction-volume, high-availability, customer-facing, online enterprise network. Coordinated complex load balancing for call and data routing from customers worldwide. Recruited and trained technology staff and call center teams, managed budgets, sourced vendors, and directed IT regulatory compliance and reporting. Managed growth from 160 to 2,000 call center employees and 3 to 26 offices.

Continued

This resume includes a detailed Technology Portfolio section at the end of the resume. Note how current consulting experience is presented, with specific projects and measurable results.

LUCILLE JANZEN ... ljanzen@gmail.com ... 617.247.9818   Page 2

REGIONAL INFORMATION TECHNOLOGY DIRECTOR / ASSISTANT VICE PRESIDENT (Continued)

- Expanded regional IT capacity to support 210,000 daily transactions and 4.6M customer accounts across multiple enterprise data centers. Total activity generated $2.5M in daily transaction revenue.
- Managed construction and outfitting of 125,000-square-foot call center/Tier IV data center supporting 10x capacity growth. Facilitated relocation of existing call center infrastructure with 100% next-business-day availability.
- Led cross-functional program teams in the design and roll-out of new technologies, applications, and enterprise-wide initiatives (e.g., single sign-on, integrated banking and brokerage, decimalization).
- Championed team learning and growth through funding of professional certifications and advanced educational programs.
- Achieved #1 enterprise ranking in company for average time-to-resolution through early adoption of ITIL best practices.

TECHNICAL OPERATIONS MANAGER   1997 to 1999
NORTHEAST LOGISTICS, Waltham, MA
Promoted from Support Services Supervisor to Technical Operations Manager during a period of accelerated growth, expansion, and acquisition. Evaluated enterprise-wide technology requirements; recruited talented technology professionals; expanded training programs; and developed standards for hardware, software, and technical support for 2,000+ users in 100 countries worldwide.

- Led technical support/help desk through a complete turnaround and revitalization, changing both the perceived and actual value of the organization. Within 90 days, reduced support requests 95% and time-to-resolution 99%.
- Spearheaded implementation of warehouse management system, sales force automation tools, and other key IT initiatives.

TECHNOLOGY CONSULTANT / PROJECT MANAGER / TRAINER   1995 to 1996
SSI, INC., South Bend, IN
Managed installation and upgrade of networks, systems, and applications for key customer accounts. Designed a portfolio of instructional materials and resources to enhance internal training capabilities.

EDUCATION & PROFESSIONAL CERTIFICATIONS

MBA (Specialization in E-business), Boston University, Boston, MA, 2006
MS (Specialization in Instructional Design & Educational Computing), Northeastern University, Boston, MA, 1994
BS (Major in Mathematics), Tufts University, Medford, MA, 1990

Certified Information Systems Security Professional (CISSP)   Certified Project Management Professional (PMP)
Certified Information Security Manager (CISM)   Microsoft Certified Systems Engineer (MCSE)
ITIL Foundations Certified   Cisco Certified Network Associate (CCNE)

TECHNOLOGY PORTFOLIO

Platforms:	Windows, Red Hat Linux, UNIX, Solaris, HP-UX, Z/OS, OS390, CICS, ISM, DB2
Development Platforms:	.NET, C#, XML, ASP, CSS, T-SQL, HTML, J2EE, JScript, VBScript, Visual Basic, Pearl, Object-Oriented (OO), Quality Assurance, C++
Networks:	WAN/LAN, TCP/IP, Wireless, 802.x, Mobile, MPLS, Satellite, Microwave, RAS, VPN, PRI, ISDN, T1, T3, DSO, DS1, DS3, POTS, Frame-Relay, OSPF, RIP, VLAN, NAT, SSH, SSL, HTTP, SMTP, Distributed
Software & Applications:	SaaS, SOA, Multitier, Bloomberg, Advent, WMS, OSM, TMS, WebSphere, Reuters, Wombat, Activ, FIX, VMware, NetApp, Citrix, SQL, Exchange, SMS, SharePoint, Cognos, OLAP, ETL, ISS, OpenView, Evault, Tivoli, Unicenter, IIS, MS Project, Visio, Remedy, Double-Take, Clusters, CenterVue, Cisco IOS, ASA, PIX Firewall, RHEL, Decision Support Systems, Warehouse Management, Supply Chain, Data Warehousing, Data Mining, Business Intelligence, Trade Order Management, Customer Relationship Management, Open Source, Enterprise Application Integration
ERP Implementations:	ORACLE RDB/ERP/CRM/E-business Suite, PeopleSoft, Dynamics
Methodologies:	SDLC, Iterative, CMM, SABSA, Zackman, UML, Waterfall, Prototyping, MOF, PCI, NIST, ISO/IEC

Cynthia Preston

cynthiapreston@gmail.com
920-555-2310 (h) • 920-505-7812 (m)
9141 Kenosha Drive, Appleton, WI 54912

Senior Executive: Information Technology

HOTEL/RESORT/TRAVEL/HOSPITALITY INDUSTRY

Strategically focused technology executive with an exemplary record of planning and delivering high-quality, dependable IT systems and services aligned with long-term business objectives. Executive team member deeply involved in business strategy, growth and acquisition planning, and alignment of business activities and initiatives to support overriding goal of increasing shareholder value.

STRENGTHS:

- **Strategic systems planning:** Ensuring the greatest ROI for technology investments; balancing needs, risks, critical priorities, and long-term goals.
- **IT/business alignment:** Building alliances, translating business objectives to IT agenda, and representing IT at the executive level.
- **Strategic sourcing:** Selecting, negotiating, and managing outsourcing relationships that deliver better service, stronger capabilities, and lower costs.
- **Team building:** Recruiting, retaining, and directing staff to provide consistent, high-quality results.

Professional Experience

Hospitality Partners, Inc.   Appleton, WI • 2007–2011

$600M nationwide hotel owner, operator, and franchisor; 600 limited-service hotels, 3 brands (Copley, Sandford, Stay Inn)

SENIOR VICE PRESIDENT/CHIEF INFORMATION OFFICER

Member of executive team that drove dramatic turnaround—delivering rapid improvements in revenue, EBITDA, share value, and customer satisfaction. Helped define and execute growth strategy that led to business revitalization (stock price soared from $2 to $11.25) and lucrative sale of the company to Eggars Associates in 2011.

As CIO, developed strategic technology plan aligned with business objectives and directed its execution across the company. Led a team of 80 IT professionals and managed strategic outsourcing relationships.

HIGHLIGHT: Transformed IT organization from the worst-performing department in the company to a national leader in customer satisfaction.

- Developed rigorous upgrading program to improve quality, responsiveness, and personnel.
- Created compensation system that rewarded performance improvement.
- Elevated satisfaction levels above 90%, far outperforming national norm of 63%.

Company-Wide Satisfaction: IT Services

ADDITIONAL ACCOMPLISHMENTS:

- Established a track record for delivering technology projects on time and within budget.
- Identified and strengthened core IT competencies (websites, data warehouse, electronic distribution) and selected strategic outsource partners to provide improved levels of noncore services. Negotiated and managed outsourcing relationships.
  - — *Data center operations* (Ambit Systems Corp.): Eradicated weekly downtime on mission-critical reservation information system, within 6 months reaching system availability of 99+%.
  - — *Telecommunications management* (Tel-Com Services Corp.): Improved service levels, reduced costs.
  - — *Critical applications support* (Strand Consulting—on-site/offshore model): Achieved quicker turnaround, higher reliability, fewer errors, improved service levels, and greater flexibility.
- Implemented full suite of Oracle PeopleSoft financial and HR systems.
- Supported 3-brand, 200-hotel acquisition, integrating all acquired properties to Copley platforms without incident within 6 months.

Continued

Notable features of this resume are the chart, showing dramatic increases in customer satisfaction, and the Highlight section of accomplishments detailed for each job. Note that business performance, as well as technical performance, is emphasized for this technology executive.

Page 2   Cynthia Preston • 920-555-2310 (h) • 920-505-7812 (m) • cynthiapreston@gmail.com

Worldwide Vacation Properties (WVP)   Chicago, IL • 2005–2006

SENIOR VICE PRESIDENT/CHIEF INFORMATION OFFICER

Recruited to join global leadership team of the market leader in vacation exchange, with more than 3,500 affiliated time-share resorts and 2.5 million member families worldwide. Directed a global team of 250+ IT professionals, with full responsibility for planning and delivering WVP's worldwide systems. Additionally, served as General Manager of Denver-based subsidiary Vacation Computer Corporation (VCC), a software company specializing in resort automation software for the time-share industry.

HIGHLIGHTS:

- Spearheaded design, development, and initial rollout of groundbreaking new exchange system to transform static week-to-week inventory to a flexible global points network (CEO's strategic priority).
- Created business case for sale of VCC subsidiary, plagued by software quality issues. Identified purchaser and directed sale that netted several million dollars to WVP.

Sheraton Hotels   Chicago, IL • 2002–2005

VICE PRESIDENT, LODGING PROPERTY SYSTEMS

Ensured the seamless provision of business systems to 1,500 domestic and international hotels, directing all aspects of IT service delivery, including systems consulting, design, development, deployment, and support. Managed 350 staff and $60M annual expense and capital projects budget.

HIGHLIGHT: Salvaged a $50M project that had floundered for 5 years. Inherited the challenge of delivering a new hotel-based sales system to all full-service Sheraton hotels.

- Reorganized the 100-member team of Sheraton employees and McKinsey consultants.
- Rescoped the project, focusing on functionality that would promote high user acceptance.
- Established accelerated completion plan, instituted project disciplines, created bonus plan to reward completion, and implemented a communications and marketing plan to drive grassroots acceptance.
- Successfully completed project within new parameters; system still in use today.

ADDITIONAL ACCOMPLISHMENTS:

- Directed flawless integration of Hi-Grade brand into Sheraton systems and operations.
- Rolled out a new property-management system for all Sheraton International properties.
- Supported launch and rapid expansion of Hostess brand, adding 400+ new properties yearly.

TravelHost International   Seattle, WA • 1996–2002

VICE PRESIDENT, RESORTS AND SALES SYSTEMS (2000–2002)
DIRECTOR, FINANCIAL/ADMINISTRATION/HUMAN RESOURCES SYSTEMS (1996–2000)

Managed development and support of systems for the sales and guest-related operational areas for 15 world-class resort and convention hotels (20,000 rooms), multiple theme parks, water parks, travel company, and hundreds of food and beverage outlets and merchandise locations.

HIGHLIGHT: Led development of a transformational technology strategy for the entire TravelHost enterprise, under executive sponsorship of TravelHost president. Blueprint remains the basis for TravelHost's systems efforts today.

- Developed vision for integrating all the business lines into common processes.
- Organized 7 teams of executive sponsors, specialty consultants, and IT and business representatives.
- Carved out 20 technology-based projects to be completed over 5 years for approximately $100M.

Early Career

SENIOR MANAGER: Deloitte   Seattle, WA
MANAGER, MANAGEMENT ADVISORY SERVICES: Deloitte   San Diego, CA
SYSTEMS ENGINEER: Electronic Data Systems   San Diego, CA

Education

B.S., Mathematics, Magna Cum Laude   University of California, Berkeley, CA

Irene G. Linitz

26 Chaucer Drive • Skokie, IL 60076
Cell: 312-892-4953 • Email: IreneLinitz58@yahoo.com

Chief Information Officer

Healthcare • Pharmaceuticals • Biotech Industries • Retail Operations

Accomplished IT executive known for willingness to take on difficult challenges. Thirteen years of experience managing global systems for extremely large enterprises. Quick advancement through the IT ranks of the world's second-largest company in healthcare products. Special expertise in global SAP implementations, M&A integration, and outsourcing.

Savvy business analyst and IT implementer who leverages strong background in retail operations and technology (Marketing M.B.A. and B.S. in Computer Science).

Experienced leader of overseas IT operations throughout Europe and the Caribbean. Bilingual Spanish and English.

Recipient of YWCA's national *Tribute to Women* award, which recognizes outstanding achievement by women executives.

ERP, SAP, and MES	Data Center Consolidation	Six Sigma (DMAIC)
Offshore Outsourcing	M&A Integration	Lean Methods (Value Steam)
Business Reengineering	SOX and HIPAA	Design Excellence (DFSS)
ITIL v3	ISO 13485:2003 (Medical Devices)	Process Excellence

Professional Experience

ABBOTT LABORATORIES, INC.   Abbott Park, IL • 1996–Present
Medical device, pharmaceutical, and packaged goods manufacturer. Approx. $31 billion annual sales and 72,000 employees.

Promoted 5 times based on ability to deliver strategically critical projects despite difficult managerial and technical challenges. Can simultaneously focus on the "big picture" while leveraging deep experience as a meticulously accurate programmer/analyst.

VICE PRESIDENT, GLOBAL DATA CENTER OPERATIONS, Abbott Park, IL • 2007–Present

Promoted and tasked to unify standards and consolidate worldwide data centers. Currently leading a 650-person organization (5 direct reports). Manage all aspects of data centers, offshore resources, worldwide IT, and a $200 million capital-and-expense budget.

Reduced costs $20 million annually via labor rationalization, platform virtualization, data center consolidation, and technology-refresh initiatives.

Consolidated and aligned disjointed tech-support groups into a single global structure, which led to contract consolidation, unified processes, and common tools and reporting.

Established a global 24/7 critical response team—based on a novel "follow-the-sun" approach—that improved responsiveness to business-critical incidents, cut downtime, exposed root causes of problems, and accelerated resolution of problems.

Planned and launched an IT standardization initiative to shrink the mainframe footprint, optimize asset utilization, and unify Abbott's global network architecture.

IT DIRECTOR, WORLDWIDE OPERATIONS/QUALITY, Palo Alto, CA • 2006–2007
Abbott Medcon, a medical-device subsidiary.

Advanced to larger scope of responsibility with the challenge to improve all aspects of IT for one of Abbott's largest business units. Concurrently contributed expertise as member of worldwide Operations, QRC, and IT Leadership Teams.

Designed global Enterprise Resource Planning (ERP) strategy for 7 operating companies. Consolidated 18 ERP platforms—over 4 years—into a single SAP environment.

Saved $1 million annually by applying *Lean Kaizen* concepts during implementation of a global Electronic Batch Records (EBR) platform for the medical-diagnostics division.

Implemented product life-cycle management (PLM) that saved $2.5+ million annually and improved effectiveness of local and off-shore resources.

Continued

Personal achievements and language skills are included in the summary to help distinguish this individual from other candidates. The resume is concise, well written, and filled with technology and business achievements.

Irene Linitz .... *(C) 312-892-4953* .... *Email: IreneLinitz58@yahoo.com* .... *Page 2*

ABBOTT LABORATORIES, continued
___

VICE PRESIDENT AND CHIEF INFORMATION OFFICER, France • 2004–2006

AbbottRX, pharmaceutical supply chain subsidiary, $12 billion annual sales.

Promoted to improve all IT aspects of a troubled subsidiary. Appointed to management board and took charge of $40 million annual budget and a European IT team dispersed across 5 countries. Created global application architecture and strategy for newly formed global supply chain organization. Meshed EMEA and U.S. technology strategies into a consolidated, enterprise-wide strategic plan for business and IT.

Decreased manufacturing cycle time 15% and saved $6 million annually by leading deployment of Electronic Batch Records (EBR) application, used throughout AbbottRX.

Cut or avoided costs—up to $12 million annually—by implementing Regional ERP (SAP) for the European Logistics Center and plants in Belgium, Switzerland, and Italy.

DIRECTOR, INFORMATION TECHNOLOGY, Italy and Portugal • 2002–2004

AbbotRX, pharmaceutical supply chain subsidiary, $6 billion annual sales.

Promoted to upgrade IT for key sites in Italy and in Portugal. Managed $7.5 million budget.

Upgraded Electronic Batch Record (EBR) system to ensure *Part 11* compliance.

Implemented SAP-based warehouse management application that controlled fully automated high-bay warehouse and 9 AGVs (automated guided vehicles).

MANAGER, OPERATIONAL EXCELLENCE AND INFORMATION MGMT, Chicago, IL • 2001–2002

Abbott USA Direct, a pharmaceutical supply chain subsidiary, approximately $5 billion annual sales.

Promoted to introduce best practices and establish Process Excellence for the North American IT organization. Trained and coached staff on Six Sigma and other process-excellence methodologies.

Led senior management during creation of 1- and 3-year strategic plans.

Saved more than $1 million annually—plus an additional $2.75 million in potential cost avoidance—by sponsoring 2 Black Belt and 6 Green Belt projects.

IT MANAGER, Puerto Rico • 1996–2001

Pharmaceutical site, $4 billion annual sales

Defined, implemented, and supported a new Manufacturing Execution System (MES). Implemented major expansion project that included building construction, material handling, and automation.

Summary of Additional Experience

ORACLE CORPORATION, Humacao, Puerto Rico (1994–1996): Programmer/Systems Administrator: Supported manufacturing system written in Visual Basic with SQL Server tables.

ERA MANAGEMENT, INC., Las Piedras, PR (1993–1994): Systems Administrator: Supervised installation of IBM 4680 Store and POS system with 6 scanning registers.

BALI FOUNDATIONS, INC., Rio Piedras, PR (1992–1993): Accounts Payable and General Ledger

MARQUETTE UNIVERSITY, Milwaukee, WI (1991–1992): Teaching and Research Assistant

M&I DATA SERVICES, INC., Milwaukee, WI (1987–1991): Programmer/Analyst I: Analyzed, estimated costs, coded, and installed enhancements for financial (trust) system written in COBOL.

Education and Professional Development

M.B.A., Marketing, Marquette University, Milwaukee, WI (1990)

B.S., Computer Science, University of Wisconsin, Platteville, WI (1987)

Harvard Business School Executive Education: Making the Case for IT Investments; Developing Strategy

RESUME 104: BY LOUISE KURSMARK

ANDREA WANG

404-229-5631 | andrea.wang@verizon.net
2991 Vista Place, Decatur, GA 30033

SENIOR OPERATING EXECUTIVE: HEALTHCARE | HEALTHCARE IT

*Driving growth and performance improvement through inspirational leadership;
clear communication; and tight focus on customer needs, business objectives, and measurable results.*

Fifteen-year record of success leading healthcare and technology organizations during periods of massive change—high growth, business transformation, downsizing, and market repositioning. Full range of executive leadership skills and exceptional ability to steer complex initiatives from concept to completion.

Built, evaluated, and transformed healthcare companies into high-quality, cost-efficient, and well-managed organizations. Inspired and mobilized business units and management teams to achieve and surpass ambitious goals. Reengineered processes for enterprises as large as $750M and managed P&L of more than $30M. Built organizational capacity and solid infrastructure to support 250% business expansion.

Wharton MBA • Princeton BA

Strategic Planning & Tactical Execution | Finance | Operations Startup & Reorganization | P&L Oversight
IT, Professional Services & Project Leadership | Healthcare Analytics | Health Information Technology
Customer Service, Client Relations & Key Account Management | Team Building & Team Leadership
Accelerated Growth & Expansion | New Business Development

EXPERIENCE AND ACCOMPLISHMENTS

MEDI-DATA, INC.   Atlanta, GA | 2005–2011
Provider of care management and analytic services to large Blue Cross Blue Shield, employer, government, and union plans.

▶ **Senior Vice President**

Drove continuous improvements in organizational capacity and efficiency during period of accelerated growth (3X revenue increase). Managed $30M capital budget and held full executive authority for multiple operating units—account management, coaching operations services, PMO, and global IT operations (including external collocation facility, internal data center, network, telephony, server, desktop, and laptop support for 1,500 employees).

- **Growth:** Managed key client relationships to retain and grow revenue of annual contracts, many exceeding **$10M** annually. Pioneered annual account-planning process and quarterly client meetings.

- **Profitability:** Automated scheduling and created daily reporting system to maximize capacity and performance of client teams—the backbone of account service and #1 opportunity to increase capacity without adding cost.

- **Business Transformation:** Drove a comprehensive culture change that created a professional environment conducive to high performance and productivity.

- **PMO:** Launched the company's first enterprise Project Management Office to address uneven execution of projects totaling **$50M** yearly in operating and capital costs. Focused on training, process redesign, and development/sharing of best practices. Radically improved on-time/on-budget results while delivering data to help all stakeholders understand and improve.

- **Performance Management:** Introduced a complete capital planning and tracking system to measure project performance against capital and operating budgets.

- **Cost Control:** Reduced operating costs **25%** during economic downturn with little impact to strategically critical deliverables by restaging work, stopping irrelevant items, and using internal staff instead of high-paid contractors.

MED SOLUTIONS, INC.   Dallas, TX | 2002–2005
Provider of IT solutions for clinical research trials and medical research.

▶ **Chief Operating Officer**

Hired to drive growth and expansion of the e-services business in North America and Europe, including IVRS, Web data capture, and clinical trial management portals. Held full P&L responsibility for the business unit.

- **Growth:** Propelled **250%** revenue surge in 3 years.

- **Profitability:** Transformed negative gross margins to **+40%,** consistently above target.

Continued

A branding statement centers a strong summary section that is supported by measurable achievements throughout the experience portion of the resume. Bold introductions to the bullet points catch the reader's attention and highlight critical areas of expertise and performance.

ANDREA WANG   404-229-5631 | andrea.wang@verizon.net

MED SOLUTIONS, continued

- **Performance:** Strengthened operations by introducing system of business measurement and culture of transparency. Boosted morale and individual performance and stemmed costly talent drain—reducing **35%** turnover rate to less than **10%.**

E-HEALTH SOLUTIONS, INC.   Dallas, TX | 1997–2001
Venture-backed provider of enterprise healthcare software and services.

▶ **Chief Operating Officer**

Repositioned company from electronic medical records provider to broad-based healthcare software company. Recruited by CEO to build development capability and operating infrastructure needed to expand scope of solutions and professional services. Provided strategic and hands-on leadership for business development and project execution.

- **Growth:** Expanded business to multiple market segments—home health, disease management, and managed care.
- **Business Development:** Built client relationships at the President and CEO levels.
- **Project Oversight:** Directed full project life cycle—from business analysis, requirements gathering, product configuration, and data conversion to user training and ongoing customer support. Maintained exceptional record of on-time completion and customer satisfaction.

SOLUTION CONSULTANTS, INC.   Atlanta, GA | 1991–1997
Provider of professional advisory services.

▶ **Vice President**

Led practice that generated more than 50% of company's overall billings, progressing rapidly from Staff Consultant and Project Manager to VP of Retirement Practice, serving large clients in finance and insurance industries.

- **Multimillion-Dollar Business Transformation:** Reengineered internal workflow and systems to reduce costs and improve customer service for a major pension firm.
- **Unprecedented Service Performance:** Redesigned policy processing operation for a **$750M** insurance company, building a multifunctional team environment that enabled company to achieve previously unmet service standards. Delivered expense reduction **2X** projections.
- **Decision-Making Data:** Designed activity-based costing model that guided **$400M** industrial products company in sales and marketing activities, product rationalization, and customer segmentation.

Prior: **National Account Representative/Regional Sales Manager,** Baxter Healthcare, Atlanta, GA, 1984–1989

EDUCATION

MBA *with highest distinction*
Wharton School of the University of Pennsylvania, 1991

BA, Economics
Princeton University, Princeton, NJ, 1984

PART III

Cover Letters for Computer and Web Jobs

CHAPTER 11

Writing a Winning Cover Letter

Now that your resume is written, you may think that you're all set to launch your job search. If it were only that easy! Just as critical to the effectiveness and success of your job search campaign is your cover letter. To begin our discussion of this vital element in your search, let's start with a concise definition:

> **Cover Letter:** A document that accompanies your resume and is used to highlight your specific skills, qualifications, competencies, achievements, and more that relate directly to the position for which you are applying.

That's right—the best cover letters are letters that are targeted to specific positions (for example, network administration position with a large university, programming and systems design position with an emerging Internet venture, technology training position with an international company). Targeted letters allow you to selectively include information about your past work experience, technical qualifications, training and education, affiliations, professional activities, and more that directly support your candidacy for a particular position. In essence, you're taking everything about your career, laying it out on the table (so to speak), and then selecting only that information which is most important to your current job objective.

Here's an example of a wonderfully written cover letter that is targeted to this candidate's specific objective—a position as a Configuration Analyst. The resume that accompanies this cover letter, resume 25, is in chapter 5.

CAROLYN HE

321 Westminster, Apt. #4
Los Angeles, CA 90020

310-787-8232
carolyn.he@ymail.com

April 9, 2011

Susie Jacobson
HR Director
Allied Industrial Technologies
823424 Southridge Park Road
Orlando, FL 32819

Re: Configuration Analyst

Dear Ms. Jacobson:

I provide a level of expertise in quality assurance and configuration management that is unmatched for its depth of knowledge, application of best practices, and delivery of project successes that are widely known and appreciated. My project capabilities are evident in the following achievements:

- Recognized as an expert in critical systems integration and customer acceptance; designed and developed FAA terminal systems air traffic programs.

- Produced on-time deliverables, meeting exact specifications for ISO 9001/AS9100B and SEI/CMMI Level 4 (progressing to Level 5) requirements.

- Designed and implemented QA and CM/DM audit checklists to satisfy ISO and CMMI requirements.

I've worked in this industry for 25 years, yet I still possess a love of learning and discovery. I'm looking for an opportunity to do what I do best. I want to work for an organization that welcomes my maturity and not only recognizes my ability to produce ongoing results, but also values my skills at nurturing and mentoring others to excel.

I believe that Allied Industrial Technologies and I are a perfect match. Please call me to schedule a convenient time to discuss my qualifications and how we might work together.

Sincerely,

Carolyn He

Attachment

A targeted cover letter (submitted by Jennifer Hay, ACRW, CRS, CPRW).

All too often, job search candidates write what we refer to as general cover letters—letters that can be used to apply for any position with any type of organization. In essence, these letters simply summarize information that is already included on your resume and tend to be not nearly as effective as targeted cover letters that are customized to each position to which you apply. Because you do not have a specific position in mind when you write a general letter, you are not able to highlight information that would be most essential in a particular situation. As such, we strongly urge that you stay away from general letters and devote the time that is necessary to develop targeted cover letters that will sell you into your next position.

Another real advantage to targeted cover letters is that the recipient will notice that you have taken the time to write an individual letter to him or her; that, of course, leaves a great impression. When you are able to integrate specific information into your letter about the company to which you are applying, it clearly demonstrates your interest in the position and the organization, before you've ever had the opportunity to speak with anyone there. Just think how impressed a prospective employer will be when he or she realizes that you've spent the time and energy necessary to research and "get to know" his or her organization. This, in and of itself, will give you a distinct advantage over the competition.

Six Steps to Writing Better Cover Letters

To help guide you in writing and designing your own winning cover letters, we've created a step-by-step process and structure that will allow you to quickly and easily write letters that will get you and your resume noticed, not passed over:

1. Identify Your Key Selling Points
2. Preplan
3. Write the Opening Paragraph
4. Write the Body
5. Write the Closing
6. Polish, Proofread, and Finalize

Now, we're going to explore each of these steps in detail to provide you with an action plan to write your letters with ease and confidence. Our most detailed discussion will be of Step 1: Identify Your Key Selling Points, which is the entire foundation for your cover letter.

STEP 1: IDENTIFY YOUR KEY SELLING POINTS

What qualifications, experiences, achievements, and skills do you bring to an organization? It's time to evaluate and quantify what it is that makes you unique, valuable, and interesting to potential employers.

Know Your Objective

The best place to start is by clearly identifying *who* you are and what your job objective is. Are you a C++ programmer, a database administrator, a Web designer, a project manager, or a CIO? It is critical that you be able to clearly and accurately define who you are in an instant. Remember, an instant is all that you have to capture your reader's attention, encouraging him not only to read your cover letter in full, but also to read your resume and contact you for a personal interview.

Summarize Your Experience

Just as important, you must be able to clearly identify why an organization would be interested in interviewing and possibly hiring you. Is it because of the schools or universities you've attended? The industries in which you've been employed? The positions you have held? The promotions you have earned? Your accomplishments? Your technical expertise? Your specific skills and qualifications? Your licenses and educational credentials? Your leadership skills? Your foreign-language skills and international experience? Why would someone be interested in you?

Sell Your Achievements

Your achievements are what set you apart from others with a similar background. They answer the reader's all-important question, "What can you do for me?" because they tell precisely what you have done for someone else. Cover letters and resumes without achievements are simply dry compilations of position titles and responsibilities. They don't sell your unique attributes, and they don't compel readers to pick up the phone and invite you in for an interview.

In thinking about your achievements, ask yourself how you've benefited the organizations where you've worked. In general terms, you can help an organization by

- **Making money** (revenues, profits, earnings, ROI/ROA/ROE increases, new customers)

- **Saving money** (cost reductions, streamlining, automating)

- **Creating new things** (courses, programs, techniques, methodologies, systems, processes, and more)

- **Improving existing things** (reengineering, redesigning, developing new processes, consolidating)

- **Improving departmental and/or organizational performance** (productivity, efficiency, quality, delivery, and customer service)

- **Winning honors, awards, and commendations**

In writing your achievements, think about the two key pieces of information you want to convey about each of your successes: what you did and how it benefited the organization. It is the combination of both of these components that will make your achievements—and, in turn, you—shine.

Who you are, what you have achieved, and why an organization would want to hire you are critical questions you must ask yourself before you ever begin to write a cover letter. The answers to those questions will directly impact what you write in your cover letter and how you present that information. You must determine what you have to offer that relates to that organization's specific needs, what will be of interest to its hiring managers, and what will entice them to read your resume and offer you the opportunity for an interview. That information then becomes the foundation for every cover letter that you write.

STEP 2: PREPLAN

Before you begin writing a single word of your cover letter, you must determine the appropriate strategy for that particular letter. You're not ready to write until you can clearly answer the following questions:

- **Why am I writing this letter?** Am I writing in response to a print or online advertisement, sending a cold-call letter to companies, contacting someone in my network, writing to an organization at the recommendation of some-one else, or writing a follow-up letter to a company to which I already sent a resume? The answer to this question will significantly impact the content of your cover letter—the introduction in particular.

- **Have I researched the organization and/or the position?** There will be instances where you know, or can find, information about an organization you are writing to, the services and products it offers, the positions that are open, the types of candidates it hires, the hiring requirements, and so much more. Do your research! The more you know about the company and the position, the more on-target you can write your letters, relating your experience to its identified needs. If you know the company has critical hardware issues, be sure to stress your success in resolving those same types of problems and restoring systems integrity. If you know that the company is struggling with its technical support organization, focus on your success in building strong customer-service centers. Your goal is to find common ground between you and the company and then leverage that to your advantage.

- **Do I have a contact name?** Have I double-checked the correct spelling of the name and the person's job title? Do I have the full mailing address or e-mail address? The fact is that if you write to the human resources department of a company, you'll never quite know where your letter and resume have landed. However, if you write to a particular individual in a particular department with particular contact information, you not only know who has your resume and cover letter, you also know whom to follow up with. This is critical for job search success in today's competitive market!

STEP 3: WRITE THE OPENING PARAGRAPH

The opening paragraph of your cover letter is your hook—your "sales pitch"—that tells your reader who you are and why you are of value to that specific organization. It should be written to entice the recipient to read your letter in its entirety and then take the time to closely review your resume. And, because it is so critical, the opening paragraph is often the section that will take you the longest to write.

> **TIP:** If you're having trouble writing the opening paragraph of your cover letter, leave it for the time being and move on to the body of the letter. Once you've written the rest, the opening paragraph will usually flow much more smoothly and quickly.

There are three specific questions you must address in the opening paragraph of your cover letter:

1. Who are you?

2. Why are you writing?

3. What message are you communicating?

Your answers to these questions, combined with the specific reason you are writing (for example, in response to an advertisement, on recommendation from a network contact, or because of an Internet job lead), will almost always dictate the type of opening you select. Review the introductory paragraphs for the sample cover letters in chapter 12 to help you get started developing your own introduction.

STEP 4: WRITE THE BODY

Now you're ready to tackle the real task at hand: writing the body of your cover letter—the substance, key qualifications, technical expertise, accomplishments, successes, and whatever other information you choose to highlight that will entice the reader to closely review your resume and offer you the opportunity for a personal interview.

In order to sell yourself (or any product) as "the answer," you must highlight the attractive *features* and *benefits* of that product. Put yourself in the shoes of the buyer and ask yourself

- What will catch my attention?

- What's interesting about this candidate?

- What's innovative or unique about this candidate?

- Why is this candidate different from (or better than) other competitive candidates?

- Do I understand the value I'll get from this candidate?

- Do I need this candidate?

- Do I want this candidate?

Whether or not you're conscious of it, every time you buy something, you ask yourself these questions and others. It's the typical process that everyone proceeds through when they're deciding whether to make a purchase. It is imperative that you remember this as you begin to write your cover letters. Understand that you must clearly communicate the answers to these questions in order to get people to want to "buy" *you*.

> **TIP:** Your cover letter should not be written as "Here I am, give me a job," but should be written as, "Here I am; this is why I am so valuable; give me a chance to solve your problems." Focusing on the value and benefits you have to offer is a good way to capture the reader's attention. Remember, the employer's most compelling question is "What can you do for me?" not "What do you want?"

Your challenge, then, is to convey your value in a short and concise document—your cover letter. Unfortunately, there are no rules to guide you in determining what to include in each specific cover letter that you write. It is entirely a judgment call based on the specific situation at hand—the position, the organization, and the required qualifications and experience. What you include in your letter is not necessarily based on what you consider to be your most significant responsibilities and achievements from throughout your career, but rather what is *most relevant to the hiring company and its needs*.

Achievements, accomplishments, contributions, and successes are the cornerstone of any effective cover letter. It goes without saying that you want to demonstrate that you have the right skills, qualifications, and experience for a particular job. However, you do not want your letter to be a "job description"—a mere listing of job responsibilities. First of all, you've addressed a great deal of that information in the resume that you'll be sending along with your cover letter. You do *not* want your letter to simply reiterate what's in your resume. The challenge is to write a cover letter that complements the resume and brings the most notable information to the forefront.

Depending on the format of your letter, you can convey this information in a paragraph format, a bullet-point format, or a combination of both. Use whichever you feel is most appropriate to convey the particular information. If you decide to use full paragraphs, make sure that they are fairly short to promote readability. Edit and tighten your copy so that every word and phrase conveys information that relates to the employer's needs and your most relevant qualifications.

STEP 5: WRITE THE CLOSING

Now that you've written your introductory paragraph and the body of your cover letter, all you have left to do is the closing paragraph. This is generally the easiest section of a cover letter to write. To get started, ask yourself these two simple questions:

- What style of closing paragraph do I want to use?

- Is there any specific personal or salary information I want to include that was requested in the advertisement to which I am responding?

When it comes to choosing style, closing paragraphs are easy. There are basically only two styles—passive and assertive—and the distinction between the two styles is evident:

- **Passive:** A passive letter ends with a statement such as "*I look forward to hearing from you.*" With this sentence, you are taking a passive approach, waiting for the hiring company or recruiter to contact you. This is *not* our recommended strategy.

- **Assertive:** An assertive letter ends with a statement such as "*I look forward to interviewing with you and will follow up next week to schedule a convenient appointment.*" In this sentence, you are asserting yourself, telling the recipient that you will follow up and asking for the interview!

We strongly recommend that you end your cover letters with an assertive closing paragraph. Remember, the only real objective of your cover letter is to get an interview, so *ask for it!* Furthermore, we also advise that you outline an agenda that communicates that you will be expecting the employer's call and, if you don't hear from the employer, you will follow up. This puts you in the driver's seat and in control of your job search. It also demonstrates to a prospective employer that once you've initiated something, you follow it through to completion. This is a valuable trait for any professional.

Inevitably, there will be instances in your job search when you will not be able to follow up:

- If you are responding to a blind advertisement with a P.O. box, you won't know whom to call.

- If you are responding to an advertisement that states "No phone calls," don't call.

- If you are sending out 1,000 letters to recruiters across the nation, don't waste your time calling them. If they're interested or have an opportunity for which you are suited, they'll call you.

- If you know that you'll never get the individual you want to speak with on the phone, don't waste your time or money.

The closing paragraph of your cover letter is also the preferred placement for any personal or salary information you will include. There are generally only two times you will want to include this type of information:

- **When it has been asked for in an advertisement.** Common requests include such things as salary history (what you have made in the past and are currently earning if you are employed), salary requirements (what your current salary objectives are), citizenship status, or geographic preference.

- **When you are writing "cold-call" letters to recruiters.** When contacting recruiters, we recommend that you at least minimally address your salary requirements (a range is fine) and any geographic preferences in the closing paragraph of your cover letter.

STEP 6: POLISH, PROOFREAD, AND FINALIZE

The process we recommend for writing your cover letters suggests that you first craft the opening, then the middle, and then the closing of each letter. Although the step-by-step process makes the task fairly quick and easy, you will probably find that your letters need final polishing, wordsmithing, and tweaking to ensure that each section "flows" into the next and that you have a cohesive-sounding whole.

Take the time to proofread your letter thoroughly and carefully. Read it for sense and flow; then read it again to check for spelling errors, punctuation mistakes, and grammatical inconsistencies. We cannot emphasize this point enough. The people who receive your cover letter and resume *do* judge your professionalism based on the quality and accuracy of these documents. In fact, in a survey of hiring authorities we conducted for a prior book, *90 percent of respondents* mentioned quality and appearance factors (such as typos, misspellings, smudged print, and low-quality paper) as reasons for *immediately discarding a resume*. Don't take a chance that your carefully written letter and resume will end up in the circular file before your qualifications are even considered.

Here are a few things to look out for during the polishing phase:

- **Spelling:** Use your computer's spell-checker, but don't rely on it totally. The spell-checker won't flag an "it's" that should be "its" or a "there" that should be "their." Make triple-certain you've correctly spelled all names: people, organizations, software programs, and so on.

- **Grammar and punctuation:** If you're not confident about your grammar and punctuation skills, purchase an all-purpose reference guide and use it as often as you need to. Don't let your cover letter be discarded because of basic grammar and punctuation errors.

- **Interesting language:** As much as possible, avoid cliches and outdated language (such as "Enclosed please find my resume"). It's difficult to find new ways to express familiar sentiments (such as "I would appreciate the opportunity for an interview"), and it's certainly not necessary to come up with unique language for every phrase. But make sure that your cover letter doesn't sound like a cookie-cutter, one-size-fits-all letter that could have been written by any job seeker.

Authors' Best Tips for Writing Winning Cover Letters

Here's our most important cover-letter advice, gleaned from our experience writing thousands of cover letters over the years.

DON'T REINVENT THE WHEEL

A great amount of our discussion has focused on the fact that your cover letters should be written individually based on the specific situation. And that is quite true. The more focused your letters, the greater the impact and the more likely you are to get a response and opportunity to interview. However, you *do not* have to reinvent the wheel with each and every cover letter you write. If you're a help-desk administrator writing in response to advertisements for other help-desk positions, you can very often use the same letter with just a few minor editorial changes to match each opportunity. Remember to use your word-processing program's "copy and paste" function. It's a great, labor-saving tool!

SELL IT TO ME; DON'T TELL IT TO ME

Just like resume writing, cover letter writing is sales—pure and simple. You have a commodity to sell—yourself—and your challenge is to write a marketing communication that is powerful and pushes the reader to action. (You want him to call you for an interview!) Therefore, it is essential that when writing your letters you "sell" your achievements and don't just "tell" your responsibilities.

Here's a quick example. If you are a Java programmer, you could "tell" your reader that you've developed more than 10 new Java scripts. Great! Or you could "sell" the fact that you've led project teams that developed and delivered new Java scripts that have supported a 200 percent increase in shopping-cart purchases within just two months. Which letter would capture your interest?

GET OVER WRITER'S BLOCK

Very often, the most difficult part of writing a cover letter is getting started. You can sit and look at that blank piece of paper or computer screen for hours, frustrated and wondering whether the whole world has such a hard time writing cover letters. If writing is part of your daily work responsibilities, the process might not be too arduous. However, if you do not have to write on a regular basis, cover letters can be an especially formidable task. That's why it is so important to follow the step-by-step process we have created. It is guaranteed to make cover letter writing faster, easier, and much less painful!

If you're still having trouble, consider this simple thought: **You do not have to start at the beginning.** Even after writing thousands and thousands of cover letters, we'll sit stumped, unable to come up with just the "right" opening paragraph. Instead of wasting time and brain power, and getting frustrated, we'll just leave it alone and move on to another section in the letter that we feel more confident writing. You'll find that once you get going, new ideas will pop into your head and the more difficult sections will come much more easily and confidently.

ANSWER THE EMPLOYER'S MOST IMPORTANT QUESTION: "WHAT CAN YOU DO FOR ME?"

A powerful cover letter can help you get what you want: a new, perhaps more advanced and more satisfying, position. It is certainly important that you understand what you want to do, the kind of organization you'd like to work for, and the environment in which you'll be most productive. Yet you must remember that employers aren't really interested in you. They're interested in *what you can do for them*. If you do not keep this thought in the forefront of your mind when writing your cover letters, you're likely to produce a self-centered-sounding "here I am" letter that probably won't do much to advance your job search.

When writing your cover letters, consider the employer's needs and make sure that you communicate that you can add value, solve problems, and deliver benefits for that employer. You can do this through a strong focus on accomplishments ("Ah, she did that for Acme Technology; she can do the same for me.") and through careful attention to the wording and tone of your letter so that you appear to be more interested in contributing to the organization than satisfying your own personal needs.

Then, be sure to review the Cover Letter Checklist on the next page to be sure that your letters meet all of our requirements for style, appropriateness, quality of text, quality of presentation, and effectiveness. Follow our rules and we guarantee that your letters will open doors, generate interviews, and help you land your next great professional opportunity.

Cover Letter Checklist

Before sending each cover letter you prepare, complete the following checklist to be sure that you have met all the rules for cover letter writing. If you cannot answer "yes" to *all* of the questions, go back and edit your letter as necessary before sending it. The only questions for which a "no" answer is acceptable are questions 5 and 6, which relate specifically to the organization to which you are writing. As we have stated previously, there will be instances when you can find this information, but there will also be instances (for example, when writing to a P.O. box) when you cannot.

		YES	NO
1.	Do I convey an immediate understanding of who I am in the first two sentences of my cover letter?	❏	❏
2.	Is my cover letter format unique, and does my letter stand out?	❏	❏
3.	Have I highlighted my most relevant qualifications?	❏	❏
4.	Have I highlighted my most relevant achievements?	❏	❏
5.	Have I included information I know about the organization or the specific position for which I am applying?	❏	❏
6.	Have I highlighted why I want to work for this organization?	❏	❏
7.	Is my cover letter neat, clean, and well-presented without being overdesigned?	❏	❏
8.	Is my cover letter error-free?	❏	❏
9.	Is my cover letter short and succinct, preferably no longer than one page?	❏	❏
10.	Do I ask for an interview in the cover letter?	❏	❏

CHAPTER **12**

Sample Cover Letters

What follows are eight more sample cover letters for your review. Look at them closely. Select opening paragraphs, closing paragraphs, formats, and styles that you like, and then model your own cover letters accordingly. You'll find that by using these sample letters for hints, your letter-writing process will be much easier and faster. To see even more samples and get more help with writing your cover letters, see our book *Cover Letter Magic* (JIST Publishing).

Vanessa Smith

6882 Leavenworth Street #3C
San Francisco, CA 94108

Mobile: 415.887.1218
van.smith@gmail.com

January 3, 2011

RE: Corporate Operations Engineer

Currently, I am employed as a Senior Application Support Specialist with the World Culture Society, and previously I worked as a Mac Genius with Apple. As such, I offer a unique combination of skills and cross-platform technical qualifications ideal for your position of Corporate Operations Engineer:

- Deep and rich technical expertise with Mac and Microsoft desktops, laptops, and remote devices, enabling user access to corporate networks and applications from sites worldwide. Solid working knowledge of Linux.

- Wealth of experience with telecommunications systems and wireless technologies, including the recent rollout of iPhones to users throughout the World Culture Society.

- Hands-on experience with numerous software programs, applications, and fonts.

- Best-in-class technical troubleshooting skills—hardware, software, networks, servers, printers, and more.

- Extensive experience facilitating project management cycles from organization and user needs assessment through technology testing, deployment, and support.

- Top-flight skills in user training and support, with an emphasis on providing personalized services to key corporate executives, board members, managers, and others throughout global organizations.

As I currently live in San Francisco, I would be most interested in your Silicon Valley Corporate Operations Engineer position. However, I am aware that Google is also recruiting for other locations and would, of course, be interested in discussing those as well.

Thank you for your time and consideration. I look forward to our interview.

Sincerely,

Vanessa Smith

Enclosure

Bullet points convey a wealth of relevant skills and experience. Notice the closing reference to specific geographic location and other opportunities with this global company (companion resume: resume 4 in chapter 4).

Irina McCarver

513-204-7382
mccarver@gmail.com

1929 Miami Lakes Drive
Loveland, Ohio 45140

Expertise: Technology Services Operations Management

January 10, 2011

RE: Operations Director, CareerBuilder posting XJK11110

Over the past 4 years, I have led a technology services company to impressive growth through a combined focus on business building, customer service, and staff training and development. The following highlights are a strong match for the capabilities you seek in your next operations director:

- Achieved a consistent annual growth rate of 35% in a competitive marketplace.

- Positioned the company as expert, service-oriented, and responsive. Focused intense efforts on improving staff knowledge, skills, and customer-service orientation.

- Improved profitability by reducing business development costs, primarily through successful referral-building efforts.

As a result of this notable growth and improved financial performance, the company was bought out late last year by Neolog, a large computer services corporation. Although my position as operations director is secure, this business change offers an excellent opportunity to look for a new challenge with an organization where I can continue to be instrumental in operational improvements, sales and marketing initiatives, staff development, and strategic planning.

May we schedule a time to discuss our mutual interests? I am confident that I can deliver similar strong results for your organization.

Thank you for your consideration.

Sincerely,

Irina McCarver

Enclosure: Resume

Although written in response to a "blind" posting (where the hiring company and manager name are not given), this letter connects to the needs expressed by the hiring company. The heading, carried over from the resume, instantly focuses the reader on the candidate's area of expertise (companion resume: resume 48 in chapter 6).

COVER LETTER 3: BY LOUISE KURSMARK

To: tgold@acme.com
Subject: Atlanta Systems Administrator

Dear Ms. Gold:

My sister, Tracy Oswald, tells me that you are looking for a Systems Administrator for your growing Atlanta operation.

I am experienced, reliable, loyal, and customer focused and would like to talk with you about joining your team.

The attached resume describes nearly 15 years of experience with Anthem Blue Cross/Blue Shield, during which I advanced to increasingly responsible technical positions. Both independently and with a team, I worked hard to provide the best possible service and support to my "customers." I was recognized for my strong technical skills, ability to guide less-experienced support people, and 100% reliability.

A recent downsizing at Anthem caused my position to be eliminated, and I am looking for a new opportunity with a company like yours, where my technical abilities, positive attitude, and dedication will be valued.

I will call you next week in hopes of getting together soon.

Yours truly,

Kevin Oswald
****
koswald@gmail.com
404-229-1109

Whenever possible, follow the example in this letter and use a referral to open the door to a possible opportunity. Written as an e-mail message, the letter shares experiences and attributes that will be of value.

Victoria Lee

NEW MEDIA & ONLINE TECHNOLOGY SECTORS

795 Center Street
Wellesley, MA 01801

victoria.lee@gmail.com
617.677.8189

January 10, 2011

Jason Wetherby
Vice President
Elephant Design
16 Quannapowitt Parkway
Wakefield, MA 01801

Dear Mr. Wetherby:

Over the past two months, I've seen a number of job postings for Elephant Design—Executive Creative Director, Executive Technology Director, and Director of Program Management. Obviously, Elephant Design is doing remarkably well in the market, and I would welcome the opportunity to help it do even better as part of the management team. As detailed in the accompanying resume, I offer a unique combination of experience and skills that make me a qualified candidate for all of these positions:

- My strong track record of success in leading fast-paced technology organizations and operations includes defining innovative technology solutions, creating new technology products, launching new technology start-ups, recruiting and training talented technology and business professionals, and transitioning technological ideas into money.

- I am able to manage from the crossroads of technology, sales, and business, working collaboratively across all business units to achieve aggressive product development, customer development, sales revenue, and ROI goals.

- My strong general management skills include P&L, sales, marketing, client relationship management, human resources, multisite operations, and project leadership.

- Throughout my career, I've spearheaded creative design, graphic design, advertising, public relations, media buying, and related programs and projects. These assignments allow me to combine my creative bent with my leadership talents to drive forward innovative campaigns that capture new clients, strengthen market positioning, and drive sustained growth.

- To date, I've had success managing start-ups, emerging ventures, and well-established companies in B2B and B2C markets.

Characterized by others as a forward-thinking, customer-centered, and compassionate business leader, I take great pride in my financial successes, technology innovations, and sales performance. However, most significantly, I believe my performance in building relationships—with employees, executives, customers, business partners, and others—is the greatest value I bring to Elephant Design.

I would welcome the opportunity to interview with you so that we can determine which of your management opportunities is most appropriate based on my experience and qualifications. I'll follow up with you next week to schedule a convenient time for us to meet. I thank you in advance for your consideration.

Sincerely,

Victoria Lee

Enclosure

This candidate has been reading about the company, and she uses what she learned in her first paragraph. Her letter is effectively opening up a conversation rather than simply responding to a job posting (companion resume: resume 73 in chapter 8).

Allison Keynes

9841 Ashburn Hill, Cincinnati, OH 45243
513-339-1101
ajkeynes@cinci.rr.com

January 10, 2011

Richard Yamamoto
CIO
National Banking Corporation
211 West Wacker Drive
Chicago, IL 60611

Dear Mr. Yamamoto:

Leading technology projects, teams, and organizations to support strategic business goals is what I do best. As Senior Project Manager for America's Bank, I guided the massive technology conversion and integration projects that followed each of its 12 acquisitions—in each case, merging hundreds of financial products, systems, and services into its central technology systems, while providing a seamless transition to customers.

Just as important, my division supported business growth from $500 million to $6 billion with only a 25% increase in staff.

Of course, technology services are only as good as the technical staff that designs, implements, and supports them. I have found that there is no "trick" to keeping staff morale high and turnover low—rather, this result relies on a top-down management attitude of respect, empowerment, continuous professional development, and teamwork. The proof of this approach can be seen in the 5% or lower turnover rate I maintained for more than a decade.

I would like to meet and discuss ways in which my leadership, technical, and managerial skills can be valuable to your organization.

Thank you for your consideration.

Sincerely,

Allison Keynes

Enclosure: resume

Using a conversational tone, this letter shares key career successes but also the leadership skills and personal attributes that made these successes possible.

Michael Roland
52 North Lake Drive
Chicago, IL 60642

mroland@chicago.us.mensa.org

773.715.4567

January 10, 2011

Mary Craft
Hiring Manager
Kewell Systems
250 Sixth Avenue
Brooklyn, NY 11235

Dear Ms. Craft:

Adaptability, determination, and innovative thinking are the key attributes that have contributed to my success during 25 years of hands-on experience with diverse technologies across a wide spectrum of solutions. I bring to the table the ability to bridge the gap between technology and business priorities to achieve extraordinary goals that impact bottom-line success. The core of my success lies in the fact that I am passionate about how a technology will benefit a business rather than technology for its own sake.

Throughout my career, I've delivered a number of critical projects that have helped shape the course of a business; these are outlined in the enclosed resume. To help you understand my management style, I offer a few insights.

As an "out-of-the-box" thinker, I maintain an open mind regarding technology solutions. My deep technological background has not narrowed my thinking, and I choose the solution that will solve the problem most cost effectively. When my company needed an effective means of communication with counterparts in India, I installed an early VoIP system. It solved the problem at a cost-efficient price.

After 9/11, the venture capital firm that provided financing for the company I worked for and 4 of the company's contracted clients went into bankruptcy. To keep the company afloat, I crafted a temporary plan to outsource development techniques and offshore resources. The company landed a 6-month contract with a Web map service vendor to completely rewrite its user interface. This project covered the company's operational costs, and it stayed in business.

I'm a good judge of skills and character, and I build strong and sustaining teams. Characterized as a straight shooter and a quick study, I quickly make sound decisions and stand by them. As a hands-on manager, I eagerly step in to perform the duties of any of my staff members.

My commitment with Quill has expired, and I am exploring opportunities for new, challenging opportunities. Nobody is better than I am at analyzing and solving business and technical issues. May I call next week for a brief conversation?

Sincerely,

Michael Roland

Enclosure: resume

This letter tells several stories that draw in the reader and provide compelling evidence of the job seeker's skills and capabilities (companion resume: resume 93 in chapter 10).

LUCILLE JANZEN

ljanzen@gmail.com

73 Granite Links Drive
Quincy, MA 02171

Mobile: 617.247.9818
Home: 508.771.4091

February 10, 2011

James Ryder
Financial Recruiters, LLC
25 State Street
Boston, MA 02101

Re: CTO / Wellfleet Financial

Dear Mr. Ryder:

Building best-in-class IT organizations is my expertise. Whether creating a new IT function to support a start-up venture, redesigning an existing infrastructure to enhance productivity and performance, or spearheading the implementation of enterprise-wide systems, my teams and I have consistently delivered innovative technology solutions.

What differentiates me from other CTO candidates is my unique blend of leadership, business, and technology qualifications:

Leadership Accomplishments
Whether leading an IT project or an entire IT organization, I have repeatedly demonstrated my ability to provide a strong vision and voice, communicate effectively with personnel through all tiers of an organization, and execute the strategic plan to achieve business objectives. Further, I have excelled in building camaraderie and collaborative relationships with my teams, colleagues, and customers.

Business Management Success
Early in my career, I learned the critical differences between leadership and business management. Fortunately, I'm able to both lead and manage—managing teams, projects, IT assets, operating budgets, capital budgets, technology facilities, call centers, and much more. Perhaps most vital is my success in allocating resources to meet multiple competing demands and obligations.

Technology Achievements
My resume highlights some of my most notable technology projects, from advanced data security to industry-leading e-commerce applications. Many of these projects have had a significant financial impact. For Beacon Financial, one IT project led to a new $300M revenue channel. For XYZ Investments, another massive IT development project resulted in more than $2.5M in daily revenues.

Currently I am exploring executive-level technology management positions where I can enhance the operational and financial success of a company by introducing new technologies, upgrading existing resources, and capitalizing on near-market solutions to provide a strong and sustainable competitive lead. I would welcome the opportunity to interview for the position of CTO with Wellfleet Financial and will follow up with you next week. Thank you in advance for your time and consideration.

Sincerely,

Lucille Janzen

Enclosure

Strengths as a technologist, manager, and business leader are equally emphasized in this letter for a CTO role with a major financial corporation (companion resume: resume 101 in chapter 10).

Irene G. Linitz

26 Chaucer Drive • Skokie, IL 60076
Cell: 312-892-4953 • Email: IreneLinitz58@yahoo.com

January 10, 2011

Kevin Jones
Spencer Stuart International
kevin.jones@spencerstuart.com

Dear Kevin:

Thank you for contacting me regarding the CEO opportunity at IOD Technologies. I am intrigued by the possibility of leading a high-growth startup that specializes in secure record storage for medical centers and clinics.

I might be an excellent fit for this position. My top skill—and one of the secrets to my success at Abbott Laboratories—is my ability to recruit, mentor, and motivate extremely high-performing IT teams. Here are three additional attributes that I could put to good use at IOD:

- **Operations and Marketing** – Although my resume emphasizes technical accomplishments, I've been deeply involved in marketing strategy and operations because "process excellence" provides a huge—and usually hidden—competitive edge in the healthcare-products market.

- **Technical Expertise** – As a technologist and senior IT leader at Abbott Laboratories, I've acquired deep expertise in all aspects of IOD's products and services, such as electronic medical records (EMR, EBR), business process outsourcing, data safeguards, storage, encryption, and privacy laws (SOX, HIPAA, PCI, ISO).

- **International Business Development** – I've built an extensive network of potential clients and complementary partners, especially while managing Abbott's IT organizations in Italy, France, Belgium, and the Caribbean. I could tap into this base and quickly catapult IOD into new and lucrative markets overseas.

During the past 13 years, I've turned around several underperforming IT operations, championed emerging technologies, and leveraged IT to galvanize marketing competitiveness. I would welcome an opportunity to combine these abilities and lead IOD to first place in the EMR/EBR market space.

Please review my resume and contact me anytime next week to discuss the next steps. I would like to learn more about this position, which sounds like a great opportunity. Thank you very much for your time and consideration, Kevin, and I look forward to our next conversation!

Sincerely,

Irene Linitz

Enclosure: Resume

Written in response to a phone call from a recruiter, this letter concisely captures the unique value the candidate brings to this opportunity—value that begins with technical expertise but goes far above and beyond (companion resume: resume 103 in chapter 10).

APPENDIX A

Resume Preparation Questionnaire

A resume is only as good as the information that it showcases. To write a great resume, you must take the time to document your complete career history, whether 2 years or 22 years. This raw data is the foundation for everything that you will write. The more raw data, the better, so be as comprehensive as possible when collecting and documenting your experience.

Keeping a running log of your career successes (for example, project highlights, revenue and profit results, productivity and efficiency improvements, customer satisfaction scores) and then updating your resume every six months is a great way to be prepared at a moment's notice when a great career opportunity presents itself.

Use the following Resume Preparation Questionnaire as a guide when assembling all of your career information—your raw data for writing a powerful and well-positioned resume.

RESUME PREPARATION QUESTIONNAIRE

Contact Information

Name:		
Address:		
City:	State:	ZIP:
Home Phone:	Mobile Phone:	
E-mail:	URL (Web portfolio):	
Willing to relocate? YES NO	Willing to travel? YES NO	
Current Salary:	Expected Salary:	

Career Objectives

Answer the following questions as completely and accurately as possible. Not all questions may apply to you. If they do not apply, mark them N/A. Use additional sheets if necessary.

(continued)

(continued)

Position/Career Objective: List your top three job title choices in order of preference:

1. _____

2. _____

3. _____

Is this a career change for you? YES   NO

_____

Long-Range Career Goals:

_____

_____

_____

What are some terms (or keywords) that are specific to your industry and profession?

_____

_____

_____

What skills do you possess that you want to highlight?

_____

_____

_____

Education

List all degrees, certificates, and diplomas you've received; the dates you received them; the school or college; and the location of the school or college. Begin with the most recent and work backward.

College/University: _____   City/State: _____

Major: _____   Degree: _____   Year: _____   GPA: _____

Honors: _____

College/University: _____   City/State: _____

Major: _____   Degree: _____   Year: _____   GPA: _____

Honors: _____

High School: _____   City/State: _____   Year: _____

Relevant Courses/Seminars/Workshops

Include names, dates, places, and sponsoring organizations.

_____

_____

_____

_____

Certifications and Licenses

Certifications: _____

_____

Professional Licenses: _____

_____

Military

Include branch of service, locations, position, rank achieved, years of service, honorable discharge, key accomplishments, special recognition, awards, and so on.

_____

_____

Professional Organizations/Affiliations

Include offices held.

_____

_____

_____

_____

_____

_____

Publications/Presentations

Include titles, names of publications, locations of public speaking engagements, and dates.

(continued)

(continued)

_____

_____

_____

_____

Computer Skills

Include hardware, software, operating systems, networks, programming languages, and so on.

_____

_____

_____

_____

_____

_____

Foreign Languages

List level of fluency—verbal/written.

_____

_____

Hobbies

Note that you will want to include on your resume only hobbies that are out of the ordinary and might make a great conversation topic.

_____

Community Activities

List names of organizations, years involved, positions held.

_____

_____

_____

_____

Work Experience

As you consider each position, ask yourself, *"How is this organization better off now than when it hired me?"* Here are some questions to get your thoughts flowing.

- Did you increase sales? If so, by what percentage or amount?

- Did you generate new business, bring in new clients, or forge affiliations?

- Did you save your organization money? If so, how much and how?

- Did you design or institute any new system or process? If so, what were the results?

- Did you meet an impossible deadline through extra effort? What difference did this make to your organization, your team members, and your customers?

- Did you bring in a major project under budget? How did you make this happen? How were the dollars you saved used?

- Did you suggest or help launch a new product or program? If so, did you take the lead or provide support? How successful was the effort?

- Did you take on new responsibilities that weren't part of your routine responsibilities? If so, did you ask for the new projects or were they assigned to you?

- Did you introduce any new or more effective techniques for increasing productivity?

- Did you improve communication? If so, with whom and what was the outcome?

- How did your organization benefit from your performance?

Begin with your present employer. If you're not currently working, you *might* want to start with your volunteer experience—treating it just like a paid position—if it relates to your current career objective. List different positions at the same organization as separate jobs (at least at this point in the information-collection process).

Name of employer:

City/State: Dates of employment:

Your title or position:

Who do you report to (title)?   Number of people you supervise:

Their titles or functions:

Briefly describe the size of the organization (volume produced; revenues; number of employees; local, national, or international?; and so on).

(continued)

(continued)

What does the organization do, make, or sell?

_____

Where does it rank in its industry in terms of competitors?

_____

Briefly describe your duties, responsibilities, and level of authority. Use numbers (size) and percentages, quantify budgets, state with whom you interacted, and so on.

_____

_____

_____

Why were you hired (or promoted or selected)? What was going on at the organization? Was there a particular challenge or problem you were brought on to solve? Did you have specific performance measurements? (If so, describe them as specifically as possible.) Where was your organization headed? Why did it need you?

_____

_____

_____

_____

_____

_____

_____

Describe four to six accomplishments, successes, project highlights, contributions, or other achievements in this position. Give plenty of details, facts, and figures.

_____

_____

_____

_____

_____

_____

_____

_____

_____

_____

Previous Employment

You will, most likely, need to make multiple copies of this section so that you have one copy for each position.

Name of organization:

_____

City/State: Dates of employment:

_____

Your title or position:

_____

Who did you report to (title)?   Number of people you supervised:

_____

Their titles or functions:

_____

_____

Briefly describe the size of the organization (volume produced; revenues; number of employees; local, national, or international?; and so on).

_____

_____

_____

What did the organization do, make, or sell?

_____

Where did it rank in its industry in terms of competitors?

_____

Briefly describe your duties, responsibilities, and level of authority. Use numbers (size) and percentages, quantify budgets, state with whom you interacted, and so on.

_____

_____

_____

Why were you hired (or promoted or selected)? What was going on at the organization? Was there a particular challenge or problem you were brought on to solve? Did you have specific performance measurements? (If so, describe them as specifically as possible.) Where was your organization headed? Why did it need you?

_____

_____

(continued)

(continued)

_____

_____

_____

_____

_____

_____

_____

_____

_____

_____

Describe four to six accomplishments, successes, project highlights, contributions, or other achievements in this position. Give plenty of details, facts, and figures.

_____

_____

_____

_____

_____

_____

_____

_____

_____

_____

APPENDIX B

Resume Verbs: Write with Power and Clarity

Here are nearly 400 of our favorite verbs for writing resumes, cover letters, thank-you letters, LinkedIn profiles, career biographies, achievement profiles, and a host of other online and offline career marketing communications. Use these verbs wisely, and remember the following tips:

- Write with verbs and stay away from phrases such as "Responsible for" and "Duties included." Verbs communicate action and results, and that's precisely what you want to accomplish when writing your resume.

- Each verb communicates a different message. For example, "manage," "coordinate," and "facilitate" seem to say the same thing; upon closer examination, however, that's not the case. Each verb has a unique meaning and very few verbs are interchangeable.

- Don't use verbs that overstate your level of responsibility for a particular company, organization, project, product, and so on. If you have to defend what you wrote, you've lost the opportunity.

- Not all verbs will be appropriate for you, your industry, or your profession. Don't use a verb just because you like it. Rather, use a verb that communicates precisely the right message.

NOTE: In descriptions and bullets for your current job, you will use verbs in the present tense, as shown here. For previous jobs, the verbs should be converted to past tense.

Accelerate	Achieve	Adjudicate
Accentuate	Acquire	Advance
Accommodate	Adapt	Advise
Accomplish	Address	Advocate

(continued)

(continued)

Align	Change	Counsel
Alter	Chart	Craft
Analyze	Clarify	Create
Anchor	Classify	Critique
Apply	Close	Crystallize
Appoint	Coach	Curtail
Appreciate	Collaborate	Cut
Arbitrate	Collect	Decipher
Architect	Command	Decrease
Arrange	Commercialize	Define
Articulate	Commoditize	Delegate
Ascertain	Communicate	Deliver
Assemble	Compare	Demonstrate
Assess	Compel	Deploy
Assist	Compile	Derive
Augment	Complete	Design
Authenticate	Compute	Detail
Author	Conceive	Detect
Authorize	Conceptualize	Determine
Balance	Conclude	Develop
Believe	Conduct	Devise
Bestow	Conserve	Differentiate
Brainstorm	Consolidate	Direct
Brief	Construct	Discern
Budget	Consult	Discover
Build	Continue	Dispense
Calculate	Contract	Display
Capitalize	Control	Distinguish
Capture	Convert	Distribute
Catalog	Convey	Diversify
Catapult	Coordinate	Divert
Centralize	Correct	Document
Champion	Corroborate	Dominate

Double	Exhibit	Import
Draft	Exhort	Improve
Drive	Expand	Improvise
Earn	Expedite	Increase
Edit	Experiment	Influence
Educate	Explode	Inform
Effect	Explore	Initiate
Effectuate	Export	Innovate
Elect	Extricate	Inspect
Elevate	Facilitate	Inspire
Eliminate	Finalize	Install
Emphasize	Finance	Institute
Empower	Forge	Instruct
Enact	Form	Integrate
Encourage	Formalize	Intensify
Endeavor	Formulate	Interpret
Endorse	Foster	Interview
Endure	Found	Introduce
Energize	Gain	Invent
Enforce	Generate	Inventory
Engineer	Govern	Investigate
Enhance	Graduate	Judge
Enlist	Guide	Justify
Enliven	Halt	Launch
Ensure	Handle	Lead
Entrench	Head	Lecture
Equalize	Hire	Leverage
Establish	Honor	License
Estimate	Hypothesize	Listen
Evaluate	Identify	Locate
Examine	Illustrate	Lower
Exceed	Imagine	Maintain
Execute	Implement	Manage

(continued)

(continued)

Manipulate	Outsource	Publicize
Manufacture	Overcome	Purchase
Map	Overhaul	Purify
Market	Oversee	Qualify
Master	Participate	Quantify
Mastermind	Partner	Query
Maximize	Perceive	Question
Measure	Perfect	Raise
Mediate	Perform	Rate
Mentor	Persuade	Ratify
Merge	Pilot	Realign
Minimize	Pinpoint	Rebuild
Model	Pioneer	Recapture
Moderate	Plan	Receive
Modify	Position	Recognize
Monetize	Predict	Recommend
Monitor	Prepare	Reconcile
Motivate	Prescribe	Record
Navigate	Present	Recruit
Negotiate	Preside	Recycle
Network	Process	Redesign
Nominate	Procure	Reduce
Normalize	Produce	Reengineer
Obfuscate	Program	Regain
Observe	Progress	Regulate
Obtain	Project	Rehabilitate
Offer	Project manage	Reinforce
Officiate	Proliferate	Rejuvenate
Operate	Promote	Remedy
Optimize	Propel	Render
Orchestrate	Propose	Renegotiate
Organize	Prospect	Renew
Orient	Prove	Renovate
Originate	Provide	Reorganize

Report	Solidify	Tabulate
Reposition	Solve	Target
Represent	Spark	Teach
Research	Speak	Terminate
Resolve	Spearhead	Test
Respond	Specify	Thwart
Restore	Standardize	Train
Restructure	Steer	Transcribe
Retain	Stimulate	Transfer
Retrieve	Strategize	Transform
Reuse	Streamline	Transition
Review	Strengthen	Translate
Revise	Structure	Trim
Revitalize	Study	Troubleshoot
Sanctify	Substantiate	Unify
Satisfy	Succeed	Unite
Schedule	Suggest	Update
Secure	Summarize	Upgrade
Select	Supervise	Use
Sell	Supplement	Utilize
Separate	Supply	Verbalize
Serve	Support	Verify
Service	Surpass	Win
Shepherd	Synergize	Work
Simplify	Synthesize	Write
Slash	Systematize	

INDEX OF CONTRIBUTORS

Index of Contributors

The sample resumes and cover letters in chapters 4 through 12 were written by professional resume and cover letter writers. If you need help with your resume and job search correspondence, you can use the following list to locate a career professional who can help.

You will notice that most of the writers have one or more credentials listed after their names. In fact, some have half a dozen or more! The careers industry offers extensive opportunities for ongoing training, and most career professionals take advantage of these opportunities to build their skills and keep their knowledge current. If you are curious about what any one of these credentials means, we suggest that you contact the resume writer directly. He or she will be glad to discuss certifications and other qualifications as well as information about services that can help you in your career transition.

Georgia Adamson, CPRW, CCM, CCMC, CEIP, JCTC
A Successful Career, a division
   of Adept Business Services
Campbell, CA
Phone: (408) 866-6859
E-mail: success@
   ablueribbonresume.com
www.ABlueRibbonResume.com

Carol Altomare, MRW, ACRW, CPRW, CCMC, CJSS
World Class Résumés
Three Bridges, NJ
Phone: (908) 237-1883
E-mail:
   carol@worldclassresumes.com
www.worldclassresumes.com

Lynn P. Andenoro, CPRW, JCTC

Ann Baehr, CPRW
Best Resumes of New York
Long Island, NY
Phone: (631) 224-9300
E-mail:
   resumesbest@earthlink.net
www.e-bestresumes.com

Mark Bartz, ACRW
Lakeland, FL
Phone: (863) 248-6105
E-mail: mark@hiringleaders.com
http://
   WhatTheHeckDoIDo.com

Janet L. Beckstrom, CPRW
President, Word Crafter
Flint, MI
Toll-free: (800) 351-9818
E-mail: janet@wordcrafter.com

Arnold G. Boldt, CPRW, JCTC
Arnold-Smith Associates
Rochester, NY
Phone: (585) 383-0350
E-mail: Arnie@ResumeSOS.com
www.NoNonsenseCareers.com

Carolyn Braden, CPRW

Paula Brandt

Alice Braxton, CPRW, CEIP
Burlington, NC
Phone: (336) 226-8195
E-mail: accutype@triad.rr.com

Jacqueline Brett, CPC, JCTC

Martin P. Buckland, CPRW, CPBS, CEIP, JCTC, CJST, CPEC
Elite Resumes
Oakville, Ontario, Canada
Phone: (905) 825-0490
Toll-free: (866) 773-7863
E-mail: martin@aneliteresume.com

Diane Hudson Burns, CPCC, CPRW, CLTMC, CCMC, FJSTC, JCTC, CEIP, CCM
Career Marketing Techniques
Boise, ID
Phone: (208) 323-9636
E-mail: dianecprw@aol.com
www.polishedresumes.com

Donald Burns, ACRW
New York, NY
E-mail:
info@Update-Your-Resume.com
www.update-your-resume.com

Freddie Cheek, M.S.Ed., CCM, CPRW, CARW, CWDP
Cheek & Associates, LLC
Amherst, NY
Phone: (716) 835-6945
E-mail:
fscheek@cheekandassociates.com
www.cheekandassociates.com

Jean Cummings, M.A.T., CPRW, CEIP, CPBS
A Resume for Today
Concord, MA
Phone: (978) 254-5492
E-mail: jc@YesResumes.com
www.aresumefortoday.com

Laura A. DeCarlo, MCD, CCM, EIC, JCTC, CERW, CECC, CCMC, CCRE, CWPP, 360Reach
A Competitive Edge Career Service, LLC
Melbourne, FL
Toll-free: (800) 715-3442
E-mail: success@acompetitiveedge.com
www.acompetitiveedge.com

Michael Davis, ACRW
Dayton, OH
E-mail: msdavis49@hotmail.com
www.linkedin.com/pub/
michael-davis/3/146/6ba

Michelle Dumas, NCRW, CPRW, CCM
Distinctive Documents
Somersworth, NH
Toll-free: (800) 644-9694
Fax: (603) 947-2954
E-mail: resumes@distinctiveweb.com
www.distinctiveweb.com

Nina K. Ebert, CPRW/CC
A Word's Worth
New Egypt/Jackson, NJ
Phone: (609) 758-7799
E-mail: nina@awordsworth.com
www.keytosuccessresumes.com

Laura Ege, CCMC, CJST, JCTC
Phone: (970) 259-2181
E-mail: laura@laura-ege.com
www.laura-ege.com

Debbie Ellis, MRW, CPRW
Phoenix Career Group
Houston, TX
Phone: (281) 458-5040
E-mail:
  debbie@phoenixcareergroup.com
www.phoenixcareergroup.com

Donna Farrise
Dynamic Resumes of Long Island, Inc.
Hauppauge, NY
Phone: (631) 951-4120
E-mail: donna@dynamicresumes.com
www.dynamicresumes.com

Robyn Feldberg, NCRW, ACRW, CCMC, CJSS, TCCS, WTVCIC
The Abundant Success Coach
Dallas/Fort Worth Area
Phone: (972) 464-1144
E-mail:
  robyn@abundantsuccesscoach.com
http://abundantsuccesscoach.com

Louise Fletcher, CPRW
Blue Sky Resumes
Bronxville, NY
Phone: (914) 595-1905
E-mail: info@blueskyresumes.com
www.blueskyresumes.com

Judy Friedler, NCRW, JCTC
CareerPro International
Toronto, Ontario, Canada and
  Amherst, NY
Toll-free: (877) 889-0094
E-mail: info@rezcoach.com
www.rezcoach.com

Louise Garver, CJSS, CPRW, CCMC, IJCTC, CMP, MCDP, CPBS, COIS, 360Reach, CLBF, Certified Retirement Coach, CEIP
Career Directions, LLC
Hartford, CT
Phone: (860) 623-9476
E-mail: Louise@careerdirectionsllc.com
www.careerdirectionsllc.com

Susan Guarneri, MS, NCC, NCCC, MCC, LPC, MPBS, CPBS, CERW, CPRW, CEIP, IJCTC
President, Susan Guarneri Associates
Three Lakes, WI 54562
Toll-free: (866) 881-4055
E-mail: Susan@Resume-Magic.com
www.resume-magic.com

Michele Haffner, CPRW, JCTC
Advanced Resume Services
Glendale, WI
Phone: (414) 247-1677
E-mail: michele@resumeservices.com
www.resumeservices.com

Beate Hait, CPRW, NCRW
President, Résumés Plus
Holliston, MA
Phone: (508) 429-1813
E-mail: bea@resumesplus.net
www.resumesplus.net

Alice Hanson, CPRW
Seattle, WA
www.linkedin.com/in/aliceehanson

Cheryl Ann Harland, CPRW
Resumes By Design
Houston, TX
Toll-free: (888) 213-1650
E-mail: CAH@resumesbydesign.com
www.resumesbydesign.com

Beverly Harvey, CPRW, JCTC, CCM, CCMC
Beverly Harvey Resume and Career
  Services
Pierson, FL
Phone: (386) 749-3111
E-mail:
  beverly.harvey@harveycareers.com
www.harveycareers.com

Jennifer Hay, ACRW, CRS, CPRW
IT Resume
Seattle Area
Phone: (425) 245-5102
E-mail: jhay@itresumeservice.com
http://itresumeservice.com

Loretta Heck
President, All Word Services
Prospect Heights, IL 60070
Phone: (847) 215-7517
E-mail: siegfried@ameritech.net

Jan Holliday, MA, NCRW, JCTC

**Gayle Howard, MRW, CPBS,
CERW, CCM, CMRS, MCP,
MRWLAA, CWPP**
Top Margin Career Marketing Group
P.O. Box 74
Melbourne, Victoria, Australia
Phone: +61 3 9726 6694
E-mail: getinterviews@topmargin.com
www.topmargin.com

**Marcy Johnson, NCRW, CPRW,
CEIP**

Ann Klint

**Myriam-Rose Kohn, CPBS, CCM,
CCMC, IJCTC, CPRW, CEIP**
JEDA Enterprises
Valencia, CA
Phone: (661) 253-0801
E-mail:
    myriam-rose@jedaenterprises.com
www.jedaenterprises.com

**Rhoda Kopy, BS, CPRW, JCTC,
CEIP**

Linsey Levine, MS
CareerCounsel
Ossining and White Plains, NY
Phone: (914) 923-9233
E-mail: linsey@linseylevine.com
www.linseylevine.com

**Abby Locke, ACRW, MRW, CJSS,
CCMC, NCRW, CPBS, 360Reach**
Premier Writing Services
Phone: (425) 608-7200
E-mail: alocke@premierwriting.com
www.premierwriting.com

**Ross Macpherson, CPRW, CJST,
CEIP, RPBS**
President, Career Quest
Whitby, Ontario, Canada
Phone: (905) 438-8548
E-mail: ross@yourcareerquest.com
www.yourcareerquest.com

Linda Matias, CIC, NCRW, JCTC
CareerStrides
Long Island, NY
Phone: (631) 456-5051
E-mail: linda@careerstrides.com
www.careerstrides.com

Wanda McLaughlin, CPRW, CEIP

Jan Melnik, MRW, CCM, CPRW
Absolute Advantage
Durham, CT
Phone: (860) 349-0256
E-mail: CompSPJan@aol.com
www.janmelnik.com

**Nicole Miller, CCM, CRW, CECC,
IJCTC**
Mil-Roy Consultants
Orleans, Ontario, Canada
Phone: (613) 834-4031
E-mail: resumesbymilroy@hotmail.com

Cheryl Milmoe, ACRW
CareerStimulus.net
New York City area
Phone: (516) 680-9055
E-mail: Cheryl@careerstimulus.net
www.careerstimulus.net

**Jacqui Barrett Poindexter, MRW,
CPRW, CEIP**
Career Trend
Overland Park, KS
Phone: (816) 584-1639
E-mail: jacqui@careertrend.net
www.careertrend.net

**Anita Radosevich, CPRW, JCTC,
CFRW, CEIP**
Career Ladders
Elk Grove, CA
E-mail: anita@abcresumes.com
www.federalresumewriter.com

Barbara Safani, MA, CERW, CPRW, NCRW, CCM
Career Solvers
New York, NY
Phone: (212) 579-7230
Toll-free: (866) 333-1800
E-mail: info@careersolvers.com
www.careersolvers.com

Mary Schumacher, ACRW, CPRW, CEIP, CPCC
TheLadders Resume Services
http://resume.theladders.com

Kelley Smith, CPRW
Advantage Resumes/Resume
  GhostWriter
Sugar Land, TX
Toll-free: (877) 478-4999
Fax: (281) 494-0173
E-mail: ksmith@resumeghostwriter.com
www.resumeghostwriter.com

Ann Stewart, CPRW
Advantage Services
Roanoke, TX
Phone: (817) 488-1448
E-mail: annstewart1@verizon.net

Reya Stevens, MA, ACRW, MRW
StandOut Resumes
Boston, MA
E-mail: reya@standoutresumes.com
http://standoutresumes.com

Marjorie Sussman, MRW, ACRW, CPRW
Dover Productions
New York City Area
Phone: (201) 941-8237
E-mail: marjorie1130@aol.com
www.visualcv.com/marjoriesussman

Sheryl Teitelbaum

Ellie Vargo, MRW, CCMC, CEQS, CFRWC, CPRW
Noteworthy Resume Services
St. Louis, MO
Phone: (314) 965-9362
E-mail: info@noteworthyresume.com
www.noteworthyresume.com

Roleta Fowler Vasquez, CPRW, CEIP
Wordbusters Resume and Writing
  Services
Fillmore, CA
Phone: (805) 524-3493
E-mail: wbresumes@yahoo.com
www.wordbusters.com

Janice Worthington, MA, CPRW, JCTC, CEIP
Worthington Career Services
Columbus, OH
Phone: (614) 890-1645
Toll-free: (877) 973-7863
  (877-9RESUME)
E-mail: Janice@worthingtoncareers.com
www.worthingtonresumes.com

INDEX